# THE 21ST CENTURY
# WEBSTER'S POCKET
# ENCYCLOPEDIA

◆ ◆ ◆

REVISED EDITION

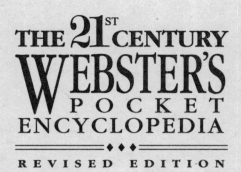

# THE 21ST CENTURY WEBSTER'S POCKET ENCYCLOPEDIA

## REVISED EDITION

Volume 1
A - Blad

Trident Press International
2000 Edition

# TRIDENT PRESS INTERNATIONAL

Copyright © 2000, Uirgeverij Het Spectrum BV

Trident Press International
801-12th Avenue South, Suite 302
Naples, Florida USA 34102
Email: tridentpress@worldnet.att.net
Web site http//www.trident-international.com

ISBN 1-58279-080-9

Printed in the United States of America

# A

**A,** first letter of the English alphabet and others that can be traced back to Semitic roots. The letter was originally drawn to represent the head of an ox and given the name *aleph* (Phoenician "ox"). In Greek this became *alpha*. The shape of the letter changed gradually as it passed into the Hebrew, Greek, and Roman alphabets. Our capital *A* is based on the Greek form. The lower-case *a* was first used in medieval manuscripts. From the first 2 letters of the Greek alphabet, alpha and beta, we derive the word *alphabet*.

**Aachen,** also Aix-la-Chapelle (pop. 243,200), city and spa in North Rhine-Westphalia, Germany. A major industrial center producing machinery, textiles, and chemicals, it is also the site of mineral springs frequented since Roman times. The emperor Charlemagne built a palace and cathedral in the city.

**Aardvark** (*Orycteropus afer*), nocturnal African mammal. Measuring up to 6 ft (1.8 m) in length and weighing up to 150 lbs (68 kg), the aardvark has a stout body with a plump, ratlike tail, elongated piglike snout, and large ears. It feeds on ants and termites, tearing open their nests with its powerful limbs and catching them with its long, sticky tongue.
*See also:* Anteater.

**Aaron,** elder brother of Moses and first Jewish high priest. In the Old Testament (Exodus) Aaron speaks for Moses before the Israelites and in the Egyptian court, after Jehovah has commanded Moses to lead his people out of Egypt.
*See also:* Moses.

**Aaron, Hank** (Henry Louis Aaron; 1934-    ), U.S. baseball player. He broke Babe Ruth's record in 1974 with his 715th career home run. He retired in 1976 with 755 homers. An outfielder with the Milwaukee (later Atlanta) Braves, Aaron also set a National League record with 2,297 runs batted in. He finished his career with the Milwaukee Brewers of the American League.

**Abacá** (*Musa textilis*), name of the plant, native to the Philippines, that yields Manila hemp.
*See also:* Manila hemp.

**Abacus,** or counting frame, ancient calculating instrument still widely used in Asia. It consists of a wooden frame containing a series of parallel rods strung with beads and divided into upper and lower portions. Each of the rods represents a power of 10; each of the beads on the lower portion counts for a power of 1 and the 2 on the upper portion for a power of 5 apiece. It can be used to solve addition, subtraction, multiplication, and division problems.

**Abadan** (pop. 295,000), Persian Gulf port city in Khuzestan province, southwestern Iran, on Abadan Island in the Shatt al Arab, the waterway formed by the confluence of the Tigris and Euphrates rivers. An important oil-refining center since 1909, Abadan was badly damaged by bombing during the Iraq-Iran war, which began in 1980 and ended in August 1988.

**Abalone**, or ear shell, marine mollusk (genus *Haliotis*) harvested as a popular seafood and for the colorful lining of its shell, which is used for making buttons and costume jewelry. The abalone is found in most mild and tropical waters clinging to submerged rocks by means of a muscular foot.

**Abbasid**, dynasty of Arab caliphs (749-1258) descended from Abbas (d. 653), uncle of Muhammad. The early years of Abbasid rule were marked by prosperity and strong government; they reached their high-water mark with the reign of the fifth caliph, Harun-Rashid (764-809). The dynasty was finally overthrown by Hulagu Khan, grandson of Genghis Khan, who sacked Baghdad in 1258.
*See also:* Muslims.

**Abbe, Cleveland** (1838-1916), U.S. meteorologist who inaugurated a system of scientific weather forecasting in the United States. After studying at the Pulkova Observatory in Russia, he became head of the Cincinnati Observatory and in 1869 began publishing official forecasts based largely on analyses of telegraphic reports on approaching storms.

**Abbey**, building of a monastic house or religious community, centered on a church. The cloistered life of medieval times grew out of the anchorite, or hermit, communities of Egypt and the Near East in the early Christian era. The first abbey in western Europe was established in France in 360, and the first in England, Bangor Abbey, in 560. Abbeys were centers of culture and the practical arts throughout western Europe.

**Abbey Theatre**, originally called Irish National Theatre. It was founded in 1902 by William Butler Yeats, Lady Gregory, and others to promote the work of Irish playwrights. The company moved to the Abbey Theatre in Dublin in 1904. It performs works in both English and Gaelic.
*See also:* Yeats, William Butler; Irish literature.

**Abbott, Robert Sengstacke** (1868-1940), journalist, editor, and publisher and founder of the *Chicago Defender*, an important newspaper in the United States. The son of former slaves, Abbott graduated from Kent College of Law in 1899, but soon left the legal profession. Utilizing previous newspaper experience he published the first issue of the *Chicago Defender* on May 15, 1905. A leading proponent of equal rights for African Americans, Abbott used the paper to encourage Southern blacks to move to the North for better jobs and opportunities during the industrial boom of World War I.

**Abbott, Sir John Joseph Caldwell** (1821-93), prime minister of Canada (1891-92). During his career as a lawyer he became involved in the Conservative Party and was an adviser to Sir John Macdonald, the first prime minister of Canada. Upon Macdonald's death in 1891, Abbott became prime minister, but he resigned after only 18 months.

**A.B.C. Powers**, loose entente between Argentina, Brazil, and Chile, initiated in 1906, taking its name from the countries' initials. The entente's mediation averted a U.S.-Mexican war in 1915. Its aims were cooperation and mutual nonaggression, but a treaty signed by the 3 countries in May 1915 had little real effect.

**Abdomen**, in vertebrates, large body cavity between the chest and the pelvis. It contains the stomach, intestines, liver, gallbladder (which are covered by the peritoneum, the thin membrane lining the cavity), kidneys, spleen, adrenal glands, pancreas, and, in the female, reproductive organs. In invertebrates, *abdomen* refers to the part of the body behind the thorax.
*See also:* Intestine; Stomach.

**Abdul-Hamid**, name of 2 sultans of the Ottoman Empire. **Abdul-Hamid I** (1725-89) succeeded his brother Mustafa III in 1774. Throughout his reign the power of Turkey was on the wane, weakened by internal revolt and continuing war with Russia. **Abdul-Hamid II** (1842-1918) succeeded his brother Murad V in 1876. The following year he began a disastrous war with Russia that resulted in Turkey's loss of control over her European provinces of Serbia, Montenegro, Bulgaria, Romania, Herzegovina, and Bosnia.After some initial gestures toward reform, he ruled harshly by decree. Sometimes called the Bloody Sultan, he roused world opinion against him and his government by the massacre of Armenians (1894-96).The Young Turks, a reform-minded political organization, forced him to accept a constitution and deposed him the following year after he attempted a counterrevolution.

**Abdul-Jabbar, Kareem** (Ferdinand Lewis Alcindor, Jr.; 1947- ), U.S. basketball player. The 7-ft 2-in (218-cm) center is considered one of the greatest players of all time. Known for his "sky hook" jump shot, Abdul-Jabbar holds records in regular season scoring (38,387 points) and games played (1,560) and received the league's most-valuable-player award 6 times. After a successful college career at UCLA, he played for the Milwaukee Bucks and Los Angeles Lakers of the NBA (1969-1989). Abdul-Jabbar legally changed his name in 1971 after adopting the Muslim religion.
*See also:* Basketball.

**Abel**, second son of Adam and Eve. His older brother, Cain, killed him in a fit of anger when God accepted Abel's offering but rejected Cain's. (Genesis 4.)
*See also:* Adam and Eve; Cain; Old Testament.

**Abelard, Peter** (1079-1142), leading medieval French scholastic philosopher and teacher. The school he founded in Paris would evolve into the University of Paris. The main thrust of Abelard's philosophy was that the power of human thinking or reason could achieve true knowledge in the natural and supernatural spheres. He excelled in his study of the nature of abstraction and in his search for the source of responsibility in human actions. The church condemned Abelard's original teachings as heretical. Abelard is probably best remembered for his love affair with Héloïse, one of his pupils. Following the birth of a child, Héloïse and Abelard married secretly, but Héloïse's vengeful uncle had Abelard castrated. After separating to take up monastic life, the couple exchanged a series of moving love letters.

**Aberdeen** (pop. 216,500), Scottish seaport and the most populous city of northern Scotland. Aberdeen is a shipbuilding and fishing center also known as the market center for the Aberdeen Angus cattle breed. In the 1970s it became the hub of the industries based on the exploitation of North Sea oil.

**Aberdeen Proving Ground**, U.S. Army test center for guns, ammunition, vehicles, bombs, and other ordnance, located in Hartford County, Md. Established in 1917, the 73,000-acre (29,200-hectare) post extends approximately 18 mi (29 km) along the upper Chesapeake Bay near the town of Aberdeen. The Army Ordnance Center, Test and Evaluation Command, Chemical Research Development, and Engineering centers as well as ordnance disposal and ballistic research and human engineering laboratories are currently located at this post.

**Abernathy, Ralph David** (1926-90), U.S. black civil rights leader and Baptist minister. In 1968 he succeeded the murdered Martin Luther King, Jr., as president of the Southern Christian Leadership Conference and led the Poor People's March on Washington D.C. that year.
*See also:* Civil rights; King, Martin Luther, Jr.

**Aberration, optical**, failure of a lens to form a perfect image of an object. The 2 types are chromatic aberration, where dispersion causes colored fringes to appear around the image, and spherical aberration, where blurring occurs because light from the outer parts of the lens is brought to a focus at a shorter distance from the lens than that passing through the center. Chromatic aberration can be reduced by using an achromatic lens; spherical aberration can be reduced by separating the elements of a compound lens.
*See also:* Lens.

**Abidjan** (pop. 1,850,000), largest city and former capital of the Ivory Coast, West Africa. Abidjan is a major port and railroad terminus, as well as one of the most modern cities of Africa. The city's main industries include canning, shipping, and the production of beer, margarine, and soap.

**Abilene** (pop. 112,600), agricultural city in central Kansas. Settled in 1856, Abilene was an important shipping point for Texas cattle brought north to the railroad over the Chisholm Trail. As marketing center for the surrounding farmlands, its chief industries are grain milling and the processing of dairy products. President Dwight D. Eisenhower lived in the town as a boy and chose it for his burial place and the site of a memorial museum.

**Ability test**, test to demonstrate a particular level of knowledge or skill. An individual general ability test consists of 8 small subtests: information test, analogies test, vocabulary, letter memory, number series, spatial relations, clock test, and sign language test.

**Abnormal psychology**, sometimes called *psychopathology*, the scientific study of disorders of the mind. Treatment for these disorders includes medication, psychoanalysis (the technique developed by Sigmund Freud), psychotherapy, and behavior modification.
*See also:* Mental illness.

**Abolitionism,** movement in the United States and other countries that aimed at abolishing slavery. The *Liberator*, an antislavery paper edited by William Lloyd Garrison, began publication in 1831. In 1833 the American Anti-Slavery Society was founded in Philadelphia. Some abolitionists used their homes as stations for fugitive slaves on the underground railroad. The movement produced much literature, including Harriet Beecher Stowe's *Uncle Tom's Cabin*. After the outbreak of the Civil War, abolitionist demands led to President Lincoln's Emancipation Proclamation (1863). The 13th Amendment (1865) completed the abolition of slavery in the United States. William Wilberforce and others led the movement in Britain to abolish the slave trade (1807) and slavery (1833).
*See also:* Douglass, Frederick; Emancipation Proclamation; Slavery; Civil War, U.S.; Underground Railroad.

**Abortion,** ending of pregnancy before the fetus is able to survive outside the womb. It can occur spontaneously (miscarriage), or it can be artificially induced. Spontaneous abortion may occur as a result of maternal or fetal disease or faulty implantation in the womb. Abortion may be artificially induced by surgical or medical means, depending on the stage of pregnancy and the patient's condition. Today, an early abortion performed in a modern facility by qualified health care professionals is relatively simple and safe. However, complications of abortion like uterine infection or injury can contribute to an inability to have children at a later time. Abortion has been long practiced in most cultures, but public opinion in the Western nations, combined with the opposition of religious leaders, led to restrictive legislation in the 19th century. By the second half of the 20th century, however, abortion was legalized in most of Europe, the USSR, and Japan. In 1973, the U.S. Supreme Court ruled in *Roe* v. *Wade* that abortions in the first or second trimester are legal, but the moral and legal controversy surrounding abortion continues.
*See also:* Roe v. Wade.

**Aboukir,** village in Egypt situated on the Mediterranean coast between Alexandria and the Rosetta mouth of the Nile. The Battle of the Nile (Aug. 1798), in which British naval forces under Nelson defeated Napoleon's fleet, took place in Aboukir Bay. A second battle (1801) was fought on land at Aboukir, and Napoleon's forces were again beaten decisively by the British. The village is the site of ancient Canopus, a thriving port in Hellenistic times.

**Abraham,** first of the patriarchs (founding fathers) of the Jews; regarded as the founder of Judaism. God promised Abraham that his people would inherit Canaan through his son Isaac. As a test of faith and obedience, God commanded Abraham to slay Isaac. Abraham unquestioningly obeyed, and Isaac was spared. (Genesis 11-25.) Muslims consider Abraham an ancestor of the Arabs through another son, Ishmael.
*See also:* Jews; Judaism; Lot.

**Abraham, Karl** (1877-1925), German psychoanalyst whose most important work concerned the development of the libido, particularly in infancy. He suggested that various psychoses should be interpreted in terms of interruption of this development.

**Abraham, Plains of,** site of the decisive battle in the Canadian theater during the French and Indian wars, in which Gen. James Wolfe defeated the French at Quebec (1759).
*See also:* French and Indian Wars.

**Abravanel (Abrabanel), Isaac** (1437-1508), Jewish theologian and states-man. Born in Lisbon, he served King Alfonso V of Portugal in state and financial affairs. Forced after the king's death to flee to Spain, he was employed by Ferdinand and Isabella until the Jews were expelled from Spain in 1492. He then lived in various Italian cities, eventually becoming a minister of state in Venice, where he died. He is best known for his extensive commentaries on the Bible.

**Absalom,** third son of King David of Israel. Absalom fled his father's court after killing his brother Amnon. He later returned and was pardoned, but he then conspired against his father, proclaimed himself king, and was killed against David's wishes. (2 Samuel 13-19.)
*See also:* David.

**Abscam,** short for "Abdul-scam," referring to Abdul Enterprises, Ltd., fake company used by the Federal Bureau of Investigations (FBI) in a 1978-80 investigation of political corruption that resulted in the convictions of 1 U.S. senator, 6 U.S. representatives, and assorted local officials. Posing as wealthy Arabs or their representatives, FBI agents secretly videotaped meetings at which they paid tens of thousands of dollars to the politicians in return for promises of social immigration legislation, government contracts, and other favors.

**Abscess,** localized accumulation of pus, usually representing a response of the body to bacterial infection. The bacteria enter the skin via a natural opening or small cut, and they can pass into the intestinal mucous membrane or the respiratory system and be swept by the bloodstream to various organs of the body. The immune, or defense, system of the body possesses 2 mechanisms for destroying the penetrating bacteria: the leukocytes (white blood cells) and antibodies. If these defense mechanisms succumb to the bacteria, an abscess forms: The bacteria destroy a large number of cells, causing tissue death and the formation of an ulcer, which forms a pussy mass. Fortunately, the tissue is usually capable of stopping the destructive work of the bacteria, forming a barrier to the spread of the bacteria by building a wall of cells and connective tissue. Such an abscess may drain spontaneously; otherwise it should be incised.
*See also:* Carbuncle.

**Absentee voting,** allowing a registered voter to cast a ballot in an election when unable to appear at a polling place. The voter sends a paper ballot to the election official before voting day. All states make provisions for absentee voting, but their laws differ on the elections in which absentee ballots are permitted and the acceptable reasons for absence.
*See also:* Voting.

**Absinthe,** common European wormwood (*Artemisia absinthium*); also, bitter, green, distilled liqueur principally flavored with an aromatic oil obtained from the wormwood. Allegation that absinthe is poisonous led to the drink's prohibition in many countries, including the United States and Canada.

**Absolute zero**, temperature (0°K [kelvin]/ -273.15°C/−459.67°F) at which all substances have zero thermal energy and thus, theoretically, the lowest possible temperature. Originally conceived as the temperature at which an ideal gas at constant pressure would contract to zero volume, absolute zero is of great significance in thermodynamics and is used as the fixed point for the absolute, or kelvin, temperature scale. In practice the absolute zero temperature is unattainable, although temperatures within a few millionths of 0°K have been achieved in cryogenics laboratories. *See also:* Gas; Temperature.

**Absolution**, in the Roman Catholic and some other churches, remission of sins pronounced by a priest in favor of a penitent.

**Absolutism**, form of government, such as a dictatorship, in which all power is held by an unchecked ruler. Monarchies in the ancient world were usually absolute. In England, in the 18th century, the Stuart attempt to rule by divine right failed, but elsewhere in Europe, especially France, absolutism flourished until the early 19th century. Examples of absolutism in the 20th century are the totalitarian governments of Adolf Hitler in Germany and Joseph Stalin in the Soviet Union. *See also:* Dictatorship; Totalitarianism.

**Absorption**, taking in of energy or molecules by a material. While in *adsorption* molecules are attracted to the surface, in absorption the energy or molecules are distributed throughout the material.

**Abstract expressionism**, U.S. art movement of the 1940s and 1950s that explored the emotional, expressive power of nonfigurative painting. It was the first significant school of U.S. painting, influencing artists in other countries. Jackson Pollock, who dipped and spattered paint on the canvas, was called, along with some other members of the movement, an "action painter." Franz Kline, Willem de Kooning, Mark Rothko, Barnett Newman, and Arshile Gorky are considered leading abstract expressionists. *See also:* Pollock, Jackson.

**Abu Bakr** (c. A.D. 573-634), first Muslim caliph of Arabia in 632, following Muhammad's death. He ordered incursions into Syria and Iraq, thus beginning the Muslim conquests. He was Muhammad's father-in-law, as well as his closest companion and adviser. *See also:* Muslims.

**Abu Dhabi** (pop. 243,000), largest (25,000 sq mi/64,750 sq km) of the 7 emirates that make up the United Arab Emirates (UAE), located on the southern coast of the Persian Gulf. The land is mostly desert, with extensive oil deposits. The city of Abu Dhabi is the capital of the UAE. *See also:* United Arab Emirates.

**Abuya** (pop.480,000) capital of Nigeria since 1991. Abuya was built to replace Lagos, predominantly to combat further overpopulation and pauperization, and to create a more centrally located capital city. Construction began in 1980.
*See also:* Nigeria.

**Abydos**, Greek name for a religious center in Middle Egypt inhabited since the early dynastic period (3100-2686 B C ) and connected with the god Osiris. It is noted for its tombs of early dynastic kings and its 19th-dynasty temple (c.3100 B C.).
*See also:* Osiris.

**Abzug, Bella** (1920-   ), U.S. feminist and political leader. While serving in Congress as a Democratic representative from New York (1971-77), she became a prominent spokesperson for the women's rights and anti-Vietnam War movements.
*See also:* Women's movements.

**Acacia**, any of a genus (*Acacia*) of mostly tropical trees and shrubs in the pea family. Various species produce catechu, gum arabic, and tannin. Acacia are characteristic of the savanna type of vegetation (grassland with some trees) in central and southern Africa. More than a dozen species grow in the United States. The flowers tend to be mostly yellow or white.

**Academic freedom**, right of members of the academic community to freedom of thought and expression. The American Association of University Professors' code of conduct proposes complete freedom of research but restricts classroom freedom to open discussion of the teacher's own subject. Despite this stand, scholastic immunity has been affected by boards of trustees, government agencies that fund some university projects, and students who object to the politics or theories of certain professors.

**Académie Française** (French Academy), literary and linguistic society officially recognized in 1635. Membership is limited to 40, the so-called immortals, and includes prominent public literary figures. It has been criticized for electing individuals with personal influence, while ignoring those with real merit. Molière and Emile Zola were never elected. Over the centuries, the Academy has produced the *dictionnaire*, the official arbiter of the French language.

**Academy Awards®** or Oscars®, annual awards given by the Academy of Motion Picture Arts and Sciences for outstanding achievement in various branches of filmmaking. The major awards are for best leading and supporting actor and actress, best direction, best screenplay, and best film. The awards were first presented in 1928, when the best picture award was presented to *Wings*.

**Acadia**, name given to Nova Scotia and neighboring regions of New Brunswick, Prince Edward Island, and parts of Quebec and Maine by the French colonists who settled there starting in 1604. All but Prince Edward Island and Cape Breton passed under British control by the Treaty of Utrecht (1713). The French colonists, dispersed by the British in 1755, are the subject

of Henry Wadsworth Longfellow's poem *Evangeline*. Those who went to Louisiana are the ancestors of the present-day Cajuns.
*See also:* Cajuns; French and Indian Wars; Nova Scotia.

**Acadia National Park**, U.S. national park covering 65 sq mi (168 sq km) in southeast Maine. The park's mountains, forests, and lakes make it an important wildlife reserve.
*See also:* National Park System.

**Acanthus**, any of a genus (*Acanthus*) of mostly tropical shrubs and herbs in the acanthus family having large, spiny leaves. Acanthus also refers to a leafy ornament used in Greek and Roman architecture.

**Acapulco** (pop. 592,200), seaport and tourist center on the Pacific coast of southern Mexico. Founded in 1550 on a natural harbor, Acapulco was a base for Spanish explorers and an important trading port. Since the 1920s it has been chiefly noted as a winter resort.

**Accelerometer**, device used to measure acceleration, working on the principle expressed by Newton's law: $a = F/m$, where $a$ = acceleration, $F$ = force, $m$ = mass. The accelerometer measures the force expressed on a spring by an object of known mass. When acceleration takes place, the object is forced back against the spring as passengers in a car are pressed against the back of their seats. The greater the acceleration, the more the object is forced back. The distance the object moves back, measured in an electrical circuit, is a measure of the acceleration.

**Accent**, vocal emphasis placed on a syllable in a word. In all languages there are two kinds of accent: (1) musical chromatic or pitch accent; (2) emphatic or stress accent.

**Acclimatization**, process of adjustment that allows an individual organism to survive under changed conditions in its environment. In a hot, sunny climate, for example, human beings acclimatize by eating less, drinking more, and wearing lighter clothes. At higher altitudes, humans adjust to the diminished oxygen by increasing production of red blood cells.
*See also:* Adaptation.

**Accordion**, portable reed organ used for jazz and folk music. Tuned metal reeds are set in vibration by air directed at them from a central bellows through valves operated by piano-type keys on the instrument's right-hand side. Buttons on the left produce chords. Although they were known in ancient China, the first modern accordions were built in 1829 in Vienna.

**Accounting**, analysis of financial records in order to reveal the financial position of an individual or firm. In the United States, an accountant who has passed a state examination becomes a certified public accountant (CPA). A financial statement is audited—that is, checked for accuracy and fairness—by an accountant who was not involved in the preparation of the statement.
*See also:* Audit.

**Accra** (pop. 965,000), capital and largest city of Ghana, on the Gulf of Guinea. The seaport, founded in the 1600s, was a center of the African slave trade until the mid-1800s. It grew in commercial importance in the 20th century after a railroad linked it with the interior.
*See also:* Africa; Ghana.

**Acerola**, commonly known as Puerto Rican, West Indian, or Barbados cherry, any of a group of subtropical and tropical trees and shrubs (genus *Malpighia*) indigenous to the West Indies, southern Texas, and parts of Mexico, Central America, and northern South America. The cherry-sized edible fruit, also called acerola, is tart, rich in vitamin C (ascorbic acid), and bright red when ripe.

**Acetaminophen**, common, over-the-counter pain-relieving and fever-reducing drug. It is sometimes taken instead of aspirin, which can irritate the stomach.
*See also:* Aspirin.

**Acetic acid** ($C_2H_4O_2$), colorless organic acid, the principal constituent of vinegar, used industrially in the synthesis of plastics. It was first isolated by George Stahl in 1700.
*See also:* Vinegar.

**Acetone** ($CH_3COCH_3$), colorless, flammable chemical used in industry as a solvent. Because of its ability to dissolve cellulose, it is used to manufacture synthetic fibers. It is also used to make compounds. Acetone is found in large amounts in the blood and urine of diabetics. It is prepared commercially by removing the hydrogen from isopropyl alcohol or by fermenting starch.
*See also:* Acetylene.

**Acetylene**, or ethyne ($C_2H_2$), colorless gas that explodes on contact with air. Acetylene and oxygen are mixed and burned in the oxyacetylene torch, producing an extremely hot flame (up to 6,300°F/3,480°C) used for welding and cutting metals. Acetylene, used to make plastics, rubber, and explosive compounds, is poisonous if inhaled.
*See also:* Acetone; Calcium carbide.

**Achaeans**, people of ancient Greece identified by Homer as the Greeks who fought in the Trojan War. Some authorities believe that the Achaeans came to Greece in the 12th century B.C , briefly dominating Mycenae before being driven by the Dorians to a region in the northern Peloponnesus, which came to be known as Achaea. The Achaean cities formed the Achaean League, which opposed the Macedonians and the Romans, in the 4th century B C. The Romans defeated the league in 146 B.C.
*See also:* Aeolians; Dorians; Iliad.

**Achaemenids**, Persian dynasty that dominated much of West Asia during the 6th-4th centuries B C. The outstanding rulers were Cyrus the Great, Darius I, and Xerxes I. It ended when Alexander the Great defeated Darius III in 330.

**Acheson, Dean Gooderham** (1893-1971), U.S. diplomat who helped re-build Europe's economic and military strength after World War II. He served Presidents Roosevelt and Truman in the State Department (1941-53), becoming secretary of state in 1949. After the war he promoted the recovery of Europe through the Marshall Plan and worked to curb Soviet expansion through the Truman Doctrine (both 1947). In 1949 he helped to formulate the North Atlantic Treaty Organization (NATO). He received the 1970 Pulitzer Prize for history for his book *Present at the Creation: My Years in the State Department*.
*See also:* Marshall Plan; North Atlantic Treaty Organization; Truman, Harry S.

**Achilles**, legendary Greek hero of the Trojan War and central figure in the *Iliad* of Homer. Dipped in the River Styx by his mother, Thetis, he was made invulnerable except at the point on his heel where she had held him. Achilles killed the Trojan hero Hector in revenge for the death of Achilles' friend Patroclus. Achilles was killed when the god Apollo guided an arrow from the Trojan warrior Paris into his heel.
*See also:* Trojan War; Iliad.

**Achilles' tendon**, tendon at the back of the ankle joining the bone of the heel to the muscles of the calf. It plays a critical role in the ability to walk, run, and stand on the toes. It is commonly injured in strenuous athletics. The name comes from the mythical Greek warrior, Achilles, who was vulnerable only in the heel.
*See also:* Achilles; Ankle; Tendon.

**Acid**, any of a class of organic or inorganic water-soluble chemical compounds that taste sour, redden vegetable substances, contain hydrogen, and readily accept electrons or give up protons. Many chemical reactions are speeded up in acid solutions, giving rise to important industrial applications. Strong acids (e.g., hydrochloric acid [HCl]), which break down easily in solution to yield hydrogen ($H^+$) ions, are good electrolytes (conductors of electricity). Amino acids, constitutive of proteins, are essential components of all living systems.
*See also:* Base.

**Acidosis**, medical condition in which the acid-base balance in the body fluids is disturbed in the direction of excess acidity. It can cause heavy breathing and weakness and lead to acidemia. Respiratory acidosis results from the underbreathing and consequent build-up of plasma carbon dioxide caused by lung disease, heart failure, and central respiratory depression. Metabolic acidosis may be caused by the ingestion of excess acids (as in aspirin overdose), ketosis (resulting from malnutrition or diabetes), heavy alkali loss (as from a fistula), and the inability to excrete acid (occurring in some kidney disorders).
*See also:* Alkalosis.

**Acid rain**, popular name for polluting rain or other precipitation caused by the combining of oxides of sulfur and nitrogen with atmospheric moisture. Although it is produced by naturally occurring combustion (volcanoes, forest fires), its serious increase is blamed on the burning of fossil fuels (oil, coal,

natural gas) by automobiles and in industry. Acid rain may pollute water, kill vegetation, and erode buildings far from its point of origin and has thus become an international as well as a local issue.
*See also:* Air pollution; Environmental pollution.

**Acne**, common skin disease caused by inflammation of the sebaceous glands, resulting in pimples on the face and upper trunk. Acne occurs most frequently between the ages of 14 and 19 years, but cases at up to 40 years may occur. An inflamed acne lesion is preceded by a noninflamed lesion (a whitehead or blackhead), which is a plugged sebaceous gland. How these lesions form is uncertain. Blackheads become inflamed either because of local production of irritant fatty acids by bacteria or because of bacterial infection.
Patients with mild acne need only topical therapy, such as the application of a preparation containing either retinoic acid (a derivative of vitamin A) or benzoyl peroxide. Patients with more severe acne require antibiotic drugs as well as topical treatment.

**Aconcagua**, highest (22,834 ft/6,960 m) mountain in the Western Hemisphere, located in the Andes of northwest Argentina. It was first climbed by E.A. Fitzgerald's expedition in 1897.
*See also:* Andes.

**Aconite**, any of a genus (*Aconitum*) of flowering plants, commonly called monkshood or wolfsbane, belonging to the crowfoot family. The species *A. napellus* produces aconite, a poisonous drug.

**Acorn**, fruit of the oak tree, an oval nut partly encased in a hard, woody cup.
*See also:* Oak.

**Acoustics**, the science of sound, dealing with its production, transmission, and effects. Acoustics may be practically applied to, for example, the designing of auditoriums, where the audience must be able to hear the speaker or performer clearly and without echoes. This is achieved by attending to the geometry and furnishings of the hall and incorporating appropriate sound absorbing, diffusing, and reflecting surfaces.
*See also:* Sound.

**Acquired characteristics**, modifications in an organism resulting from interaction with its environment. In 1801 Jean Baptiste Lamarck proposed an evolutionary theory in which the inheritance of acquired characteristics provided the mechanism for species divergence. In later editions of *The Origin of Species*, Charles Darwin moved toward accepting this explanation along with that of natural selection, but eventually the Lamarckian mechanism was entirely discounted. Geneticists currently believe that inheritance is determined by reproductive cells.

**Acromegaly**, rare disease associated with the overgrowth of bone, especially in the jaws, hands, and feet. An endocrinological disorder or chronic hyperpituitarism may be the cause.

**Acropolis** (Greek, "high city"), fortified hilltop of an ancient Greek city, serving as its military and religious center. The most famous is the acropolis of Athens, with its many temples, including the Parthenon.
*See also:* Athens.

**Acrylic**, group of versatile and durable synthetic products manufactured from petroleum as fibers, plastics, and resins for use in fabrics, glass substitutes, and protective paints. The molecules of a petroleum-based synthetic chemical or substance, acrylonitrile or acrylate, are polymerized (combined in a long, repetitive chain) to form acrylic. Orlon, Lucite, and Plexiglas are trademark names for some common acrylic products.
*See also:* Polymer; Polymerization.

**ACTH** (adrenocorticotrophic hormone), or corticotropin, hormone produced by the pituitary gland that stimulates the cortex of the adrenal gland to produce corticosteroids, which regulate many biochemical reactions in the body. Too much ACTH induces growth of the adrenal glands and provokes increased secretion of hydrocortisone. Lack of ACTH gives rise to a wasting away of the adrenal cortex; skin pigmentation is reduced, and the function of other endocrine glands, such as the thyroid, testes, and ovaries, is inhibited. The secretion of ACTH is largely controlled by the release of chemicals to the pituitary gland by the brain.
*See also:* Gland; Hormone.

**Actinide** *See:* Rare earth; Element.

**Actinium**, chemical element, symbol Ac; for physical constants see Periodic Table. Actinium was discovered by André Debierne in 1899. It is radioactive and occurs naturally in minute amounts in uranium minerals. Actinium is synthesized by irradiating radium with neutrons. A reactive metal, it is obtained by reducing its fluoride with lithium vapor. It is about 150 times as active as radium and valuable in the production of neutrons. There are 26 known isotopes. Actinium-227, a beta emitter and a powerful source of alpha rays, has the longest half-life (21.77 years). Chemically, actinium is similar to lanthanum. It is the first of the actinides, a series of homologous elements analogous to the lanthanide transition series.

**Actinomycosis**, chronic infectious disease caused by *Actinomyces israeli*, a microorganism often (and usually harmlessly) present on the gums, tonsils, and teeth. The characteristic lesion is a hard area of multiple small communicating abscesses surrounded by granulation tissue. Other similar bacteria are usually also present.

**ACTION**, federal agency founded in 1971 to coordinate U.S. government volunteer programs. Over 400,000 volunteers assist seniors, residents of low income communities, and young people through food distribution, health care, drug prevention and education, and other programs. The Retired Senior Volunteer Program and Volunteers in Service to America (VISTA) are part of ACTION. The Peace Corps, which coordinates U.S. volunteers abroad, was administered under ACTION, but became independent in 1982.

**Actium**, now Ákra Nikólaos, promontory on the west coast of Greece. In a great sea battle fought near it in 31 B C , Octavian's naval forces crushed those of Marc Antony and Cleopatra. Victory gave mastery of the Roman world to Octavian, who later became the first Roman emperor, Augustus.

**Act of Settlement**, English parliamentary act of 1701 securing the succession of the Hanoverian line. It increased parliamentary control over the monarch, who was also required to belong to the Protestant Church of England.

**Act of Union**, 4 acts of the British Parliament uniting England with Wales (1536), Scotland (1707), and Ireland (1801) and uniting Upper and Lower Canada (1840).

**Acton, Lord** (John Emerich Edward Dalberg Acton, 1st Baron Acton; 1834-1902), English historian and moralist. Lord Acton introduced German research methods into English history and launched the monumental *Cambridge Modern History* (1899- 1900). He is famous for the remark, "All power tends to corrupt, and absolute power corrupts absolutely."

**Actors Studio**, professional workshop for actors, established in New York City in 1947; Lee Strasberg became director in 1948. The school's training, often called the Method, is based on the teachings of Constantin Stanislavski, stressing an actor's psychological interpretation of a role and emotional identification with the personality of the character.

**Acts of the Apostles**, fifth book of the New Testament, the only history of the early Christian Church. Probably written between A D. 60 and 90 by the evangelist Luke, it is a continuation of St. Luke's Gospel and deals mainly with the deeds of the apostles Peter and Paul.
*See also:* Bible.

**Acupressure** (Japanese *shiatsu*), treatment system comparable to acupuncture. Pressure is applied to specific points on the surface of the body to eliminate fatigue and to stimulate natural curative abilities. Seven interrelated effects may stimulate the body to operate normally and help maintain good health: (1) invigoration of the skin, (2) stimulation of the circulation of body fluids, (3) promotion of function of striated muscles, (4) correction of disorders of the skeletal system, (5) promotion of harmonious functioning of the nervous system, (6) regulation of the operation of endocrine glands, and (7) stimulation of the normal function of internal organs.

**Acupuncture**, ancient Chinese medical practice in which fine needles are inserted into the body at specified points. It can be used as a pain reliever, an anesthesia, and a treatment for a variety of conditions, including arthritis, ulcers, and migraine. Research has shown that acupuncture has a specific effect on the release of certain chemical transmitters— natural painkillers known as endorphins—from nerve cells in the brain. Acupuncture is not fully accepted in the United States.
*See also:* Endorphins.

**A.D.**, abbreviation for *anno Domini* (Latin, "in the year of our Lord"). The monk Dionysius Exiguus started a system of reckoning years in A D 532, using the year in which he believed Christ was born at the beginning of the Christian era. A D. refers to events that took place after the birth of Christ, and B.C (before Christ) refers to events that took place before his birth.

**Adam and Eve**, first man and woman, according to the Bible (Genesis 2-3). They were created in God's image and placed in the Garden of Eden to care for the earth and its inhabitants. According to the story, Adam and Eve ate the fruit from the forbidden tree of knowledge of good and evil and were exiled from Eden by God to live a mortal life. Man was destined to a life of toil and woman to the pain of childbirth, and both were subject to death.
*See also:* Abel; Cain; Genesis.

**Adam, Robert** (1728-92) and **James** (1730-94), Scottish architect brothers. Robert's studies of ancient Roman architecture helped to inspire their joint designs of graceful interiors, furnishings, and buildings, notably Syon House (1762-69) and Osterley Park House (1761-80) in London.

**Adams, Abigail Smith** (1744-1818), wife of John Adams, the second president of the United States, and mother of John Quincy Adams, the sixth president. Largely self-educated but highly intelligent, she wrote letters giving a lively account of contemporary society.
*See also:* Adams, John.

**Adams, Ansel** (1902-85), U.S. photographer known for his dramatic black-and-white photos capturing the beauty of California's Sierra Nevada and of the American Southwest. He founded the first college photography department in 1946 at the California School of Fine Arts (now the San Francisco Art Institute).

**Adams, Brooks** (1848-1927), U.S. historian, son of U.S. diplomat Charles Francis Adams, grandson of President John Quincy Adams, and brother of historian Henry Adams. He saw history as a series of economic growth cycles, a theory developed in his chief work, *The Law of Civilization and Decay* (1895).

**Adams, Charles Francis** (1807-86), U.S. diplomat and son of President John Quincy Adams. As minister to Great Britain (1861-68), he helped to keep Britain neutral during the Civil War. In 1871-72 he represented the United States in the Alabama Claims settlement.

**Adams, Henry Brooks** (1838-1918), U.S. historian, brother of Brooks Adams. His autobiography, *The Education of Henry Adams*, in which he attempted to show how ill- prepared his generation was for the 20th century, won a Pulitzer Prize in 1919. His other works include *Mount-Saint- Michel and Chartres* (1913)and the 9-volume *History of the United States* (1885-91).

**Adams, John** (1735-1826), second president of the United States and father of the sixth president, John Quincy Adams. Adams was a brilliant political thinker who helped lead the nation's struggle for independence.

**John Adams**

| | |
|---|---|
| 2nd U.S. president | |
| Born: | Braintree (later Quincy), Massachusetts; October 30, 1735 |
| Term: | March 1797-March 1801 |
| Vice President: | Thomas Jefferson |
| Political Party: | Federalist |
| Spouse: | Abigail Smith Adams |
| Children: | 5 |
| Died: | Quincy, Massachusetts; July 4, 1826 |

*Early life.* Adams grew up on a small farm and attended Harvard University, graduating in 1755. He taught school briefly and then became a lawyer, moving to Boston in 1768. In 1764, he married Abigail Smith, the daughter of a minister.

*Revolutionary leader.* Adam's opposition to the British Parliament's Stamp Act of 1765 first brought him to political prominence. The Act, which imposed taxes on all printed materials, was Britain's first attempt to tax the colonies directly. Adams and others argued that the taxes were illegal since the colonists had no representation in Parliament. Adams risked political disfavor in 1770 when he acted as defense lawyer for the British captain and 8 soldiers accused of firing into the crowd in the Boston Massacre. But many admired him for his fairness, and in 1771 the people of Boston elected him to the colonial legislature.

In 1774 the First Continental Congress met in Philadelphia to protest the Intolerable Acts, further harsh laws enacted by the British government. Adams, representing Massachusetts, helped draft a declaration of rights and a petition to the king.

The following year, during the Second Continental Congress, he recommended the creation of the Continental Army, nominating George Washington as its commander-in-chief. In 1776 he served on the committee that prepared the Declaration of Independence.

*Diplomat.* From 1778 to 1788, with the exception of a brief return home in 1779-80, Adams lived abroad, serving the new United States in various diplomatic posts. In 1782 he helped negotiate the Treaty of Paris, which marked formal British recognition of the former colonies' independence.

*President.* In 1789 Adams became the nation's first vice president, serving under President George Washington for 2 terms. In 1796 he was elected president. Adams was a leader of the Federalist party, which supported strong central government. But many members of Adams's own cabinet were more loyal to another Federalist leader, Alexander Hamilton, than they were to Adams.

A split developed within Adams's administration over foreign policy. After the French Revolution, Britain and France were at war. Some U.S. leaders, including Vice President Thomas Jefferson, wanted the United States to join the war on the side of France. Others, led by Hamilton, wanted to go to war *against* France. In 1799 President Adams sent ministers to France in a successful attempt to negotiate a peace accord. Adams lost the support of his own party by seeking peace with France, and he angered the opposing

Democratic-Republicans by allowing passage of the Alien and Sedition Acts, which limited the rights of both foreigners and U.S. citizens. As a result, Adams lost the 1800 election and was succeeded by Thomas Jefferson as president. A few weeks before the end of his term, in what proved to be one of his most important acts, Adams appointed John Marshall as Chief Justice of the Supreme Court. Adams lived for another 26 years. In 1825 his son, John Quincy Adams, became the nation's sixth president. John Adams died on July 4th, 1826—the 50th anniversary of the Declaration of Independence.

**Adams, John Quincy** (1767-1848), sixth president of the United States and son of the second president, John Adams. Adams also served as diplomat, secretary of state, senator, and representative.

*Early life.* As a boy, Adams accompanied his father on various diplomatic missions in Europe, where he was educated. After returning home in 1785, he studied at Harvard, graduating at the age of 19. He became a lawyer and settled in Boston to practice, but he spent much of his time writing newspaper articles on political topics.

*Diplomat.* In 1794 Adams was appointed ambassador to the Netherlands by President George Washington, who had been favorably impressed by Adams's political essays. He later served in diplomatic posts in London, Lisbon, and Berlin.

In 1809 President James Madison appointed Adams the first U.S. ambassador to Russia, a post he held until 1814. Adams helped to negotiate the Treaty of Ghent (1814), which ended the War of 1812 between the U.S. and Britain. From 1815 to 1817, he was ambassador to England.

*Secretary of State.* John Quincy Adams became secretary of state in 1817, under President James Monroe. He helped develop the Monroe Doctrine, which stated U.S. opposition to involvement by European countries in the Americas. He also negotiated the treaty with Spain (1819) that ceded Florida to the United States and established a border with Mexico.

*President.* Adams's presidential term (1825-29) was probably the least successful phase of his public life and certainly the unhappiest. His political enemies accused him of having made a suspicious deal with one of the other candidates, Henry Clay, in order to become president by vote of the House of Representatives. These accusations haunted him throughout his term.

As president, Adams advocated a strong national bank, protective tariffs, conservation of public lands, and protection of Native American tribes. He

---

### John Quincy Adams

6th U.S. president

| | |
|---|---|
| Born: | Braintree (later Quincy), Massachusetts; July 11, 1767 |
| Term: | March 1825 - March 1829 |
| Vice President: | John Caldwell Calhoun |
| Political Party: | Initially Federalist, later Democratic-Republican |
| Spouse: | Louisa Catherine Johnson Adams |
| Children: | 4 |
| Died: | Washington, D.C.; Feb. 23, 1848 |

pushed for other national projects and improvements such as highways, canals, and railroads, but Congress rejected most of these ideas.

A tariff act passed during his term was so unpopular that it was called the Tariff of Abominations. Adams ran for reelection in 1828 but was defeated by Andrew Jackson.

*Return to Congress.* In 1830 Adams was elected to the U.S. House of Representatives, where he served until his death in 1848. Known as Old Man Eloquent, he fought vigorously for the right of the people to petition for the redress of wrongs, as well as against the extension of slavery. He was one of the first to claim that the federal government could free slaves during time of war, an argument that later supported President Abraham Lincoln's Emancipation Proclamation of 1862.

Adams died at the age of 80, 2 days after suffering a stroke at his desk in the House of Representatives.

**Adams, Maude** (1872-1953), U.S. actress best remembered for her leading roles at the turn of the century in plays by James Barrie, Edmond Rostand, and William Shakespeare.

**Adams, Roger** (1889-1971), U.S. chemist and teacher whose work included research on the molecular structure and laboratory synthesis of organic compounds. He contributed to medicine and industry by determining the organic composition of gossypol, the toxic cottonseed pigment; cannabinol, a compound in marijuana; and chaulmoogric, used in treating leprosy and by developing catalytic hydrogenation, a petroleum-refining process using a platinum oxide.

**Adams, Samuel** (1722-1803), American Revolutionary leader and signer of the Declaration of Independence. His oratory and writings increased colonial discontent with British rule. Adams opposed the Sugar and Stamp acts (1764-65), helped organize the Boston Tea Party (1773), and urged independence at the First Continental Congress (1774). He served as governor of Massachusetts from 1794 to 1797.

*See also:* Boston Tea Party; Continental Congress; Intolerable Acts; Revere, Paul; Stamp Act.

**Adams, Samuel Hopkins** (1871-1958), U.S. writer. As a newspaper and magazine journalist Adams attacked dishonesty in medicine, business, and government, and his collected articles, *The Great American Fraud* (1906), furthered the passage of the Pure Food and Drug Act. His novels include *The Clarion* (1914) and *Revelry* (1926).

**Adams, Sherman** (1899-1986), U.S. Republican congressional representative (1945-47), governor of New Hampshire (1949-53), and White House Chief of Staff (1953-58). Adams resigned from President Dwight D. Eisenhower's administration after political leaders condemned him for accepting gifts from industrialist Bernard Goldfine, who was under government investigation.

*See also:* Eisenhower, Dwight David.

**Adams-Onís Treaty**, or Transcontinental Treaty, U.S.-Spanish agreement (1819) defining the western boundary of the United States, negotiated by

Secretary of State John Quincy Adams and the Spanish minister to the United States, Luis de Onís. Spain ceded Florida to the United States in return for the abandonment of U.S. claims to Texas.

**Adaptation**, an organism's adjustment to its environment in order to survive, believed to arise from transmitted genetic variations preserved by natural selection. Successful and versatile adaptation in an organism leads to wide-spread distribution and long-term survival. Examples include the development of lungs in amphibians and of wings in birds and insects.
*See also:* Acclimatization; Evolution.

**Addams, Jane** (1860-1935), U.S. social reformer. With Ellen Gates Starr she founded Chicago's Hull House (1889) to provide social and cultural activities for the neighborhood poor. An ardent pacifist, she served as president of the Women's International League for Peace and Freedom from 1915 to 1929 and was cowinner of the 1931 Nobel Peace Prize.
*See also:* Hull House; Settlement house.

**Addax** (*Addax nasomaculatus*), North African desert antelope of the family Bovidae. The addax stands about 3.5 feet (1 m) at the shoulder and has spirally twisted horns and broad hoofs.

**Adder**, common name for several species of venomous and harmless snake found in different parts of the world. Examples are the European viper (*Vipera berus*) and the puff adder (*Bitis arietans*) of Africa, deadly members of the viper family, and the hognose snake (genus *Heterodon*), a harmless species found in North America.

**Adder's tongue** *See:* Dogtooth violet.

**Addis Ababa** (pop. 1,425,000), capital of Ethiopia (since 1889). The modern city, standing on an 8,000-ft (2,438-m) central plateau, is Ethiopia's center for trade, communications, and administration and houses the headquarters of the Organization of African Unity.
*See also:* Ethiopia.

**Addison, Joseph** (1672-1719), English writer and statesman, including service as secretary of state (1717-18). Author of plays and poems, it was for his lasting contribution to the English essay form that he is best remembered, especially those essays published in the *Tatler* and the *Spectator*, which he co-founded with Sir Richard Steele.
*See also:* Steele, Sir Richard.

**Addison, Thomas** (1793-1860), English physician and teacher who described Addison's disease (atrophy of the adrenal cortex) and Addison's anemia (now *pernicious anemia*).
*See also:* Addison's disease; Anemia.

**Addison's disease**, progressive disease resulting from atrophy of the cortex (outer layer) of the adrenal glands. Deficient secretion of the hormones aldosterone or cortisol causes lowered blood volume and pressure, anemia, low blood sugar, gastrointestinal upsets, and brownish pigmentation of the

skin. The cause is unknown. The disease, which occurs in all age groups and in both sexes, is often successfully treated today with adrenocortical hormones, reversing its previously fatal effects.
*See also:* Gland.

**Ade, George** (1866-1944), U.S. newspaper humorist and playwright whose *Fables in Slang* (1899) used colloquialisms and down-to-earth characters to poke fun at society.

**Adelaide** (pop. 1,049,900), capital of the state of South Australia in Australia. Located near the mouth of Torrens River, the city is an industrial center for automobiles and textiles and the commercial hub of a large region, exporting wool, grains, and dairy products. Adelaide accounts for almost two-thirds of the state's population and has many notable buildings and parks.
*See also:* Australia.

**Aden** (pop. 407,000), former capital and chief port of the People's Democratic Republic of Yemen (Southern Yemen), on the Gulf of Aden. Sana became the capital upon the creation of the Republic of Yemen (May 22, 1990) which merged the two Yemens. Under British rule from 1839 to 1967, it became a coaling station for ships sailing between Europe and India with the opening of the Suez Canal in 1869. Chief trade center of southern Arabia, it is also the country's industrial center, with an oil refinery.
*See also:* Yemen.

**Aden, Gulf of,** arm of the Arabian Sea, 550 mi (885 km) long, lying between the Republic of Yemen on the north and Somalia on the south and connected with the Red Sea by the Strait of Bab-el Mandeb. It forms part of the sea route from the Mediterranean through the Suez Canal to the Indian Ocean.

**Adenauer, Konrad** (1876-1967), first chancellor of West Germany (1949-63). A politician since World War I, he was twice imprisoned by the Nazis. He became leader of the Christian Democratic Union Party in 1947, and as chancellor he led West Germany through its postwar recovery into membership in the North Atlantic Treaty Organization (NATO) and the European Common Market.

**Adenoids,** or pharyngeal tonsils, mass of lymph tissue in the nasopharynx (above the soft palate in the back of the throat) that acts as a filter against disease. Adenoidal enlargement is the most common cause of nasal obstruction in the young and follows recurrent infections in that region.
*See also:* Tonsil.

**Adhesion,** force of attraction between surfaces of different substances, such as glue and wood or water and glass, due to intermolecular forces.
*See also:* Cohesion; Tissue.

**Adirondack Mountains,** forested range in northeast New York, source of the Hudson River, and southern extension of the Laurentian (Canadian) Shield. Mt. Marcy (5,344 ft/1,629 m), the highest peak, towers over scenic lakes and millions of acres of woodland, all contributing to make this an important resort region.
*See also:* New York.

**Adjutant**, either of 2 species of scavenger storks of India and southeast Asia. The adjutant has a naked pink neck and head, a white body, and gray wings, back, and tail. The greater adjutant (*Leptoptilos dubius*) stands about 5 ft (1.5 m) high and has a respiratory pouch hanging from the throat. The lesser adjutant (*L. javanicus*) measures about 4 ft (1.2 m).
*See also:* Stork.

**Adler, Alfred** (1870-1937), Austrian psychiatrist who founded the school of individual psychology. Adler believed that feelings of inferiority account for the maladjustment of certain individuals to society. He saw the overcoming of these feelings as the basic human drive for power.
*See also:* Psychology.

**Adler, Dankmar** (1844-1900), German-born U.S. architect and engineer whose partnership with Louis Sullivan from 1881 helped to create the famous Chicago School of Architecture. Adler's first important work was the Chicago Central Music Hall (1879).
*See also:* Sullivan, Louis Henri.

**Adler, Felix** (1851-1933), German-born U.S. educator and social reformer, founder of the Ethical Culture movement. He held professorships in Semitic literature and social and political ethics and championed educational, housing, and child-labor reforms.

**Admiral**, in several countries, including the United States, the highest rank in the navy. In the U.S. Navy, grades are fleet admiral, admiral, vice admiral, and rear admiral.
*See also:* Rank, military.

**Admiralty Islands**, group of about 40 volcanic and coral-reef Melanesian islands in the South Pacific, some 200 mi (320 km) northwest of New Guinea, in the Bismarck Archipelago.
*See also:* Bismarck Archipelago; Pacific Islands.

**Adobe**, Spanish name for sun-dried clay and straw bricks of Mexico and the southwest United States; also, a structure made of adobe brick. Because the brick will crumble if exposed to excessive moisture or cold, it is used for building only in hot, dry climates. Material similar to adobe has been used in arid climates throughout the world since ancient times.

**Adolescence**, period of life between childhood and full adulthood (between 12 and 20 years of age). Its physical manifestation is puberty, the development of sex characteristics, making possible sexual union and reproduction. Physical changes include the development of breasts in girls, changes in voice in boys, and the appearance of pubic hair in both. Adolescence is of psychological interest because of the changes in attitudes, emotional responsiveness, and social behavior that accompany this sexual maturation.
*See also:* Developmental psychology; Growth.

**Adonis**, in Greek mythology, beautiful mortal beloved of Aphrodite and Persephone. In an effort to resolve the problem of who would keep Adonis, Zeus commanded that he spend 6 months of every year on earth with

Aphrodite, during which crops flourished, and 6 months in the underworld with Persephone, during which the earth was barren. This myth was used by the Greeks to explain the changing of the seasons. In another myth, Adonis is killed by Aphrodite's husband who is disguised as a boar.
*See also:* Aphrodite.

**Adrenal glands,** or suprarenal glands, small endocrine glands closely attached to the upper part of each kidney, each comprising a central medulla and a surrounding cortex. The adrenal medulla secretes the hormones epinephrine (adrenaline) and norepinephrine. Release of these hormones follows stress-related stimuli such as pain, emotional disturbance, hypotension (low blood sugar), exposure to severe cold, and muscular exertion. The adrenal medulla is not essential to life; a person can survive in good health after total removal of the glands if adequate substitution therapy is provided. The adrenal cortex secretes about 30 steroid hormones that are separated into 3 main groups. The glucocorticoids, including cortisol, enhance glucose formation in the tissues and cells. The mineralocorticoids, including aldosterone, are steroids that promote retention of sodium and excretion of potassium by the kidney. The androgens are sex hormones that have a weaker effect than those produced by the (male) testes and (female) ovaries. Disorders of the adrenal cortex, such as Addison's disease or Cushing's syndrome, may be due to either defective or excessive secretion of hormones.
*See also:* Epinephrine; Gland; Hormone.

**Adrenalin** *See:* Epinephrine.

**Adrian IV** (Nicholas Breakspear; 1100?-59), only Englishman to become pope (1154-59). He crowned Frederick Barbarossa as Holy Roman Emperor in 1155, but angered Frederick by his persistent demands for papal supremacy and also by excommunicating the crowned king of Sicily, William I the Bad. Adrian then invested William upon his pledge of allegiance and service to him. He also promised excommunication for Frederick when the latter declared himself ruler of northern Italy, but he died before carrying out his threat.

**Adriatic Sea,** arm of the Mediterranean Sea between Italy and former Yugoslavia and Albania. The Adriatic extends for about 500 mi (800 km), with an average width of 110 mi (177 km) and a depth of up to 4,201 ft (1,250 m). The Strait of Otranto links it to the Ionian Sea to the south.

**Adsorption,** adhesion of molecules to a surface, to be distinguished from absorption.
*See also:* Absorption.

**Adult education,** or continuing educaton, learning undertaken by adults. Originally offering adults the educational opportunities missed in youth, adult education is now seen more as part of an ongoing process, enhancing the education already received. In the United States adult education started with the Lyceum Movement, early in the 19th century. After the Civil War, important advances were made by the Chautauqua Movement and in various federal agricultural education acts. During the Depression the Works Projects Administration (WPA) provided education programs for 2 million adults, and after World War II the G.I. Bill of Rights made advanced learning available for veterans. In the 1960s federal funds provided for basic literacy programs under the Economic Opportunity Act.

**Advent** (from Latin *adventus*, "arrival"), first season of the Christian church year. It begins on the Sun. nearest Nov. 30 (St. Andrew's Day) and ends on Christmas Eve. Advent has been observed since the 6th century as a period of meditative preparation for the celebration of Christ's birth and second coming.
*See also:* Christmas.

**Adventists**, members of Christian sects, mainly in the United States, who believe in the imminent second coming of Christ. Adventism grew from the teachings of William Miller (1782-1849). Members of the largest Adventist sect, the Seventh-Day Adventists, formally organized in 1863, observe Saturday as the Sabbath and support an extensive missionary program.
*See also:* Seventh-day Adventists.

**Advertising**, paid publicity designed to persuade people to buy a product or service or to adopt a viewpoint. U.S. advertising in magazines, newspapers, radio, and television provides these media with most of their income. Advertisers pay advertising agencies to conduct market research, formulate advertising campaigns, buy the necessary time or space in the medium or media chosen, and produce the actual advertisements. The United States spends more money on advertising than any other country in the world.

**Aegean civilization**, collective term for the Bronze Age civilizations surrounding the Aegean Sea. These cultures, which flourished from 3000 to 1200 B C, are the Mycenaean, or Helladic, culture of the Greek mainland; the Cycladic culture of the Cyclades; the Minoan culture of Crete; and the Trojan culture. Archeological work in the area was begun in the 1870s-80s by Heinrich Schliemann, who located Troy.
*See also:* Crete; Mycenae; Schliemann, Heinrich; Troy.

**Aegean Sea**, arm of the Mediterranean Sea between mainland Greece and Turkey, the heart of the classical Greek world. About 400 mi (640 km) long and 200 mi (320 km) wide, its numerous islands, known as the Grecian Archipelago, include the Sporades, Dodecanese, and Cyclades groups. Islanders live by fishing and tourism; the Aegean also contains deposits of natural gas.
*See also:* Mediterranean Sea.

**Aeneas**, mythological Trojan prince. son of Venus and Anchises and hero of the Roman poet Vergil's *Aeneid*. After the fall of Troy he rescued his father and son and fled to Carthage and then to Italy. Rome was said to be founded by his descendants, Romulus and Remus.
*See also:* Aeneid; Vergil.

**Aeneid**, epic Latin poem, 12 books in length, depicting the life of the mythical Trojan hero Aeneas. The poem, written by Vergil between 30 and 19 B C., describes the great achievements of Aeneas as he sought to create a new nation. Vergil selected his theme to bring glory to the emperor, Augustus, and to reconfirm the integrity of religious values in ancient Rome.

**Aeolian harp**, ancient musical instrument, the strings of which are vibrated ("played") by the wind. It is constructed of a wooden box with 2 low wood bridges, across which the strings are loosely stretched. The harp is named for the ancient Greek god of the winds, Aeolus.

**Aeolians**, an ancient Greek people. They lived in east-central Greece until c.1150 B C, when invading Dorians forced many from their land. They moved to what is now Turkey and the nearby islands of Lesbos and Tenedos. *See also:* Greece, Ancient.

**Aerobics**, exercise program specifically focused on improving physical fitness by forcing the lungs and heart to work hard for a long period, thus improving cardiovascular functioning. Running, swimming, and cycling are common aerobic activities.

**Aerodynamics**, branch of physics dealing with the motion of air and other gases and their flow around a body in motion, used particularly in the development of the airplane and other aircraft. Aerodynamic forces depend on the body's size, shape, and velocity and on the density, compressibility, viscosity, temperature, and pressure of the gas. At low velocities flow around the body is streamlined and causes low drag; at higher velocities turbulence occurs, with fluctuating eddies, and drag is much greater. Additional drag is created by friction. Pressure impulses radiate at the speed of sound ahead of the moving body; at supersonic velocities these impulses pile up, producing a shock wave—the "sonic boom." In airplane design all of these factors must be considered. In normal cruising flight the lift provided by the wings must equal the aircraft's weight; the forward thrust of the engine must balance the forces of drag. Lift occurs because the wing's upper surface is more convex, and therefore longer, than the lower surface, creating a difference in air speed and thus pressure, according to Bernoulli's principle. *See also:* Wind tunnel.

**Aeronautics**, technology of aircraft design, manufacture, and performance. *See also:* Aerodynamics; Airplane.

**Aerosol**, suspension of small liquid or solid particles in a gas. Examples include smoke, fog, and clouds. Aerosol particles can remain in suspension for hours, or even indefinitely. Aerosols are also manufactured for the dispersion of insecticides, air fresheners, paints, cosmetics, etc. The use of the most common aerosol propellants, the fluorocarbons, has been curtailed because they have been implicated in the destruction of the ozone layer of the atmosphere. *See also:* Fluorocarbon; Ozone.

**Aertsen (Aertszen), Pieter** (1508-75), Dutch painter of finely detailed still-lifes and domestic interiors. He is regarded as one of the founders of genre painting.

**Aeschylus** (525-456 B C.), earliest of the 3 great dramatists of ancient Greece, preceding Sophocles and Euripides. He is often regarded as the originator of tragedy. Only 7 of at least 80 plays survive, including *The Persians, Prometheus Bound,* and the *Oresteia,* which concerns the murder of Agamemnon by his wife, Clytemnestra, and the subsequent revenge of their son, Orestes. Aeschylus elaborated Greek dramatic form by adding a second actor (previously the poet had spoken all roles) and exploiting the dramatic possibilities of dialogue.

**Aesculapius** *See:* Asclepius.

**Aesop,** in tradition, Greek author of animal fables, said to have been a slave on 6th-century B.C. Samos, but perhaps a wholly legendary figure. Some fables attributed to Aesop are known in versions by La Fontaine and other writers.
*See also:* Allegory; La Fontaine, Jean de.

**Affidavit,** voluntary statement reduced to writing and sworn to or affirmed before an authorized magistrate or officer. Affidavits are not testimony in courts of law because the makers cannot be cross-examined, but a person who makes a false affidavit may be punished for perjury.

**Affirmative action,** U.S. program designed to increase the numbers of minority group members or of women in jobs or schools from which they were previously wholly or partly excluded. Affirmative action flourished in the 1960s under the leadership of Presidents Kennedy and Johnson and was institutionalized by the Equal Employment Opportunity Act of 1972. Critics have charged that the racial quotas and timetables of some affirmative action plans bring about reverse discrimination. Affirmative action was dealt a sharp blow in 1978, when the Supreme Court, in the Bakke case, ruled against the use of strict racial quotas.
*See also:* Bakke case.

**Afghan hound,** breed of dog known for speed and agility, used as a hunter in Afghanistan for centuries. It stands 24-28 in. (61-71 cm) in height at the shoulder and weighs 50-60 lb (23-27 kg), has long ears, a slim body, large feet, and a coat of long silky hair. The breed originated in Egypt c. 3000 B C , was perfected in Afghanistan to hunt the leopard and gazelle, and was discovered by Europeans in the 1800s and brought to England after World War I.

**Afghanistan,** land-locked country in central Asia.
*Land and climate.* The high rugged mountains of the Hindu Kush cover three quarters of the country. The winters are extremely cold (as low as 15°F/–9°C) and the summers extremely hot (up to 120°F/49°C). There is very little rainfall, but the Hindu Kush is a major watershed containing fertile river valleys.
*People.* The majority of the people live in the fertile mountain valleys. About 2.5 million are nomadic. Islam is the most important factor in the everyday life of the country. The two principal languages are Pashtu and Dari.
*Economy.* Less than 15% of the country is good for cultivation. Main crops are wheat, corn, barley, rice, and fruits. Sheep are also raised. Fruits, wool,

## Afghanistan

| | |
|---|---|
| Capital: | Kabul |
| Area: | 251,825 sq mi |
| | (652,225 sq km) |
| Population: | 24,792,000 |
| Language: | Pashto; Dari Persian |
| Government: | Islamic republic |
| Independent: | 1747 |
| Head of gov.: | Prime minister |
| Per capita: | U.S. $765 |
| Mon. unit: | 1 Afghani (AF) |
| | = 100 puls |

skins, and various handicrafts are important sources of foreign exchange. Coal and salt have been mined for some years, and the country has long been famous for its lapis lazuli. Iron ore is plentiful, and vast deposits of natural gas have been exploited. The lack of an infrastructure is a major obstacle to economic development; there are few paved roads, and there is no railroad. *History.* Afghanistan was conquered by Alexander the Great in 330 B C and thrived as the Kingdom of Bactria (250-150 B.C.). The Arabs conquered Afghanistan in the 7th century, and Islam took root. Genghis Khan and Tamerlane invaded, and Babur (1143-1530) used Kabul as his base for establishing the Mogul Empire in India. Afghanistan became a united state under Ahmed Shah in 1747. Amanullah (1919-29) seized control of foreign policy from the British, began modernizing, and proclaimed a monarchy in 1926. The last king, Mohammed Zahir Shah, was overthrown in 1973 by Lt. Gen. Sardar Mohammed Daud Khan, who became president and prime minister of the new republic. Daud was overthrown in 1978 and replaced by the pro-Soviet government of Noor Mohammed Taraki. Taraki was overthrown by Hafi-zullah Amon, who was in turn overthrown by Babrak Karmal. In December 1979, 100,000 Soviet troops invaded. In 1979 Soviet troops invadede Afghanistan in order to contain the rebellion. Despite the withdrawal of the Soviet troops in 1989 and various steps towards a transition to a new government the fighting continued into the 1990s. At the end of the 1990s the Taliban (radical-islamic militia) was almost entirely in control of the country. Taliban laws and regulations made it difficult for the European Union to provide aid, and as a result this aid was discontinued in July 1998.

**AFL** *See:* American Federation of Labor and Congress of Industrial Organizations.

**Africa,** world's second-largest continent, 11,672,639 sq m (30,232,135 sq km). Africa includes Madagascar and many smaller offshore islands. With the completion of the Suez Canal in the 19th century, Africa was severed from Asia and is completely surrounded by water. Its coastline has few indentations, bays, or inlets, thus, few good harbors. From narrow coastal plains the land rises steeply to form the immense African plateau about 2.000 ft (610 m) above sea level. Apart from the coastal plains, the Congo Basin is the only sizable lowland region. The Atlas Mountains form the continent's major system, including Africa's highest peak, Mt. Kilimanjaro (19,340 ft/5,895 m) in Tanzania.The Great Rift Valley of East Africa is the continent's major geological feature, with its long narrow depressions forming some of the world's largest lakes: Lake Victoria (26,828 sq mi/69,485 sq km), third largest lake in the world; Lake Tanganyika (5,715 ft/1,742 m deep), the largest freshwater lake in the world; and Lake Nyasa (360 mi/579 km long and 50 mi/80 km wide). The great rivers of Africa include the Nile (4,157 mi/6,690 km), the world's longest; the Niger; the Congo; and the Zambesi, which has been dammed at the Kariba Gorge, where it forms a lake 120 mi (193 km) long.The great mass of Africa lies within the tropics, but contains a variety of climates. The equatorial rain forest of the Congo Basin, which receives up to 200 in. (508 cm) of rain per year, and the tropical rain forest along the Gulf of Guinea and in west Central Africa account for 20% of the continent. The humid subtropical regions have up to 43 in (109 cm) of rainfall per year. Temperate grasslands known as savannah or veldt cover 40% of Africa and usually have one dry and one rainy season per year with 20-50 in (51-127 cm) annual rainfall. The deserts cover more than 40% of the continent and include the Sahara, the world's largest, in the north and the Kalahari in the south. Finally, Africa's Mediterranean coast and the area south and southwest of Cape Province enjoy the most moderate climate, with average annual rainfall of 15-30 in (38-76 cm), hot summers, and warm pleasant winters.

Africa's richly varied animal life is largely preserved in national parks. Poaching, the increase in human populations, and economic development have reduced the animal population, leading to the extinction of many species and threatening more.

Africa's population consists of many distinct peoples and cultures. The northern part of the continent, from Morocco in the west to Egypt in the east, is primarily Arab, with minorities of Berbers and Tuaregs. South of the Sahara the population is overwhelmingly black. Excluding European languages introduced by colonizers, there are nearly 1,000 different languages or distinct dialects. Most people in North Africa speak Arabic; major languages in black Africa include Swahili, Hausa, Yoruba, Xhosa, and Amharic. Besides those who practice the native religions of the black African majority, there are more than 100 million African Muslims and about 35 million Christians, 5 million of them belonging to the ancient Coptic church of Egypt and Ethiopia.

The countries of Africa are Algeria, Angola, Benin, Botswana, Burkina Faso, Burundi, Cameroon, Cape Verde, Central African Republic, Chad, Comoros, Congo Republic, Djibouti, part of Egypt, Equatorial Guinea, Eritrea, Ethiopia, Gabon, Gambia, Ghana, Guinea, Guinea-Bissau, Ivory Coast, Kenya, Lesotho, Liberia, Libya, Madagascar, Malawi, Mali, Mauritania, Mauritius, Morocco, Mozambique, Namibia, Niger, Nigeria, Rwanda, São Tomé and Principe, Senegal, Seychelles, Sierra Leone, Somalia Republic, Republic of South Africa, Sudan, Swaziland, Tanzania, Togo, Tunisia, Uganda, Western Sahara, Zaïre, Zambia, and Zimbabwe.

**African Americans**, preferred term to designate Americans of African descent, who account for about 12 percent of the U.S. population, a major minority group in society. Most African Americans live in the South and in the large cities of the North, in many of which they constitute a large portion, or even a majority, of the population.

The first African Americans were brought to North America as indentured servants, under contract to work for a particular master for a specified period, after which they were free. But from the early 1600s, the expansion of the slave trade brought larger and larger numbers of Africans who were forced to work on the expanding plantations in the South.

The institution of slavery was recognized by the U.S. Constitution, and the importance of slaves increased after 1793, when the invention of the cotton gin gave southern plantations a new financial viability. Conflict between slave society in the South and industrial development in the North led eventually to the Civil War, which ended slavery in the United States. During the period of Reconstruction (1865-77), newly freed African Americans, despite extreme poverty, played a major role in political life, 16 serving in Congress. But Reconstruction was followed by the reimposition of discriminatory legislation and practices, denying African Americans the right to vote and segregating them socially. The system of segregation, sanctioned by the Supreme Court in its *Plessy* v. *Ferguson* decision of 1896, kept the African American population in conditions of social, economic, and political oppression. That system began to break down only after World War II. In 1954 the Supreme Court outlawed "separate but equal" facilities in its historic *Brown* v. *Board of Education* decision. The struggle for equal rights and the abolition of segregation soon took a new turn.

In the 1950s and 1960s African Americans developed a broad-based civil rights movement to end discrimination in education, jobs, public facilities, and voting rights. The successes of this movement eliminated most formal barriers to the incorporation of African Americans into U.S. society, but socioeconomic discrimination remained; the gap between white and black average incomes, for example, widened during the 1980s, despite the emergence of an African American middle class. African Americans have made major contributions to U.S. society in many areas. They fought in all the nation's wars, though in integrated units only after World War II. Notable African American historical figures include Frederick Douglass and George Washington Carver, who made significant contributions to politics and science in the 19th century. In the early 1900s, Booker T. Washington, W.E.B. DuBois, and Marcus Garvey were major political leaders. The towering figures of the 1950s and 1960s included Martin Luther King, Jr., and Malcolm X. More recently, African Americans have made their mark in the political sphere (Mayor David Dinkins in New York City), the military (General Colin Powell, Chairman of the Joint Chiefs of Staff), and as members of federal, state, and local legislatures. They have achieved nationwide recognition for outstanding contributions in literature, the arts, sports, entertainment, business, and education.

**African Methodist Episcopal Church** (A.M.E.), black Protestant denomination akin to, but separate from, white Methodist denominations. Founded in Philadelphia (1815) by the Rev. Richard Allen, it is the largest black Methodist body, with about 6,000 churches and 2,000,000 members. *See also:* Allen, Richard.

**African Methodist Episcopal Zion Church** (A.M.E. Zion), independent Methodist denomination founded in New York City in 1796 by blacks disaffected by white prejudices. The church has over 1,000,000 members.

**African National Congress**, black African organization devoted to the "creation of a united democratic South Africa" and the political empowerment of blacks. Founded in 1912 as the Native National Congress, the organization encouraged passive resistance to the "pass" laws and other instruments of apartheid. After an outbreak of violence, it was banned in 1961 by the government of South Africa. Its leader, Nelson Mandela, was sentenced to life imprisonment, but he was released Feb. 1990 and the ban was lifted. The ANC won the majority of the votes in the first democratic elections in South Africa in 1994.
*See also:* Apartheid; Mandela, Nelson; South Africa.

**African violet**, any of a genus (*Saintpaulia*) of perennial herbs with velvety heart-shaped leaves and purple, pink, or white violetlike flowers, native to tropical East Africa.

**Afrikaans**, one of the 11 official languages of South Africa. Afrikaans evolved from the form of Dutch spoken by 17th-century Boer settlers, but incorporates Bantu, Khoisan, Malayo-Portuguese, and English words.

**Afrikaners** *See:* Boers.

**AFS Intercultural Programs**, nonprofit organization providing student exchange programs to promote living and learning experience in foreign countries. Founded in 1914 as the American Field Service and originating as a volunteer ambulance corps during World War I, the AFS became a student exchange program in 1947. Active in about 70 countries, its programs primarily involve high school age students and young professionals.

**Afterbirth** *See:* Placenta.

**Aga Khan**, spiritual leader of the Ismaili sect of Shi'te Muslims; a hereditary title. His millions of followers are dispersed through the Near East, India, Pakistan, and parts of Africa and are descended from 14th-century Hindus converted by Persian Ismails. **Aga Khan I** (Hasan Ali Shah; 1800-81), a Persian provincial governor who emigrated to India in 1840, was invested as leader of the sect in 1866. **Aga Khan II** (Ali Shah) held the title from 1881 until his death in 1885. **Aga Khan III** (Sultan Sir Mahomed Shah; 1877-1957) represented British India at numerous conferences and as first president of the All-Indian Muslim League worked for Indian independence. **Aga Khan IV** (H.H. Shah Karim; 1936-   ) inherited the title in 1957.
*See also:* Islam.

**Agamemnon**, in Greek legend, son of Atreus and king of Mycenae who organized the expedition against Troy recounted in Homer's *Iliad*. Before setting sail he was forced to sacrifice his daughter Iphigenia. He was murdered on his return home by his wife Clytemnestra and her lover, his cousin Aegisthus. His death was avenged by his son, Orestes, and his daughter Electra.
*See also:* Iliad; Mycenae; Trojan War.

**Ágana** (pop. 900), capital and political center of the island of Guam, a U.S. territory in the western Pacific Ocean.

**Agassiz, Louis** (Jean Louis Rodolphe Agassiz; 1807-73), Swiss-American naturalist, geologist, and educator who first proposed (1840) that large areas of the northern continents had been covered by ice sheets in the geologically recent past. He is also noted for his studies of fishes. He became a professor of zoology and geology at Harvard in 1848, where he founded the Museum of Comparative Zoology in 1859.

**Agate**, variety of the quartz chalcedony, found chiefly in Brazil and Uruguay. Agates form as layers in the cavities of older rocks, creating characteristic bands of colors. Semiprecious stones, they are used to make ornaments and grinding equipment.

**Agave**, any of a genus (*Agave*) of economically important U.S. tropical plants of the amaryllis family. Different species are used to produce soaps, foods, and drinks.

**Agee, James** (1909-55), U.S. writer whose works include *Let Us Now Praise Famous Men* (1941), a portrayal of Depression-era white sharecroppers done in collaboration with photographer Walker Evans, and a partly autobiographical novel, *A Death in the Family* (1957), which won a Pulitzer Prize. Agee was an influential film critic and also wrote screenplays, including *The African Queen* (1951) and *The Night of the Hunter* (1955).

**Agency for International Development** (AID), U.S. government agency formed in 1961 to administer nonmilitary foreign aid. It promotes long-range economic programs that help developing countries become self-sufficient, chiefly in the areas of health, education, and agriculture.

**Agent Orange**, herbicide used by the United States during the Vietnam War to defoliate the jungle. Agent Orange was contaminated with dioxin, a substance discovered to be toxic to human beings and animals. Use of the chemical was abandoned in the late 1970s. In postwar years, 60,000 veterans complained to the Veterans Administration that they had suffered lasting damage from Agent Orange poisoning. In 1984 the manufacturers of Agent Orange created a relief fund for the victims of Agent Orange.
*See also:* Vietnam War; Chemical and biological warfare.

**Age of Reason**, or the Enlightenment, a period in history in which accepted social, political, and religious doctrines were challenged by a new, rational view of the universe. Beginning in the 1600s and lasting until the late 1700s, the movement was led by such philosophers as, in France, René Descartes, Denis Diderot, Jean Jacques Rousseau, and Voltaire, and, in England, John Locke. Scholars of the period produced many breakthroughs in the fields of anatomy, astronomy, chemistry, mathematics, and physics. Their ideas about human dignity and progress influenced the future leaders of the French Revolution.
*See also:* Locke, John; Rousseau, Jean-Jacques.

**Aggression**, behavior characterized by physical or verbal attack. Aggression is defined by psychoanalysts as a manifestation of the will to have power over other people (Alfred Adler) or as a projection of the death impulse (Sigmund Freud). Unable to find a satisfactory explanation for the human

readiness for hatred and aggression, Freud believed that it may be instinctual. Thus, the violent and strenuous behavior shown by infants may not be oriented toward a goal. Still, in many instances aggression that serves no apparent goal is associated with emotional disorder.
*See also:* Psychology.

**Agincourt**, now Azincourt, village in northwest France, scene of a decisive battle in the Hundred Years' War. On Oct. 25, 1415, English forces under Henry V routed the French under Claude d'Albret, demonstrating the power of the English longbow over a heavily armored enemy. The French lost over 7,000 men, the English only a few hundred.
*See also:* Hundred Years War.

**Agnes, Saint**, 4th-century virgin martyr of the Roman Catholic Church and patron saint of young girls. For refusing to sacrifice to pagan gods, she was disgraced, miraculously saved, and martyred. On her feast day, Jan. 21, the pope blesses 2 lambs in the church of St. Agnes; their wool is used to weave palla (items of ceremonial dress) for archbishops.

**Agnew, Spiro Theodore** (1918-96), U.S. vice president under Richard Nixon (1969-73). Agnew was elected Republican governor of Maryland (1966) and gained a reputation as a moderate liberal, though he later took a conservative stand toward civil rights demonstrations and urban unrest. He resigned from the vice presidency in 1973 following revelations of political corruption in his Maryland administration and pleaded no contest to a charge that he had failed to report income from payoffs by Maryland business people, for which he was fined $10,000. A Maryland court later fined him $248,000 for taking bribes while in office.
*See also:* Nixon, Richard Milhous.

**Agnon, Shmuel Yosef** (Samuel Josef Czaczkes; 1888-1970), Israeli writer remembered for his novels and stories of Jewish life in his native Galicia and in Palestine. In 1966 he shared the Nobel Prize for literature (with Nelly Sachs of Sweden) for works that include *The Bridal Canopy* (1937) and *The Day Before Yesterday* (1945).

**Agnosticism**, doctrine that one cannot know about things beyond the realm of one's experience, in particular about God. Unlike atheism, which is a rejection of divine order, agnosticism is a skeptical holding back of judgment in the absence of proof.
*See also:* Atheism.

**Agra** (pop. 891,800), historic city in the northern Indian state of Uttar Pradesh, which is situated on the Jumna River, 110 mi (177 km) southeast of Delhi. An important military and commercial center, it produces cotton, grain, raw silk, sugar, and rugs. It was the capital of the Mogul empire during the late 16th and the first half of the 17th centuries. The city has several beautiful and important Mogul buildings, including the Taj Mahal, built by Shah Jahan.
*See also:* Taj Mahal.

**Agribusiness**, the business of agriculture, extended to include supply, management, information, and machine services, as well as processing and distribution. A rapidly growing industry in the United States, agribusiness employs about one-fourth the U.S. work force.

**Agricola, Gnaeus Julius** (A D. 37-93), Roman general. As proconsul of Britain (77-84) he defeated the Caledonians and extended Roman rule into Scotland. His son-in-law, the historian Tacitus, wrote the famous biography of Agricola.

**Agricultural education**, as an organized field of study began only at the end of the 18th century, when a number of agricultural societies grew up in the United States and Great Britain. In the United States the first steps on the national level began with the Morrill Act (1862), which gave grants of land to the states to assist them in setting up colleges for mechanical and agricultural training. In 1917 the federal government also began to sponsor agricultural education in secondary schools. The Future Farmers of America and 4 H clubs have also been developed to encourage agricultural interest among boys and girls.

**Agriculture**, science and practice of farming, including the production of crops, the rearing of livestock, and the care of soil. The storing and sowing of seeds, central to agriculture, developed in the Neolithic period. Tools and techniques developed gradually over the centuries. The organization of farming, especially the ownership of land, was crucial in determining the prevailing social, economic, and political structures of civilizations as diverse as those of Egypt and Babylonia, China, Rome, and Japan. In medieval Europe the self-contained manorial system shaped the agricultural village. Late in the Middle Ages communal subsistence farming gave way to farms organized to produce salable surpluses. The agricultural revolution of the 16th and 17th centuries saw advances in horticultural techniques, and by the dawn of the industrial revolution, farming was concentrated in fewer hands and was geared to feeding the cities and supplying raw materials for manufactures. During the 19th century the United States led the world in agricultural development. The transportation revolution, new machines such as McCormick's reaper, the introduction of artificial fertilizers, and increased specialization all helped raise productivity. In the late 20th century agriculture in most industrialized countries is highly specialized and relies upon pesticides, growth-stimulating antibiotics for livestock, fertilizers, and artificial insemination. By contrast, agriculture in much of the Third World is not mechanized, crop yields are not high, and famine still occurs.

**Agriculture, U.S. Department of**, executive department of the U.S. government concerned with the promotion and regulation of agriculture. Established in 1862, the department operates research, credit extension, conservation, crop control, distribution, and other programs.

**Agrimony**, any of a genus (*Agrimonia*) of woodland plants of the rose family, native to Europe, Asia, North America, and the Andes Mountains of South America. The agrimony plant has featherlike hairy leaves and clusters of small yellow flowers on long spikes; the fruit is a cone-shaped burr.

**Agrippa, Marcus** *See:* Augustus.

**Agrippina The Younger** (A D 15-59), mother by her first marriage, of Nero and second wife of the Roman emperor Claudius. Agrippina persuaded Claudius to adopt Nero as his son and heir and then poisoned the emperor. When she interfered with Nero's rule, he had her murdered.
*See also:* Claudius; Nero.

**Agronomy,** branch of agricultural science dealing with production of field crops and management of the soil. The agronomist studies crop diseases, selective breeding, crop rotation, and climatic factors and also tests and analyzes the soil, investigates soil erosion, and designs land reclamation and irrigation schemes.

**Aguinaldo, Emilio** (1869-1964), leader of the Philippine independence movement. After helping the United States capture the Philippines during the Spanish-American War (1898), he led Filipino guerilla warfare against U.S. occupation. He was defeated in 1901.
*See also:* Philippines.

**Ahmadabad,** or Ahmedabad (pop. 2,800,000), capital of the state of Gujarat in northwest India, situated on the Sabarmati River, north of Bombay. One of the largest and most important cities of India in Mogul times, Ahmadabad was ceded to the British in 1818. The modern city is an important trade center, particularly for cotton textiles, and a railway junction.
*See also:* India.

**Ahmad Shah** (1724-73), Afghan ruler who founded the Durrani dynasty. Through several successful invasions of India he acquired a huge empire. Although unable to hold his empire together, he succeeded in strengthening and uniting Afghanistan and is thus often thought of as founder of the modern nation.

**Ahura Mazda** *See:* Zoroastrianism.

**AIDS** (Acquired Immune Deficiency Syndrome), viral disease that compromises the body's immune system, leaving the victim susceptible to dangerous diseases and infections. The virus, known as HIV (human immunodeficiency virus), uses certain white blood cells, known as T-helper cells, as hosts and eventually destroys them. Those with AIDS are likely to suffer from Kaposi's sarcoma (a rare and usually fatal skin cancer), *pneumocystis carinii pneumonia* (a lung infection caused by parasites), chronic herpes simplex (a virus that can cause ulcerating anal and oral herpes), as well as infections that attack the bone marrow, liver, or brain. Early flu-like symptoms of AIDS are fatigue, fever, night sweats and chills, and weight loss. During the next stage, patients display symptoms specific to diseases that appear with the breakdown of the immune system. Later symptoms are likely to include skin lesions, shortness of breath, seizures, and mental disorientation. Those currently at highest risk of infection in the United States are intravenous drug users, prostitutes, hemophiliacs and others who have required repeated transfusion, and babies of infected women. Although AIDS used to be known as a disease which occurred primarily among homosexuals, AIDS can be contracted just as easily by heterosexuals. The virus is transmitted through blood and semen. Saliva, tears, and urine also contain the virus, but so far have not been found to be effective vectors. Preventive measures include avoiding sexual contact with those who are infected, using condoms, using only sterilized needles and not sharing them with anyone, and avoiding contact with blood or sores of those infected. The education of children and adults is an important preventive measure in the battle against the disease. There is at present no cure for AIDS, but since its detection in 1981, care of AIDS patients has improved. AZT (azidothymide) has proven the most effective drug to date in inhibiting the virus's ability to reproduce, but it is a retardant, not a cure, and its side effects can include anemia, dementia, and blindness. Research for effective treatment and cure continues. Since 1997, combination therapy is used in the struggle against AIDS. A cocktail of three drugs ( AZT, 3TC, and Ritonavir), is able to remove the virus from the blood and lymph node tissue of previously untreated seropositive patients. The originator of this therapy is David Ho. The first positive results were presented in Amsterdam, in November 1997, by researchers of the Academic Medical Center. The therapy is expensive and hard, and must be maintained. If not, resistent virusses will develope. There are people who get into contact with the virus, but do not get ill for a long period of time, or not at all. In 1997 scientists stated that a defect of the CCR5 gene is the cause of this natural defense. As a result of this defect, the virus is not able to invade the T-cells. Other gene defects might have the same result.

**Aiken, Conrad Potter** (1889-1973), U.S. writer. His *Selected Poems* (1929) won a Pulitzer Prize (1930). His critiques and essays on poetry were published in *A Reviewer's ABC* (1958). Other prose works include the novel *Great Circle* (1933) and his autobiography, *Ushant* (1952).

**Ailanthus**, any of a genus (*Ailanthus* ) of tropical-looking deciduous trees native to Asia and Australia but now widely cultivated in Europe and North America. The best-known species, *A. altissima*, grows up to 60 ft (18 m) high and thrives in polluted urban conditions in almost any kind of substrate.

**Ailey, Alvin** (1931-89), U.S. dancer and choreographer. Ailey was a pupil of Lester Horton, with whom he made his debut in 1950. He began choreographing in 1953 and formed his own company, the Alvin Ailey American Dance Theater, in 1958. *Creation of the World* (1954), *Blues Suite* (1958), and *Revelations* (1960) are among his most noted works.

**AIM** *See:* American Indian Movement.

**Ainu**, Japanese aborigines, possibly of Caucasoid descent, distinguished by stockiness, pale skin, and profuse body hair. Most Ainu live on Hokkaido, the northernmost of Japan's major islands. Ainu speech, little used today, bears no relation to any other language. The Ainu are few in number, many having been assimilated into Japanese society.
*See also:* Japan.

**Air**, heterogeneous mixture of tasteless, odorless, colorless, and invisible gases surrounding the earth, consisting of about 78% nitrogen, 21% oxygen, and 1% argon, carbon dioxide, hydrogen, krypton, neon, helium, and xenon.

Air is what we breathe and what is essential to all plant and animal life. It is kept close to the surface of the planet by the force of gravity.
*See also:* Air pollution; Climate; Gas; Nitrogen; Oxygen; Weather.

**Airborne troops**, or paratroops or sky soldiers, soldiers brought into a combat area by parachute drop or airplane. Airborne troops have been a part of military strategy since World War II, often figuring in surprise attacks. After landing behind enemy lines, the troops may be used to destroy bridges, communications, and supplies or for hand-to-hand combat.The airborne troops of the U.S. Army are all volunteers.
*See also:* Parachute.

**Airbrush**, pencil-like painting tool that uses compressed air to apply a fine spray. A smaller, more delicate version of the spray gun, the airbrush is often used to shade drawings, retouch photographs, or accent highlights in prints. The operator creates different effects by varying the air pressure passing through the brush.

**Air compressor**, device used to compress air, which is then used to power air brakes, pneumatic tools, and other machinery. Commonly, air compressors work like a piston pump, with a cylinder moving within to compress air and force it into a closed chamber.
*See also:* Pump; Turbine.

**Air conditioning**, regulation of the temperature, humidity, circulation, and composition of the air in a building, room, or vehicle. In warm weather an air-conditioning plant, working like a refrigerator, cools, dehumidifies, and filters the air. In colder weather it may be reversed to run as a heat pump.

**Aircraft** *See:* Airplane; Airship; Balloon; Glider; Helicopter; Rocket; Autogiro.

**Aircraft, military**, airplanes, helicopters, and other flying machines used for military purposes: to attack enemy forces, transport troops and supplies, and defend territory. Aircraft range in size from small electronically powered devices to huge transport planes designed to carry tanks or trucks. Speeds can reach as high as 2,000 mph (3,200 kmph). Varieties include bombers, fighters, reconnaissance aircraft, transports, special-mission aircraft, and helicopters.

**Aircraft carrier**, warship equipped to launch and land airplanes. Planes are launched by steam catapults, and arresting cables are used to bring landing aircraft to a halt. Each ship is equipped with antiaircraft guns and missiles and is protected by its own planes and sister ships. The U.S. Navy's first aircraft carrier went into service in 1922. The U.S. Navy's first nuclear-powered aircraft carrier is the *Enterprise*, launched in 1961, which can carry about 50 airplanes.
*See also:* Navy; Navy, United States.

**Air cushion vehicle** (ACV), or hovercraft or ground effect machine, vehicle that rides on a cushion of compressed air. ACVs have fans that pull air inside and then force it beneath the vehicle, trapping the air between the ground

surface and a rubberized skirt on the ACV. This invisible, compressed air cushion enables the ACV to maneuver over rough terrain smoothly because it eliminates friction between the craft and the surface. Though some can reach speeds of over 100 mph (160 kmph), ACVs are designed for short distances. ACVs are most often used to transport passengers and heavy freight over land or water like the one in service across the English Channel.
*See also:* Ship.

**Airedale terrier**, breed of large terriers. Weighing from 50 to 60 lb (23 to 27 kg), the Airedale was first bred in England in the 1880s. Considered to be fearless and loyal to their owners, Airdales are commonly used as watchdogs.

**Air Force Academy, U.S.**, center that trains students to become officers in the U.S. Air Force. Established in 1954, it is located in Colorado Springs, Colo. Graduates are awarded a B.S. degree and are commissioned as officers in the air force.

**Air Force, U.S.**, branch of the Department of Defense responsible for air warfare and defense and military space research. Prior to 1947 it was a branch of the U.S. Army. Air force personnel are organized into different commands. Among those responsible for actual fighting are the Strategic Air Command (SAC), which is the long-range bombardment and reconnaissance force, and the Tactical Air Command (TAC), which supports land and sea forces in action. Other commands are devoted to communications, intelligence, and training.

**Air Force, U.S. Department of the**, division of the U.S. Department of Defense that controls U.S. military aviation, including missile and aerospace programs.
*See also:* Defense, Department of; Air Force, U.S.

**Airline** *See:* Airport; Aviation.

**Air lock**, mechanism that allows people to pass between areas of different atmospheric pressures. The air lock chamber has 2 airtight doors sandwiched between the 2 pressure regions. The atmosphere in the air lock is gradually adjusted to match the pressure of the next space to be entered. Air locks are used when transferring people between the outside air and compressed air spaces such as underground tunnels and pneumatic caissons (watertight chambers) and between space vehicles in outer space.
*See also:* Bends.

**Airmail**, the transporting of mail by aircraft. A revolutionary 20th-century postal development, airmail is used for almost all first-class mail traveling more than 200 mi (320 km). The first official U.S. airmail delivery was in 1911, from Garden City to Mineola, N.Y.; regular airmail service began in 1918.
*See also:* Postal Service, U.S.

**Airplane**, powered heavier-than-air craft that obtains lift from the aerodynamic effect of the air rushing over its wings. Besides wings, the typical

airplane has a cigar-shaped fuselage that carries the pilot and payload, a power unit to provide forward thrust, stabilizers and a tail fin for controlling the plane in flight, and landing gear for supporting it on the ground. The plane is piloted using the throttle and the 3 basic control surfaces: the elevators on the stabilizers, which determine *pitch* (whether the plane is climbing, diving, or flying horizontally), the rudder on the tail fin, which governs *yaw* (the rotation of the plane about a vertical axis), and the ailerons on the wings, which control *roll* (the rotation of the plane about the long axis through the fuselage). In turning the plane, both the rudder and the ailerons must be used to *bank* the plane into the turn. The airplane's control surfaces are operated by moving a control stick or steering column (elevators and ailerons) in conjunction with a pair of footpedals (rudder).
*See also:* Aerodynamics; Wright brothers; Aviation.

**Air pollution,** contamination of the atmosphere by harmful vapors, aerosols, and dust particles, resulting principally from the activities of humans, but to a lesser extent from natural processes. Natural pollutants include pollen particles, saltwater spray, wind-blown dust, and fine debris from volcanic eruptions. Pollution attributable to humans includes the products of fossil fuel combustion (from municipal, industrial, and domestic furnaces and automobiles): carbon monoxide, lead, oxides of nitrogen and sulfur dioxide, and smoke particles; crop spraying; and atmospheric nuclear explosions. Most air pollution arises in the urban environment, with a large portion coming from the automobile. Pollution control involves identifying the sources of contamination, developing improved or alternative technologies and sources of raw materials, and persuading industries and individuals to adopt these, if need be under the sanction of legislation. Key areas for current research are automobile emission control, the recycling and thorough oxidation of exhaust gases, the production of lead-free gasoline, and the development of alternatives to the conventional internal combustion engine.

**Airport,** site where airplanes and other aircraft take off and land. Consisting of passenger terminals, hangars, and cargo terminals, large-city airports also include related services such as shops, hotels, restaurants, movie theaters, police and fire-fighting forces, medical facilities, and sewage plants. Although many small airports in the United States are privately owned, most large ones are owned by cities or public corporations. The Federal Aviation Administration (FAA) licenses aircraft, establishes requirements for pilots, and determines safety regulations. The International Civil Aviation Organization (ICAO) establishes airport operation and air-traffic-control standards for its 150 member countries, which include the United States and Canada.
*See also:* Air traffic control; Aviation.

**Air rights,** rights to the use of building space above a piece of property, especially railroad tracks, highways, and bridge and tunnel approaches. As urban land has grown scarcer, such rights have become increasingly valuable for housing developments and office construction.

**Airship,** or dirigible, lighter-than-air, self-propelled balloon whose buoyancy is provided by hydrogen or helium. The internal gas pressure causes the nonrigid type of airship, or blimp, to maintain its form. The first successful airship was designed by Henri Giffard, a French engineer, in 1852.

In 1900 Count Ferdinand von Zeppelin of Germany built the first rigid airship. It used hydrogen, which is flammable, as the lifting gas and had a metal-lattice frame that held its shape. The vulnerability of rigid airships in storms and a series of spectacular fires, including the *Hindenburg* disaster in 1937, brought an end to their use.
*See also:* Zeppelin, Ferdinand von.

**Air traffic control**, system by which airplanes are monitored and guided. Relying on radar and other electronic equipment, air traffic controllers on the ground instruct pilots on landing and take-off patterns and on use of runways for taxiing.

**Aisne River**, northeastern French river that rises in the forests of Argonne near Vaubecort and flows northwest and west to join the Oise river near Compiègne. The Aisne is about 180 mi (290 km) long. The valley of the Aisne was the scene, during World War I, of prolonged trench warfare and was crossed in World War II by the U.S. Army during its Aug. 1944 offensive.
*See also:* World War I; World War II.

**Aix-en-Provence** (pop. 124,800), city in southern France, in the department of Bouches-du-Rhône, about 20 mi (32 km) north of Marseilles. As the Roman settlement Aquae Sextiae, it was colonized by the proconsul C. Sextius Calvinus in 123 B C Known from antiquity for its mineral baths, in medieval times Aix became the capital of the region of Provence, as well as a famous literary center. In 1536 it was the temporary residence of the Holy Roman Emperor Charles V.Present-day industries include the production of olive oil, food processing, the manufacture of textiles, and the milling of flour.

**Aix-la-Chapelle** *See:* Aachen.

**Aix-la-Chapelle, Congress of**, meeting (1818) of the rulers of Austria, Prussia, and Russia and representatives from Great Britain and France at Aachen (Aix-la-Chapelle), Germany, after the Napoleonic Wars. The nations sought to preserve the peace established by, and resolve problems arising from, settlements made at the Congress of Vienna (1814-15).
*See also:* Vienna, Congress of.

**Ajax**, the name of 2 figures in Greek mythology. Ajax the Greater was the son of King Telamon and one of the greatest Greek heroes of the Trojan War. Informed that the arms of the slain Achilles had been awarded to Odysseus, Ajax went mad and committed suicide. The Greek warrior Ajax the Lesser also fought in the Trojan War. As punishment for raping Cassandra in Athena's temple, Ajax was shipwrecked and then killed.

**Akbar** (1542-1605), greatest of the Mogul emperors of India (1556-1605). He extended Mogul power over most of Afghanistan and India. An excellent administrator, he pursued a policy of religious toleration and also improved social laws, commerce, and transportation.
*See also:* India.

**Akhenaton**, or Ikhnaton, title taken by Amenhotep IV, king of Egypt (c. 1379-50 B C.). Akhenaton started the cult of the sun god Aton, despite the opposition of the priesthood of Amon-Ra. He moved the capital from Thebes, city of Amon, to Akhetaton (now Tell el-Amarna), where he fostered a naturalistic school of art and literature. After his death the old religion was reestablished. Akhenaton was married to Nefertiti.
*See also:* Egypt, Ancient.

**Akihito** (1933-   ), emperor of Japan (1989-   ). He married a commoner, Michiko Shodo, in 1959, the first member of the royal family to do so.

**Akita**, powerful hunting dog originating in northern Japan in the 17th century. Standing 20-27 in (51-69 cm) high at the shoulder and weighing 75-110 lbs (34-50 kg), the Akita possesses a solid body and a short, stiff coat. Sometimes called the royal dog of Japan, the Akita is considered a symbol of good health and has been designated a national treasure by the Japanese government.

**Akiva Baer ben Joseph** (c.   A D 50-135), Jewish rabbi, one of the greatest compilers of Hebrew Oral Law, whose work later formed the basis of the Mishnah. The Mishnah is part of the Talmud, a collection of writings constituting Jewish civil and religious law. After supporting a revolt against the Romans, he was executed as a rebel
*See also:* Talmud.

**Akron** (pop. 226,700), industrial city, seat of Summit County, Ohio, located on the Cuyahoga River, 36 mi (58 km) south of Cleveland. Akron was settled early in the 19th century and incorporated in 1865. Among the city's historical buildings is the home of John Brown, the abolitionist. B.F. Goodrich founded his pioneer rubber factory in Akron in 1870. With the invention of the automobile, Akron developed some of the world's largest tire and automobile plants. In addition, the city manufactures aircraft, matches, plastics, and clay and wood products.

**Akutagawa, Ryunosuke** (1892-1927), Japanese writer of short stories, poetry, and plays. From medieval themes he turned to autobiographical subjects. His work's fantastic and morbid nature reveals susceptibilities that led to his suicide. His most famous story is *Rashomon* (1915).

**Alabama**, state in the southeast United States; bordered by Tennessee in the north, Georgia in the east, Florida and the Gulf of Mexico in the south, and Mississippi in the west.
*Land and climate.* The Appalachian Mountain chain ends in northern Alabama, where it forms a plateau covering a third of the state. The rest of the state is largely lowland plains, the most important of which is the famous Black Belt. Forests cover more than 60% of Alabama's land surface. Among the most important rivers are the Tennessee, the Tombigbee, the Alabama, the Coosa, the Black Warrior, and the Chattahoochee. Alabama has a generally moderate climate. Principal cities are Birmingham, Mobile, and Montgomery.
*Economy.* Manufacturing is the largest contributor to Alabama's economy. Leading goods are paper products, chemicals, and steel. Coal, natural gas, petroleum, and limestone are the state's most valuable minerals. Although

## Alabama

| | |
|---|---|
| Capital: | Montgomery |
| Statehood: | Dec. 14, 1819 (22nd state) |
| Familiar name: | Heart of Dixie |
| Area: | 51,705 sq mi (133,915 km$^2$; ranks 29th) |
| Population: | 4,319,000 (1997; ranks 22nd) |
| Elevation: | Highest—2,407 ft (734 m), Cheaha Mountain |
| | Lowest—sea level |
| Motto: | Andemus jura nostra defendere |
| | (We Dare Defend Our Rights) |
| State flower: | Camellia |
| State bird: | Yellowhammer |
| State tree: | Southern pine |
| State song: | "Alabama" |

cotton, which once ruled Alabama's 1-crop economy, is still an important crop, livestock, poultry, soybeans, and peanuts have supplanted it in revenue earned. Alabama's forests support a large lumber industry.

*Government.* Alabama's constitution was adopted in 1901. The governor serves a 4-year term. The state legislature is composed of a senate of 35 members and a house of representatives of 105 members elected for 4-year terms. Alabama sends 7 representatives and 2 senators to the U.S. Congress.

*History.* Choctaws, Creeks, and other members of the Five Civilized Tribes originally peopled Alabama. Spain's Hernando De Soto explored the region in 1540, and France's Sieur de Bienville founded the first permanent European settlement in the Mobile area in 1702. The defeat of the Creeks by Andrew Jackson at the Battle of Horseshoe Bend (1814) opened south Alabama to settlers, who developed a slave-based plantation economy. At the outbreak of the Civil War Montgomery became the first Confederate capital. Alabama was readmitted to the Union in 1868. One-crop farming and the sha-

recropping system brought widespread agricultural depression and poverty, accentuated during the early 20th century by the infestation of the cotton-fields by the boll weevil. Tennessee Valley Authority projects (begun in 1933) and World War II boosted industry. The 1954 Supreme Court decision outlawing school segregation led to a period of racial tension. In 1965, black civil rights leader Dr. Martin Luther King, Jr., led a march from Selma to Montgomery in protest of voter discrimination. Alabama suffered financially in the 1970s and 1980s, although industry continues to grow.

**Alabama**, Confederate warship built in England (1862) for use in the U.S. Civil War. Under the command of Capt. Raphael Semmes, the *Alabama*

attacked, captured, or destroyed over 60 Union commerce ships, before being sunk near Cherbourg, France (June 19, 1864) by the U.S.S. *Kearsarge*, commanded by Capt. John Winslow.
*See also:* Washington, Treaty of.

**Alabaster,** soft, usually white, semitransparent variety of the mineral gypsum, used to make decorative objects. Gypsum is composed of calcium sulfate. The alabaster used in ancient times is composed of calcium carbonate and is harder than gypsum.
*See also:* Gypsum.

**Aladdin,** boy hero of one of the stories of the *Thousand and One Nights*, a collection of folk tales from the Middle East preserved in Arabic in the 16th century. Aladdin, the son of a poor widow, comes into possession of a magic ring and lamp. As the master of the lamp and of the 2 genies, or jinns, who reside within, Aladdin amasses great wealth and becomes a sultan.
*See also:* Arabian Nights.

**Alain-Fournier** (Henri Alban Fournier; 1886-1914), French writer whose one novel, *The Wanderer* (1913), is the haunting tale of a boy's attempt to rediscover the dreamlike setting of his meeting with a beautiful girl.

**Alamo,** Spanish mission fortress in San Antonio, Tex. It was the site of a heroic defense (1836) by fewer than 200 Texans in the struggle for independence from Mexico. All the defenders, including Davy Crockett and Jim Bowie, died in a lengthy siege by 4,000 Mexicans under Gen. Santa Anna. The famous phrase "remember the Alamo" refers to the siege.
*See also:* Texas.

**Alamogordo,** (pop. 27,600)   town in south-central New Mexico, seat of Otero County. It is the center of an agricultural, timber, and recreation area that includes the White Sands National Monument and Lincoln National Forest. The first atomic bomb was exploded near Alamogordo in a test on July 16, 1945.
*See also:* Nuclear weapon.

**Alanbrooke, Lord** (Alan Francis Brooke, 1st Viscount; 1883-1936), one of the leading British military strategists of World War II and chief of the Imperial General Staff (1941-46).

**Alarcón, Pedro Antonio de** (1833-91), Spanish regional writer best known for his novel *The Three-Cornered Hat* (1874). His work is distinguished by sharp realistic observation and picturesque effects.

**Alaric,** name of 2 Visigothic kings. **Alaric I** (c.  A D 370-410) was commander of the Visigothic auxiliaries under the Roman Emperor Theodosius, upon whose death Alaric was proclaimed king of the Visigoths. After invading Greece and northern Italy, he captured and sacked Rome in 410. **Alaric II** (d. 507), ruled Spain and South Gaul from 484 and in 506 issued the Breviary of Alaric, a Visigothic code of Roman law, for his Roman subjects. He was slain in battle by Clovis I, king of the Franks.
*See also:* Goths.

**Alaska**, largest state in the United States, located at the extreme northwest corner of North America, separated from the rest of the continental United States by northwest Canada; bordered by British Columbia and Yukon Territory in the west, the Pacific Ocean in the south, the Bering Sea in the west, and the Arctic Ocean in the north.

*Land and climate.* Alaska's general coastline is 6,640 mi (10,686 km) long, longer than the coastlines of the other 49 states combined. In the southeastern part of the Alaskan mainland is the mountainous Panhandle region, which is paralleled by the Alexander Archipelago. The Alaska Range, in the south-central part of the state, contains the highest peak in North America, Mt. McKinley. Extending southwest from the Alaska Range are the Alaska Peninsula and the Aleutian Islands. The Aleutian Range, which extends over the peninsula to Attu Island, near the Asian continent, has many active volcanoes. Between the mountain chains along the Pacific Coast and the Brooks Range, an extension of the Rockies, lies the central plateau of Alaska, crossed by the Yukon River. Alaska's northernmost settlement is Point Barrow, lying in the frozen tundra of the Arctic Coastal Plain. Southern Alaska has a relatively mild climate, with brief but hot summers. Winters are much colder in central Alaska. Principal cities are Anchorage, Fairbanks, and Juneau.

*Economy.* Oil is Alaska's valuable natural resource. Prudhoe Bay, on the Arctic Coastal Plain, is believed by engineers to be the largest oil field in North America. Alaska's other major mineral products are gold, sand and gravel, and natural gas. Alaska's fishing industry is the largest in the United States. Salmon is the most important catch. Alaska's leading manufactures are food, petroleum, and paper products. Furs were the original motive for Alaska's colonization and are still important.

---

## Alaska

| | |
|---|---|
| Capital: | Juneau |
| Statehood: | Jan. 3, 1959 (49th state) |
| Familiar name: | Last Frontier |
| Area: | 591,004 sq mi (1,530,700 km²; ranks 1st) |
| Population: | 609,000 (1997; ranks 48th) |
| Elevation: | Highest —20,320 ft (6,194 m), Mt McKinley |
| | Lowest—sea level |
| Motto: | North to the Future |
| State flower: | Forget-me-not |
| State bird: | Willow ptarmigan |
| State tree: | Sitka spruce |
| State song: | "Alaska's Flag" |

*Government.* Alaska's constitution was adopted in 1956. The governor is elected for a 4-year term. The state senate has 20 members elected for 4-year terms, and the house of representatives is composed of 40 members serving 2-year terms. Alaska sends 1 representative and 2 senators to the U.S. Congress.

*History.* Russia claimed Alaska after Vitus Bering sighted it in 1741. Gregory Shelikof founded the first permanent white settlement in 1784 on Kodiak Island. U.S. Secretary of State William H. Seward bought Alaska in 1867 for $7.2 million—about 2 cents an acre. Economic growth remained slow until the 1896 Klondike gold rush in the Yukon and after subsequent deposits were discovered in Nome in 1899 and Fairbanks in 1902. Alaska was established as a U.S. territory in 1912. World War II brought economic change to Alaska, with the United States sending thousands of workers to the territory to build defense installments and the Alaska Highway.In 1942 the Japanese occupied the Aleutian Islands of Agattu, Attu, and Kiska, the only part of North America to be invaded during the war. In 1968 the Prudhoe Bay oil field was discovered, transforming the economy. The Trans-Alaska Pipeline, which carries petroleum from Prudhoe Bay to the port of Valdez, was completed in 1977. In 1980 the federal government, which controls most of the state's land, set aside more than 104 million acres 42 million hectares) for wilderness areas, wildlife refuges, and national parks and preserves. In 1989 the Exxon *Valdez* accidentally discharged 10 million gal (39 million l) of oil into Prince William Sound, in North America's worst oil spill.

**Alaska Boundary Dispute,** disagreement concerning the demarcation of the border between the Alaska Panhandle and Canada, which arose in 1898 during the Klondike gold rush. Skagway and the head of the Lynn Canal, through which supplies reached the Yukon, were claimed as Canadian territory. The question was settled in favor of the United States by a joint U.S.-British commission in 1903.

**Alaska Highway,** road extending 1,422 mi (2,288 km) from Delta Junction, Alaska, to Dawson Creek, British Columbia. It was built by the United States as a strategic all-weather military route in 1942. In 1946 Canada took control of the 1,221 mi (1,965 km) passing through its territory.

**Alaskan malamute,** strong sled dog developed by the Malemiut Eskimos. The malamute's thick coat is gray or black with white markings and a bushy tail curls across its back. Weight ranges from 75 to 85 lb (34 to 39 kg).

**Alaska pipeline,** oil pipeline running 789 mi (1,270 km) from Alaska's Prudhoe Bay to the port of Valdez. Finished in 1977, it was bitterly opposed by environmentalists for adversely affecting the ecology.
*See also:* Petroleum; Pipeline.

**Al-Azhar University,** in Cairo, Egypt, one of the world's oldest universities (founded in c. A D 970) and a major center of Islamic learning. Women gained admittance in 1962.

**Alba, Duke of** *See:* Alva or Alba, Fernando Alvarez de Toledo, Duke of.

**Alban, Saint** (d. c. 304), first Christian martyr in Britain. Martyred during the persecutions of the Emperor Diocletian, he is said to have performed many miracles. A monastery was built in his memory in 795 by the king of Mercia, near the presumed place of his execution. St. Alban's feast day is celebrated on June 22 by Roman Catholics and on June 17 by the Church of England.

**Albania,** one of the smallest countries in the Balkans, 210 mi (338 km) long, and less than 100 mi (161 km) wide.

*Land and climate.* The country is mountainous, with isolated fertile basins and a narrow coastal plain. The climate is Mediterranean, but summers can bring prolonged droughts and winters can be harsh.

*People.* Albania's population is largely Muslim, with a Roman Catholic and Greek Orthodox Christian minority.

*Economy.* Albania is a poor country with slow development. Farming yields grapes and olives as well as grains, fruits, tobacco, and cotton. Albania is rich in chromium, copper, nickel, and coal, and mining provides most of the country's income. Industries produce food and petroleum products, textile-sand building materials.

*History.* As part of ancient Illyria, Albania was successively under Greek, Roman, and Byzantine influence and control. In succeeding centuries it was invaded by Goths, Bulgars, Slavs, and Normans. Later, the national hero Scanderberg (1403?-68) delayed but failed to stop Ottoman Turkish conquest. Turkish rule Islamized Albania and suppressed nationalist aspirations until the First Balkan War (1912). Occupied in World War I, ruled by the self-proclaimed King Zog I (1928-39), then annexed by Italy and occupied in World War II, Albania regained independence under the antifascist guerilla leader Enver Hoxha, a Communist, who proclaimed a republic in 1946. The death of Hoxha in 1985 marked the beginning of a period of political and economic liberalization. In 1991 free elections took place. The new government was unable to improve the economic situation of the country. Towards the end of the 1990s, tensions developed between Albania and its neighbor Yugoslavia, regarding the ethnic Albanian population of Kosovo.

### Albania

| | | |
|---|---|---|
| Capital: | Tiranë | |
| Area: | 11,100 sq mi | |
| | (28,748 sq km) | |
| Population: | 3,330,000 | |
| Language: | Albanian | |
| Government: | Presidential republic | |
| Independent: | 1912 | |
| Head of gov.: | Premier | |
| Per capita: | U.S. $670 | |
| Mon. unit: | 1 Lek = 100 qindars | |

**Albany** (pop. 874,304), capital of New York since 1797 and seat of Albany County, located on the west bank of the Hudson River about 145 mi (233 km) north of New York City. An important industrial center, Albany's products include chemicals, paper, and textiles. Many people are also employed in state and county government offices. The opening of the Erie and Champlain canals in the 1820s and the first railroad connection with Schenectady in 1831 established Albany's position as a commercial and shipping center.
*See also:* New York.

**Albany Congress**, meeting (1754) of 25 representatives from 7 British colonies at Albany, N.Y., aimed at conciliating the Iroquois and improving the common defense of the colonies against the French. The congress adopted a plan, chiefly designed by Benjamin Franklin, providing for greater colonial unity, one of the first significant attempts at colonial cooperation. The colonial governments later rejected the plan.
*See also:* Revolutionary War in America.

**Albany Regency**, group of politicians with headquarters in Albany who controlled the New York State Democratic party (1820-54), with the first U.S. political machine. Among its members were Martin Van Buren, William L. Marcy, Silas Wright, and John A. Dix. Marcy's slogan, "To the victors belong the spoils," was its guiding principle; it rewarded the party faithful with government jobs. Starting in 1842, opposition groups (Barnburners and Hunkers) developed similar strategies, ultimately having a divisive effect on the party and diminishing the prestige of the Albany Regency.

**Al Basrah**, or Basra (pop. 616,700), second-largest city in Iraq and an important port, lying on the Shatt al Arab River approximately 55 mi (90 km) from the Persian Gulf. Arabs founded Al Basrah in A D 636, after which it became a trade center. Under Ottoman rule (1534-1918) the city declined in importance. From 1918 to 1932, the years Great Britain ruled Iraq, Al Basrah served as a military center. Located near major oil fields, it became a center for oil refining and export. Because it was the site of heavy fighting, the city's importance as a port decreased during the Iran-Iraq War of 1980-88.
*See also:* Persian Gulf War.

**Albatross**, any of 14 species of large, long-winged, gliding, hook-billed seabirds forming the family Diomedeidae. Two species form the genus *Phoebetria*, the other 12 the genus *Diomedea*. Most albatrosses are white with darker markings on the back, wings, and tail. The wandering albatross (*D. exulans*) has the broadest wingspan of any living bird —up to 12 ft (3.7 m).

**Albee, Edward Franklin** (1928-    ), U.S. playwright who gained international fame with *Who's Afraid of Virginia Woolf?* (1962), a penetrating look at contemporary American marriage. His other plays include *The Zoo Story* (1958) and *The American Dream* (1961), both one-act plays, and *Tiny Alice* (1964). He won Pulitzer Prizes for *A Delicate Balance* (1966) and *Seascape* (1975).

**Albéniz, Isaac** (1860-1909), Spanish composer and pianist. He is best remembered for his later piano works, including the suite *Iberia* (1906-9), which is based on Spanish folk themes and popular music forms.

**Albert I** (1875-1934), king of the Belgians (1909-34); nephew and successor of Leopold II. During World War I Albert commanded the armed forces. He did much to improve conditions in the Belgian Congo, and he strengthened national defense and the merchant fleet and introduced social reforms in Belgium.

**Albert II** (1934-   , sixth king of Belgium. He succeeded his brother, King Baudouin, who died in 1993. Married Paola Ruffo di Calabria (1937-   ) in 1959. They have three children: Philip (1960-   ), Astrid (1962-   ), and Laurence (1963-   ).

**Alberta**, westernmost of Canada's Prairie Provinces; bordered by Saskatchewan (in the east), the Northwest Territories (in the north), British Columbia (in the west), and the U.S. state of Montana (in the south).*Land and Climate.* Alberta is a plateau sloping gradually upward and westward to the Rocky Mountains and the Continental Divide. The south is treeless prairie, the central region is partly wooded, and the north is densely forested. The prairie is drained by the Athabasca, Saskatchewan, and Slave rivers, among others. Temperatures range from an average of 59°F (15°C) in summer to 5°F (−15°C) in winter.*People.* About half of Alberta's inhabitants live in the metropolitan areas of Edmonton and Calgary. There are also some 300,000 Native Americans, three-quarters of whom live on reservations. The largest religious denomination is the United Church of Canada.
*Economy.* Alberta's principal crops are wheat and sugar beets; livestock raising, dairying, logging, fishing, and fur trapping also contribute to the province's wealth. Petroleum, natural gas, and coal have made Alberta one of Canada's richest provinces. The Leduc oil field was discovered in 1947, and the province contains about half of Canada's reserves of coal. Since the 1960s the leading industries have been in mineral exploitation.
*History.* In 1670 unexplored Alberta was granted to the Hudson's Bay Company. Few European settlers arrived until after 1869, when the Canadian government bought the land. The arrival of the Mounties (1874) and the completion of the Canadian Pacific Railway (1885) encouraged immigration. Alberta became a province in 1905.

**Albert, Carl Bert** (1908-   ), Oklahoma Democrat, Speaker of the U.S. House of Representatives (1971-77). Albert graduated from the University of Oklahoma in 1931, after which he studied at Oxford University in England on a Rhodes scholarship, earning 2 law degrees. After practicing law for 6 years, he served in the U.S. Army (1941-46). A member of the U.S. House of Representatives (1947-77), Albert served as majority whip (1955-62). He was platform chair of the 1964 Democratic National Convention and chair of the 1968 Democratic National Convention. In the mid-1960s Albert supported President Lyndon Johnson's civil rights proposals despite opposition from his district.

**Albert, Prince** (Francis Charles Augustus Albert Emmanuel; 1819-61), prince consort of Great Britain, husband of Queen Victoria. German-born son of the Duke of Saxe-Coburg-Gotha, he married Victoria in 1840 and served as her trusted adviser. He was active in promoting fine arts.

**Alberti, Leon Battista** (1404-72), Italian Renaissance scholar, architect, painter, and art theorist. His architectural works include the Palazzo Rucellai in Florence and the church of San Francesco in Rimini. Alberti is noted for his literary contributions during the Italian Renaissance, including *Della pittura*, the first formulation of the aesthetic and scientific attitudes of Renaissance painting; it idealized the imitation of nature and served as a foundation for modern perspective. His architectural influence was presented in his treatise *De re aedificatoria*, which provided the Renaissance with an original program for architectural design. Alberti also wrote on a variety of subjects involving domestic animals, religion and the priesthood, jurisprudence, politics, government, mathematics, mechanics, literature, and language. He was the prototype of the Renaissance man.

**Albertus Magnus, Saint** (1206?-80), German scholastic philosopher and scientist and teacher of St. Thomas Aquinas. He helped establish Aristotelianism and the study of the natural sciences in Christian thought, and he was possibly the first to isolate arsenic.

**Albigenses,** members of a heretical sect that flourished in the 12th and 13th centuries in southern France. The Albigenses believed that the principles of good and evil are in constant struggle and that matter is evil and only the human spirit is good. A crusade proclaimed by Pope Innocent III in 1208 broke the hold of the heresy, and a special inquisition was created in 1233 to convert the Albigenses.

**Albino,** organism lacking normal pigmentation. The skin and hair of albino animals (including humans) is uncolored, and the irises of the eyes appear pink. Albinism, which may be total or only partial, is generally inherited. Because albino plants contain no chlorophyll and thus are unable to perform photosynthesis, they rapidly die.

**Albright, Ivan Le Lorraine** (1897-1983), U.S. painter of microscopically detailed canvases that focus on decay and human dissolution. His works include *That Which I Should Have Done I Did Not Do* (1941) and a series of paintings for the film *The Picture of Dorian Gray* (1944).

**Albright, Madeleine Korbel** (1937-    ), American politician, born in Czechoslovakia. At the age of 11 she and her family moved to the United States. A professor of international affairs, she started to work for the White House in 1978 where she dealt with foreign policy legislation. She is a former president of the Center for National Policy and a former member of the National Security Council staff. In 1993 she became ambassador to the United Nations. In 1997, she succeeded Warren Christopher as Secretary of State. Albright is the most highly placed woman in the American government.

**Albumin,** protein that occurs in its most well-known state in the white of an egg. Albumin appears in animal and plant tissues. It is the primary constituent of the protein in blood serum. Albumins are used in the dyeing industry and in making photographic chemicals.

**Albuquerque** (pop. 398,500), largest city in New Mexico and seat of Bernalillo County, situated on the Rio Grande. Founded in 1706, it is an important commercial and industrial city, a center for nuclear energy and defense research, and a transcontinental air and land route hub. Its dry, sunny climate and nearby mountains and Native American reservations have made it a popular tourist center.

**Alcan Highway** *See:* Alaska Highway.

**Alcatraz**, rocky island in San Francisco Bay, famous as the site from 1933 to 1963 of a federal maximum security prison, nicknamed "the Rock." It is now part of the Golden Gate National Recreation Area.

**Alchemy**, blend of philosophy, mysticism, and chemical processing that originated before the Christian era. Practitioners sought the conversion of base metals into gold using the "philosopher's stone." Other goals were the prolongation of life and the secret of immortality. Alchemy began in Hellenistic Egypt and passed through the writings of the great Arab alchemists to the Latin West. In the early 16th century Paracelsus set alchemy on a new course toward chemical pharmacy, although other alchemists—including John Dee and Isaac Newton— continued to work along quasi-religious lines. *See also:* Chemistry; Metallurgy.

**Alcibiades** (c. 450-404 B C), Athenian statesman and general, nephew of Pericles, and student of Socrates. He fell in and out of favor with the Athenian people during the era of the Peloponnesian War. He was eventually exiled and assassinated.
*See also:* Peloponnesian War.

**Alcindor, Lew** *See:* Abdul-Jabbar, Kareem.

**Alcock and Brown**, pioneer British aviators, who made the first nonstop flight across the Atlantic Ocean in 1919. Pilot Sir John William Alcock (1892-1919) and navigator Sir Arthur Whitten Brown (1886-1948) began their transatlantic flight near St. John's, Newfoundland, in a twin-engine, converted bomber, landing in a bog near Clifden, Ireland, the next day, having traveled 1,950 mi (3,138 km).

**Alcohol**, class of compounds containing a hydroxyl group bonded by a carbon atom. Alcohols occur widely in nature and are used as solvents and antifreezes and in chemical manufacture. They are obtained by fermentation, by oxidation or hydration of alkenes from petroleum and natural gas, and by reduction of fats and oils. The simplest alcohols are methanol and ethyl alcohol, or ethanol (the intoxicating constituent of alcoholic beverages); others include benzyl alcohol, ethylene glycol, and glycerol.
*See also:* Solvent.

**Alcoholics Anonymous** (A.A.), international organization founded in 1935 to help people suffering from alcoholism overcome their addictions. The practice of sharing recovery experiences among its members is a successful part of the treatment plan.

**Alcoholism,** chronic illness marked by compulsive drinking of alcohol, leading to physical and psychological addiction. Alcohol is a depressant that acts on the central nervous system to reduce anxiety and inhibition. It is a potent and addictive substance that impairs physical coordination, judgment, and perception and, in sufficiently high dosages, can cause unconsciousness or death. Alcohol is nearly unique among potent drugs in that moderate, self-induced levels of intoxication are socially acceptable. Because alcohol is so readily available and its use so generally accepted, its abuse remains by far the most serious drug problem in the United States. Alcohol abuse is the direct cause of crime, delinquency, and accidents that cost billions of dollars, as well as considerable physical and psychological suffering and loss of life.Prolonged alcohol abuse causes cirrhosis of the liver, damages other organs, including the brain and heart, and may contribute to cancer of the esophagus. Drinking during pregnancy is harmful to the fetus. For the severely addicted alcoholic, withdrawal from alcohol is more dangerous and potentially more life-threatening than withdrawal from heroin and must be done under medical supervision. Treatment most often includes individual or group psychological counseling, but may also include prescriptions of Antabuse (disulfiram), which causes unpleasant physical responses, such as nausea, in patients who drink alcohol while they are taking the drug. Research continues into the causes of alcoholism, including findings that indicate a genetic component in the disease suggesting heredity.
*See also:* Alcoholics Anonymous; Drug abuse.

**Alcott, (Amos) Bronson** (1799-1888), U.S. educator, philosopher, and author, father of Louisa May Alcott. Founder of the progressive Temple School in Boston, his teaching methods were too advanced to be popular. A leading transcendentalist along with Ralph Waldo Emerson and Henry David Thoreau, his writings include *Concord Days* (1872) and *Table Talk* (1877).
*See also:* Transcendentalism.

**Alcott, Louisa May** (1832-88), U.S. author; daughter of Bronson Alcott. Her best-known work is the autobiographical *Little Women* (1869). Another important work, *Hospital Sketches* (1863), was based on her experiences as a Union nurse in the Civil War.

**Alcuin,** or Albinus (c. A D. 735-804), English prelate and educator whose scholarship influenced medieval teaching of the liberal arts. He supervised Charlemagne's program of ecclesiastical and educational reform.

**Aldehyde,** any of a class of highly reactive organic chemical compounds characterized by a CHO group; especially, acetaldehyde ($C_2H_4O$). Formaldehyde ($CH_2O$) is a pungent gaseous aldehyde used commonly as a disinfectant and preservative and in making resins and plastics.
*See also:* Formaldehyde.

**Alden, John** (1599-1687), one of the leaders of Plymouth Colony. He is best known through Henry Wadsworth Longfellow's fictional poem *The Court-*

*ship of Miles Standish* (1858), in which Alden courts Priscilla Mullens on behalf of Standish but marries her himself.

**Alder,** any of a genus (*Alnus*) of shrubs and small trees of the birch family. Found in moist, temperate regions at high altitudes, they are indigenous to the Americas, Asia, and North Africa. One variety, the red alder (*A. rubra*), is used commercially as timber.

**Aldridge, Ira Frederick** (1805-67), first African American to achieve fame as an actor in the Western Hemisphere. Because of limited opportunities in the United States due to racial prejudice, he was forced to go to Europe, where he became known for his bold interpretations of Lear, Othello, and Macbeth.

**Aldrin, Buzz** (Edwin Eugene Aldrin, Jr.; 1930-   ), U.S. astronaut. Aldrin was the second man to walk on the moon, during the Apollo 11 space flight in 1969. In 1966 he was the pilot of the Gemini 12 flight, which included rendezvous maneuvers and his record 5-hour space walks.

**Aldus Manutius** (Teobaldo Mannucci or Manuzio; 1450-1515), Venetian founder of the Aldine Press, whose scrupulous editions of Greek and Roman classics (including the works of Aristotle) advanced Renaissance scholarship. He was the first to use italic type (1501) to produce cheap, pocket-sized editions of the Latin classics.

**Aleatory music** (from Latin *alea*, "dice"), music dependent on chance, applied to the post-1950 tendency of composers, such as John Cage, to leave elements in their work to the performer's decision or chance.

**Aleichem, Sholem** *See:* Sholem Aleichem.

**Aleixandre, Vicente** (1898-1984), Spanish poet. His collections of poetry include *Destruction or Love* (1935) and *Shadow of Paradise* (1944). He won the 1977 Nobel Prize for literature.

**Alembert, Jean le Rond d'** (1717-83), French philosopher, physicist, and mathematician, a leading figure in the French Enlightenment, and coeditor with Denis Diderot of the *Encyclopédie*. His early fame rested on his formulation of d'Alembert's principle in mechanics (1743). His other works treat calculus, music, philosophy, and astronomy.

**Aleppo** (pop. 1,400,000), second-largest city of Syria. It flourished in Byzantine times as a trade center on the caravan route to Baghdad. An important manufacturing center, its industries include textile- and carpet-making. The cultural center of Syria, Aleppo contains the National Museum, a medieval citadel, and numerous mosques with many fine examples of Islamic art.

**Aleut,** native of the Aleutian Islands and western Alaska. Descended from an Eskimo people, Aleuts have their own language. Traditionally, Aleuts hunted land animals, such as caribou and bear, and sea animals, such as whales and seals. They traveled in skin-covered kayaks, made spears and fishhooks, and dressed in parkas made from animal furs and skins. Under

Russian domination, which began in the 18th century, the Aleutian population dropped dramatically, dropping further with Japanese occupation of the Aleutians during World War II. Through the Alaska Native Claims Settlement Act of the U.S. Congress (1971), the Aleuts won the rights to their homeland.

**Aleutian Islands**, chain of rugged Alaskan islands of volcanic origin, extending westward 1,200 mi (1,900 km) from the Alaska Peninsula and separating the Bering Sea from the Pacific. Fishing is the chief occupation. During World War II the Japanese occupied the islands Agattu, Attu, and Kiska.
*See also:* Alaska.

**Alewife** (*Alosa pseudoharengus*), fish in the herring family. Alewives travel in large schools along the Atlantic coastline of the United States. They grow up to 15 in (38 cm) in saltwater and, in the freshwater of the Great Lakes, up to 6 in (15 cm). After maturity, saltwater alewives travel from the Atlantic to freshwater, where they lay their eggs.

**Alexander**, name of 3 Russian tsars. **Alexander I** (1777-1825) succeeded his father, Paul I, in 1801. In 1805 he joined England and Austria against Napoleon. After French victories Napoleon proposed Franco-Russian domination of Europe, but mutual mistrust came to a head, and Napoleon invaded Russia in 1812. The French were defeated, and in 1815 Alexander formed a coalition with Austria and Prussia, the Holy Alliance. At his death, Russia faced economic ruin and rebellion. **Alexander II** (1818-81) succeeded his father, Nicholas I, in 1855. He was responsible for the emancipation of the serfs in 1861, but he was assassinated when his domestic reforms did not satisfy populist groups. In foreign policies he was a moderate, making peace in the Crimea and extending Russian power in the Far East as well as in Central Asia. **Alexander III** (1845-94) succeeded his father, Alexander II, in 1881. He discarded the latter's proposals for moderate reform in favor of rigid repression and persecution of minorities.

**Alexander I** (1888-1934), king of Yugoslavia from 1921 to 1934. Yugoslavia, which has been formed as a country in 1918, was home to several peoples, including Serbs, Croats, and Slovenes. To ensure Serb dominance, Alexander declared himself dictator in 1929. He was assassinated by a Croatian terrorist in 1934.

**Alexander III** (Orlando Bandinelli; d.1181), pope (1159-81). He continued a longstanding conflict with the Holy Roman Emperor Frederick I. Opposed also by 3 antipopes, he was victorious over Frederick at the Battle of Legano in 1176. He convened the Third Lateran Council (1179) and forced King Henry II of England to recognize papal supremacy.

**Alexander IV** (Rodrigo Borgia; 1431-1503), pope (1492-1503). The most notorious of the Renaissance popes, he directed his efforts at increasing the temporal power of the papacy and creating great hereditary domains for his children, among them Cesare and Lucrezia Borgia.

**Alexander, Grover Cleveland** (1887-1950), U.S. baseball player. One of the greatest right-handed pitchers in baseball history, in 1916 he set the major league record for shutouts in a season (16). Third on the career win list with 373, Alexander's 90 career shutouts are the second most in major league history. Alexander played with the Philadelphia Phillies, Chicago Cubs, and St. Louis Cardinals from 1911 to 1930. He was inducted into the National Baseball Hall of Fame in 1938.

**Alexander Archipelago**, group of more than 1,100 islands lying along the coastline of the Alaska Panhandle. They are the peaks of a submerged coastal range. Sitka, on the island of Baranof, was once capital of Alaska. The islands were discovered by Vitus Bering in 1741 and were acquired by the United States as part of the Alaska purchase in 1867. Fish, furs, gold, and timber are important items in their economy.

**Alexander of Tunis, 1st Earl** (Harold Rupert Leofric George Alexander; 1891-1969), last British-born governor of Canada (1946-52). He was known for his military achievements in both world wars and, in 1944, was named commander in chief of all Allied forces for Italy. Knighted (1942) and made Viscount Alexander of Tunis (1946), he then served as minister of defense for Britain (1952-54).

**Alexander the Great**, or Alexander III (356-323 B C ), king of Macedonia (336-323 B C.). At 20 Alexander succeeded his father, Philip II of Macedon, and executed Philip's plans for freeing the Greeks of Asia Minor from Persian rule. After his defeat of the Persian king Darius III at Issus in 333, Alexander subdued Phoenicia and Egypt, founding Alexandria. In 331 Alexander again defeated Darius in the battle of Guagamela, after which the principal cities of the Persian Empire fell easily to his attack. He was proclaimed king of Asia and moved on eastward. He intended to conquer India, but his soldiers refused to follow him. Though he lived to be only 33, he conquered the greatest empire yet known in Western civilization and prepared the way for the Hellenistic Age.

**Alexandria** (pop. 105,000), city and port of entry in Virginia, located on the Potomac River. The home of Robert E. Lee, the city was, in part, designed by George Washington. From 1791 to 1846 it was part of the capital district. The Lee home, Arlington House, is now the site of Arlington National Cemetery. Predominantly a residential suburb of the nation's capital, Alexandria also has railroad yards and produces structural steel, chemicals, and fertilizers.

**Alexandria** (pop. 3,295,000), chief port and second-largest city of Egypt. Founded by Alexander the Great c. 332 B.C., it was the capital of Ptolomaic Egypt and a center of trade and learning in the Hellenistic and Roman worlds. The city has grown into Egypt's principal channel for foreign trade.
*See also:* Seven Wonders of the Ancient World.

**Alexandrian Library**, in antiquity, the greatest collection of manuscripts, first assembled in the 3rd century B C The library, containing more than 400,000 scrolls, was housed in Alexandria, Egypt. It was probably destroyed in stages during sieges starting with Julius Caesar's in 47 B C ; its destruction is thought to have been complete by 400 A.D

**Alexandrite**, variety of the mineral chrysoberyl, discovered in 1833 and named for Tsar Alexander II. It has brilliant luster and is predominantly green, but changes colors when viewed from different directions or in different light.

**Alfalfa**, or lucerne (*Medicago sativa*), legume widely grown for pasture, hay, and silage. The high protein content of this perennial makes it an excellent food for livestock, and the nitrogen-fixing bacteria on its roots are important in enriching depleted soil.

**Alfonso XIII** (1886-1941), king of Spain from birth until 1931. Because of the unrest during his reign, Alfonso supported Primo de Rivera's establishment of a military dictatorship in 1923. The dictator fell from power in 1930, however, and the outcome of the elections in 1931 was so pro-republican that Alfonso, although not abdicating the throne, left Spain, and a republic was established.
*See also:* Juan Carlos I.

**Alfred the Great** (A D 848-899), king of the West Saxons from 871. He halted the Danish invasions with his victory at Edington (878), making his kingdom of Wessex the nucleus of a unified England. He also introduced educational and legal reforms, translated Latin works into English, and began the *Anglo-Saxon Chronicle*, an important source for Anglo-Saxon history.

**Algae**, large and diverse group of nonvascular (rootless and stemless) aquatic plants that contain chlorophyll and carry on photosynthesis, including some of the simplest organisms known. They range in size from microscopic single-celled organisms to strands of seaweed several yards long. Most species of green algae, which are found mainly in freshwater, are microscopic. Brown algae include the familiar seaweeds found on rocky shores. Red algae, found mostly in warmer seas, include several species of economic importance. Algae are important as the basis of food chains. Many of the larger algae are used in foodstuffs, in medicine, and as manure.
*See also:* Eutrophication; Seaweed.

**Algebra**, branch of mathematics in which relationships between known and unknown quantities are represented symbolically. For a relationship to satisfy the fundamental theorem of algebra it must consist of a finite number of quantities and must have a solution. An example of such a relationship taken from elementary algebra is: $ax^n + bx^{n-1} + cx^{n-2} + \ldots + z = 0$
This is an "$n$ degree" polynomial equation (of order $n$). Here $x$ is a variable denoting an unknown quantity to be found, and $a$, $b$, $c\ldots z$ represent known values. Elementary algebra, the algebraic system most familiar to the general public, uses operations of arithmetic to solve equations from sets of numbers. Abstract algebra developed from elementary algebra by mathematicians attempting to solve specific problems. Mathematical structures such as fields, rings, and groups were devised. Concepts of abstract algebra have been used by theoretical physicists in the development of quantum theory as well as by digital communications engineers in the development of coding theory.

Linear algebra is used to solve simultaneous linear equations and is applied extensively in economics and psychology. Manipulations of equations are accomplished through the use of matrices and vectors. Boolean algebra is a symbolic representation of classical logic developed in 1854 by George Boole. Operations such as union and intersection are used. This algebraic system is used in computer science.

Gradual introduction of algebraic symbols occurred between 2000 B.C. and 1550 A.D. *Arithmetica*, regarded as the first treatise on algebra, was written by Diophantus of Alexandria in the 3rd century A.D. The Arabs became leaders in the field in about the 9th century. It was not until the 16th and 17th centuries in Europe that algebra underwent a complete transformation and became almost completely symbolic, much as it is today. Abstract algebra developed in the early 19th century, with major contributions by Niels Abel and Evariste Galois.

**Alger, Horatio** (1834-99), U.S. author of more than 100 books whose heroes rise from rags to riches through virtue and hard work, including *Ragged Dick* (1867), *Luck and Pluck* (1869), and *Sink or Swim* (1870).

**Algeria**, country in northwest Africa; bordered by Mauritania, Morocco, and Western Sahara in the west, the Mediterranean Sea in the north, Tunisia and Libya in the east, and Niger and Mali in the south.
*Land and climate.* The Atlas Mountains divide the large country (919,590 sq mi/2,381,741 sq km) into the coastal region (Tell), the steppe, and the desert. Some 75% of the Algerians live in the narrow fertile coastal area.
*People.* Algeria's population is predominantly Arab and 99% follows the Sunni denomination of Islam. Berbers are an important minority. More than half of the population is literate. Most Algerians still live on their land, and farms yield citrus fruits, grapes, grain, and vegetables.
*Economy.* Algeria is an important oil-producing countries and a primary exporter of liquified natural gas. However, the economy is burdened with high levels of debt repayment.
*History.* The Phoenicians settled North Africa around 1200 B.C. The area belonged to Carthage, then to Rome, and in 201 B.C. became the Roman

| Algeria | |
|---|---|
| Capital: | Algiers |
| Area: | 919,595 sq mi (2,381,741 sq km) |
| Population: | 30,480,000 |
| Language: | Arabic |
| Government: | Republic |
| Independent: | 1962 |
| Head of gov.: | Prime minister (appointed by president) |
| Per capita: | U.S. $1,600 |
| Mon. unit: | 1 Algerian dinar (DA) = 100 centimes |

province of Numidia. Subsequently, Algeria was conquered by Vandals, Byzantines, and Arabs. From the 16th to the 18th centuries, Algeria was home to the Barbary pirates and the slave trade. The French took colonized Algeria (1830-1909), governing until the nationalist revolt (1954-62) led by the National Liberation Front (FLN), in which at least 100,000 Muslims and 10,000 French soldiers died. Algeria became independent on July 3, 1962. In the 1990s Algeria had to deal with severe economic problems. This situation was aggravated by the continuous assaults made by fundamentalist Muslims, in which about half a million civilians lost their lives.

**Algiers** (pop. 1,483,000), capital, major port, and largest city of Algeria. Founded by Berbers in A.D. 935 on the site of the Roman settlement of Licosium, it was taken by the French in 1830. The modern city lies at the base of a hill overlooking the Bay of Algiers; higher up the slope is the old Moorish city, dominated by the Casbah, a citadel built by the Turks.

**Algonquins**, or Algonkins, North American Native Americans. They were driven out of their territory along the St. Lawrence and Ottawa rivers by the Iroquois in the 17th and 18th centuries.

**Algren, Nelson** (1909-81), U.S. naturalistic novelist, best known for his fiction describing Chicago slum life. Among his works are *Never Come Morning* (1942), *The Man with the Golden Arm* (1949), and *A Walk on the Wild Side* (1956).

**Alhambra** (Arabic, "The Red"), 13th-century citadel and palace dominating the city of Granada, the finest large-scale example of Moorish architecture in Spain.
*See also:* Moors.

**Ali, Muhammad** (Cassius Marcellus Clay; 1942-  ), U.S. boxer. Ali won an Olympic gold metal in 1960 and the heavyweight championship from Sonny Liston in 1964. He was stripped of this title in 1967 by the World Boxing Association while appealing a conviction for draft evasion, later overturned. One of the greatest and most outspoken heavyweights in boxing history, he defeated George Foreman for the title in 1974, lost it in 1978 to Leon Spinks, and won it back from Spinks later that year. Larry Holmes defeated Ali in 1980. Ali changed his name after adopting the Black Muslim religion in 1964.

**Ali Baba**, main character in the story in *1,001 Nights*, "Ali Baba and the Forty Thieves." A poor woodcutter, he discovers that the magic words "Open, Sesame" will open the door to a secret cave containing stolen treasure. The thieves plan to kill him but are outwitted by the slave girl Morgana.

**Alien and Sedition Acts**, 4 unpopular laws passed by the U.S. Congress in 1798 in response to the threat of war with France. The laws empowered the president to expel or imprison aliens, made naturalization more difficult, and punished those who wrote or spoke against the government.
*See also:* Kentucky and Virginia Resolutions.

**Alienation**, one's estrangement from society and from oneself. According to the 19th-century social and economic philosopher Karl Marx, the sale of labor power and the general conditions of production and exchange under capitalism deprive the individual of his or her essential humanity.

**Alimentary canal**, passage from the throat to the anus functioning in digestion and absorption of food.
*See also:* Digestive system.

**Alinsky, Saul David** (1909-72), U.S. pioneer in community organization, known for his early community action work in the Chicago stockyards area (1939). He founded a school for community organization in Chicago.

**Alkali**, water-soluble compound of an alkali metal that acts as a strong base and neutralizes acids. Common alkalis are sodium hydroxide (NaOH), ammonia ($NH_3$), and sodium carbonate ($Na_2CO_3$). Alkalis are used to manufacture glass, soap, paper, and textiles.

**Alkaloid**, any of a group of organic alkali compounds found in certain plants and fungi, containing carbon, hydrogen, and nitrogen. Many alkaloids are poisonous; others, such as morphine, nicotine, and cocaine, can be addictive. Other alkaloids are caffeine and quinine. In small doses alkaloids are powerful medicines, used as analgesics, tranquilizers, and cardiac and respiratory stimulants.

**Alkalosis**, condition wherein the concentration of alkali in the body cells and tissues is higher than normal.
*See also:* Acidosis.

**Allah**, Arabic name (*al-ilah*) for the supreme being, used by the prophet Muhammad to designate the God of Islam.

**Allahabad** (pop. 806,500), city in the state of Uttar Pradesh, northern India. Situated at the confluence of the sacred rivers Ganges and Jumna, Allahabad is the goal of many Hindu pilgrims and the site of India's oldest universities.

**All-American Canal**, waterway, completed 1940, that brings water 80 mi (130 km) from the Imperial Reservoir on the Colorado River to irrigate 500,000 acres (200,000 hectares) of the Imperial Valley, Calif. The canal also supplies water to San Diego. A branch delivering an equal amount of water to the Coachella Valley was opened in 1958.
*See also:* Imperial Valley.

**Allegheny Mountains**, central Appalachian range extending from southwest Virginia into north-central Pennsylvania. The Alleghenies average heights of 2,000 ft (610 m) in the north and more than 4,500 ft (1,372 m) in the south.

**Allegheny River**, river in west Pa., important transportation route before the railroads were built. In Pittsburgh, it joins the Monongahela to form the Ohio River.

**Allegory,** literary work in which characters and concrete images are used to represent abstract philosophical or moral notions. John Bunyan's *Pilgrim's Progress* and Edmund Spenser's *Faerie Queene* are classic English-language allegories.

**Allen, Ethan** (1738-89), American Revolutionary hero, leader of the Green Mountain Boys of Vermont. In 1775 he seized the British fort at Ticonderoga but was captured in an attack on Montreal. He unsuccessfully petitioned Congress for Vermont's statehood.
*See also:* Green Mountain Boys.

**Allen, Richard** (1760-1831), first bishop and founder of the African Methodist Episcopal Church. Born a slave, he was raised on a plantation in Delaware, becoming a Methodist at age 17. He bought his freedom (1786) and moved to Philadelphia, where he organized an Independent Methodist Church to better serve black people. He was ordained a minister in the Methodist Church (1799) and later founded the African Methodist Episcopal Church (1816), the first black denomination in the United States.
*See also:* Jones, Absalom.

**Allen, Woody** (Allen Stewart Konigsberg; 1935- ), U.S. comedian, author, and film director. A self-effacing wit established him as a major comedic talent of the 1960s and 1970s. Following a nightclub career he broke into films (1965) and wrote, directed, and starred in successes like *Bananas* (1971), the Academy Award-winning *Annie Hall* (1977), and *Crimes and Misdemeanors* (1989). *Deconstructing Harry* was the opening film at the 1997 Venice Film Festival. In December 1997 Allen married Soon-Yi.

**Allenby, Edmund Henry Hynman, 1st Viscount** (1861-1936), British field marshal who directed the campaign that won Palestine and Syria from the Turks in World War I. From 1919 to 1925 he was British high commissioner in Egypt.

**Allende Gossens, Salvador** (1908-73), Marxist founder of the Chilean Socialist Party, president of Chile (1970-73). His radical reform program disrupted the economy; strikes and widespread famine led to a military coup and to his death, reportedly by murder or suicide.

**Allentown** (pop. 686,688), commercial and industrial city in eastern Pennsylvania, seat of Lehigh County, situated on the Lehigh River about 50 mi (80 km) northwest of Philadelphia. Founded in 1762, Allentown has many Revolutionary War associations. Settled by German immigrants, the city lies on the perimeter of the "Pennsylvania Dutch" region. There is considerable light industry, and factories produce trucks, buses, electronic equipment, cement, and textiles. Located in the city are Muhlenberg and Cedar Crest colleges.

**Allergy,** abnormal sensitivity to specific foreign material (an allergen). The allergy sufferer produces an antibody that combines with antigens, causing certain chemicals to be released, producing allergy symptoms. In the skin, this appears as eczema or urticaria (hives); in the nose and eyes, hay fever results; in the gastrointestinal tract, diarrhea may occur. In the lungs, there may be a spasm of the bronchi (airways), leading to the wheezing and breathlessness of asthma. Common allergens include drugs (penicillin, aspirin), foods (shellfish), plant pollens, animal furs or feathers, insect stings, and the house dust mite.

**Alliance for Progress,** program to aid the economic and social development of Latin America, instituted by President John F. Kennedy in 1961 and brought into being when 22 nations and the United States signed the Charter of Punta del Este. The Latin American countries drew up development plans and guaranteed the larger part of capital costs, the United States meeting the remainder. Most U.S. funds are administered by the Agency for International Development, and since 1970 the Organization of American States (OAS) has also reviewed and coordinated programs.
*See also:* Organization of American States.

**Allies,** during World War I, nations bound together in opposition to the Central Powers. The Allies included the members of the Triple Entente, as well as Serbia, Belgium, Japan, Italy, and, as an "associated power," the United States. During World War II "Allies" was the popular term for some 25 nations that opposed the Axis powers. The major nations among the Allies were the United States, Britain, Russia, China, and later, the Free French. These 5 became the permanent members of the UN Security Council, established in 1945.

**Alligator,** either of 2 species of aquatic, carnivorous, lizardlike reptiles (genus *Alligator*) belonging to the crocodile family. The American alligator (*A. mississipiensis*), which lives in the southeastern United States, generally reaches a length of 9 ft (2.7 m), but the rare Chinese alligator (*A. sinensis* ) is much smaller. An adult American alligator is gray and dark green in color, weighs about 500 pounds, and lives to 50 or 60 years old. The females make excellent mothers and protect the newborn for over a year. Alligators like to eat fish, frogs, turtles, birds, and small mammals.

**Alliluyeva, Svetlana** (1926-    ), daughter of Joseph Stalin and his second wife Alliluyeva. She defected from the USSR to the United States in 1966. Her *Twenty Letters to a Friend* (1967) described her life in Moscow and the reasons for her departure. *Only One Year* (1969) tells of her life after her defection. In 1984 she returned to the USSR.

**Allopathy,** standard form of medical practice, producing a condition incompatible with or antagonistic to the condition being treated; the opposite of homeopathy.
*See also:* Homeopathy.

**Allotropy,** occurrence of an element in 2 or more forms (allotropes) that differ in their crystalline or molecular structure. Allotropes may have strikingly different physical or chemical properties. Allotropy in which the forms are stable under different conditions and are reversibly interconvertible at certain temperatures and pressures is called anantiotropy. Notable examples of allotropy are diamond and graphite (allotropes of carbon) and oxygen and ozone.

**Alloy**, combination of metals with each other or with nonmetals, such as carbon or phosphorus, and formed by mixing the molten components. An alloy's properties can be adjusted by varying the proportions of the constituents. Very few metals are used today in a pure state. The most common alloys are the different forms of steel, all of which contain a large proportion of iron and small amounts of carbon and other elements. Brass and bronze, 2 well-known alloys of copper, are still used in industry.
*See also:* Metallurgy; Permalloy.

**Allspice**, dried berry of the pimento, an evergreen tree (*Pimenta officinalıs*) of the myrtle family, used as a spice and for medicinal purposes.
*See also:* Pimento.

**Allston, Washington** (1779-1843), U.S. painter. After studying in London and Rome, he lived in the Boston area. He was noted for paintings on biblical and classical themes, such as *Belshazzar's Feast* and *The Deluge*. He was one of the first romantics in the United States to show a preference for classical landscapes in the style of Claude Lorrain and Salvator Rosa.

**Alluvial fan,** fan-shaped deposit of sediment composed of gravels, sands, and silts. When a stream suddenly diminishes in speed before entering a large body of water or a valley, an alluvial fan is formed.

**Alluvium**, sand, mud, or other earthly material deposited by rivers and streams, especially in the lower parts of their courses. The deltas of some rivers, for example, the Ganges, the Nile, and the Mississippi, consist of great masses of alluvial deposits. The meadows or plains flanking many rivers have been built up of alluvium and often receive further accumulations during floods.

**Almagro, Diego de** *See:* Pizarro, Francisco.

**Almanac**, originally, a calendar giving the position of the planets, the phases of the moon, etc., particularly as used by navigators (nautical almanacs), but now any yearbook of miscellaneous information, often containing abstracts of annual statistics.
*See also:* Banneker, Benjamin.

**Almond**, tree (*Prunus amygdalus*) of the rose family, the seed of whose fruit is used as food and flavoring and for medicinal purposes. It usually grows 10-20 ft (3-6 m) high and has spear-shaped, finely serrated leaves on thorny branches. The large flowers usually occur in pairs and are rose to white in color. It is native to Asia but grows well in California and the Mediterranean region.

**Aloe**, any of the succulent plants (genus *Aloe*), of the lily family. Aloes are natives of warm climates and especially abundant in Africa. Some aloes are used medicinally for treatment of burns, as insect repellents, and for pigment.

**Alpaca** (*Lama pacos*), South American hoofed herbivorous mammal, closely related to the llama. It has a long body and neck, and is about 3 ft (1 m) high at the shoulder. Its long, thick coat of black, brown, or yellowish

hair provides valuable wool. All alpacas are domesticated, living in the Andes above 13,000 ft (3,962 m).
*See also:* Llama; Vicuña.

**Alphabet** (from first 2 Greek letters, *alpha* and *beta*), set of characters intended to represent the sounds of spoken language. The chief alphabets of the world are Roman (Latin), Greek, Hebrew, Cyrillic (Slavic), Arabic, and Devanagari (used for Sanskrit). Alphabets probably originated around 2000 B C Hebrew, Arabic, and other written languages sprang from an alphabet that appeared around 1500 B.C Greek was derived from the Phoenician alphabet, which appeared around 1700 B C. Roman letters were derived from Greek and from Etruscan, also a descendant of the Greek. Most of the letters used in English are from the Latin alphabet. The Cyrillic alphabet, used for Slavic languages, also derives from the Greek.

**Alpha Centauri**, star 4.3 light-years (about 26 trillion miles) from the earth; only the sun is nearer. It is the brightest star in the constellation Centaurus and the third brightest star in the sky.

**Alpha Orionis** *See:* Betelgeuse.

**Alpha particle** (α-, or alpha ray), one of the particles emitted in radioactive decay. It is identical with the nucleus of the helium atom, consisting of 2 protons plus 2 neutrons bound together. A moving alpha particle is strongly ionizing and so loses energy rapidly in traversing through matter. Natural alpha particles will traverse only a few centimeters of air before coming to rest.
*See also:* Radiation; Radioactivity; Nuclear energy.

**Alphonsus Liguori, Saint** (1696-1787), Italian priest who founded the Congregation of the Most Holy Redeemer (Redemptorist Order), a society of missionary preachers working with the rural poor. He was canonized in 1839.

**Alps**, Europe's largest mountain system, 650 mi (1000 km) long and 30-180 mi (50-290 km) wide. Its fold mountains resulted from earth movements in the Tertiary period. The Western Alps run along the French-Italian border and include Mont Blanc, the highest Alpine peak at 15,771 ft (4,807 m). The Central Alps run northeast and east through Switzerland. The Eastern Alps extend through southern Germany, Austria, and northern Italy into Yugoslavia. Peaks are snowy and etched by ice action. The Alps are known for their many glaciers, glacially deepened valleys, and magnificent scenery.

**Alsace-Lorraine** (pop. 4,000,000), region in northeast France occupying 5,608 sq mi (14,525 sq km) west of the Rhine. It produces grains and grapes; timber, coal, potash, and salt (Vosges Mts.); iron ore; and textiles. Metz, Nancy, Strasbourg, and Verdun are the chief cities. The people are of French and German origin. France and Germany have long disputed control of the area. In medieval times both Alsace and Lorraine were part of the Holy Roman Empire. France took Alsace after 1648 and Lorraine in 1766. Germany seized most of the region in 1871 in the Franco-Prussian War, lost it to France after World War I, regained control in World War II, then lost it again.

**Alston, Walter Emmons** (1911-84), baseball manager. The low-keyed man of baseball, he led the Brooklyn (later Los Angeles) Dodgers to 7 National League pennants and 4 World Series championships (1955, 1959, 1963, and 1965).

**Altai Mountains**, mountain system in central Asia stretching across part of the USSR and the Mongolian People's Republic. Consisting of a number of parallel ranges, the Altai region is similar in geological character to the Alps but covers a larger area. The highest peak is Mt. Belukha (15,157 ft/4,620 m). Rich in minerals (gold, silver, copper, tin, lead, zinc, iron), the Altai Mountains supply the Soviet Union with large quantities of metals, particularly lead and zinc.

**Altamira**, cave near Santander, northern Spain, inhabited during the Aurignacian, upper Solutrean, and Magdalenian periods (14,000 B C.-10,000 B C). In 1879 the daughter of an amateur archaeologist discovered the striking cave paintings, believed to date from the Magdalenian period. They skillfully depict larger-than-life bulls, boars, and horses, among other paleolithic animals.

**Alternating current**, electrical signal that reverses direction at regular intervals. The frequency of alternation is measured in cycles per second (hertz); U.S. household current is 60 hertz.

**Alternation of generations**, in many lower plants and animals, alternation of 2 distinct forms. One form reproduces sexually and gives rise to the other form, which reproduces asexually. The offspring of the generation that reproduces asexually usually reproduce sexually again, but under certain conditions several asexual generations may follow each other. *See also:* Plant.

**Altgeld, John Peter** (1847-1902), U.S. political leader and jurist who sought to defend the individual against abuses of governmental power and vested interests. As a Cook County, Ill. superior court judge, he argued that legal practice was weighted against the poor. Elected Democratic governor of Illinois (1892), he backed labor and championed reform, arousing controversy by freeing three anarchists imprisoned for Chicago's Haymarket Affair Riot of 1886 and by opposing President Cleveland's use of troops to crush the Pullman strike of 1894.

**Altimeter**, instrument used for estimating the height of an aircraft above sea level. Most are modified aneroid barometers and work on the principle that air pressure decreases with increased altitude, but these must be constantly recalibrated during flight to take account of changing meteorological conditions (local ground temperature and air pressure). Radar altimeters, which compute absolute altitudes (the height of the aircraft above the ground surface immediately below) by measuring the time taken for radar waves to be reflected to the aircraft from the ground, are essential for blind landings. *See also:* Barometer.

**Altoona** (pop. 130,542), city in Blair County, south-central Pennsylvania, at the foot of the Allegheny Mountains, about 90 mi (145 km) east of

Pittsburgh. First settled in 1849 as a construction camp for the Pennsylvania Railroad, it was incorporated as a city in 1868. Altoona is noted for the manufacture and repair of locomotives and railway cars. Bituminous coal deposits are found nearby.

**Alum**, class of double sulfates containing aluminum and such metals as potassium, ammonium, and iron.
*See also:* Salt, chemical.

**Alumina**, or aluminum oxide, chemical compound ($Al_2O_3$). Found in bauxite ore, it is used in the production of aluminum, and also as an abrasive in ceramics.
*See also:* Aluminum.

**Aluminum**, chemical element, symbol Al; for physical constants see Periodic Table. Aluminum in the form of its compounds has been used for hundreds of years. Potassium aluminum sulfate, the most common alum, continues to be used in medicine as an astringent, and as a mordant in dyeing. Aluminum was first isolated by Oersted in 1825 although in an impure form. It occurs primarily in the form of complex silicates, and is the third most abundant element on earth. The principal ore of aluminum is *bauxite*, a hydrated oxide. Aluminum is a soft, tin-white, reactive, metal, the most abundant metal in the earth's crust. Aluminum is prepared by electrolysis of *alumina* (aluminum oxide) in fused *cryolite*, a procedure known as the Hall-Héroult process. Aluminum oxide occurs naturally in other important and useful forms as ruby, sapphire, corundum, and emery. Aluminum has many valuable properties which account for its wide use. It is second in malleability and sixth in ductility of all metals. It is light and a good electrical conductor. Since aluminum is soft, it is almost always alloyed with small amounts of other elements. It is the second most important metal after iron.

**Alva or Alba, Fernando Alvarez de Toledo, Duke of** (1507?-82), Spanish general who tyrannized the Netherlands. During his brutal campaign against rebellious Dutch Protestants (1567-73), he executed some 18,000 people. Hated for his atrocities and harsh taxes, and harassed by William the Silent's liberation army, Alva was recalled to Spain in 1573. In 1580 he conquered Portugal for Spain.

**Alvarado, Pedro de** (1485-1541), Cortés's chief lieutenant in the conquest of Mexico (1519- 21) and leader of the force that seized what are now Guatemala and El Salvador (1523-24). As governor of Guatemala he instituted forced Indian labor and founded many cities.
*See also:* Cortés, Hernando.

**Alvarez, Luis Walter** (1911-88), U.S. physicist awarded the 1968 Nobel Prize for physics for work on subatomic particles, including the discovery of transient resonance particles. He helped develop much of the hardware of nuclear physics. During World War II he worked on the development of radar and on the Manhattan (atomic bomb) Project.
*See also:* Bubble chamber.

**Alzheimer's disease**, progressive, incurable disease of the brain, the most common cause of premature senility. Its symptoms may include loss of memory, changes in personality, impaired language and motor skills, loss of control of bodily functions, and unresponsiveness. Currently it is difficult to diagnose and there is no specific treatment.
*See also:* Senility.

**AMA** *See:* American Medical Association.

**Amadís of Gaul**, Spanish romance of chivalry. Garci Ordóñez de Montalvo is credited with the first known version, *The Four Books of the Virtuous Knight Amadís* (1508), although some evidence suggests that the story of Amadís, the medieval knight, may have been in circulation since the late 14th century. Cervantes' *Don Quixote* owes much to *Amadís*.

**Amado, Jorge** (1912-    ), Brazilian novelist, author of *The Violent Land* (1942), *Gabriela, Clove and Cinnamon* (1958), and *Doña Flor and Her Two Husbands* (English, 1969). His books are particularly concerned with the plight of the poor.

**Amalfi** (pop. 6,000), seaport in the Campania region of Italy, on the Gulf of Salerno, near Naples. Built on a steep mountain slope and having a mild climate, it is a popular tourist center along the Amalfi Drive from Sorrento to Salerno. Amalfi became an important commercial and maritime center during the Middle Ages, for a time even rivaling Venice.

**Amalgam**, alloy of mercury with another metal, commonly used for tooth fillings.
*See also:* Metallurgy.

**Amaranth**, common name for plants of genus *Amaranthus*, including pigweed as well as plants grown as cereal and as ornamentals; also, a poetical name for a flower that never fades.
*See also:* Pigweed; Tumbleweed.

**Amarillo** (pop. 187,547), largest city and commercial center of the Texas Panhandle. Amarillo's industries include oil, natural gas, and copper refining, as well as livestock and grains. The city offers various music and art facilities and is home to several colleges and universities. Amarillo was founded in 1887 and rapidly grew in the early 1900s with the discovery of oil .

**Amaryllis**, family of bulbous-rooted plants with lilylike flowers. Among the best-known of the 1,200 species are the true amaryllis, the narcissus, and the snowdrop.
*See also:* Narcissus.

**Amasis II** (569-525 B C.), Egyptian pharaoh of the 26th dynasty. During his long reign, he developed strong ties with Greece, using mercenaries and maintaining relations with various Greek states. Egypt prospered under his enlightened rule and skilled diplomacy. He thwarted an invasion by Nebuchadnezzar, added Cyprus to his kingdom, and through marriage became very influential in Cyrene. He was the last great Egyptian ruler before the Persian conquest, which occurred soon after his death. Amasis (or Ahmose) is also the name of the lesser-known pharaoh (c.1580-87 B.C ) who rid Egypt of the Hyksos conquerors.

**Amateur Athletic Union** (AAU), U.S. nonprofit organization, founded in 1888, that promotes and encourages amateur sports. The AAU sponsors the annual Junior Sports and Junior Olympic Games and other athletic competitions and presents the James E. Sullivan Award annually to the country's outstanding amateur athlete.

**Amazon River,** world's second-longest river (3,900 mi/6,280 km). The Amazon rises in Andean Peru near the Pacific Ocean and flows east through the world's largest equatorial rain forest to the Atlantic Ocean. It is also the world's largest river in volume and drainage area. Its basin drains 40% of South America, and it has hundreds of tributaries. Most of the Amazon is navigable, and oceangoing vessels can travel 2,300 mi (3,700 km) to Iquitos in Peru. Other ports are Belém and Manaus in Brazil. The Amazon is important for commerce in hardwoods and other forest products.
*See also:* Brazil.

**Amazons,** in Greek mythology, race of warrior women living in the Black Sea area. Their name derives from the Greek word for "breastless," due to their alleged practice of removing the right breast to aid archery. For his ninth labor, Heracles (Hercules) was required to take the girdle of the Amazonian queen Hippolyta. Amazons fought on the side of Troy in the Trojan War.

**Amber,** fossilized resin from prehistoric evergreens. Brownish-yellow and translucent, it is highly valued and can be easily cut and polished for ornamental purposes. Its chief scientific importance is that fossil insects up to 20 million years old have been found embedded in it.
*See also:* Resin.

**Ambergris,** waxy solid formed in the intestines of sperm whales, perhaps to protect them from the bony parts of their squid diets. When obtained from dead whales, it is soft, black, and foul-smelling, but on weathering (as when found as flotsam) it becomes hard, gray, and fragrant, and is used as a perfume fixative and in the East as a spice. The heaviest piece of ambergris found in the intestine of a sperm whale weighed 1,003 lb (455 kg).
*See also:* Whale.

**Amberjack** (genus *Seriola*), large, elongated fish found in tropical oceans. The amberjack's superior swimming and fighting abilities make it a popular game fish. Of the approximately 12 species of amberjacks, the greater amberjack (*S. dumerili*) is the largest, reaching a weight of more than 150 lb (68 kg) and a length of more than 5  ft (1.5 m).

**Ambrose, Saint** (c. A.D. 340-397), important Father of the Latin Church. A Roman governor who became the influential bishop of Milan, he attacked imperial moral standards and strengthened the position of the Church amid the ruins of the Roman Empire by his preaching and writing. St. Augustine was one of his converts.

**Ambrosia,** fabled food of the ancient Greek gods, which conferred immortality on those who partook of it; hence, anything pleasing to the taste or smell.
*See also:* Nectar.

**Ameba,** or amoeba, microscopic, one-celled organism that lives in moist earth, water, and parasitically in the bodies of animals. The ameba is a shapeless cell of jellylike material (protoplasm) encased in a thin membrane. It constantly changes shape by forming temporary projections called pseudopods (false feet) used for feeding and locomotion. The ameba reproduces by fission (splitting). Amebas are harmless to people, except for a type that inflames the lining of the large intestine, causing a disease called amebic dysentery.

**Amendment,** in legislation, change in a bill or motion under discussion, or in an existing law or constitution. In the U.S. Congress a bill already passed by one house may be amended by the second house. If the first house does not agree to this amendment, a conference committee, made up of members of both houses, is called to work out a compromise.
*See also:* Parliamentary procedure; Constitution of the United States; Bill of rights.

**America,** the 2 major continents of the Western Hemisphere, North and South America (although the name is sometimes used to mean the United States). In 1507 the German geographer Martin Waldseemüller first gave the name to the area that is now Brazil in honor of the Italian navigator Amerigo Vespucci, who supposedly discovered much of South America.
*See also:* Vespucci, Amerigo.

**America,** patriotic song written in 1832 by the Massachusetts minister, Rev. Samuel Francis Smith, to the tune of the British national anthem, "God Save the Queen (King)."

**America First Committee,** organization that opposed U.S. involvement in World War II. Founded in 1940, it vigorously opposed the politics of President Franklin Delano Roosevelt. Much of its support came from the Hearst newspapers and the *Chicago Tribune.* The committee advocated isolationism and neutrality in European affairs. The Japanese attack on Pearl Harbor abruptly ended support for its activities.
*See also:* World War II.

**American Academy and Institute of Arts and Letters,** organization to promote literature, music, and the fine arts in the United States. Based in New York City, it was formed in 1976 from the merger of the National Institute of Arts and Letters (founded 1898) and the American Academy of Arts and Letters (founded 1904). The organization, consisting of 250 members who serve for life, makes awards to American writers, artists, and composers, sponsors exhibits of their works, and purchases works to donate to museums.

**American Academy in Rome,** institute for independent work and advanced research in the arts, architecture, art history, and archaeology by U.S.

artists and scholars in Rome, established in 1894 by the neoclassical architect Charles F. McKim as a school of architecture in Italy. By an act of Congress, the academy was officially incorporated in 1905.
*See also:* McKim, Charles Follen.

**American Association of Retired Persons**(AARP), private, nonprofit organization for people aged 50 and older. AARP's purpose is to improve the quality of life for the elderly through educational programs and other special services, including travel benefits, health insurance, a credit union, and pharmaceutical information. AARP, with headquarters in Washington, D.C., was founded in 1958.

**American Automobile Association** *See:* Automobile Association, American.

**American Bar Association** (ABA), voluntary national organization for members of the U.S. legal profession. Founded in 1878 at Saratoga Springs, N.Y., the group promotes the study and practice of jurisprudence and improvements in the administration of justice, and works to uphold the honor and standards of the profession. National headquarters are in Chicago. Its general policy-making body is made up of representatives from all state bar associations and acts through a board of governors. Standing committees study current legal issues. Official association publications include a legal yearbook and a monthly law journal.

**American Booksellers Association** (ABA), trade group primarily comprising bookstore owners and publishers, first founded in 1900 in New York City. It is active in defending First Amendment rights, providing education, research, and publications for people in the book business, as well as administering the annual ABA convention and tradeshow.

**American Cancer Society** *See:* Cancer Society of America.

**American Civil Liberties Union** (ACLU), organization founded in 1920 and dedicated to defending constitutional freedoms in the United States. Its work centers on providing legal aid in cases of violated civil liberties, especially those of political, religious, and racial minorities. From its founding the ACLU has participated in the nation's most important civil rights cases: the Scopes trial (1925), which challenged a Tennessee law barring the right to teach Darwin's theory of evolution in schools; the federal court test (1933) that ended censorship of James Joyce's *Ulysses*; and the landmark *Brown* v. *Board of Education* (1954), which successfully challenged the constitutionality of racially segregated schools. The organization generated controversy in 1978 by upholding the American Nazi Party's right to march in Skokie, Ill., and to display swastika symbols.

**American Expeditionary Forces** (AEF), name given to the U.S. forces serving in Europe during World War I. Its commander was General John Pershing. The first U.S. troops arrived in June 1917 and saw major action in May 1918, when they relieved the French at Château-Thierry and stopped a German advance. In June, some 6,000 U.S. marines were killed at Belleau Wood. U.S. forces were important in stemming the German counteroffensive in the second Battle of the Marne (July-Aug. 1918). By the end of the war the AEF held one-fourth of the line and had taken part in 13 battles, most of them major encounters. U.S. troops were at the front for a total of 200 days, with 1,993,000 men fighting at the end of the war. Over 100,000 members of the AEF were killed in action, a similar number died of disease (especially influenza), and more than 200,000 were wounded.

*See also:* Pershing, John Joseph; World War I.

**American Federation of Labor and Congress of Industrial Organizations** (AFL-CIO), powerful federation of labor unions created in 1955 by the merger of the AFL and CIO. Over 100 constituent unions in the United States, Mexico, Canada, and Panama represent about 15 million members. A national president, secretary-treasurer, and vice-presidents make up the executive council, which enforces policy decisions made at biennial conventions attended by several thousand delegates.

The organization's main objectives are more pay, shorter working hours, and better working conditions for employees, obtained by union-management agreements that preserve industrial harmony and prosperity. Each affiliated union conducts its own collective bargaining and determines much of its own policy. The AFL-CIO lobbies on such issues as social welfare, conservation, education, and international problems, and has backed political candidates. The AFL, founded in 1886 under the leadership of Samuel Gompers, originally comprised only craft unions, excluding unskilled and semiskilled workers, whose numbers multiplied as mass production increased in the early 1900s. To cater to these workers, AFL dissidents in 1935 formed the Committee for Industrial Organization, later the Congress of Industrial Organizations, led by John L. Lewis. Laws hostile to organized labor led to the cooperation between and, in 1955, the merger of the AFL and CIO, with George Meany (head of AFL) as president. Despite the union membership of a large number of women, it was only in 1980 that a woman, Joyce Miller, was named to the AFL-CIO executive council.

**American Indian Movement** (AIM), civil rights organization in the United States and Canada, founded in 1968 to establish equal rights and improve living conditions of Native Americans. AIM has demanded the return of property rights as specified in U. S. and Canadian government treaties with various tribes, legal reform, and reform of education, employment, and health services for Native Americans.

**American Labor Party**, New York State left-wing political party (1936-56). Founded by labor leaders, it helped elect its member Fiorella LaGuardia mayor of New York in 1937 and 1941 and Herbert Lehman governor in 1938. In World War II it split over attitudes to the USSR: The right under David Dubinsky accused Sidney Hillman's left of being communist-controlled. The party disbanded in 1956.

**American Legion**, organization fostering the welfare, and protecting the rights of United States veterans of World War I, World War II, the Korean War, and the Vietnam War. Ongoing activities of the legion include building and maintaining community centers, parks, and recreation facilities; providing equipment for hospitals and other health care endeavors; care and help for disabled United States veterans; sponsorship of scout troops; annual oratory contests for high school students to promote study of the United States Constitution; and furtherance of education and employment services.

**American Library Association,** society "to extend and improve library service throughout the world." Founded in Philadelphia (1876) by Melvil Dewey, it is the world's oldest and largest library association and has had great influence on library development in English-speaking countries, as well as in Scandinavia, the Netherlands, and Germany. With headquarters in Chicago, the organization has more than 50,000 members.

**American literature,** see: United States literature.

**American Medical Association** (AMA), U.S. federation of state medical organizations. It was established in 1847 for the purpose of advancing medical knowledge, raising standards of medical education and practice, improving public health, and furthering the interests of the medical profession in general. AMA national headquarters are in Chicago Ill. Its various sections publish the weekly *Journal of the American Medical Association* (*JAMA*) and other specialized periodicals. Through its powerful national and state lobbies, the AMA has great influence on legislation.

**American Museum of Natural History,** institution in New York City founded in 1869 and dedicated to research and public education in anthropology and natural science. It is noted for its mounted specimens of birds and other animals from all over the world, fossil collections including dinosaur skeletons, its gem collection, and the Hayden Planetarium.

**American Party,** conservative U.S. political party, originally called the American Independent Party. Established in 1968, the party's purpose was to support the presidential candidacy of George C. Wallace, governor of Alabama. Wallace's platform was based largely on his opposition to desegregation of Alabama schools. The name was also used by the Know-Nothing Party of the 1850s.

**American Philosophical Society,** oldest surviving U.S. learned society, based in Philadelphia, where it was founded by Benjamin Franklin (1753). The U.S. counterpart of the Royal Society of London, it has nearly 600 U.S. and foreign members. It has an extensive library, much relating to Colonial science.

**American Red Cross** *See:* Red Cross.

**American Revolution** *See:* Revolutionary War in America.

**American Samoa,** unincorporated U.S. territory in the South Pacific, about 2,300 mi (3,700 km) southwest of Hawaii, with a total area of 76 sq mi (197 sq km). The territory consists of 7 islands: Tutuila (site of the capital, Pago Pago), the Manua group (Aununu, Ofu, Tau, Olosega), Rose, and Swains. The region is mountainous and tropical. The native Polynesians speak Samoan and English, live in villages, and practice Christianity. The leading industry is tuna canning. Agricultural products include coconuts, bananas, and taro. Samoa was divided between the United States and Germany, by treaty, in 1899; the eastern portion was administered by the U.S. Navy until 1951, when it passed to the jurisdiction of the Department of the Interior. American Samoans are nationals, but not citizens of the United States. They elect a governor, a legislature, and a nonvoting delegate to the U.S. Congress. *See also:* Pacific Islands.

**Americans for Democratic Action** (ADA), independent political organization, founded in 1947, that supports liberal policies in government, promoting civil rights and opposing U.S. military involvement in developing countries. The ADA campaigns to elect liberal politicians. Its headquarters are in Washington, D.C.

**American Society for the Prevention of Cruelty to Animals** (ASPCA), organization founded in 1866 to prevent maltreatment of animals by enforcing laws designed to protect them, disseminating information, maintaining animal hospitals, and providing shelters and veterinary facilities. Its charter was granted by the New York State legislature and its operations are limited to that state. More than 600 organizations of a similar purpose exist in the United States.

**American Society of Composers, Authors and Publishers**   (ASCAP), association that serves as a clearinghouse between creators and users of music. Founded in 1914, ASCAP grants licenses and collects fees to protect members from copyright infringement, covering performance as well as publication of music. The national headquarters are in New York City.

**American System,** term used by Henry Clay (1777-1852) for his program of economic nationalism, which provided protective tariffs and internal improvements such as roads and canals. For a time the American System had considerable support, and in President James Monroe's second term tariffs were increased and a national bank was reestablished. President John Quincy Adams's ideas went far beyond Clay's, but they antagonized westerners, who wanted the price for the public lands lowered, and Southerners, who were fearful of interference with slavery and who needed cheap imported manufactures. After Andrew Jackson became president in 1829, the provisions of the American System were not put into effect.
*See also:* Clay, Henry; Monroe, James.

**America's Cup,** international yachting trophy. The cup, the oldest trophy in international sports, was held continuously by the United States from the first race in 1851 until 1983, when the *Australia II* defeated the U.S. yacht *Liberty.* The U.S. yacht *Stars & Stripes* defeated Australia's *Kookaburra* in 1987 to regain the cup. In 1988 controversy surrounded the U.S. use of a 60-ft (20-m) catamaran, *Stars & Stripes,* which defeated the challenger, the 133-ft (44.4-m) monohull *New Zealand. New Zealand's* team claimed the catamaran was illegal, but after several U.S. court rulings *Stars & Stripes* was awarded the cup. To avoid future controversy, all competitors will use 75-ft (25-m) monohulls with a 110-ft (36.6-m) mast in the May 1992 America's Cup competition.

**America the Beautiful,** patriotic song, with words written in 1893 by Katherine Lee Bates, and music by Samuel A. Ward.

**Americium**, chemical element, symbol Am; for physical constants see Periodic Table. Americium was synthesized by Glenn Seaborg and co-workers in 1944 by bombardment of plutonium-234 with alpha particles at the wartime Metallurgical Laboratory of the University of Chicago (now the Argonne National Laboratory). It is produced in quantity by neutron irradiation of plutonium isotopes in a nuclear reactor. Americium is a reactive, radioactive, metal, obtained by reducing its trifluoride with barium vapor. It is a member of the actinide series. The element must be handled with special care because of its great alpha and gamma activity. Americium is used in gamma radiography, glass thickness gages, and in smoke detectors. Thirteen isotopes of americium are known.

**Amerigo Vespucci** *See:* Vespucci, Amerigo.

**Amethyst**, transparent violet or purple variety of quartz, thought to be colored by iron or manganese impurities. A semiprecious gem, it is used to make jewelry. Amethysts are mined in Brazil, Uruguay, North America, and the USSR.

**Amherst, Jeffrey Amherst Baron** (1717-97), British major-general who helped take Canada from the French. He commanded British forces at the capture of Louisburg on Cape Breton Island (1758), Ticonderoga and Crown Point (1759), and Montreal (1760). While governor-general of British North America (1760-63), he crushed a pro-French Indian uprising led by Pontiac.

**Amiens** (pop. 136,400), city in northern France, capital of the Somme department on the Somme River 80 mi (130 km) north of Paris. An important trade and manufacturing center, Amiens has been noted since the 16th century for its linens, woolens, silks, and velvets. Its Cathedral of Notre Dame, begun c.1220, is one of the finest examples of French Gothic architecture.

**Amin Dada, Idi** (1925-    ), president of Uganda (1971-79). He led the military overthrow of President Milton Obote in 1971. A flamboyant and dictatorial ruler, he expelled Uganda's Asian middle class in 1972, called for the extinction of Israel in 1975, and purged many opponents. In 1975-76 he was president of the Organization of African Unity. Insurrectionists, aided by Tanzanian forces, drove out Amin in 1979. After his exile to Saudi Arabia, his whereabouts were uncertain.

**Amine**, chemical compound formed from ammonia ($NH_3$) by replacing 1 or more hydrogen atoms of the ammonia molecule with a corresponding number of hydrogen-carbon groups.

**Amino acids**, class of organic acids containing a carboxyl group (COOH) and 1 or more ($NH_2$) groups. Amino acids are synthesized in cells and are the basis of proteins. Amino acids are white crystalline solids that are soluble in water; they can act as acids or bases depending on the chemical environment. All amino acids (except glycine) contain at least 1 asymmetric carbon atom to which are attached the carboxyl group, the amino group, a hydrogen atom, and a fourth group that differs for each amino acid and determines its character. Amino acids can exist in 2 mirror-image forms. Generally only

L-isomers (left-turning) occur in nature, but a few bacteria contain D-isomers (right-turning). Organisms link amino acids in chains called polypeptides and proteins. Digestion breaks down these linkages.
*See also:* Protein.

**Amis, Kingsley** (1922-95), English novelist, poet, and critic. He emerged as a sharp satirist in *Lucky Jim* (1953), an attack on social and academic pretensions. Among his other works are *New Maps of Hell* (1960), *One Fat Englishman* (1964), *The Green Man* (1969), and *Jake's Thing* (1979).

**Amish**, conservative group of the Mennonite sect, founded by Jacob Ammann in Switzerland in the 1690s. In the 18th century members settled in what are now Indiana, Ohio, and Pennsylvania. Their farm communities reject modern life, including electricity, telephones, and cars.
*See also:* Mennonites; Pennsylvania Dutch.

**Amman** (pop. 1,573,000), largest city, capital, and commercial and industrial center of the kingdom of Jordan. Industries include food and tobacco processing, textiles, cement, and leatherware. It is a busy transport junction, with good rail and road connections to major Middle Eastern cities and an international airport. Arab refugees from Israel and Israeli-held territories of Jordan have greatly enlarged its population in recent years. Amman was the scene of heavy fighting between government troops and guerilla forces of the Palestine Liberation Organization in 1970.
The modern city is built on the site of the Rabbath Ammon, the capital of the ancient Ammonites. Named Philadelphia in the third century B C., it prospered under Greek, Roman, and Byzantine rule. During the Middle Ages, after coming under Muslim control, it gradually declined to the status of a caravan village. Part of the Ottoman Empire until World War I, Amman became the capital of Transjordan, established as a British mandate in 1920. Amman remained the capital and royal residence when Jordan became independent in 1946. Its extensive Greco-Roman ruins include baths, a fortress, a temple dedicated to Hercules, a huge theater, and a Byzantine basilica.

**Ammann, Othmar Hermann** (1897-1965), U.S. engineer. He designed the George Washington Bridge in New York City (1931), the San Francisco Golden Gate Bridge (1935), and the Verrazano-Narrows Bridge in New York (1964).

**Ammeter**, instrument for measuring amperes of electric current. The most commonly used ammeter is of the permanent-magnet moving-coil type.
*See also:* Ampere; Electromagnetism.

**Ammonia**, chemical compound ($NH_3$), colorless acrid gas. Ammonia is used as a cleaning fluid (with water), as a fertilizer, a refrigerant, and to make ammonium salts, urea, and many drugs, dyes, and plastics.

**Amnesia**, partial or complete loss of memory. It can result from concussions, senility, severe illness, or physical or psychological trauma, and is of varying duration.

**Amnesty International,** organization founded in 1961 to aid political prisoners and others detained for reasons of conscience throughout the world. With thousands of members in the United States and around the world, it has advisory status with the UN and other international organizations. Amnesty International received the Nobel Prize for peace in 1977.

**Amniocentesis,** procedure of sampling the amniotic fluid surrounding a fetus by puncturing the abdomen of the pregnant woman with a very fine, hollow needle. Cells and other substances shed into the amniotic fluid by the fetus are used for detecting the presence in the fetal genes of such disorders as Down's syndrome, Tay-Sachs disease, and spinal malformations.Amniocentesis also can be used to determine the sex of an unborn child with 98% accuracy.
*See also:* Genetic counseling.

**Amoeba** *See:* Ameba.

**Amon,** ancient Egyptian deity, sometimes depicted as a ram or a human with a ram's head. Chiefly worshipped in Thebes, he was identified with the sun god Re, and became known as Amon-Re, king of the gods. In Hellenistic times his temple and oracle were visited by many Greeks, who identified Amon with Zeus.

**Amos** (8th century B C ), Hebrew prophet; also, a book of the Old Testament containing his life and teachings. A shepherd from Judah, Amos proclaimed that there was one God for all peoples. In neighboring Israel, he denounced corruption until expelled by the king.

**Ampere** (amp or A), unit for measuring the rate of flow of an electric current. One ampere is defined as the current in each of 2 parallel wires when the magnetic force between them is $2 \times 10^{-7}$ newtons per meter. It is named after André Marie Ampère, the French scientist.
*See also:* Ammeter; Ohm's law.

**Ampère, André Marie** (1775-1836), French mathematician, physicist, and philosopher best remembered for many discoveries in electrodynamics and electromagnetism. He expanded Hans Oersted's experiment on the interaction between magnets and electric currents and investigated the force set up between current-carrying conductors. He also made contributions in the fields of statistics, chemistry, optics, and crystallography.
*See also:* Ampere; Electromagnetism.

**Amphetamine,** any of a group of stimulant drugs, including Benzedrine and Methedrine, derived from the chemical compound amphetamine ($C_9H_{13}N$). Amphetamines counteract fatigue, suppress appetite, speed up performance (hence the slang "speed"), and give the taker a false sense of confidence. Pronounced depression often follows use, encouraging psychological and then physical addiction. A paranoid psychosis resembling schizophrenia may result from prolonged use. Amphetamines have been used in the treatment of obesity and narcolepsy (a rare condition of abnormal sleepiness).

**Amphibian**, class of cold-blooded vertebrates, including frogs, toads, newts, salamanders, and caecilians. Typically they spend part of their life in water, part on land. They are distinct from reptiles in that their eggs must be laid in moist conditions, and that their soft, moist skins have no scales. The larval amphibian is usually solely aquatic; the adult is partly or entirely terrestrial, generally 4-legged, and carnivorous.

**Amphibious warfare**, coordinated use of land and sea forces to seize a beachhead, an area from which to carry on further military action. Although naval and ground forces have often cooperated since the earliest days of warfare, the strategy of modern amphibious military operations did not develop fully until World War II. Specially outfitted ocean vessels were constructed, and landing craft were designed, capable of making long voyages to transport troops, weapons, and supplies, and then unload them ready for combat if they met concentrated enemy opposition. Allied operations against the Japanese in the Pacific and in the landings in Italy and Normandy during World War II were typical of this strategy.

**Amphibole**, any of a group of silicate minerals with similar chemical compositions and characteristic optical properties. Amphiboles are usually found in lava or very old rock strata. They form long slender crystals, which in asbestos become fine fibers. Hornblende is the most common amphibole.

**Amphioxus**, or lancet, a small, primitive, fishlike sea animal (genus *Branchiostoma*), important as a possible descendant of the evolutionary link between invertebrates and vertebrates.

**Amphitheater**, open edifice built in the Roman Empire for public viewing of contests and spectacles (e.g., the Colosseum in Rome). Usually oval in form, it comprises a central arena surrounded by ascending rows of seats. Gladiators and animals used in the spectacles were held under the arena. The term is now used loosely for any large auditorium.

**Ampicillin**, semisynthetic antibiotic that is a derivative of penicillin, used to treat a wide range of bacterial infections. Ampicillin can kill some bacteria not effectively killed by other forms of penicillin, and is used to treat severe ear and sinus infections, meningitis in children, and various infections of the urinary, respiratory, and intestinal tracts. Among the microorganisms susceptible to ampicillin are *Salmonella*, several species of which cause a type of food poisoning, and *Salmonella typhosa*, the cause of typhoid fever. Although penicillin is still widely prescribed, its effectiveness has decreased somewhat since its introduction in 1961, because certain bacteria have begun to develop resistance to it.
*See also:* Penicillin.

**Amritsar** (pop. 708,800), city in Punjab state in northwest India. The center of the Sikh religion, it is the site of the *Amritsar* or sacred "pool of immortality" in which Sikhs immerse themselves as an act of purification. The city is also an important industrial center, known for textiles and carpets.

**Amsterdam** (pop. 721,600), capital and largest city of the Netherlands, and one of Europe's great commercial, financial, and cultural centers. In the province of North Holland, it lies on the IJ and Amstel rivers, at the south end of Lake IJsselmeer. The city center is built on a series of concentric semicircular canals. Other canals link it to the Rhine River and the North Sea and make Amsterdam one of Europe's major ports. It is also a major rail center and has an international airport. Amsterdam is a diamond-cutting center and produces chemicals, machinery, bicycles, electronics, beer, and textiles. It has an important stock exchange, two universities, and about 50 museums, and is home to major collections of works by Rembrandt and Van Gogh. Amsterdam grew from a medieval fishing village, becoming a major city by the 17th century. Amsterdam was under German occupation 1940-45. *See also:* Netherlands.

**Amtrak**, official nickname of the National Railroad Passenger Corp., established by Congress in an effort to halt the deterioration of railroad passenger service. Amtrak began operations on May 1, 1971, with 150 intercity trains. It improved service and increased ridership but, like the private carriers it replaced, accumulated large deficits, and has required government subsidies. *See also:* Railroad.

**Amundsen, Roald** (1872-1928), Norwegian polar explorer. He was the first person to reach the South Pole (Dec. 14, 1911), his party beating the ill-fated Robert F. Scott expedition by one month. In the Arctic he was the first to navigate the Northwest Passage (1903-6), later crossing the North Pole in the dirigible *Norge* (1926). He was killed in the Arctic during an air search for the Italian explorer Umberto Nobile. *See also:* Antarctica.

**Amur**, river in northeastern Asia. Formed by the Shilka and Argun rivers in Mongolia, it flows east through the USSR for 2,700 mi (4,300 km) to empty into the Pacific. For more than half its course it forms the boundary between the USSR and China.

**Amyotrophic lateral sclerosis**, or Lou Gehrig's disease, progressive fatal disease in which there is degeneration of the motor nerve cells of the brain and spine, resulting in progressive muscular atrophy, paralysis, and death from asphyxiation. *See also:* Gehrig, Lou.

**Anabaptism**, movement advocating baptism of adult believers rather than infants. The first group was formed in 1523 at Zürich by dissatisfied followers of Ulrich Zwingli. Most stressed the dictates of individual conscience, and urged nonviolence and separation of church and state. Despite widespread persecution, their doctrines spread, forming the basis of belief for the Mennonites in the Netherlands and the Hutterites in Moravia. *See also:* Reformation.

**Anabolic steroid**, any of a group of steroids derived from the male sex hormone testosterone. They affect growth, muscle bulk, and protein buildup, and may be used in treating patients after major surgery or severe accidents or with debilitating disease, when there may be a breakdown of body protein. However, these drugs have been abused by athletes, and for this reason they are only prescribed by hospital doctors and are not available on normal prescriptions.

**Anaconda,** semiaquatic subfamily of the boa family. *Eunectes notaeus* is found in Paraguay and *Eunectes murinus*, probably the largest snake in the world—up to 25 ft (8 m) long and 3 ft (1 m) in circumference— throughout Brazil. Anacondas do not have a poisonous bite, but kill prey by constriction. *See also:* Boa constrictor.

**Anacreon** (572-485? B.C), Greek lyric poet who celebrated wine and love in mellow, simple verses. These were copied in the so-called Anacreontics, fashionable in the Hellenistic Age and again in 18th-century Europe. His main patrons were the tyrants of Samos and Athens.

**Anaheim** (pop. 2,410,556), city in Orange County, southern California, southeast of Los Angeles. Settled in the 1850s by German immigrant grape growers, it became a prosperous center for handling the local citrus fruit. Now a tourist center, it is home to Disneyland (built 1955), the California Angels baseball team, and the Los Angeles Rams football team. Its diversified industry includes chemicals, hardware plants, electronics, and aircraft engineering.

**Analog computer,** computer that operates on data by representing them with physical quantities such as voltages. Most computers are now digital rather than analog.

**Anarchism,** political belief that government should be abolished and the state replaced by the voluntary cooperation of individuals and groups. Like socialists, anarchists advocate the abolition of the institution of private property. But unlike socialists, they believe that government is unnecessary and intrinsically harmful.
Pioneers of modern anarchism included England's William Godwin (1756-1836), France's Pierre Joseph Proudhon (1809-65), and the Russian revolutionary Mikhail Bakunin (1814-76). Emma Goldman (1869-1940) and Alexander Berkman (1870?-1936) were activeU.S. anarchists who were deported for their actions (1919). After President William McKinley was assassinated by an anarchist in 1901, anarchists were barred from entering the United States. Although anarchism is now more important philosophically than politically, it has recently become linked with student radicalism in Europe and America.
*See also:* Nihilism.

**Anastasia** (1901-18?), Russian grand duchess. Daughter of the last tsar, Nicholas II, she was probably murdered with her family during the Revolution. Several women later claimed to be Anastasia, but none could prove her identity.
*See also:* Russian Revolution.

**Anatomy,** study of the structure of plants and animals. The word is derived from a Greek verb meaning to cut up, since dissection was the main source of anatomical knowledge. Anatomy is closely related to physiology, the investigation of the functions and vital processes of living organisms. Gross

anatomy is the study of the structures that can be seen with the naked eye, and microscopic anatomy, the investigation of minute parts of organs and tissues with the aid of a microscope. Comparative anatomy systematically compares the structures of different organisms.
*See also:* Human body.

**Anaxagoras** (500-428 B.C), Greek philosopher of the Ionian school, resident of Athens, who taught that the elements were infinite in number and that everything contained a portion of every other thing. He also postulated a basic moving force of the universe, *Nous* or Mind. He was the teacher of Pericles, Euripides, and reputedly, of Socrates.
*See also:* Socrates.

**Anaximander** (611?-547? B C.), Greek philosopher, first to give a naturalistic, rather than mythological, explanation to natural processes. He believed that the origin of all things was a formless matter, which he called "indefinite." His later works anticipated the theory of evolution and certain laws of astronomy.

**Anchorage** (pop. 235,000), largest city in Alaska, located in the southern part of the state at the head of Cook Inlet. Founded in 1915 as the headquarters for the Alaska Railroad and incorporated in 1920, it is now the commercial and transportation center of Alaska, serving the state's coal, gas, and oil industries. During World War II, Anchorage became an important military and air defense center. Its international airport services heavy traffic in jets bound for the Orient, Canada, and other parts of the United States and for Europe by the transpolar route. Anchorage was severely damaged by an earthquake in 1964 that killed 131 people.
*See also:* Alaska.

**Anchovy**, small fish of the family Engraulidae, related to the herring family, exported from the Mediterranean for use as a seasoning and garnish. It is also found on the coast of Peru.

**Ancient civilization**, term used to describe history and culture prior to the fall of the Roman Empire. Achievements in art, mathematics, literature, and architecture from those times still influence the modern world. The cultures of Egypt, Mesopotamia, Greece, and Rome are instances of ancient civilizations.

**Andersen, Hans Christian** (1805-75), Danish writer, best remembered for his 168 fairy tales. Based on folklore and observation of people and events in Andersen's life, they have a deceptively simple, slyly humorous style and often carry a moral message for adults as well as children. Among his best known stories are "The Ugly Duckling," "The Emperor's Clothes," and "The Red Shoes."

**Anderson, Carl David** (1905-91), U.S. physicist who shared the 1936 Nobel Prize in physics for the discovery of the positron (1932). Later he was codiscoverer of the first meson.
*See also:* Dirac, Paul Adrien Maurice.

**Anderson, Dame Judith** (1898-1992), Australian-born actress who worked in the United States. She is best known for her tragic roles in the plays of Eugene O'Neill and Shakespeare and in Robinson Jeffers's version of *Medea* (1947).

**Anderson, Elizabeth Garrett** (1836-1917), one of the first English women to become a doctor (1865). She helped establish the place of women in the profession and founded a women's hospital and a medical school for women.

**Anderson, John Bayard** (1922-    ), U.S. politician. He represented an Illinois district in the House of Representatives 1961-81, serving as chairman of the House Republican Conference 1969-79. Always a fiscal conservative, he gradually became a liberal on social and defense issues. After losing a bid for the Republican presidential nomination in 1980, he ran for president as an independent and polled about 7% of the popular vote.

**Anderson, Marian** (1902-93), U.S. contralto. Overcoming the handicaps of poverty and discrimination, she became an international singing star in the 1930s. In 1939, Anderson was refused permission to perform in the DAR Constitution Hall, in Washington, D.C. Through the sponsorship of Eleanor Roosevelt and Secretary of the Interior Harold Ickes, Anderson sang from the steps of the Lincoln Memorial to a massive crowd of people of all races. She was awarded the Springarn Medal by the National Association of Colored People for the highest achievement by a black American (1939). In 1955 she became the first African American to sing a leading role with, and be named a permanent member of, the Metropolitan Opera. She also served as alternate delegate to the UN in 1958, and won the UN peace prize in 1977.

**Anderson, Maxwell** (1888-1959), U.S. playwright. After early realistic plays, he concentrated on the revival of verse drama, achieving some success with such plays as *Elizabeth the Queen* (1930), *Winterset* (1935), *High Tor* (1936), and *The Bad Seed* (1954).

**Anderson, Sherwood** (1876-1941), U.S. writer whose novels and short stories deal largely with the rebellion of individuals against contemporary industrial society. He is best remembered for the novel *Winesburg, Ohio* (1919), which details the frustrations of small-town Midwestern life, and such story collections as *The Triumph of the Egg* (1921) and *Horses and Men* (1923). Other novels include *Poor White* (1920) and *Dark Laughter* (1925).

**Andes,** South America's largest mountain system, 4,500 mi (7,200 km) long and averaging 200-250 mi (320-400 km) wide, near the west coast and running almost the entire length of the continent. Aconcagua (22,835 ft/6,960 m) is the highest peak in the Western Hemisphere. The Andes rose largely in the Cenozoic era (the last 70 million years), and volcanic eruptions and earthquakes suggest the range is still rising. The South Andes divide Chile and Argentina. The Central Andes form 2 ranges flanking the high Bolivian plateau (the Altiplano), once home to the Incan civilization. The North Andes divide in Colombia and form four ranges ending in the Caribbean area. Many high Andean peaks are jagged and snowy, and glaciers fill some southern valleys. The region is an important source of copper, silver, and tin, and oil has been found in the north.

## Andorra

| | |
|---|---|
| Capital: | Andorra la Vella |
| Area: | 180 sq mi |
| | (465 sq km) |
| Population: | 65,000 |
| Language: | Catalan |
| Government: | Parliamentary co-principality |
| Independent: | 1278 |
| Head of gov.: | President of government |
| Per capita: | U.S. $9,000 |
| Mon. unit: | 1 Franc = 100 centimes |
| | 1 Peseta = 100 centimos |

**Andorra** (pop. 61,000), tiny European principality (180 sq mi/465 sq km) in the eastern Pyrenees along the border between France and Spain. The Andorrans speak Catalan, French, and Spanish. Andorra uses both the French franc and the Spanish peseta as currency. The country attained autonomous status under Charlemagne, and since 1278 has been a co-principality, under the joint sovereignty of the Bishop of Urgel in Spain and, in modern times, the French chief of state. Andorra's terrain is extremely mountainous, pocketed by gorges and a few fertile valleys; the average altitude of the whole country is above 6,000 ft (1,800 m). The Valira River, flowing into Spain, has a sizable hydroelectric potential, still little exploited. Tobacco is Andorra's main money crop; rye and barley, grapes, potatoes, and sheep and cattle are also important. Other assets include iron and lead deposits, quarries, trout and lake salmon, and extensive pine woods. In recent decades tourism has brought new commercial affluence. The capital is the township of Andorra la Vella (Andorra-la-Vieille).

**Andrada é Silva, José Bonifácio de** (1763-1838), Brazilian geologist and statesman, known as the father of Brazilian independence. He helped create an independent monarchy under Pedro I, whom he served as prime minister (1822-23) until exiled for his democratic views. He was later tutor to Pedro II.

**Andrea del Sarto** (1486-1531), leading 16th-century Florentine painter, influenced by Michelangelo and Albrecht Dürer and renowned for delicately colored church frescoes. He rivaled Raphael's classicism but foreshadowed Mannerism through his pupils Jacopo da Pontormo, Il Rosso, and Giorgio Vasari. Two of his well- known paintings are *Madonna of the Harpies* and *Holy Family*.

**Andrea Doria**, Italian luxury liner that sank on July 26, 1956, following an inexplicable collision with the *Stockholm*, a Swedish liner, about 45 mi (72 km) south of Nantucket Island; 51 people died. In 1981 a salvage operation run by Peter Gimbel and his wife, Elga Andersen, raised the ship's safe; further work was abandoned because of dangerous conditions.

**André, John** (1750-80), English army officer, hanged as a spy by the Americans during the Revolutionary War. He secretly met Benedict Arnold behind American lines to arrange Arnold's surrender of West Point but was caught in civilian clothes, with incriminating papers.
*See also:* Revolutionary War in America.

**Andretti, Mario** (1940-    ), Italian-born U.S. race car driver. His many achievements include winning the United States Auto Club national driving championship (1965, 1966, 1969) and the Grand Prix world driving championship (1978). Andretti also finished first in the Daytona 500 (1967) and Indianapolis 500 (1969).

**Andrew, John Albion** (1818-67), U.S. statesman and antislavery proponent. A Unitarian, he became a staunch but moderate abolitionist and was active in organizing both the Free-Soil Party (1848) and the Republican Party (1854). He helped form the first regiment of free blacks in the North (54th Massachusetts) and ensured that black troops received the same pay as white soldiers. During Reconstruction he favored leniency toward the defeated Confederacy and opposed giving former slaves immediate citizenship.

**Andrew, Saint** (1st century A D), one of Jesus's 12 Apostles, formerly a fisherman and disciple of John the Baptist. He reputedly preached in what is now Russia and was martyred in Patras, Greece, on an X-shaped ("St. Andrew's") cross. He is the patron saint of Russia and of Scotland.
*See also:* Apostles.

**Andrews, Charles McLean** (1863-1943), U.S. historian. He stressed Colonial America's dependence upon Britain in works like *The Colonial Period of American History* (1943-41), the first volume of which won a Pulitzer Prize.

**Andrews Air Force Base**, headquarters for Air Force Systems Command. Established in 1943, this command, located in Camp Springs, Maryland, houses passenger aircraft for use by the president and other officials. Aircraft, missiles, and weapons systems for the United States Air Force are bought by the command at this base.

**Andrews, Roy Chapman** (1884-1960), U.S. naturalist, explorer, and author. From 1906 he worked for the American Museum of Natural History (later becoming its director, 1935- 41) and made important expeditions to Alaska, the Far East, and Central Asia. In Mongolia he discovered the first known fossil dinosaur eggs.

**Andreyev, Leonid Nikolayevich** (1871-1919), Russian novelist, short-story writer, and playwright. His work, including *The Seven That Were Hanged* (1908), reflects a basic pessimism and preoccupation with death.
*See also:* Russian literature.

**Andric, Ivo** (1892-1975), Yugoslav novelist who won the Nobel Prize for literature in 1961, largely for the epic quality of The Bridge on the Drina. His themes are humanity's insecurity and isolation in the face of change and death.

**Androcles**, in Roman legend, slave who was thrown to the wild animals in the Roman arena but was spared by a lion from whose paw he had once extracted a thorn. Amazed at the lion's behavior, the Roman officials pardoned Androcles and presented him with the lion.

**Androgen** *See:* Hormone.

**Andromache**, in Greek mythology, wife of Hector, prince and hero of Troy. After the fall of Troy, Achilles' son Neoptolemus took her as a slave to Epirus and later married her. After he divorced her, she became the wife of Hector's brother Helenus. Her farewell to Hector and mourning of his death are among the most celebrated passages in Homer's *Iliad*. Euripides also based a tragedy on her story.

**Andromeda**, spiral galaxy visible in the Andromeda constellation. The most distant object visible to the naked eye in northern skies, it is the nearest galaxy external to our own, but larger (120,000 light-years in diameter), and about 2 million light-years from earth.
*See also:* Astronomy.

**Andromeda**, in Greek mythology, daughter of Cassiopeia and Cepheus, king of Ethiopia. Her mother boasted that she was more beautiful than the Nereids (sea nymphs). Out of revenge for this insult, Poseidon inundated the land and sent a sea monster to ravage the shore. Andromeda was rescued by Perseus, whom she then married.
*See also:* Mythology.

**Andropov, Yuri Vladimirovich** (1914-84), Soviet political leader, who became general secretary of the Communist party in 1982 after the death of Leonid Brezhnev and also, in 1983, chief of state. Earlier he had served as ambassador to Hungary (1954-57) and as head of the KGB, the Soviet security service (1967-82). In 1973 he became a full member of the Politburo, the governing body of the Communist party. As party leader, Andropov fought bureaucratic corruption, adopted a conciliatory attitude toward China, and tried to create a division between Western Europe and the United States on trade and military issues. After August 18, 1983, he was not seen in public.

**Andros, Sir Edmund** (1637-1714), British governor of New York (1674-81) and the Dominion of New England (1686-89). His attempt to curb the colonists' rights caused a rebellion. Imprisoned and sent to England for trial, he was acquitted and became governor of Virginia (1692-97).

**Anemia**, deficiency in the number of red blood cells or their hemoglobin content (the red substance that binds with oxygen), or both. Causes vary, but symptoms include pallor, fatigue, difficulty breathing, giddiness, heart palpitations, and loss of appetite.

**Anemometer**, instrument for measuring wind speed. The rotation type of mechanical anemometer estimates wind speed from the rotation of cups mounted on a vertical shaft. The sonic or acoustic anemometer depends on the velocity of sound in the wind. In laboratories, air flow is estimated from the change in resistance it causes by cooling an electrically heated wire.

**Anemone**, genus of wild or cultivated perennial herbs of the buttercup family (*Ranunculaceae*). Up to 3 ft (1 m) high, anemones have deeply cut, whorled leaves and white, pink, red, blue, or rarely, yellow flowers.

**Anesthesia**, loss of sensation, especially the sensation of pain. The loss of sensation following injury or disease is known as pathological anesthesia, but anesthesia, either general or local, can also be drug-induced. General anesthesia is a reversible state of unconsciousness accompanied by muscle relaxation and suppression of reflexes. It is indispensable for many surgical procedures. Injections of short-acting barbiturates such as sodium pentothal are frequently used to speed the onset of anesthesia; inhaled agents, including halothane, ether, nitrous oxide, trichlorethylene, and cyclopropane, are then used to induce and maintain general anesthesia. Local anesthesia is induced by the chemical action of cocaine derivatives like novocaine or lidocaine. Regional anesthesia may be induced by blocking one or more large nerves or spinal nerve roots, as in epidural anesthesia for childbirth.
*See also:* Anesthesiology.

**Anesthesiology**, branch of medicine that deals with the administration before and during childbirth or surgery of anesthetics, drugs that dull or block sensation or anxiety. Anesthesiologists (physicians who administer anesthetics) use various techniques to anesthetize all or part of the patient's body during surgery, while monitoring and maintaining important body functions; their work may also involve resuscitation and intensive respiratory care.
*See also:* Anesthesia.

**Aneurysm**, localized dilation of a blood vessel, usually an artery, due to local fault in the wall through defect, disease, or injury, producing a pulsating swelling over which a murmur may be heard. Generally the structural integrity of the arteries enables them to resist the destructive effects of the repetitive hydraulic stress of circulation. Sometimes, however, the wall of an artery gives way, and a segment of the artery expands to form a balloon-like dilation: an aneurysm. If left untreated, the aneurysm may burst, causing death or grave disability. Even an unruptured aneurysm can lead to damage by interrupting the flow of blood or by impinging on and in some cases eroding nearby blood vessels, organs, or bone. The incidence of aneurysm rises with age.
*See also:* DeBakey, Michael Ellis; Stroke.

**Angel**, supernatural messenger and servant of the deity. Angels figure in Christianity, Judaism, Islam, and Zoroastrianism. In Christianity angels traditionally serve and praise God, but guardian angels may protect the faithful against the evil of the devil (the fallen angel, Lucifer). The hierarchy of angels is said to have 9 orders: cherubim, seraphim, thrones, dominions, virtues, powers, principalities, archangels, and angels.

**Angel Falls**, world's highest known waterfall (3,212 ft/979 m), on the Churin River in southeastern Venezuela, discovered by U.S. aviator Jimmy Angel in 1935. Its longest unbroken drop is 2,648 ft (807 m).

**Angelfish**, any of a group of freshwater tropical fish, and of several fish found in warm seas (family Chaetodontidae). The colorful freshwater angelfish is native to the Amazon basin.

**Angell, Sir Norman** (1874-1967), English economist and internationalist, awarded the Nobel Peace Prize in 1933. A journalist most of his life, he argued in *The Great Illusion* (1910) that war was futile and best prevented by the mutual economic interest of nations.

**Angelou, Maya** (1928-    ), U.S. author best known for her autobiographical books *I Know Why the Caged Bird Sings* (1970) and *Gather Together in My Name* (1974), which recount her struggles for identity as an African American in a hostile world.

**Angevin**, name of 2 medieval royal dynasties originating in the Anjou region of western France. The first ruled in parts of France and in Jerusalem and England. Henry II, son of Geoffrey of Anjou, became England's first Angevin (or Plantagenet) ruler in 1154. His descendants held power in England until 1485. The second branch, which began in 1266 when Charles, brother of Louis IX of France, became king of Naples and Sicily, ruled in Italy, Hungary, and Poland until the end of the 15th century.

**Angina pectoris**, severe but temporary attack of heart pain that occurs when the demand for oxygen by the heart muscle exceeds the ability of the coronary vessels to supply oxygen, due to narrowing or blockage of the vessels. The discomfort of angina pectoris, although highly variable, is most commonly felt beneath the sternum (breastbone). Pain may radiate to the left shoulder and down the inside of the left arm, straight through to the back, into the throat, the jaws, and the teeth. Anginal discomfort may be felt in the upper and lower abdomen, and occasionally in the right arm. Angina pectoris is characteristically triggered by physical activity and usually persists for no more than a few minutes, subsiding with rest.
*See also:* Heart.

**Angiography**, technique allowing visualization of blood vessels on X rays after injection of a radiopaque substance (one that shows up on X ray). It is usually performed on arteries or veins connected with organs such as the brain, heart, or kidneys, when a narrowing or blockage is suspected. Angiography is used to determine if deposits of substances such as cholesterol or calcium, known as plaque, are causing vessel narrowing, and has developed into a relatively safe and useful diagnostic technique. A typical angiographic procedure involves the passing of a catheter through the skin and into a vein or artery, where it is advanced to the structure being evaluated. Contrast material is injected into the area, making the section visible on X ray.

**Angioplasty**, set of techniques used in reconstructing damaged blood vessels, which may involve surgery, lasers, or tiny inflatable balloons. Usually, arteries that have become blocked by deposits of such substances as cholesterol or calcium—substances known as plaque—are reopened by inserting a catheter with an attached balloon into the diseased vessel where inflation of the balloon compresses or splits the deposits that clog the artery. Angioplasty is an important alternative to surgery for patients whose clogged coronary arteries predispose them to risk of a heart attack.

**Angiosperm**, member of a large class of seed-bearing plants (the flowering plants), its seeds developing completely enclosed in the tissue of the parent plant (rather than unprotected, as in the only other seed-bearing group, the gymnosperms). Containing about 250,000 species distributed throughout the world, from tiny herbs to huge trees, angiosperms are the dominant land flora. There are 2 subclasses: monocotyledons (with 1 leaf) and dicotyledons (with 2).

**Angkor**, extensive ruins from the ancient Khmer Empire in northwestern Cambodia, covering 40 sq mi (100 sq km). Dating from the 9th to the 13th century, the remains were found by the French in 1861. The city of Angkor Thom, with its temples and palace, is intersected by a canal system and lies within a perimeter wall. Angkor Wat, a massive complex of carved Hindu temples, is the foremost example of Khmer art and architecture.

**Angle**, in plane geometry, the figure formed by the intersection of two straight lines. The point of intersection is known as the vertex. If the two lines are viewed as radii of a circle of unit radius, the magnitude of an angle can be defined in terms of the proportion of the circle's circumference cut off by the two lines. Angles are measured in radians or degrees. One radian is the magnitude of an angle whose two sides cut off an arc of circumference equal in length to the radius. A degree is the magnitude of an angle whose two sides cut off 1/360 of the circumference. An angle of $\pi/2$ rad (90°), whose sides cut off one-quarter of the circumference, is a right angle, the two lines being said to be perpendicular. An angle of $\pi$ rad, or 180°, whose sides cut off one-half of the circumference, is a straight angle or straight line. Angles less than 90° are termed acute; those greater than 90° but less than 180°, obtuse; greater than 180°, reflex. Pairs of angles that add up to 90° are complementary; those that add up to 180°, supplementary. In solid geometry, angles have definitions that are specific to the solids.
*See also:* Geometry; Trigonometry.

**Angles**, Germanic tribe from which England derives its name. Coming from the Schleswig-Holstein area of northern Germany, the Angles, with the Saxons and Jutes, invaded England in the 5th century and founded kingdoms including East Anglia, Mercia, and Northumbria.
*See also:* Anglo-Saxons.

**Anglicans**, community of churches developed from the Church of England. The Church of England split from the Roman Catholic Church in the 1500s, during the Reformation. It was formed by King Henry VIII, who broke with the Roman Catholic Church because he was denied permission to divorce his second wife, Anne Boleyn. The Anglican Communion is made up of the Church of England, the Anglican Church of Canada, and the Episcopal Church in the United States.

**Anglo-Saxons**, collective name for the Germanic peoples who dominated England from the 5th to the 11th centuries. They originated as tribes of Angles, Saxons, and Jutes who invaded England after Roman rule collapsed, creating kingdoms that eventually united to form the English nation. In modern usage, Anglo-Saxons are the English or their emigrant descendants in other parts of the world.

**Angola** (Republic of), independent state in southwest Africa; bordered by the Atlantic Ocean in the west, Zaire in the north, Zambia in the east, and Namibia in the south.

*Land and climate.* Angola is dominated by the Bié Plateau, some 4,000 ft (1,219 m) above sea level, which occasionally rises to altitudes of 8,000 ft (2,438 m) or more. To the north are tropical rain forests; to the south, semiarid or desert regions. In the east, the plateau drops off to the basins of the Zambezi and Congo rivers. The narrow coastal plain to the west, though humid, receives little rainfall. Savanna wildlife is abundant.

*People.* The overwhelming majority of Angolans are Africans belonging to several Bantu tribes. More than half of the population are Christians (chiefly Roman Catholic) and a significant minority follows traditional religions.

*Economy.* Crude oil is Angola's principal export, followed by coffee, diamonds, and iron ore. There is also some light industry, including food processing and production of cotton, textiles, and paper.

*History.* Angola was a Portuguese colony from 1576 onward, and the export of slaves to Brazil caused severe depopulation. Portuguese colonization and economic development grew in the early 20th century, coupled with repression of the native peoples. Nationalists began the fight for independence in 1961, and by the 1970s some 50,000 Portuguese troops were engaged in fighting nationalist guerrillas. Angola became independent on November 5, 1975, and conflict erupted among three rival groups for control of the government. The Popular Liberation Movement (MPLA), backed by Soviet and Cuban troops, prevailed. Angola has been sympathetic to liberation groups from neighboring countries and, since 1979, has been the focus of attacks by South African troops stationed in Namibia. A 1988 accord was reached by which Cuban troops withdrew from Angola and South African troops from Namibia. However the political situation remained unstable. Towards the end of

**Angola**

| | |
|---|---|
| Capital: | Luanda |
| Area: | 481,354 sq mi |
| | (1,246,700 sq km) |
| Population: | 10,865,000 |
| Language: | Portuguese |
| Government: | Republic |
| Independent: | 1975 |
| Head of gov.: | Prime minister |
| Per capita: | U.S. $410 |
| Mon. unit: | 1 Kwanza (Kz) = |
| | 100 lwei |

the 1990s, Angola became closely involved in the power struggle in Congo (the former Zaire).

**Angora** *See:* Ankara.

**Angora**, term used for the long-haired varieties of goats, cats, and rabbits. Originally it referred to goats bred in the Angora (now Ankara) region of Turkey. The silky white hair of Angora goats has long been used for fine yarns and fabrics, especially for making mohair cloth.
*See also:* Ankara.

**Ångström, Anders Jonas** (1814-74), Swedish physicist, one of the founders of spectroscopy (spectrum analysis) and the first to identify hydrogen in the solar spectrum (1862). The Ångstrom unit is named in his honor.
*See also:* Ångstrom (Å).

**Ångström (Å)**, unit used to measure the length of light waves and other extremely small dimensions, named for Swedish physicist Anders Jonas Ångstrom. It is equivalent to one ten-millionth of a millimeter (1 x 10-10m).
*See also:* Ångström, Anders Jonas.

**Anguilla** (pop. 9,000), island in the West Indies, 35 sq mi (90 sq km), lying 150 mi (240 km) east of Puerto Rico. Local industries include boat building, fishing, and salt. Discovered by Columbus, it became a British colony in 1650. Anguilla was part of the West Indian Associated States of St. Kitts, Nevis, and Anguilla, but it seceded in 1967 and is again under British rule.

**Anhinga**, also called darter, snakebird, or water turkey, large bird of the anhinga family that feeds in waters from southeast and southcentral United States to Argentina. Measuring about 3 ft (91 cm) long, it is glossy black, with silver and brown markings. The anhinga is a strong swimmer and flier. It has webbed feet and swims mostly submerged, with its snakelike neck visible, spearing fish with its long, sharp beak. It perches in an upright position, often with wings and long fan-shaped tail spread. Similar species are the cormorant and the darters of the Eastern Hemisphere.

**Anhydride**, oxide that forms an acid or base when it reacts with water. Metal oxides such as calcium oxide produce hydroxides (bases) and are termed basic anhydrides. Oxides of nonmetals such as phosphorus, carbon, and sulfur produce acids on being dissolved in water and are acid anhydrides. Organic anhydrides are used in the manufacture of solvents, paints, and dyes. Acetic anhydride is used in large quantities during the production of acetic acid and various plastics.

**Anhydrous ammonia**, dry or liquid form of ammonia, made by compressing pure ammonia gas ($NH_3$) and used as nitrogen fertilizer and as a refrigerant.
*See also:* Ammonia.

**Ani**, or tickbird, any of a genus (*Crotophaga*) of long-tailed black cuckoos native to the warm regions of the Americas. About 12 in (30 cm) in length and having flattened, blade-like beaks, anis live in flocks and build a single communal nest.

**Aniakchack**, volcano on the Alaska Peninsula, in the Aleutian mountain range. It is one of the largest craters in the world, with a diameter of about 6.5 mi (10.5 km). Thought to be extinct when discovered in 1922, it erupted in 1931 and is now classified as dormant.

**Aniline**, chemical compound ($C_6H_5NH_2$) obtained from indigo or other organic substances, or from benzol, and used in the production of dyes. *See also:* Dye.

**Animal**, living organism distinguished from plants by locomotion, environmental reactivity, nutrient absorption, and cell structure. Animals move freely using a wide variety of mechanisms to do so, whereas plants are rooted to one place. Animals sense their environments and react to them. In the case of multicellular animals, they react by means of the nervous system; in more highly developed animals reactions to the environment are mediated by the nervous system combined with sense organs of touch, smell, taste, hearing, and sight. Plants may react to light, chemicals, and other stimuli, but such reactions are automatic and not nervous. Plants usually contain chlorophyll, which helps them build, from inorganic material, the organic substances of which they consist. Animals must consume organic food. And while both plants and animals are made up of cells, plants have a cell wall strengthened with cellulose (a woodlike substance), but animals contain no cellulose. Other minor distinctions include the ability of plants, lacking in animals, to periodically form new organs from undifferentiated cells.

**Animation**, cinematographic technique creating the illusion of movement by projection of a series of drawings or photographs showing successive views of an action. The first animated cartoons were made by Emile Cohl in France in 1907. Walt Disney pioneered in the use of sound and color and in producing cartoons that aimed at suspense and drama as well as broad humor. In classic animation, drawings on transparent celluloid (cels) are superimposed to form each picture; only cels showing motion are changed from frame to frame. *See also:* Disney, Walt; Schulz, Charles Monroe.

**Animism**, term first used by anthropologist E.B. Tylor in 1871 to designate a general belief in spiritual beings, which belief he held to be the origin of all religions. A common corruption of Tylor's sense interprets animism as the belief that all natural objects possess spirits. The psychologist Jean Piaget proposed that a growing child passes through an animistic phase. *See also:* Piaget, Jean; Tylor, Sir Edward Burnett.

**Anise**, herb of the carrot family that yields seeds with a spicy, licorice flavor. The seeds, and the oil produced from them, are used to flavor foods, candy, and liquors like ouzo and Pernod. Anise is native to the eastern Mediterranean.

**Ankara** (pop. 2,559,500), capital of Turkey and of Ankara province in Asia Minor. It produces textiles, cement, flour, and beer, and trades in local

Angora wool and grain. Ankara (formerly Ancyra or Angora), once a Hittite trade center, later became capital of a Roman province in 25 B C. It replaced Istanbul as Turkey's capital in 1923.

**Ankle**, joint connecting the foot and the leg. Sprained ankle is a common acute injury, causing considerable discomfort and disability. The ankle joint may also be affected in rheumatoid arthritis. Pain is often due to inflammation of the sheaths of the peroneal tendon and of the bursa.
*See also:* Anatomy.

**Anna**, in the New Testament (Luke 2), Jewish prophetess, daughter of Phanuel of the tribe of Asher. Widowed at an early age, she served God in the temple by continual prayer and fasting. At the age of 84 she witnessed the presentation of Jesus in the temple.

**Anna Ivanovna** (1693-1740), empress of Russia from 1730. Elected puppet empress by the nobles' supreme privy council, she overthrew the council and, with German advisers, waged costly wars against the Poles and Turks and opened Russia's way to Central Asia.

**Annapolis** (pop. 31,700), capital of Maryland, seat of Anne Arundel County on the Severn River near Chesapeake Bay. It was settled in 1649 by Puritans from Virginia and given its present name in 1694. It is the site of St. John's College (founded 1696) and the U.S. Naval Academy (established 1845). Local industries include seafood processing and boat building.
*See also:* Maryland.

**Annapolis**,
*See also:* United States Naval Academy.

**Annapolis Convention** (1786), meeting in Annapolis, Md., to discuss interstate commerce. Alexander Hamilton and James Madison wanted its scope broadened to discuss revision of the Articles of Confederation. But only 5 of the 13 states were represented, and thus a full-scale meeting was called for, leading to the Constitutional Convention at Philadelphia.
*See also:* Articles of Confederation; Constitution of the United States.

**Annapolis Royal** (pop. 630), town on the Annapolis River, west coast of Nova Scotia, near the site of the earliest permanent French settlement in Canada. The original town of Port Royal grew up around a French fort built in 1605. After nearly a century of fighting, the British finally captured Port Royal in 1710 and changed its name to Annapolis Royal in honor of Queen Anne. Until Halifax was founded in 1749, it was the capital of Nova Scotia. Today it is the center of a prosperous farming area and a summer resort.

**Annapurna**, Himalayan mountain in Nepal with the world's 11th-highest peak (26,391 ft/8,044 m). Its conquest in 1950 by Maurice Herzog's team was the first such success involving any great Himalayan peak.

**Ann Arbor** (pop. 282,937), city in southeastern Michigan, seat of Washtenaw County, and home of the University of Michigan since 1841. It is situated on the Huron River about 40 mi (65 km) west of Detroit. Once mainly a farming and fruit-growing center, Ann Arbor has also become a center of light industry since World War II. The city was settled in 1824, incorporated as a village in 1833, and given its city charter in 1851.

**Anne** (1665-1714), queen of Great Britain and Ireland (1702-14), last of the Stuart monarchs. Her reign was dominated by the War of the Spanish Succession, also known as Queen Anne's War in the colonies (1702-13). It also saw the Act of Union (1707), uniting England and Scotland to form the kingdom of Great Britain, and the growth of the parliamentary system.

**Anne, Saint**, mother of the Virgin Mary and wife of St. Joachim. Though not mentioned in Scripture, she was venerated in Early Christian times. According to an apocryphal writing of St. James, long after St. Anne had despaired of bearing a child, an angel appeared to her and foretold the birth of Mary. Often represented in art in such scenes as the Birth of the Virgin, St. Anne is the patron saint of women in labor. Her feast day is July 26. *See also:* Sainte-Anne-de-Beaupré.

**Annenberg, Walter** (1908-), U.S. publisher. He inherited a Philadelphia-based publishing empire that included the *Philadelphia Inquirer*, founded *Seventeen* magazine and *TV Guide*, and bought the *Philadelphia Daily News*. He was appointed ambassador to Great Britain by President Richard Nixon (1969).

**Anne of Austria** (1601-66), queen consort and regent of France. The daughter of King Philip III of Spain, Anne married King Louis XIII of France in 1615. Her position at court was precarious because of France's involvement in the Thirty Years' War against Spain and Austria. After her husband's death in 1643, Anne served as regent for her young son, King Louis XIV, relying on Cardinal Mazarin, the successor of Cardinal Richelieu, for guidance. In 1651 she had her 13-year-old son proclaimed of age, but she remained powerful until the death of Mazarin in 1661, when Louis personally took control of the state. *See also:* Mazarin, Jules Cardinal.

**Anne of Brittany** (1477-1514), duchess of Brittany and queen of France. Anne was married to King Charles VIII of France in 1491 and after his death became the wife of his successor, King Louis XII. Through the marriage of her daughter to the future King Francis I of France, the duchy of Brittany, the last of the great feudally held territories of France, was permanently united to the crown of France.

**Anne of Cleves** (1515-57), queen consort and fourth wife of England's Henry VIII. She was the daughter of a powerful German noble, and Henry married her (1540) on Thomas Cromwell's advice to forge international bonds, but 6 months later he had Parliament annul the marriage. *See also:* Henry (England).

**Annexation**, acquisition by a country of a territory previously outside its jurisdiction. The term is generally used to refer to the extension of a country's sovereignty by conquest or threat of force, rather than by treaty.

**Anno Domini** *See:* A.D.

**Annual,** plant that completes its life cycle in one growing season, as contrasted with biennials (two seasons) and perennials (more than two). Annuals include garden flowers and food plants such as cornflowers and tomatoes. Preventing seeding may convert an annual to a biennial or a perennial.

**Annual rings,** rings of dark and light wood seen across the trunk of a tree that has been cut down. The lighter rings are formed during the spring and are made up of cells with large cavities. The darker rings are formed during the summer, when less new wood is laid down and the cells have smaller cavities. In hot countries the rings represent dry and wet seasons. The size of the rings tells a great deal about the conditions under which the tree was growing, and the number of rings can be used to measure the age of the tree. The science of dating things by counting annual rings is dendrochronology.

**Annuity,** yearly payment a person receives for life or for a term of years, the person usually being entitled to such payment in consideration of money advanced to those who pay.

**Annulment,** decree to the effect that a marriage was invalid when contracted. Grounds for annulment include fraud, force, and close blood links between the parties. The Roman Catholic Church recognizes annulment but not divorce.

**Annunciation,** in Christian belief, the archangel Gabriel's announcement to the Virgin Mary that she would give birth to the Messiah. The Roman Catholic Church celebrates the Annunciation on March 25. The Annunciation is the theme of many Christian paintings.

**Annunzio, Gabriele d'** *See:* D'Annunzio, Gabriele.

**Anodizing,** electrolytic method of producing a corrosion-resistant or decorative layer of oxide on a metal, usually aluminum. The metal to be coated is used as an anode (positive pole), suspended in an electrolyte (usually an aqueous solution of sulfuric, chromic, or oxalic acid). When an electric current is passed through this solution, a coating of oxide builds up on the anode.
*See also:* Electrolysis.

**Anorexia nervosa,** psychological disorder characterized by a disturbed sense of body image and exaggerated anxiety about weight gain, manifested by abnormal refusal to eat, leading to severe weight loss, and, in women, amenorrhea (loss of period). The onset is usually in adolescence, and the disorder affects females predominantly; only about 5% of the cases occur in males.

**Anouilh, Jean** (1910-87), French playwright, whose highly theatrical dramas emphasize the dilemma of modern times, in which individuals are forced to compromise their dreams. His works include *Antigone* (1944), *The Lark* (1953), and *Beckett* (1959).

**Anoxia,** severe hypoxia (lowered oxygen levels in body tissues), whether due to lack of oxygen in air inhaled or lack of oxygen available in the blood or tissues. Anoxia can be of such severity as to cause permanent damage. Anemic anoxia, resulting from deficient amounts of hemoglobin in the blood, may be caused by hemorrhage or anemia or by poisoning with carbon monoxide, nitrites, or chlorates. Anoxic anoxia occurs when blood flowing through the lungs does not pick up enough oxygen, possibly caused by high altitudes or foreign gases or by abnormalities in pulmonary tissues. Stagnant anoxia, in which slow blood circulation results in loss of oxygen before the blood reaches tissues, is often associated with congestive cardiac failure or postoperative shock.

**Anselm, Saint** (1033?-1109), archbishop of Canterbury (from 1093), a founder of Scholasticism. He endured repeated exile for challenging the right of English kings to influence church affairs. Anselm saw reason as the servant of faith and was the author of an ontological "proof" of God's existence: the human idea of a perfect being itself implies the existence of such a being. Saint Anselm's Day is celebrated on April 21.

**Ansermet, Ernest** (1883-1969), Swiss orchestral conductor who directed many premieres of Stravinsky ballets. He founded the Orchestre de la Suisse Romande in 1918, conducting it until his death.

**Ansky, Shloime** (Solomon Samuel Rapoport; 1863-1920), Russian Yiddish author and playwright, best known for *The Dybbuk* (1916), a tragedy of demonic possession. He was active in Russian Jewish socialism, but left Russia after the Revolution and died in Poland.

**Anson, Adrian Constantine** (1851-1922), U.S. baseball player, also known as "Cap" or "Pop." In 1939 he was elected to baseball's Hall of Fame as "the greatest hitter and greatest National League player-manager of the 19th century."

**Ant,** insect of order Hymenoptera (which also includes bees and wasps), family Formicidae, living in communities consisting of males, females, and infertile worker females. An ant colony may contain thousands and even millions of ants organized into a highly socialized community. The queen ant's function is to produce eggs. The female worker ant (there are no male worker ants) is responsible for food, protection, and building the nest. The male's singular function is to mate and die quickly. Ants are found in all parts of the planet but prefer warmer climates. An ant is usually under 1 inch (2.5 cm) in height and black, brown, or red in color. It usually lives in tunnels beneath the earth or mounds of its own making. The two antennae on the head provide the ability to hear, smell, touch, and taste, although other areas of the body can taste and touch. The ant has no ears. It has acquired a reputation for remarkable strength because it can lift 50 times its own weight. The ant produces a humming or buzzing sound capable of detection by the human ear.

**Antananarivo,** or Tananarive (pop. 803,400), capital and largest city of Madagascar. Located near the center of the island of Madagascar on a mountain ridge and linked to other areas by railroad, it is a manufacturing and communications center. The University of Madagascar and the 200-year-old palace of the Merina rulers are located in the city.

**Antarctic** *See:* Antarctica.

**Antarctica,** fifth largest continent, almost 6,000,000 sq mi (17,400,000 sq km). Antarctica is almost entirely covered by an ice cap up to 14,000 ft (4,267 m) thick except where the ice is pierced by mountain peaks.

The Vinson Massif is Antarctica's highest mountain (16,900 ft /5,150 m). The continent is circular, indented by the arc-shaped Weddell Sea (south of the Atlantic Ocean) and the rectangular Ross Sea (south of New Zealand). Pack ice virtually surrounds the rest of the continent. The western half of Antarctica, including the Antarctic Peninsula, is structurally related to the Andes; the eastern half geologically resembles Australia and South Africa. Antarctica is almost entirely within the Antarctic Circle (66°30' S) and the climate is intensely cold, with winter temperatures as low as −80° F (−62° C), and winds up to 100 mph (161 kmph).

Capt. James Cook was the first to attempt a scientific exploration of the region (1773). The mainland was probably first sighted in 1820 by the American sea captain, Nathaniel Palmer. The Englishman James Weddell led an expedition to the area in 1823 and another Englishman, James Clark Ross, discovered the sea later named for him. The Norwegian Roald Amundsen was the first to reach the South Pole on Dec. 4, 1911 and Admiral Richard Evelyn Byrd became the first to fly over the pole on Nov. 29, 1929. Since the International Geophysical Year (1957-58), international cooperation in Antarctica has increased. On Dec. 1, 1959, 12 nations signed the 30-year Antarctic Treaty reserving the area south of 60° S for peaceful scientific investigation. In 1985, 32 nations agreed to limit access of humans to Antarctica to specific research sites. Antarctica is home to over 25 scientific installations, three of which are from the United States. During the 1980s scientists began to detect a deterioration in the ozone level above Antarctica which created great environmental concern for the region and the planet. The ozone layer protects the planet from destructive sun rays. Because of this new awareness and increasing accessibility to the region, tourism to Antarctica is rising.

**Antarctic Circle,** imaginary boundary, 66°30' S lat., marking the northernmost latitude of the Antarctic region at which the sun remains above the horizon at least one day a year, the December solstice, and the southernmost latitude at which the sun is visible at the June solstice. Most of the continent of Antarctica lies within the circle.

**Antarctic Ocean,** ocean surrounding the Antarctic continent, also called the Southern Ocean; sometimes not considered to be a separate ocean but rather a part of the Atlantic, Indian, and Pacific oceans. Its width varies from 700 mi (1,100 km) at the tip of South America to 2,400 mi (3,860 km) off the tip of Africa. Pack ice and icebergs drift in the ocean's 29°F (−2°C) waters.

**Antares,** one of the brightest stars in the southern sky, in the constellation Scorpio. It is over 400 light years from earth. It is a visual binary, or double, star; the main star is a red (thus, cool) giant, 480 times the size of the sun; its

companion star is blue (hot) and too small to be visible without a powerful telescope.
*See also:* Astronomy.

**Anteater,** any of 3 genera of Central and South American mammals, family Myrmecophagidae, order Edentata, including the giant anteater and the tamandua. They have long snouts, tubular, toothless mouths, and long, sticky tongues with which they catch their food, chiefly termites.
*See also:* Aardvark.

**Antelope,** swift-moving hollow-horned ruminant of the family Bovidae, order Artiodactyla. Common features include a hairy muzzle, narrow cheek teeth, and permanent, backward-pointing horns. Distribution is throughout Africa and Asia. Antelopes range in size from the royal antelope, probably the smallest hoofed mammal, standing about 10 in (25 cm) high at the shoulders, to the giant eland, which may be as tall as 6 ft (1.8 m).

**Antenna,** or aerial, component in an electrical circuit that radiates or receives radio waves. A transmitting antenna is a combination of conductors that converts AC electrical energy into electromagnetic radiation. The simple dipole consists of 2 straight conductors energized at the small gap which separates them. It can be made directional by adding electrically isolated director and reflector conductors in front and behind. Other configurations include the folded dipole, the highly directional loop antenna, and the dish type used for microwave links. A receiving antenna can consist merely of a short dielectric rod or a length of wire for low-frequency signals. For VHF and microwave signals, complex antenna configurations similar to those used for transmission must be used.

**Antennae,** paired sensory appendage on the head of most insects, crustaceans, and other arthropods. Nerves on the antennae are sensitive to vibrations, heat, water vapor, or chemicals. Hairs on the antennae of male mosquitoes pick up female sounds as far as one-quarter mi (0.4 km) away, while June bugs have pits in their antennae that help them smell. Most insects have 1 pair of antennae; crustaceans, such as lobsters and crabs, have 2 pairs.

**Antheil, George** (1900-59), U.S. composer. He studied under Ernest Bloch and brought popular motifs into serious music in works such as *Jazz Symphonietta* (1926) and the opera *Transatlantic* (1928-29). In later work he was more traditional, and after World War II he developed a neoclassical style influenced by Igor Stravinsky.

**Anthemius of Tralles** (d. c.534), Byzantine architect, mathematician, and physicist. With Isidorus of Miletus, he designed the Hagia Sophia in Constantinople at the order of the Byzantine emperor Justinian. It is likely that he also designed the Church of Saints Sergius and Bacchus in the same city.

**Anthony, Susan Brownell** (1820-1906), major U.S. leader and organizer of the fight for women's rights. A schoolteacher who backed the temperance and abolitionist movements, she later worked with Elizabeth Cady Stanton for women's suffrage and other political and economic rights. She cofounded the National Woman Suffrage Association (1868) and served as president of the National American Woman Suffrage Association (1892-1900). She also helped to write the first 3 volumes of *The History of Woman Suffrage*. In 1979, Anthony became the first woman to have her image on a coin of general circulation in the United States. The Susan B. Anthony dollar became an immediate collectible. *See also:* Women's movements.

**Anthony of Padua, Saint** (1195-1231), Franciscan friar, theologian, and preacher. He was born near Lisbon but taught and preached in France and Italy. Patron saint of the poor, his feast day is June 13.

**Anthony of Thebes, Saint** (c.250-350), Egyptian hermit, considered the founder of Christian monasticism. He founded a desert community of ascetics near Fayum, then lived alone in a mountain cave near the Red Sea and died aged over 100. He supported St. Athanasius in the Arian controversy. His feast day is Jan. 17.

**Anthrax**, infectious disease affecting livestock and, more rarely, humans, causing skin pustules and lung damage. Anthrax spores, which can survive for years, may be picked up from infected animals or bone meal. It was the first disease shown (by Robert Koch in 1876) to be caused by bacteria. A vaccine effective on sheep and cattle was developed by Louis Pasteur. Anthrax is now rare in developed countries.
*See also:* Pasteur, Louis.

**Anthropoid** *See:* Primate.

**Anthropology**, study of the origins, evolution, and development of human beings and their various cultures and societies. Physical anthropology is concerned with human beings as physical organisms, the place of Homo sapiens in the framework of evolution, and the classification of early humans based upon the study of fossil remains. Cultural anthropology examines the specific knowledge, values, and behaviors that are characteristic of members of a particular society, emphasizing the uniqueness of cultures while attempting to compare them. Cultural anthropology shares with social anthropology an emphasis upon understanding behaviors within a particular context and rejects any attempt to classify or explain particular behaviors in the abstract. Social anthropology studies the structures of a society through the detailed and direct examination of patterns of relations among its classes, generations, and religious and political institutions. One of the major contributions of social anthropology has been to discredit the idea that preliterate societies are lacking in complexity or that the peoples in them lack the same intellectual abilities as peoples in industrialized societies.

**Antiaircraft defense**, method of protection from attack by enemy aircraft or missiles, involving early detection and interference and destruction. Radar is an early detector but can be foiled if the enemy confuses the radar by dropping metal strips called chaff. Interference with incoming missiles is accomplished with chaff, decoys, and electronic jamming devices. Radar is also used in coordination with guns or missiles on ships or on the ground to destroy the attackers. Some antiaircraft missiles use homing devices attracted to heat from enemy planes, guiding the missiles to the target.
*See also:* Radar.

**Antibiotic,** any of the substances, usually produced by microorganisms, that kill or prevent the growth of other microorganisms, especially bacteria and fungi. Louis Pasteur noted the effect in the 19th century, and in 1928 Alexander Fleming showed that the mold *Penicillium notatum* produced penicillin, a substance able to destroy certain bacteria. Other early discoveries of antibiotics include the isolation of streptomycin (by Selman Waksman), gramicidin (by René Dubos), and the cephalosporins. Semisynthetic antibiotics, in which the basic molecule is chemically modified, have increased the range of naturally occurring substances.
*See also:* Penicillin; Bacteria.

**Antibody** *See:* Immunity.

**Antichrist,** in Christian belief, the human antagonist of Christ. The term appears in the Epistles of St. John. While the concept is sometimes interpreted as a lawless but impersonal power, others consider the Antichrist a personal incarnation of evil. Roman Catholic writers commonly interpret the term to mean any adversary of Christ and of the Church's authority, specifically the last and greatest antagonist of the Christian Church, whose coming will precede the end of the world.

**Anticoagulant,** substance that interferes with blood clotting, used to treat or prevent strokes and embolism. The 2 main types are heparin, which is injected and has an immediate but short-lived effect, and the coumarins, which are taken orally and are longer lasting.
*See also:* Coagulant.

**Anti-Defamation League** *See:* B'nai B'rith.

**Antidote,** remedy that neutralizes a poison or counteracts its effects. A chemical antidote unites with a poison to produce a harmless chemical, a mechanical antidote prevents the absorption of a poison, and a physiologic antidote produces effects contrary to those of the given poison. Most antidotes are effective against only one kind of poison, although specific antidotes are available in less than 2% of poisonings.
*See also:* Antitoxin; Poison.

**Antietam, Battle of** *See:* Civil War, U.S.

**Anti-Federalists,** opponents of the ratification of the Federal Constitution of 1787. The Anti-Federalists argued that centralized power would become despotic. After Washington's inauguration, the Anti-Federalist group helped to form the Democratic-Republican Party under Jefferson.
*See also:* Federalist Party.

**Antifreeze,** substance added to a solvent to prevent it from freezing in cold weather. Antifreeze used in the cooling system of automobiles is generally made of water mixed with ethylene glycol, methanol, ethanol, or other substances that lower the freezing point.
*See also:* Glycol.

**Antigen**, foreign substance introduced into an organism, stimulating the production of antibodies that combat the intruder. Antigens may be viruses, bacteria, or the non-living toxins they produce.

**Antigone**, in Greek mythology, daughter of Oedipus and Jocasta. When her brothers Eteocles and Polynices killed each other in combat, Creon, king of Thebes and Jocasta's brother, refused to allow the burial of Polynices, whom he regarded as a traitor. When Antigone defied him, Creon sentenced her to death. She is the subject of tragedies by the ancient Greek playwright Sophocles and the modern French playwright Jean Anouilh.
*See also:* Mythology.

**Antigonid dynasty**, line of kings that ruled Macedonia (northern Greece) 294 B C.-168 B C. **Antigonus I**, a general under Alexander the Great, was the first of the dynasty to rule Macedonia (294-283 B.C.). He was succeeded by **Antigonus II** (r. 283-239) and grandson **Demetrius II** (r. 239-229). **Phillip V**, son of Demetrius II, challenged Rome but was defeated in 197 B.C Antigonid rule ended 168 B.C. with the defeat and capture of Philip's successor, **Perseus**.

**Antigravity**, hypothetical force of repulsion described in science fiction but never scientifically observed. The opposite of gravity, antigravity would cause objects to repel one another rather than to be attracted to one another. Earth's gravity pulls objects toward the planet's center, antigravity would push objects away from earth's center.

**Antigua**, also called Antigua Guatemala (pop. 15,800), city in south central Guatemala, once the capital. After an earthquake and flood leveled an earlier capital, Antigua was founded in 1542, quickly becoming one of the richest cities in the New World, only to be destroyed itself by an earthquake in 1773. Today Antigua is a trading and tourist center in a coffee-growing area.

**Antigua and Barbuda**, island nation in the West Indies, largest and most developed of the Leeward Islands.

### Antigua and Barbuda

| | |
|---|---|
| Capital: | Saint John's |
| Area: | 170.5 sq mi |
| | (441.6 sq km) |
| Population: | 64,000 |
| Language: | English |
| Government: | Parliamentary monar- |
| | chy in the British |
| | Commonwealth |
| Independent: | 1981 |
| Head of gov.: | Prime minister |
| Per capita: | U.S. $9385 |

*Land and climate*. The islands of Antigua, Barbuda, and Redonda (uninhabited), are of volcanic origin. White sandy beaches fringe the coasts; few places rise to more than 1,000 ft (2,048 m) above sea level. The climate is tropical with a dry season July-Dec.

*People and economy*. The population is predominantly of African and British origins. St. John's is the largest town and chief port, and tourism is the principal economic activity. In the 19th century, cotton replaced sugarcane as the main crop, and some tropical fruits are also grown. The United States maintains large naval and army bases near Parham.

*History*. Antigua was named by Christopher Columbus in 1493. The island passed from Spanish to French control in the 17th century and was taken over by the British in 1632. With Barbuda and Redonda as dependencies it became a self-governing West Indies Associated State in 1967 and independent in 1981.

**Antihistamine,** drug used to neutralize the effects of histamine (an organic compound released by certain cells that causes tissue swelling, hives, and severe itching). It is used to relieve the symptoms of allergies.

**Antilles, The,** islands of the West Indies, with the exception of the Bahamas. Shaped like an arc that stretches from Cuba to the coast of South America, the Antilles separate the Caribbean Sea from the Atlantic Ocean.

The Greater Antilles include the large islands of Cuba, Jamaica, Hispaniola, and Puerto Rico. The Lesser Antilles include the Virgin Islands, the Leeward and Windward Islands, Trinidad and Tobago, Barbados, the Netherlands Antilles, and the Margarita Islands of Venezuela. Cuba, Haiti, and the Dominican Republic have long been independent nations. Three of the large islands formerly held by the British—Barbados, Jamaica, and Trinidad—gained their independence in the 1970s. All other islands of the Antilles are colonies, self-governing affiliates, or integral parts of other nations.

**Anti-Masonic Party,** U.S. political party (1827-36), formed to oppose Freemasons in politics. The Masons were accused, without proof, of murdering the author of a book claiming to reveal the secrets of Masonry.

The Anti-Masons held the first national nominating convention (1831) and were the first to issue a written party platform. They eventually helped form the Whig Party.

*See also:* Whig Party.

**Antimatter,** material composed of antiparticles, which are identical in mass and behavior to electrons, protons, and neutrons but have opposite electrical charges.

Matter and antimatter are both annihilated when they collide, and other particles, such as photons (quanta of energy) are released. Antimatter is rare and short-lived in our part of the universe, where matter predominates. The first antiparticle, the positron (antielectron), was discovered by Carl D. Anderson in 1932. In 1997 three scientists received the Nobel prize for developing a method to cool off antimatter using a laserbeam, in order to make particles more managable and to prevent annihilation.

*See also:* Antigravity.

**Anti-Monopoly Party**, U.S. political party opposing monopolies in business in 1884. The party joined with the Greenback Party in supporting Benjamin F. Butler of Massachusetts for president, but disbanded after Butler received only 175,000 votes.
*See also:* Butler, Benjamin Franklin.

**Antimony**, chemical element, symbol Sb; for physical constants see Periodic Table. Substances containing antimony have been used for thousands of years as medicines and cosmetics. It was first characterized accurately by Nicolas Lémery in 1707. Its principal ore is stibnite, a sulfide. Antimony is obtained by roasting the sulfide to the oxide, which can be further reduced with carbon. It is an extremely brittle, bluish-white metalloid and a poor conductor of heat and electricity. Two allotropes of antimony are known. Antimony greatly increases the hardness and mechanical strength of lead. It is used in batteries, antifriction alloys, type metal, infrared detectors, diodes, and Hall-effect devices. Its compounds are used in safety matches, flame-proofing agents, paints, ceramic enamels, glass, and pottery. Antimony and its compounds are toxic.

**Antioch** (pop. 94,900), ancient city in Asia Minor, now known as Antakya, in southern Turkey on the Orontes River. Founded by Seleucus I in 301 B C, it became the capital of the Seleucid Empire and was one of the great commercial centers of the ancient world. In 64 B C. control of the city passed to Rome, which made "Antioch the Golden" capital of the empire in Asia, surpassed in splendor only by Rome and Alexandria. It was the most important center of early Christianity outside Palestine. After the decline of the Eastern Roman Empire, Antioch came under Arab and then Ottoman Turkish rule. After World War I, it was incorporated into French-administered Syria, but in 1939 it was restored to Turkey. The city is a trade and agricultural center.

**Antipodes** (Greek, "foot-to-foot"), 2 places exactly opposite each other on the globe, so that a straight line connecting them would pass through the center of the earth. The region around Australia and New Zealand is the antipode of England, and is thus sometimes called the Antipodes.

**Antique**, object that has acquired value through a combination of age, rarity, craft, and historic interest. Generally, the term applies to objects over 100 years old, though by the 1980s even those of the 1890s and early 1900s, particularly in the art nouveau style, were becoming sought-after. The U.S. 1939 Tariff Act defined antiques as "artistic antiquities" made before 1830. Certain categories of objects are favorites, notably furniture, china, rugs, and other useful and decorative articles.

**Antirenters**, group of tenant farmers in New York State who protested against paying rent to landlords (1839–1847). The tenant families had lived on the disputed land for generations and considered it theirs. When, in 1839, the heirs of the Dutch merchant Van Rensselaer tried to collect $400,000 in back rents. The Antirenters rose up in protest, rioting and terrorizing the landlords. In 1846, a new state constitution guaranteed ownership to the tenants.

**Anti-Semitism,** systematic hostility to Jews. Until the 19th century, anti-Jewish prejudice was basically religious in nature, stemming from the claim that the Jews were responsible for Christ's death. In the late 1800s, particularly in eastern Europe, religious hostility acquired a racist rationale, based on the idea that Jews were a distinct, and evil, race. In Tsarist Russia the Jewish population was subjected to brutal physical attacks (pogroms). Anti-Semitism became a cornerstone of the ideology of Nazi Germany under Adolf Hitler, culminating in the murder of some 6 million Jews during World War II.
*See also:* Concentration camp; Holocaust; Jews; Racism.

**Antiseptic,** substance that kills or prevents the growth of microorganisms (particularly bacteria and fungi), especially used to avoid sepsis (infection) from contamination of body surfaces and surgical instruments. Vinegar and cedar oil have been used since early times to treat wounds and for embalming. Commonly used antiseptics and disinfectants include iodine, chlorine, alcohol, isopropanol, formaldehyde, and hydrogen peroxide. Heat, ultraviolet, and ionizing radiations also have antiseptic effects.
*See also:* Disinfectant; Lister, Sir Joseph.

**Antitoxin,** antibody released into the bloodstream to counteract the poisonous products (toxins) of invading bacteria. When a small amount of a bacterial toxin is injected into the blood, the body produces its own antitoxins to combat infection. The body may also accept blood serum injected from another organism that has already formed the antitoxin. This technique is effective in fighting such diseases as diphtheria and tetanus.

**Antitrust laws,** legislation designed to protect competition among businesses. By preventing large firms from controlling the price or supply of goods and services, these laws work to ensure that smaller firms are not forced out of business. Congressional antitrust action includes the Sherman Antitrust Act (1890), which was used to end unfair restraint of trade practices of the Standard Oil Company and American Tobacco Company in the early 1900s. The Clayton Antitrust Act (1914) is a supplement to the Sherman Act which outlaws price discrimination, non-complete agreements, price cutting, and certain mergers. The Federal Trade Commission (FTC) was established in 1914 to enforce antitrust laws. In 1950 the Clayton Act was enhanced by the Celler-Kefauver Act. Antitrust legislation has recently been complicated by the growth of huge conglomerates that control businesses in many industries.

**Anti-war movement,** opposition to U.S. involvement in the Vietnam war. From a relatively small group of protesters during the Kennedy administration, the movement proliferated and gained a broad base, its popularity widely believed responsible for President Lyndon B. Johnson's decision not to run for a second term in 1968. Hundreds of thousands demonstrated their opposition in protest marches in 1968-69. Anti-war pressure intensified under President Richard M. Nixon and strongly influenced his decision to settle for peace without victory.

**Ant lion,** or doodlebug, larval form of any of several insects of the Myrmeleontidae family that traps ants and other prey in pits dug in sandy soil. It uses its plump, hairy body to dig by backing into the soil in a narrowing spiral path. When prey slides into the pit, the ant lion, hiding under sand at the bottom, kills the prey with its long sharp jaws, and sucks its nourishment from the victim.

**Antofagasta** (pop. 228,000), major Pacific seaport in northern Chile, capital of Antofagasta province. An important industrial center, it is also the shipping point for the copper, nitrates, and sulfur mined in the surrounding region, as well as being the crossroads for rail and highway connections to southern Chile and across the Andes to Bolivia and Argentina. Antofagasta was ceded to Chile by Bolivia after the War of the Pacific (1879-83).

**Antoinette, Marie** *See:* Marie Antoinette.

**Antonioni, Michelangelo** (1912-    ), Italian film director. His work includes *L'Avventura* (1959), *La Notte* (1961), *Eclipse* (1962), *The Red Desert* (1964), *Blow-Up* (1966), *Zabriskie Point* (1969), and *The Passenger* (1975).

**Antonius Pius** (A.D 86-161), Roman emperor (138-161), tolerant of Christians, the last to achieve relative stability in the empire. Chosen consul in 120, he adopted Marcus Aurelius and Lucius Verus as successors.

**Antony, Marc** (Marcus Antonius; 82-30 B.C.), Roman politician and general. A member of Caesar's family, he became a tribune in 50 B C.; after Caesar's murder in 44 B.C, Antony, then consul, joined the Triumvirate, including his brother-in-law Octavian and Lepidus, dividing the empire among them.Antony controlled the east from the Adriatic to the Euphrates, but soon alienated Octavian by falling in love with the Egyptian queen, Cleopatra, and combining forces with her. As a result, the senate stripped Antony of his powers (32 B.C ), certain the insult would invite civil war. Octavian attacked and defeated Antony in a naval battle at Actium; Antony returned to Egypt, pursued by Octavian, and committed suicide. Cleopatra, too, died by her own hand.
*See also:* Rome, Ancient.

**Antwerp** (pop. 462,900), city and leading port, on the Scheldt River in northern Belgium. It is the capital of Antwerp province, the commercial and cultural center of Flemish Belgium, and an important manufacturing   city, with oil, metal, automobile, and diamond industries. It was the center of the great Flemish school of painting: artists like Brueghel, Rubens, and Van Dyck worked there in the 16th and 17th centuries.

**Anubis**, ancient Egyptian god of the dead, usually portrayed as having the head of a dog or jackal. In Egyptian belief, Anubis guided the dead to the underworld, where he symbolically weighed their hearts on the scales of justice.
*See also:* Mythology.

**Anxiety**, unpleasant and disturbing emotion, ranging from ill-defined discomfort to panic or a profound sense of impending doom.
Anxious people may be irritable, restless, and agitated, or have impulses for physical activity that may be purposeless and aimless. Physical symptoms

may include an increase in heart rate and blood pressure, generalized or localized muscle tension, rapid and shallow breathing, sighing or shortness of breath, dizziness, or nausea.

Anxiety may be acute, lasting a few minutes to a few hours, or chronic, with symptoms mild to moderate in intensity but almost constantly present. The chronic state may be intermittently and unpredictably accompanied by acute increases in the severity of the symptoms.

Anxiety is usually brought on by stress, which may be well defined and external or ill defined and internal. While it is often thought that anxiety is always undesirable and to be avoided, human personality development studies have demonstrated that tolerable levels of age-appropriate anxiety are largely responsible for individuals' gradual establishment of sophisticated, self-reliant behavior, attitudes, and values.
*See also:* Phobia.

**Anzio** (pop. 27,100), Italian fishing port and seaside resort about 30 mi (48 km) south of Rome. As ancient Antium, it was the birthplace of the emperors Caligula and Nero. Anzio was the site of Allied landings in Jan. 1944, during World War II, leading to a bloody battle in which casualties were high.

**Anzus Pact**, treaty signed Sept. 1, 1951, by Australia, New Zealand, and the United States for mutual defense in the Pacific. The name consists of the initials of the participating countries, which meet annually.

**Aorta**, the body's main artery, carrying blood from the left ventricle of the heart to the branch arteries that spread throughout the body.

**Apache**, Native American tribe of North America's Southwest (since c.1100), from Athabascan linguistic family. Members of a nomadic hunting culture whose men lived with and worked for their wives' families, these strong fighters repelled the Spanish, only to face the Comanches and other tribes and eventually the westward expansion of the European Americans. They rejected repeated federal attempts to confine their tribes to reservations. In the bloody conflicts that followed, they were decimated, and in 1896 Geronimo, their chief, was captured. Most present-day Apaches live on 3 million acres of federal reservations in Oklahoma, New Mexico, and Arizona, supported by income from timber, tourism, cattle, and mineral resources. In 1982 the Apaches won an important Supreme Court case that tested their right to tax resources taken from their lands.

**Apartheid** (Afrikaans, "apartness"), policy of racial segregation as employed by the Republic of South Africa, enforced by the dominant white minority. The system separates whites from nonwhites (i.e., Coloreds, or mulattoes; Asiatics; and Africans, or Bantu), nonwhites from each other, and each individual Bantu group. The policy also involves the "separate development" of 10 Bantu homelands, where the majority of the population lives on a very small portion of poor land. Segregation and discrimination of nonwhite peoples is imposed by denying the rights to vote, own land, travel, or work without permits. In addition, workers are often separated from their families, which undermines family structure. Although dissent, led largely by the formerly outlawed African National Congress, is met with imprisonment, exile, or house arrest, resistance to apartheid continues, both inside the country (where thousands have been killed or imprisoned) and outside (in the form of nearly worldwide economic and political sanctions against South Africa). Since the 1970s and 1980s many apartheid laws have been repealed. In the early 1990s the system was completely dismantled, democratic structures were introduced, and a black majority rule was established in 1994. *See also:* African National Congress; Mandela, Nelson.

**Apatosaurus**, see: Brontosaurus.

**Ape**, primate, family Pongidae, closely related to human beings. These forest dwellers, whose brain structure allows for fairly advanced reasoning, range in size from the gibbon (3 ft/0.9 m, 15 lb/6.8 kg) of southeast Asia to the gorilla (6 ft/1.8 m, 500 lb/227 kg) of Africa. The chimpanzee (5 ft/1.5 m, 150 lb/68 kg), also of Africa, is the animal most closely related to humans. It is a member of the ape family.

**Apennines**, mountain chain forming the backbone of the Italian peninsula and extending into Sicily, about 800 mi (1,287 km) long and 25-80 mi (40-129 km) wide. The predominant rocks are limestone and dolomite; sulfur and cinnabar are mined in the volcanic area near Vesuvius. Olives, grapes, and grains are widely grown, although lack of fertile topsoil prevents intensive agriculture.

**Apennine Tunnel**, 11.5-mi (18.5-km) train tunnel in Italy on the Florence-Bologna line; one of the longest train tunnels in the world, built from 1920-34.

**Aphasia**, partial or total language impairment, in which the comprehension or expression of words is diminished as a result of injury to the brain. Reeducation is the only proven treatment.

**Aphid**, destructive sap-feeding insect of the aphid family, also known as greenfly or plant louse. Because of the damage caused by their piercing of plant tissue and because many of the 4,000 species carry viruses, aphids are one of the world's greatest crop pests. They are an important food source for ants and other insects.

**Aphrodite**, in Greek mythology, goddess of love, fertility, and beauty. The daughter of Zeus and Dione in some versions, in others she is described as having risen from the sea. Her intensely sensual beauty aroused jealousy among other goddesses, particularly after the Trojan Paris chose her as the most beautiful over Hera and Athena. Wife of the crippled smith Hephaestus, she took both divine and mortal lovers, giving birth to Aeneas and Eros. The Greeks honored her with many major shrines. The Romans called her Venus.

**Apia** (pop. 36,000), capital and main port of Western Samoa, on the northern coast of Upolu Island. Apia's Government House was once the home of Robert Louis Stevenson, author of *Treasure Island*, who died there in 1894 and is buried nearby.

**Apocalypse**, prophetic revelation, usually about the end of the world and the ensuing establishment of a heavenly kingdom. Jewish and Christian apocalyptic writings appeared in Palestine between 200 B.C. and 150 A.D. and offered hope of liberation to a people under alien rule.

**Apocrypha,** appendix to the King James Version of the Old Testament. Protestants use the term mainly for books written in the 2 centuries before Christ and included in the Septuagint and the Vulgate, but not in the Hebrew Bible. These include Esdras I and II, Tobit, Judith, additions to Esther, the Wisdom of Solomon, Ecclesiasticus, Baruch, the Song of the Three Holy Children, Susanna and the Elders, Bel and the Dragon, the Prayer of Manasses, and Maccabees I and II.

**Apollinaire, Guillaume** (Wilhelm Apollinaris de Kostrowitzky; 1880-1918), influential French avant-garde poet and critic. The friend of Derain, Dufy, and Picasso, he helped to publicize Cubist and primitive art. In his lyric poems *Alcools* (1913) and *Calligrammes* (1918), he anticipated Surrealism with his use of startling associations and juxtapositions.

**Apollo,** in Greek mythology, the son of Zeus and Leto, twin of Artemis, and second only to Zeus in that he had the power of the sun as giver of light and life. He was the god of justice and masculine beauty, purifier of those stained by crime, divine patron of the arts, leader of the Muses, and god of music and poetry. Apollo was considered a healer who could also send disease. He spoke through the oracle at Delphi. The Romans adopted Apollo, honoring him as healer and sun god.

**Apollo Project,** U.S. space program initiated by President John F. Kennedy on May 25, 1961, to place a person on the moon by the end of the 1960s. The program's mission was accomplished (at a cost of over $24 billion) when the Apollo 11 Lunar Excursion Module (LEM) carrying astronauts Neil Armstrong and Buzz Aldrin touched down on the moon's surface on July 20, 1969. Subsequent flights allowed exploration of various areas of the moon. The program ended in 1972 with Apollo 17.
*See also:* National Aeronautics and Space Adminstration.

**Apostles,** the 12 disciples closest to Jesus, whom he chose to proclaim his teaching: Andrew, John, Bartholomew, Judas, Jude, the two Jameses, Matthew, Peter, Philip, Simon, and Thomas. When Judas died, Matthias replaced him. Paul and Barnabas became known as apostles for their work in spreading the gospel.
*See also:* Bible.

**Apostles' Creed,** statement of belief ascribed to Jesus's apostles and maintained in its present form since the early Middle Ages. The Roman Catholic Church uses it in the sacraments of baptism and confirmation. It is also used by various Protestant denominations.
*See also:* Apostles.

**Apothecaries' weight,** system of weights once widely used in Great Britain and the United States by druggists, now replaced by the metric system. Apothecaries' weight divides the pound into 12 ounces, the ounce into 8 drams, the dram into 3 scruples, and the scruple into 20 grains.
*See also:* Weights and measures.

**Appalachian Mountains,** mountain system of Northeastern America, about 1,800 mi (2,897 km) long and 120-375 mi (193-603 km) wide, stretching south from Newfoundland to central Alabama. Major ranges of the north include the Notre Dame, Green, and White mountains. The central area has the Allegheny Mountains and part of the Blue Ridge Mountains. The south contains the south Blue Ridge, Cumberland, Black, and Great Smoky mountains. The highest peak is Mt. Mitchell (6,684 ft/2,037 m) in North Carolina. Appalachian forests yield much timber, and rich deposits of coal and iron have stimulated growth of industrial areas like Birmingham, Ala., and Pittsburgh, Pa. In the early years of the United States, the Appalachians were a barrier to westward expansion, but the Connecticut, Hudson, Delaware, and other rivers have cut deep gaps in the ranges.

**Appalachian National Scenic Trail,** longest marked hiking trail in the world, stretching over 2,000 mi (3,219 km) along the crest of the Appalachian Mountains from Mt. Katahdin in northern Maine to Springer Mountain in northern Georgia.

**Appeal,** in law, transfer of a case that has been decided in a lower court to a higher court for review. In most U.S. jurisdictions, if the appeals court finds that the lower court (or administrative agency) made legal errors, it may decide in favor of the party making the appeal (appellant) or order a new trial in the lower court. The highest appeals court of the land is the Supreme Court in Washington, D.C., which will only hear cases in which a substantial federal or constitutional question is involved. Otherwise, the state supreme court is the highest authority.

**Appellate court** *See:* Court; Trial.

**Appendicitis,** inflammation of the appendix, often caused by obstruction to its narrow opening, followed by swelling and bacterial infection. Acute appendicitis can lead to rupture of the organ, formation of an abscess, or peritonitis. Symptoms include abdominal pain (usually in the right lower abdomen), nausea, vomiting, and fever. Early surgical removal of the appendix is essential; any abscess requires drainage of pus and delayed removal. *See also:* Appendix.

**Appendix,** in biology small, hollow, closed tube located where the small and large intestines meet. While it aids digestion in certain rodents, it no longer has a function in humans and is considered a vestigial organ. The disease appendicitis results when the appendix becomes inflamed. *See also:* Appendicitis.

**Appia, Adolphe** (1862-1928), Swiss stage designer whose ideas revolutionized early 20th-century theater. He stressed the use of 3-dimensional settings and of mobile lighting with controlled intensity and color.

**Appian Way,** oldest Roman road, constructed by the censor Appius Claudius Caecus in 312 B.C At first stretching from Rome to Capua (about 130 mi/209 km), by the mid-third century B.C. the road had been extended to the site of present-day Brindisi, making it the main artery to southern Italy.

**Apple,** tree (genus *Malus*) of the rose family, widely cultivated in temperate climates; also, the fruit of the tree. Over 7,000 varieties are known, but only about 40 are commercially important, the most popular U.S. variety being the Delicious. Some 15 to 20% of the world's crop is produced in the United States, mostly in the states of Washington, New York, California, Michigan, and Virginia. There are 3 main types of apples: cooking, dessert, and those used in making cider.

**Apple of Sodom** (*Solanum sodomeum*), spiny plant of the nightshade family, native to Palestine, that bears yellow fruit resembling small apples. It is named for the biblical apple of Sodom, which looked tempting but turned to ashes in the mouth.

**Appleseed, Johnny** (John Chapman; 1774-1845), U.S. folk hero. A pioneer in the Ohio River region, he wandered for 40 years, planting and tending apple orchards.

**Appleton, Sir Edward Victor** (1892-1965), English physicist who discovered the Appleton layer (now resolved as 2 layers, $F_1$ and $F_2$) of ionized gas molecules in the ionosphere. His work in atmospheric physics won him the 1947 Nobel Prize for physics and contributed to the development of radar. During World War II he helped develop the atomic bomb.
*See also:* Ionosphere.

**Appolonius of Rhodes** (3rd century B C.), Greek poet, pupil of Callimachus, and later head of the library at Alexandria. In addition to shorter works, he wrote the epic *Argonautica*, describing the expedition of Jason and the Argonauts. The poem uses much of Homer's style and meter, and its portrayal of Medea is thought to have influenced the Roman poet Vergil in the creation of Dido, a character in the *Aeneid*
*See also:* Homer; Vergil.

**Appomattox Courthouse,** settlement in central Virginia where the Civil War ended with Confederate General Robert E. Lee's surrender to Union General Ulysses S. Grant on Apr. 9, 1865. The site became a national historical park in 1954.
*See also:* Civil War, U.S.

**Apportionment, legislative,** distribution of voters' representation in the lawmaking bodies. Representation can be apportioned according to population or political units. For example, although each U.S. state, whatever size, elects 2 senators, the number of seats each state holds in the House of Representatives is based on the state's population. There is a reapportionment of seats each decade when the census is taken.

**Apprentice,** person who works for an accomplished craftsperson to learn a trade. An apprentice normally works regular hours and earns a salary. The system of apprenticeship, begun in ancient times, reached its peak in medieval Europe with the organization of guilds representing individual crafts. Following the Industrial Revolution, guilds were gradually replaced by smaller, newer fields of apprenticeship, particularly among machine workers and electricians.
*See also:* Guild.

**Apricot** (*Prunus armeniaca*), tree of the rose family, native to China but grown throughout temperate regions; also, the orange-colored fruit of the tree. Over 90% of the U.S. crop of apricots comes from California. They are eaten fresh or preserved by drying or canning; the kernels are used to make a liqueur.

**April Fools' Day**, or All Fools' Day, Apr. 1, the traditional day for practical jokes. The custom probably began in France in 1564, when New Year's Day was changed from Apr. 1 to Jan. 1. Those continuing to observe Apr. 1 were ridiculed.

**Apuleius, Lucius** (c.A.D 125-185), Latin writer. His *Metamorphoses* or *The Golden Ass* is the only complete extant Latin novel. The adventures of the novel's hero, who has been turned into an ass, provide insight into Imperial Roman society.

**Aqaba, Gulf of**, northeastern arm of the Red Sea, between the Sinai Peninsula and Saudi Arabia. Geologically part of the Great Rift Valley of Africa and Asia, it is about 110 mi (177 km) long and 5-17 mi (8-27 km) wide. At the northern end of the gulf stand the ports of Aqaba (Jordan) and Elat (Israel). The Egyptian blockade of Elat sparked the 1967 Arab-Israeli Six-Day War.

**Aquaculture**, controlled raising of marine animals and seaweed for harvest. Aquaculture takes place in enclosures built on land or in natural bodies of water. China has practiced aquaculture for 4,000 years and is still the leading world producer of cultivated freshwater fish. Production in the United States is growing rapidly. In addition to fish, Asian sea farmers cultivate seaweed, from which are produced agar, algin, and carrageenan, used in food thickeners and in drugs.

**Aqualung** *See:* Skin diving.

**Aquamarine**, transparent blue or pale blue-green semiprecious stone, a variety of the mineral beryl. The most important deposits are in Brazil, but aquamarine is also found in Siberia, Madagascar, and sections of the United States. Other bluish gemstones are sometimes incorrectly called aquamarine, including a blue variety of corundum called Oriental aquamarine. *See also:* Beryl.

**Aqua regia** (Latin, "royal water"), mixture of concentrated nitric and hydrochloric acids used since the Middle Ages to dissolve gold, the "royal metal," and other substances that are difficult to get into solution.

**Aquarium**, tank, bowl, or pool in which aquatic animals and plants are kept. Aquariums originated in ancient Egypt and Asia. Romans used them not for decorative purposes, but as a source of fresh fish for the dinner table. The ornamental aquarium made its appearance in the West in the 18th century, when the goldfish became popular in France. The first public aquarium was opened in London in 1853, and Vienna and Paris soon followed. Today they are found in many of the major cities of the world, including, in the United States, Chicago, New York, and San Francisco. Giant aquariums, or oceanariums, large enough to hold a small whale, have been built in Los Angeles and at Marineland, Fla. These collections provide entertainment for the public as well as valuable information for students of marine life.

**Aqueduct**, artificial conduit for water. Ancient Rome was supplied with fresh drinking water from mountain springs by 14 aqueducts. In the south of France the Pont du Gard still stands. The longest aqueduct today is the California State Water Project aqueduct (826 mi/1,329 km), completed in 1974.

**Aquinas, Saint Thomas** (1225-74), Italian scholastic theologian and philosopher. Known as the Angelic Doctor, St. Thomas reconciled Christian faith with Aristotelian reason. His teachings are basic to Roman Catholic theology. His greatest work is the *Summa Theologica* (1267-73).
*See also:* Scholasticism.

**Aquino, Corazon** (1933-), first woman president of the Philippines (1986-92). The widow of slain Philippine opposition leader Benigno Aquino, she was the major opposition candidate in the 1986 presidential elections. The National Assembly—controlled by supporters of President Marcos—declared Marcos winner of the election, although there were major signs of fraud. After rioting broke out, Marcos left the Philippines on board a U.S. plane, and Aquino was recognized as president.

**Arab**, one whose language is Arabic and who identifies with Arab culture. The term originally referred to inhabitants of the Arabian Peninsula, but the Arab world today includes the countries Algeria, Egypt, Iraq, Jordan, Lebanon, Libya, Morocco, Sudan, Syria, and Tunisia. Arab culture spread after the successful campaigns of Mohammed (c.A.D. 570). In the 7th century the Arabs extended their hegemony from northwestern Africa and Spain to Afghanistan and northern India, where many non-Arabic peoples were converted to the Arabic religion of Islam. Non-Muslim peoples who are also Arabs include Palestinian, Lebanese, and Syrian Christians. In the 20th century the discovery and exploitation of petroleum in Arab lands has resulted in sudden wealth and modernization for many Arab countries. Arab hostility to the state of Israel has strengthened Pan-Arab nationalism.
*See also:* Islam; Middle East; Muslims.

**Arabesque**, elaborate decorative style characterized by curved or intertwining shapes, with grotesque, animal, human, or symbolic forms and delicate foliage.

**Arabia** *See:* Arabian Peninsula; Saudi Arabia.

**Arabian Desert**, one of the greatest desert regions in the world, comprising almost all of the deserts of the Arabian Peninsula in southwest Asia. The desert covers approximately 900,000 sq mi (2,331,000 sq km) and is surrounded by the Syrian Desert, the Persian Gulf, the Gulf of Oman, the Arabian Sea, the Gulf of Aden, and the Red Sea.

**Arabian Nights**, or *The Thousand and One Nights*, collection of ancient Persian, Indian, and Arabian folktales, written in Arabic and arranged in its

present form during the early 16th century. The stories, which include the tales of Aladdin, Ali Baba, and Sinbad the Sailor, are linked by a framing story about Scheherazade. She marries a king who executes his wives on the second day of their marriage. Each night, she tells him part of a story but leaves the ending for the next night. The king must spare her for another day if he is to learn the ending. By the 1,001st night, the king has learned to love his wife, and Scheherazade is spared.
*See also:* Burton, Sir Richard Francis.

**Arabian Peninsula**, vast land, largely desert, in southwest Asia, surrounded by the Red Sea, the Arabian Sea, and the Persian Gulf. Saudi Arabia takes up the greatest part of land. Other countries are the Republic of Yemen, Oman, United Arab Emirates, Qatar, and Kuwait. The arid area, approximately 1,162,000 sq mi (3,009,600 sq km), is economically and politically important because of its great petroleum resources.

**Arabian Sea**, northwestern sea of the Indian Ocean, between India and Arabia. It is connected with the Persian Gulf by the Gulf of Oman and with the Red Sea by the Gulf of Aden. Its ports include Bombay and Karachi.

**Arabic**, one of the Semitic languages. The Arabic alphabet comprises 28 consonants, vowels being expressed either by positioned points or, in some cases, by insertion of the letters *alif*, *waw*, and *ya* where they would not otherwise occur, thereby representing the long *a*, *u*, and *i* respectively. Arabic is written from right to left. Classical Arabic, the language of the Koran, is used occasionally in writing, rarely in speech; a standardized modern Arabic is used in newspapers. Arabic played a large part in the dissemination of knowledge through medieval Europe because many ancient Greek and Roman texts were available solely in Arabic translation.
*See also:* Semitic languages.

**Arabic numerals**, also called Hindu-Arabic numerals, the most common symbols for numbers. These basic symbols or digits (Latin, "fingers") are: 0, 1, 2, 3, 4, 5, 6, 7, 8, and 9. The position of the digit determines its value. For example, in the Arabic numeral 846, the digit 8 has a value of 8 x 100, the digit 4 has a value of 4 x 10, and the digit 6 has a value of 6. Exactly how Arabic numerals originated is unknown. The Hindus in India probably developed 1 through 9 in about 200 B C ; they developed zero after A D 600. Traders and merchants helped spread the Arabic numeral system into Europe.
*See also:* Numeration systems.

**Arab-Israeli Wars**, several conflicts between Israel and the Arabs. In 1948, when Israel was established as an independent state on what the Arabs regarded as Arab land, Egypt, Iraq, Transjordan (Jordan), Lebanon, and Syria attacked, but within a month Israel had occupied the greater part of Palestine. By July 1949, separate ceasefires were concluded with the Arab states.
On Oct. 29, 1956, with the Suez Canal and Gulf of Aqaba closed to its ships, Israel invaded Egypt, which had nationalized the canal in July. British and French supporting troops occupied the canal banks but were replaced by a UN force after international furor. By Mar. 1957 all Israeli forces had left Egypt in exchange for access to the Gulf of Aqaba. In 1967 Egypt again closed the gulf to Israel, and on June 5, at the start of the Six-Day War, Israeli

air strikes destroyed the Arab air forces on the ground. Israel won the West Bank of the Jordan River, the Golan Heights, the Gaza Strip, the Sinai Peninsula, and the Old City of Jerusalem. A ceasefire was accepted by June 10. On Oct. 6, 1973, Yom Kippur, Egypt and Syria attacked Israel to regain the lost territories. A ceasefire was signed on Nov. 11, 1973. Although Israeli troops penetrated deep into Syria and crossed onto the west bank of the Suez Canal, initial Arab success restored Arab confidence. Talks between Egypt and Israel led to a peace treaty in 1979. But tension ran high elsewhere, especially in Lebanon, which was used as a guerrilla base by the Palestinians and became a target for Israeli attacks. In June 1982 Israel invaded Lebanon to destroy strongholds of the Palestine Liberation Organization (PLO) guerrillas. Subsequently, under a U.S.-sponsored plan, the guerrillas left Beirut for other countries willing to accept them, and a multinational peacekeeping force, including U.S. marines, landed in Lebanon.

**Arab League**, organization promoting economic, cultural, and political cooperation among Arab states, founded in 1945. Its members include 21 of the Arab states and the PLO. In 1948 the members attacked the new state of Israel, which had been established on what the Arabs considered Arab land. The league broke with Egypt, an original member, in 1979 after the country signed a peace treaty with Israel. Egypt rejoined the league in 1989.

**Arachne**, in Greek mythology, mortal so expert in weaving that she challenged Athena to a contest. Arachne's tapestry, which depicted the foibles of the gods, angered the goddess, who tore it up. Arachne hanged herself in despair and was transformed into a spider.

**Arachnid**, insectlike arthropod of the class Arachnida. Spiders, mites, and scorpions are arachnids. While an insect's body consists of head, thorax, and abdomen, an arachnid's body has only 2 main parts: abdomen and cephalothorax, which combines head and thorax. Also unlike insects, arachnids have no wings or antennae, and they have simple rather than compound eyes.

**Arafat, Yasir** (1929-), Palestinian political figure. After organizing the anti-Israel Al Fatah guerrillas in the 1950s, Arafat became chairman of the Palestine Liberation Organization (PLO) in 1969. In 1974 Arafat opened a debate on Palestine at the UN, where he led the first nongovernmental delegation to take part in a General Assembly plenary session. It is generally believed that Arafat authorized terrorist actions to accomplish the goals of the PLO. In 1991, the PLO sided with Iraq in the Persian Gulf War which led to a weakening of its position. Arafat regained esteem when he signed an agreement with Israel regarding limited Palestinian autonomy in the Gaza Strip and Jericho (1993). This resulted in him getting the Nobel Peace prize, together with Yitzhak Rabin and Shimon Peres (1994). In September 1995, Arafat and Rabin signed an agreement regarding the withdrawal in stages of the Israeli troops from six important cities on the West Bank. The agreement also provided for elections for a Palestinian council and a president. In 1996 Arafat was elected president of the council.
*See also:* Palestine Liberation Organization.

**Aragón**, historic region of northeastern Spain, stretching from the central Pyrenees to south of the Ebro River. The medieval kingdom of Aragón comprised what are now the provinces of Huesca, Teruel, and Saragossa, although the influence of the kings of Aragón was more extensive. King Ferdinand II of Aragón's marriage to Isabella of Castile (1479) laid the foundations of a unified Spain. Aragón's sovereignty was ended 1707-9 by Philip V during the War of the Spanish Succession (1701-14).

**Aral Sea,** inland sea or saltwater lake covering 24,904 sq mi (64,501 sq km) in Kazakhstan and Uzbekistan. It is the fourth largest lake in the world and is fed by the Amu Darya and Syr Darya rivers. The sea is commercially important for its bass, carp, perch, and sturgeon. In the last 30 years, the irrigation needed for the extensive cultivation of cotton, has led to a considerable reduction of the water supply. This, together with pollution resulted in an environmental disaster which also threatened public health in the surrounding areas. In 1997, the Worldbank granted a loan for the construction of water pipes and water treatment plants.

**Aramaic,** Semitic language. It spread throughout Syria and Mesopotamia from the 8th century B.C. on, and was the official language of the Persian Empire. Aramaic was probably spoken by Jesus and the apostles, and parts of the Old Testament are in Aramaic. Aramaic survives only in isolated Lebanese villages and among some Nestorians of northern Iraq and eastern Turkey.
*See also:* Semitic languages.

**Arapaho,** North American tribe of the Algonquian family. They lived as nomadic buffalo hunters on the Great Plains. Fierce enemies of European-American settlement, they were forced onto reservations at the end of the 19th century. The Arapaho are divided into 3 groups: the Southern Arapaho, the Northern Arapaho, and the Gros Ventre. Less than 5,000 Arapaho remain, mostly on reservations in Oklahoma and Wyoming.

**Ararat, Mount,** dormant volcanic mountain in eastern Turkey with 2 peaks, 16,950 ft (5,166 m) and 13,000 ft (3,962 m) high. According to the Bible, Noah's Ark landed on Mount Ararat (Genesis 8:4). The Armenians venerate the mountain as the "Mother of the World."
*See also:* Noah.

**Araucanians,** South American tribes famous for their resistance to the Spaniards, beginning with the 16th-century Spanish invasion of what is now central Chile. Many Araucanians crossed the Andes into Argentina on stolen Spanish horses. The tribes were defeated in the late 19th century. Today over 200,000 Araucanians live in Chile.

**Arawak,** group of often culturally distinct South American tribes, now living mostly in Brazil, the Guyanas, and Peru. Arawak inhabited several West Indian islands when Columbus landed in 1492. The Caribbean Arawak were wiped out by the mid-16th century by a combination of disease and forced labor brought on by Europeans.

**Arbitration,** process for settling disputes in which the parties submit the controversy to an impartial arbitrator. In conciliation or mediation, the impartial person tries to persuade the parties to accept a settlement; in arbitration, by prior agreement the arbitrator imposes a final and binding decision, called an award. Experienced tribunals established by trade associations arbitrate commercial disputes between business organizations. Industrial arbitration settles disputes between labor and management. Collective bargaining agreements generally provide for an impartial arbitrator to settle conflicts arising from different interpretations of the agreement. Arbitration in international affairs is one of the oldest ways of settling disputes. It was used by the Greek city-states and is today included as a provision in many treaties between nations.

**Arboretum,** place in which trees and shrubs are cultivated for scientific or educational purposes.

**Arcadia,** ancient Greek region in central Peloponnesus, enclosed by mountains. The simple life of its rustic inhabitants was idealized by classical pastoral poets and later writers, notably the English poet Sir Philip Sidney, as the embodiment of innocent, virtuous living.

**Arc, electric** *See:* Electric arc.

**Arc, Joan of** *See:* Joan of Arc, Saint.

**Arcaro, Eddie** (George Edward Arcaro; 1916-    ), U.S. jockey. The first to have won the Triple Crown twice (1941,1948) and the Kentucky Derby 5 times, and the third jockey to win more than 4,000 races. Arcaro's purses totaled more than $30 million during his career (1931-62).

**Arc de Triomphe,** Napoleon's triumphal arch in the Place Charles de Gaulle at the end of the Champs-Elysées, Paris. It was built 1806-36 and is 163 ft (49 m) high and 147 ft (45 m) wide. Inspired by Roman triumphal arches, it bears reliefs celebrating Napoleon's victories. The arch is also the site of the tomb of France's Unknown Soldier.

**Arch,** structural device to span openings and support loads. In architecture the simplest form of the arch is the round (semicircular), in which wedge-shaped stones, or voussoirs, are fitted together, receiving the stresses in the arch exerted outward onto them. Downward forces from the load combine with these to produce a diagonal force, or thrust. The voussoirs at each end of the arch are called springers; the one in the center, usually the last to be placed, is the keystone. Although the arch was known in ancient Egypt and Greece, it was not until Roman times that its use became popular.

**Archaeopteryx,** prehistoric feathered reptile the size of a crow, with 2 claws representing the thumb and forefinger projecting from its wing and about 20 tail vertebrae.
*See also:* Prehistoric animal.

**Archangel** (pop. 419,000; Russian, *Arkhangelsk*), city in northwestern Russian Federation, near the mouth of the North Dvina River. Archangel is a major White Sea port, exporting lumber, resin, turpentine, and furs. Other industries include sawmilling, shipbuilding, and papermaking. Established as a trading post called Novo-Kholmogory in 1584, it later became a leading

Russian port, declining after 1703, when St. Petersburg was founded. The port expanded in World War II, when it received tons of supplies shipped by the Allies.

**Archbishop**, metropolitan bishop of the Roman Catholic, Anglican, or Eastern Orthodox church, or of the Lutheran churches of Finland and Sweden, having jurisdiction over the bishops of a church province, or archdiocese. The archbishop consecrates bishops and presides over synods.

**Archeoastronomy**, study of the astronomy of ancient peoples and its relation to other aspects of culture. The field includes the work of archeologists, astronomers, historians, and anthropologists. Archeoastronomers in Great Britain have studied the circles of large stones laid more than 5,000 years ago, and believe the circles may have been calendars or a way of predicting eclipses. Also of interest are Mayan buildings, which were constructed in a direct line with Venus on the horizon.
*See also:* Archeology; Astronomy; Stonehenge.

**Archeology**, study of the past through identification and interpretation of the material remains of human cultures. Archeology uses the knowledge and techniques of such disciplines as anthropology, history, paleography, and philology. Its keystone is fieldwork. Archeology began in the early 18th century with excavations of Roman and other sites. The famous Rosetta Stone, which provided the key to Egyptian hieroglyphics, was discovered in 1799 and deciphered in 1818. In the 19th century archeology became a systematized science through the work of Heinrich Schliemann, Arthur Evans, C. L. Woolley, Howard Carter, and others. In the United States archeologists have studied the culture of early Native Americans as well as settlements of colonial America—an example of historic archeology, which deals with peoples who left behind written documents.

Suitable sites may be revealed as a result of war damage or during construction of buildings and roads. Because unusually shaped hills or mounds are sometimes artificial, they are often investigated. Ancient writings may help in locating sites. Aerial photography has sometimes revealed the existence of buried structures. The archeological team then recovers objects or fragments lying loose on the ground or inside caves, or, more often, excavates (digs) to find the artifacts. Great care is required not to damage any object or trace of an object. Small hoes, spades, trowels, penknives, brushes, and fingers are used. Archeologists record the spatial relationships artifacts have to one another and to the layers in which they are found. Notes and drawings are made, each item is numbered, and photographs are taken.

Archeologists use 2 dating systems: absolute dating and relative dating. Early inscriptions, and especially, mention of an eclipse or other astronomical phenomena, make it easy to date a monument or site. Tree-ring chronology can help date wood remains. Pollen, an extraordinarily durable organic substance, is also a useful date indicator. Radiocarbon dating uses the known half-life of radioactive carbon-14, found in all organic matter, as a yardstick. Stratigraphy, the most important method for relative dating, uses the principle that objects found near the surface are more recent than those found lower within the ground. Because pottery styles sometimes overlap on several sites, information gained from one site can be applied to another. Chemical changes in bones can also help differentiate younger ones from older ones.

**Archerfish,** any of several species of Indo-Pacific fishes of the family Toxotidae with the ability to eject water from their mouths to knock insect prey to the surface; especially, *Toxotes jaculator*. The archerfish has a flat, elongated body and inhabits both fresh and salt water.

**Archery,** competitive and recreational sport, using bows and arrows. The three major types of archery are target, field and flight. Target and field archery involve firing arrows at set targets, while flight archery is a contest of distance shooting. An Olympic event, archery's popularity worldwide led to the formation of the International Archery Federation (1931).

**Arches National Park,** 82,953 acres (33,571 hectares) in eastern Utah containing natural rock arches formed by weathering and erosion. The park was established in 1929.

**Archimedes** (c.287-212 B.C.), Greek mathematician and physicist who spent most of his life in Syracuse, Sicily, where he was born. In mathematics he worked on the areas and volumes of conic sections, determined the value of $\pi$ as lying between 3-1/7 and 3-10/71, and defined the Archimedean spiral. He founded the science of hydrostatics with his enunciation of Archimedes' principle, that the force acting to buoy up a body partially or totally immersed in a fluid is equal to the weight of the fluid displaced. He is also credited with the invention of Archimedes' screw, a machine for raising water that is still used to irrigate fields in Egypt. In physics he was the first to prove the law of the lever.
*See also:* Calculus; Physics.

**Archipelago** (Greek, "chief sea"), name originally applied to the Aegean Sea, which is studded with many small islands; by extension, any space of water interspersed with islands or the group of islands itself. The greatest archipelago is the 3,200-mile (5,100-km) crescent of more than 3,000 islands that form Indonesia.

**Architecture,** art or science of designing and building structures. While the beginnings of architecture are traceable to areas around the Nile, Euphrates, and Tigris rivers, the Greeks and Romans created the styles that we rely on today. Greek architecture used post-and-lintel construction: a rectangle formed by beams and columns. The Romans were the first to fully use the arch and to use concrete as a building material, making possible structures with enormous roof spans.
Byzantine architecture, which arose in the Eastern Roman Empire and later influenced Russia, introduced the dome. Islamic architecture featured interior courtyards surrounded by colonnades. At the end of the Middle Ages, European churches and monasteries were stoutly built, for defensive purposes. Starting at the end of the 12th century, stained glass, high pillars, and thin arches of Gothic architecture were held in equilibrium by exterior buttresses. The Renaissance brought a revival of classical (Greek and Roman) architecture. In the Baroque period, rich ornamentation and curves replaced the straight lines of the Renaissance. The 18th century saw a revival of classical architecture in Europe and America, and a Gothic revival began in the 19th century. Starting in the last half of the 19th century, the use of iron, steel, and reinforced concrete allowed skyscrapers to be built.

**Archon**, administrator of ancient Athens and other Greek city-states. Originally a life term open only to nobles, by 682 B C the archonship was shared by 9 members elected from the population for 1 year, and included a civil ruler, a religious head, a military commander, and 6 lawmakers. The archons lost influence with the rise of democracy.

**Arc light**, device in which electrical current flowing between poles or electrodes produces the electric arc, yielding an intensely bright light. Arc lights are used in searchlights and movie projectors. The mercury arc is the basis for modern fluorescent lamps.
*See also:* Electric light.

**Arctic**, region north of the Arctic Circle (66°30' N); alternatively, regions north of the tree line.
*Land and climate.* The Arctic comprises the Arctic Ocean, Greenland, Spitsbergen and other islands, extreme northern Europe, Siberia, Alaska, and northern Canada. The area's central feature is the Arctic Ocean, opening south into the North Atlantic Ocean and Bering Strait. The Arctic Ocean comprises 2 main basins and has a shallow rim floored by the continental shelves of Eurasia and North America. Much of the ocean's surface is always covered with ice.
The Arctic climate is cold. In midwinter the sun never rises and the mean Jan. temperature is -33° F (-57.6° C), far lower in interior Canada and Siberia. Snow and ice never melt in the high altitudes and latitudes of the Arctic, but elsewhere the short mild summer, with 24 hours of sunlight a day, thaws the sea and the topsoil. In spring, melting icebergs floating south from the Arctic Ocean endanger North Atlantic shipping. Vegetation in the Arctic is varied but confined mainly to shrubs, flowering herbaceous plants, mosses, and lichens. Wild mammals include polar bears, reindeer, musk oxen, moose, wolves, weasels, foxes, and lemmings. Geese, ducks, gulls, cranes, falcons, auks, and ptarmigan all nest in the Arctic, and its seas harbor whales, seals, cod, salmon, and shrimp.
*People.* Inuits (Eskimos), Lapps, Russians, and others make up a human population of several million. Eskimos have lived in the Arctic for at least 9,000 years. Once exclusively hunters and fishers, Eskimos now also work in towns and on oil fields.
*Economy.* The Arctic is home to scattered agricultural, mining, and fishing industries, and the United States, Canada, and the Russian Federation maintain air bases and meteorological stations there. In 1978, oil production began at Prudhoe Bay, an inlet of the Arctic Ocean in northern Alaska, the oil moving south to Valdez, Alaska, through the Alaskan Pipeline.
*History.* Vikings were the first recorded Arctic explorers. Norwegians visited the Russian Arctic in the 9th century and the Icelander Eric the Red established a Greenland settlement in A D. 982. In the 16th and 17th centuries exploration was encouraged by the search for a northwest passage (a water route along the northern coast of North America, between the Atlantic and Pacific oceans) and a northeast passage (a water route between the same oceans but along the northern coast of Europe and Asia). In the 16th century Martin Frobisher reached Baffin Island, and Willem Barentz explored Novaya Zemlya and saw Spitsbergen. Henry Hudson probed eastern Greenland and the Hudson Strait in the early 17th century. But the longed-for passages remained undiscovered, and interest in Arctic exploration declined until

Canadian and Russian fur traders revived it late in the 18th century. Early in the 19th century the British naval officers John and James Ross, W. E. Perry, John Rae, and Sir John Franklin traveled to unexplored areas, and James Ross discovered the north magnetic pole. N.A.E. Nordenskjöld of Sweden navigated the Northeast Passage (1878-79) and R. Amundsen the Northwest Passage (1906). In 1909 Robert E. Peary reached the North Pole. Richard E. Byrd and Floyd Bennett flew over the Pole in 1926, pioneering polar air exploration and transpolar air travel. In 1958 the U. S. nuclear submarine *Nautilus* reached the Pole.

**Arctic Circle**, imaginary circle at 66 30′ N lat. roughly defining the tree line and marking the southernmost point of the polar area at which the midnight sun is seen. The sun never rises on the Arctic Circle at the winter solstice on or about Dec. 21.

**Arctic fox** (*Alopex lagopus*), tundra dweller of the family Canidae. In summer, it is brown or gray; in winter it is white or slate blue. The Arctic fox is about 2 ft (60 cm) long, with a long tail and short, rounded ears. A true scavenger, it eats any available food and follows polar bears to eat the remains of their kills.

**Arctic Ocean**, the smallest ocean, centering on the North Pole and connecting with the Atlantic through the Greenland Sea and with the Pacific through the Bering Strait. It covers about 4 million sq mi (10.3 million sq km), has an average depth of 4,362 ft (1,330 m), and includes an abyss with a known depth of 17,880 ft (5,450 m) and a continental shelf extending up to 1,000 mi (1,600 km) from the coast. Most of the Arctic Ocean is frozen all year. It was probably discovered by Greek sailors around 400 B.C. and was sailed by Vikings in the 800s. Norwegian explorer Fridtjof Nansen conducted the first scientific study in 1893-96.

**Arctic tern** (*Sterna paradisaea*), a coast-dwelling, long-distance migrant bird of the family Laridae. The Arctic tern winters in Antarctica, then flies north to breed on Atlantic coasts from New England to the northernmost islands of the Arctic Ocean. It is about 17 in (43 cm) long, with gray, black, and white feathers and a red bill and feet.
*See also:* Tern.

**Arcturus** (*Alpha Bootes*), brightest and fourth -largest star, orange-red in color. It is located in the constellation Boötes. Arcturus is about 40 light-years from earth and is moving toward earth at 3 mi (5 km) per second. Its luminosity is about 100 times that of the sun.

**Ardennes**, forested plateau in southeastern Belgium, northern Luxembourg, and northern France. The area is sparsely populated, with some agriculture and quarrying. It was a major battleground in World War I and World War II.

**Arendt, Hannah** (1906-75), German-born U.S. political philosopher. In 1959 she became the first woman appointed a full professor at Princeton University; she later taught at the University of Chicago and the New School for Social Research in New York. In *The Origins of Totalitarianism* (1951) she traced Nazism and Communism back to 19th-century anti-Semitism and imperialism. Her controversial *Eichmann in Jerusalem* (1963), with its theory of the "banality of evil," analyzed Nazi war crimes and the 1960 trial of Adolph Eichmann by the Israeli government.

**Areopagus**, small hill northwest of the Acropolis in Athens, where the supreme council of the city passed judgment on matters of state, religion, and morality. The name came to refer to the council itself. The Areopagus tried homicide cases, and it had a legislative veto and powers of impeachment.
*See also:* Solon.

**Arequipa** (pop. 634,800), city in southern Peru, capital of Arequipa department. Located at an altitude of 8,000 ft (2,400 m), between the Pacific Ocean and the Andes, Arequipa has a mild, dry climate. An important wool market and a crossroads of trade and transportation, its industries produce textiles, food, and shoes. Arequipa has frequently suffered severe damage from earthquakes.

**Ares**, in Greek mythology, the god of war. He was known to the Romans as Mars.

**Argentina**, second-largest country in South America (1,072,157 sq mi/2,776,889 sq km). Only Brazil is larger. Argentina borders on the Atlantic Ocean in the southeast; Uruguay, Brazil in the east, Paraguay in the northeast, Bolivia in the north, and Chile in the west.
*Land and climate.* The Andes Mountains form a natural border with Chile. The Gran Chaco region, in the north, is an extensive forested plain. Also in the north is the Paraná Plateau. The fertile Pampa in the heart of Argentina is the country's most important region economically. Semiarid Patagonia to the south yields oil. In the west, the Andes include Mt. Aconcagua (22,834 ft/6,960 m), the highest peak in South America. The climate of Argentina varies from damp and subtropical in the north to cool and dry in the south.
*People.* About 90% of the people are descended from Southern European immigrants, with a small Native American population. The national language is Spanish and about 90% of the population is Roman Catholic, with 87% living in urban areas like Buenos Aires.
*Economy.* Grain-growing and cattle-raising dominate the pampas, and agriculture is the basis of the country's wealth. Oil and other minerals come from the north and south. About 25% of the labor force works in the country's well-developed industrial sector, much of which is located in and around Buenos Aires. High inflation is chronic and persistent.
*History.* Colonized by the Spanish in the 16th century, Argentina won its independence in 1816. The 19th century saw increased European immigration, economic progress, and political instability and strife with repercussions well into the 20th century. In 1944, Col. Juan Perón seized power and ruled until 1955. His dictatorship was supported by nationalists, the army, and the Roman Catholic church. However, his rule depended in large measure upon the popularity of his wife, Eva Duarte de Perón, and her death (1952), combined with a bad economy, led to Perón's ouster (1955). The Perónist movement remained popular, and in 1973 Perón was restored to power. He died in 1974 and was succeeded by his wife, Isabel Perón, but the

## Argentina

| | |
|---|---|
| Capital: | Buenos Aires |
| Area: | 1,068,302 sq mi |
| | (2,766,889 sq km) |
| Population: | 36,265,000 |
| Language: | Spanish |
| Government: | Federal presidential |
| | republic |
| Independent: | 1816 |
| Head of gov.: | President |
| Per capita: | U.S. $8,030 |
| Mon. unit: | 1 Pesos = 100 centavos |

economy worsened and violence between left and right increased. Isabel Perón was overthrown in 1976 by military juntas. In reaction to terrorism from the left, the juntas, through their agents and surrogates, kidnapped and murdered some 20,000-30,000 Argentine citizens suspected of leftist sympathies. In 1982, Argentina occupied the Falkland Islands and was defeated by Britain in the subsequent war. Gen. Leopoldo Galtieri resigned and Raúl Alfonsin was elected president of a civilian government in 1983. Nine members of the juntas stood trial for murder and human rights abuses and were sentenced to long prison terms. Carlos Raúl Menem, a Perónist, was elected president in 1989 and started an austerity program to devitalize the economy. This program led to a decline of inflation, but at the same time increased unemployment.

**Argon**, chemical element, symbol Ar; for physical constants see Periodic Table. Argon was discovered by Lord Rayleigh and Sir William Ramsay in 1894. It is prepared by fractionation of liquid air, the atmosphere containing almost 1% of the element. Argon is a colorless, odorless, and chemically inert gas. It is not known to form chemical compounds, as do krypton, xenon, and radon. It is available in high purity, and is used in electric light bulbs, as a nonreactive shield in arc welding and in the production of reactive metals, and as a protective atmosphere for growing silicon, and germanium crystals.

**Argonaut**, or paper nautilus, small marine animal (genus *Argonauta*), a cephalopod which is native to the Mediterranean and other warm seas. Eggs are laid in a semitransparent, papery spiral shell that can be carried by the female. The male seldom reaches an inch in length, but the female may be as long as 6 in (15 cm) or more.

**Argonauts**, heroes of Greek mythology who set sail in the ship *Argo* under Jason to find the Golden Fleece. With many illustrious members (Orpheus, Hercules, Castor and Pollux, Theseus), they sailed for Colchis, where the fleece was guarded by a dragon. After averting many perils, they obtained the fleece and returned home.

**Argonne National Laboratory,** nuclear-power research center 25 mi (40 km) south of Chicago. The University of Chicago operates it for the U.S. Energy Research and Development Administration.

**Argus,** or Argos, in Greek mythology, (1) the designer of the Argonauts' ship *Argo*; (2) the old dog who died after recognizing his master, Odysseus, returning in disguise to his home in Ithaca after an absence of 19 years; (3) the monster called Panoptes (the all-seeing) because of the great number of eyes in his head and over his body. He was ordered by Hera to watch Io, who had been transformed into a cow, but Hermes killed him, and by Hera's orders, Argus's eyes were sprinkled as decorations through the tail of the peacock.

**Århus** (pop. 271,300), port and Denmark's second largest city. Developed by the 9th century. Århus is a commercial and industrial center producing textiles, machines, beer, and timber. It is the site of the Cathedral of St. Clemens, built around 1100, and of the University of Århus, foundened in 1928.

**Ariadne,** in Greek mythology, daughter of Minos, king of Crete. She loved the hero Theseus and gave him thread that helped him find his way out of the labyrinth. After Theseus killed the Minotaur, he married Ariadne but later deserted her. The god Bacchus gave her a crown of seven stars, which became a constellation.

**Arianism,** 4th-century Christian heresy founded in Alexandria by the priest Arius. He taught that Christ was not coequal and coeternal with God the Father, for the Father had created him. To curb Arianism, the Emperor Constantine called the first Council of Nicaea (A.D 325), and the first Nicene Creed declared that God the Father and Christ the Son were of the same substance.
*See also:* Nicene Councils.

**Arias Sánchez, Oscar** (1941- ), Costa Rican politician. He served as the president's financial adviser (1970-72), minister of national planning (1972-77), and president (1986-90). Arias Sánchez denied U.S.-supported Nicaraguan contras operating bases in Costa Rica, and promoted peaceful regional negotiations, for which he was awarded the Nobel Peace Prize in 1987.

**Ariosto, Ludovico** (1474-1533), Italian poet best remembered for the epic *Orlando Furioso* (1532), which continued the Roland legend, depicting the hero as a love-torn knight. The work greatly influenced later poets such as Edmund Spenser and Lord Byron.

**Aristarchus of Samos** (310-230 B.C.), Alexandrian Greek astronomer who recognized that the sun is larger than the earth. According to Archimedes, he taught that the earth orbited a motionless sun.
*See also:* Archimedes.

**Aristides** (530?-468? B.C ), called the Just, Athenian politician and general, a founder of the Delian League. He fought at the battle of Marathon (490 B.C ) and was elected archon for 489. Ostracized in 482, he was recalled in

480 and helped repulse the Persians. Later he fixed Greek cities' contributions to the Delian League.
*See also:* Themistocles.

**Aristocracy** (from Greek *aristos*, "the best," and *kratos*, "rule"), originally, the ruling of a state by its best citizens in the interest of all; used by the philosophers Plato and Aristotle in this sense. The term later came to mean a form of government dominated by a small privileged class. Today the term refers to members of a class that has hereditary privileges.

**Aristophanes** (450-385 B.C.), comic dramatist of ancient Greece. His works feature political, social, and literary satire, witty dialogue, vigorous rivalry, cleverly contrived comic situations, and choral lyrics. Eleven of his 40 plays survive, notably *The Frogs* (satirizing Euripides), *The Clouds* (satirizing Socrates), *Lysistrata* (a plea for pacifism), and *The Birds* (a fantasy about a sky city).
*See also:* Greece, Ancient; Theater.

**Aristotle** (384-322 B.C.), Greek philosopher, one of the most influential thinkers of the ancient world. He studied at Plato's academy in Athens in 343 B C and became the tutor of the young Alexander the Great. In 335 Aristotle set up his own school at the Lyceum in Athens. His works, covering a vast range of subjects, include *Physics*, *Metaphysics*, *On the Soul*, *On the Heavens*, *Poetics*, *Politics*, *Nicomachean Ethics*, and works on biology, aesthetics, rhetoric, and other subjects. Aristotle's writings reached the West through Latin translations in the 11th and 13th centuries, and had a prevailing influence on medieval and later thought. His emphasis on observation and analysis of the physical world, revolutionary for his time, underlies modern science. He developed the system of logic in use in the West until recent times.
*See also:* Greece, Ancient; Philosophy.

**Arithmetic** (Greek *arithmos*, "number"), science of numbers. Until the 16th century arithmetic was viewed as the study of all the properties and relations of all numbers; in modern times, the term usually denotes the study of the positive real numbers and zero under the operations of addition, subtraction, multiplication, and division.
*See also:* Mathematics.

**Ariyoshi, Sawako** (1931-84), Japanese writer of short stories, murder mysteries, and historical novels that explore the culture, traditions, social structure, and domestic problems of classical and modern Japan. Among her works are *Kokotsu No Hito*, *The Twilight Years*, *The River Ki*, *Compound Pollution*, *The Doctor's Wife*, *Diary of Princess Kazu*, and *The Curtain-Raising Bell Sounds Beautiful*.

**Arizona**, state in the southwest United States; bordered by Utah in the north, New Mexico in the east, Mexico in the south, and, across the Colorado River, Nevada and California in the west.
*Land and climate.* The Colorado Plateau to the north contains the Grand Canyon, the Painted Desert, the Petrified Forest, and Monument Valley. A mountain chain extends northwest to southeast through the Basin and Range

## Arizona

| | |
|---|---|
| Capital: | Phoenix |
| Statehood: | Feb. 14, 1912 (48th state) |
| Familiar name: | Grand Canyon State |
| Area: | 114,000 sq mi (295,260 km$^2$; ranks 6th) |
| Population: | 4,555,000 (1997; ranks 23th) |
| Elevation: | Highest—12,633 ft (3,851 m), Humphreys Peak |
| | Lowest—70 ft (21 m), Colorado River |
| Motto: | Didat deus (God Enriches) |
| State flower: | Saguaro (Giant Cactus) |
| State bird: | Cactus wren |
| State tree: | Paloverde |
| State song: | "Arizona" |

Region, while desert occupies the southwestern region. The most important river in Arizona is the Colorado. Although the desert climate is hot and dry, the mountain areas often have winter temperatures below 0°F (−18°C). Thirty-eight percent of all native American tribal lands are in Arizona. Principal cities are Phoenix, Tucson, and Tempe.

*Economy.* Manufacturing is the leading contributor to the state's wealth. The major manufactures are machinery, electronic and aeronautical products, and transportation equipment. With the aid of irrigation, Arizona's deserts become rich farmland. About 45% of farm income is from livestock products. Cotton is the principal cash crop.

Arizona is also rich in minerals, supplying half the nation's copper. The state's scenic attractions, native American reservations, and climate bring in millions of tourists each year.

*Government.* The state constitution, adopted in 1911, provides for an executive branch headed by a governor, who is elected for a 4-year term.

The state legislature is composed of 30 senators and 60 representatives, who serve 2-year terms. Arizona sends 2 senators and 5 representatives to the U.S. Congress.

*History.* Evidence of the cultures of the ancient Hohokam and Anasazi peoples is found in deserted cliff dwellings and irrigation works throughout the state.

The first European known to have visited Arizona was Marcos de Niza, a Franciscan friar, in 1539. In the late 17th century Spanish missionaries began to penetrate Arizona. Mexico gained control of the region in 1821. At the end of the Mexican War (1846-48), the terms of the Treaty of Guadalupe Hidalgo awarded Arizona north of the Gila River to the United States. The Gadsden Purchase in 1853 added the territory south of the Gila to form the present boundary between the United States and Mexico.

## Arkansas

| | |
|---|---|
| Capital: | Little Rock |
| Statehood: | June 15, 1836 (25th state) |
| Familiar name: | Land of Opportunity |
| Area: | 53,187 sq mi (137,754 km$^2$); ranks 27th) |
| Population: | 2,523,000 (1997; ranks 33rd) |
| Elevation: | Highest—2,753 ft (839 m), Magazine Mountain |
| | Lowest—55 ft (839 m), Ouachita River |
| Motto: | Regnat populus (The People Rule) |
| State flower: | Apple blossom |
| State bird: | Mockingbird |
| State tree: | Pine |
| State song: | "Arkansas" |

In 1863 Arizona Territory was created. The early period of U.S. rule in Arizona was troubled by a succession of Native American wars, ending with the surrender of the Apache chief, Geronimo, in 1886. During the first third of the 20th century, a series of federal dams and irrigation systems were developed, including the Hoover Dam in 1936, but the boom following World War II (1939-45) strained Arizona's water resources. In 1974 construction began on the Central Arizona Project, which is expected to bring water to Tucson in the early 1990s.

**Ark**, biblical vessel Noah built for protection from the great flood (Genesis 6-9); also, the Ark of the Covenant, the sacred chest of the Hebrews representing God's presence (Exodus 25). The word can refer to a basket, box, or coffer, and in the United States, to the flat riverboats used for transport during western expansion.
*See also:* Noah.

**Arkansas**, state in the south-central United States; bordered by Tennessee and Mississippi (east), Louisiana (south), Texas and Oklahoma (west), and Missouri (north).
*Land and climate.* Arkansas' major rivers include the Arkansas River, which bisects the state, and the Ouachita. The Ozark Plateau, or Mountains, in the northwest and Ouachita Mountains in the west-central part of the state make up the highland region, an area of rugged hills and valleys. Between these mountains lies the Arkansas Valley, which contains Magazine Mountain. Along the Mississippi River covering the eastern third of the state is vast alluvial plain. Hot Springs National Park is a famous resort. Arkansas has a mild, rainy climate. Principal cities are Little Rock, Fort Smith, and Pine Bluff.

*Economy.* The most important economic activity in Arkansas, manufacturing, includes processed foods, electrical equipment, and paper and wood products. Soybeans, rice, and cotton are the principal cash crops of the state. About a third of the nation's rice is grown in Arkansas. Livestock and poultry provide the largest part of the farm income. The state's leading mineral products are natural gas, oil, and bauxite. The only active diamond field in America is at Murfreesburo.

*Government.* Arkansas is governed by the constitution of 1874, which provides for 35 senators serving 4-year terms and 100 representatives serving 2-year terms. The governor is elected for a 2-year term. Arkansas sends 2 senators and 4 representatives to the U.S. Congress.

*History.* Hernando de Soto, the first European to explore Arkansas, led an expedition into the region in 1541. René-Robert Cavelier, Sieur de la Salle claimed the entire Mississippi Valley for France during his voyage down the river in 1682. Henri de Tonti established the first permanent white settlement in the region, Arkansas Post, in 1686. The area was acquired by the United States as a part of the Louisiana Purchase in 1803. Arkansas Territory was organized in 1819. In 1861 Arkansas joined the Confederacy. A group of Arkansans formed a union government 3 years later, giving the state 2 governments. Arkansas was readmitted to the Union in 1868. Manufacturing grew after World War II (1939-45) until the income derived from it passed the state's farm income in the early 1960s. In 1957 President Dwight D. Eisenhower sent federal troops to enforce a court order to integrate Central High School in Little Rock. Today, while Arkansas faces many problems, including an unstable farm economy, it continues to attract new residents.

**Arkansas River,** the longest tributary of the Mississippi-Missouri system, rising in the central Colorado Rocky Mountains and flowing SE 1,459 mi (2,339 km) to join the Mississippi near Greenville, Miss. The Arkansas is controlled by dams and reservoirs and is navigable to Tulsa, Okla.

**Ark of the Covenant,** wooden chest, overlaid inside and out with gold, containing the original Ten Commandments. The Ark was the most sacred religious object of ancient Israel, for the divine presence was believed to dwell within. It was installed in Solomon's temple but disappeared after the fall of Jerusalem and the destruction of the temple by Nebuchadnezzar in 586 B C

**Arkwright, Sir Richard** (1732-92), English industrialist and inventor of cotton carding and spinning machinery. In 1769 he patented a spinning frame that was the first machine able to produce cotton thread strong enough to use in the warp. He was a pioneer of the factory system of production, building several water- and later steam-powered mills.

**Arlington National Cemetery,** U.S. national cemetery in northern Virginia, established in 1864. More than 175,000 U.S. war dead and public figures are buried here. Monuments include the Tomb of the Unknown Soldier and the grave of John F. Kennedy, with its eternal flame.

**Armada,** fleet of armed ships, in particular Spain's "Invincible Armada," 130 ships carrying 30,000 men sent by Philip II in 1588 to seize control of the English Channel for an invasion of England. After battles with Charles

Howard and Sir Francis Drake, the Spaniards took refuge off Calais. Driven out by fire ships, the surviving vessels battled storms as they attempted to return home. Only half of the ships survived.

**Armadillo**, armored mammals (family Dasypodidae) of the order Edentata, native to warm regions of the Western Hemisphere. There are 20 species, ranging in length from about 5 in. (12 cm) to about 5 ft (1.5 m). Largely insectivorous (insect-eating), they are usually nocturnal and live in burrows either excavated by themselves or deserted by other animals. Armadillos generally produce several identical offspring from a single fertilized egg. *See also:* Edentate.

**Armageddon**, according to the Bible, the site of the world's last great battle, in which the powers of good will destroy the forces of evil (Revelation 16:16). The word derives from the name of an ancient city called "Megiddo" because of the many battles fought on its soil.

**Armagnac**, hilly farming area of southwestern France noted for its brandy. Count Bernard VII of Armagnac was virtual ruler of France in 1413-18. Armagnac passed to the French crown in 1607. The chief city, Auch, is a commercial center.

**Armenia**, republic in western Asia, bordered by Turkey, Azerbaijan, and Georgia.
*Land and climate*. Armenia is mountainous and the landscape extends from subtropical lowland to snow-covered peaks. Small mountain pastures provide rich grazing for sheep and cattle, and the valleys are fertile when irrigated. The climate is continental, with cold winters and hot summers.
*People*. The population is mainly Armenian (90%) with minorities of Kurds, Russians, Ukrainians, Greeks and Georgians. The majority of the inhabitants are Christians.
*Economy*. Armenia was highly industrialized during the Soviet period. The economy suffered severely as a result of the Nagorno-Karabach conflict with Azerbaijan.

---

### Armenia

| | |
|---|---|
| Capital: | Yerevan |
| Area: | 11,500 sq mi |
| | (29,800 sq km) |
| Population: | 3,422,000 |
| Language: | Armenian |
| Government: | Republic |
| Independent: | 1991 |
| Head of gov.: | President |
| Per capita: | U.S. $730 |
| Mon. unit: | 1 Dram= 100 luma |

*History*. Armenia was conquered in 328 B C by Alexander the Great and in 66 B.C. by Rome. In A D 303 it became the first country to make Christianity its state religion. Later it was successively under Byzantine, Persian, Arab, Seljuk, Mongol, and Ottoman Turkish control. An Armenian republic emerged after World War I but was swiftly absorbed by the USSR. In 1991 Armenia regained its independence. Armenia is part of the Commonwealth of Independent States. President Levon Ter-Petrosjan eliminated the opposition and had the press monitored by the state. In 1998, Robert Kocharian became the new president.
*See also:* Union of Soviet Socialist Republics.

**Armor**, protective body covering used in armed combat. The earliest armor consisted of boiled and hardened animal skins, but Roman soldiers wore armor made of iron. By the end of the 11th century, chain mail, a fabric of interlocking metal rings, was the standard form of armor. It provided poor protection against heavy blows, however, and the Middle Ages saw the development of full suits of metal plates with chain mail joints for flexibility. Full armor was used in Europe only until the 16th century. Modern armor employs nylon, fiberglass, and other synthetic materials.
*See also:* Knights and knighthood.

**Armory Show**, officially the International Exhibition of Modern Art, the first show of its kind in the United States, held at the 69th Regiment Armory, New York City, Feb.-Mar. 1913. Comprising over 1,300 works, it included a large section of paintings by contemporary Americans and works by modern European artists, including Constantin Brancusi, Georges Braque, Paul Cézanne, Marcel Duchamp, Henri Matisse, and Pablo Picasso. The avant-garde paintings caused much controversy but also the acceptance of modern art in the United States.

**Arms control** *See:* Disarmament; Strategic Arms Limitation Talks.

**Armstrong, Anne Legendre** (1927-    ), U.S. political figure. Appointed by President Richard M. Nixon in 1972, Armstrong was the first woman to hold the Cabinet-level position of counselor to the president, serving under Presidents Nixon and Gerald R. Ford. She was also the first woman to serve as U.S. ambassador to Great Britain, appointed by Ford in 1976 and 1977.

**Armstrong, Edwin Howard** (1890-1954), U.S. electronic engineer who developed the feedback concept for amplifiers (1912), invented the super-heterodyne circuit used in radio receivers (1918), and perfected FM radio (1925-39).
*See also:* Frequency modulation.

**Armstrong, Henry** (1912-88), U.S. boxer. Nicknamed "Perpetual Motion" for his aggressive style, he was the only fighter to hold 3 world championships (featherweight, welterweight, and lightweight) simultaneously (1938).

**Armstrong, Louis "Satchmo"** (1900-71), U.S. jazz musician renowned as a virtuoso trumpeter and singer. A master of improvisation, he was one of the most important figures in the early history of jazz. Satchmo grew up in New Orleans, moved to Chicago in 1922, and by the 1930s was internation-

ally famous. In later life he played at concerts around the world as goodwill ambassador for the U.S. State Department.
*See also:* Jazz.

**Armstrong, Neil Alden** (1930-   ), U.S. astronaut, first human to set foot on the moon. He studied aeronautical engineering at Purdue University (1947-55) with time out on active service in the Korean War. He joined NASA in 1962, commanding *Gemini 8* (1966) and landing the *Apollo 11* module on the moon on July 20, 1969.
*See also:* Astronaut.

**Armstrong, Samuel Chapman** (1839-93), U.S. educator and philanthropist. Colonel of a black regiment in the Civil War and agent of the Freedmen's Bureau (Virginia), Armstrong founded the Hampton Institute (1868), an industrial school for blacks and Native Americans.

**Armstrong, William Howard** (1914-   ), U.S. author. Armstrong is best known for the children's novel *Sounder*, the story of an African American sharecropping family in the Depression-era South, for which he won the 1970 Newbery Medal. Other works include *Barefoot in the Grass* (1970) and *Sour Land* (1971).

**Army,** land fighting force of a nation; more narrowly, a large unit of ground forces under a single commander. Primitive armies consisted of raiding parties that waged individual combat using stones and clubs. Later, horses and chariots increased the mobility of armies, while the development of artillery extended their range. Formation tactics evolved with the Macedonian phalanx and Roman legion. The 20th-century army depends upon technology. Because of the ongoing development of weapons and detection systems, modern armies must be highly mobile, a need that has blurred the traditional distinctions between army, navy, and air force. Nuclear weaponry has taken the range of firepower to its limits, and the value of tactical formations has largely been eliminated by radar, making unconventional units (guerrillas, paratroops) increasingly important.
*See also:* Army, U.S.

**Army, Department of the,** division of the U.S. Department of Defense. Headed by the secretary of the Army, the department serves as U.S. Army headquarters and directs the U.S. land forces. It is located in Washington, D.C.
*See also:* Defense, Department of; Army, U.S.

**Army, U.S.,** branch of U.S. armed forces organized to fight any war, local or global, conventional or atomic. The highest ranking officer is the chief of staff, answerable to the secretary of the army, a civilian who in turn is responsible to the secretary of defense and the president. Under the chief of staff come several major commands: the Continental Army Command, responsible for U.S. ground defense; the Air Defense Command; the Army Materiel Command, charged with procuring equipment and weapons for army units; and the Army Combat Development Command, which equips and organizes army units. The total strength of the all-volunteer U.S. Army in 1989 was 760,000. In addition, an almost equal number of men and women serve in the Army Reserve and National Guard. Members of active and reserve units were used extensively in the 1991 Persian Gulf War.

**Army War College**, senior educational institution of the U.S. Army, founded 1901 in Washington, D.C., by Elihu Root, then secretary of War. Its curriculum is designed to prepare students, usually high-ranking officers, to deal with security issues, military strategy, war operations, and Army doctrine.
*See also:* Root, Elihu.

**Army worm**, any of several species of voracious caterpillars that travel in masses, causing severe crop damage; especially the common army worm (*Pseudaletia unipuncta*). The common army worm is the larva of a brown moth found in North America east of the Rocky Mountains. The eggs, laid in grass or on small grains, hatch into small worms that, if not controlled by parasites or pesticides, devour everything within reach and then migrate in armies to new feeding grounds.

**Arnhem** (pop. 134,700), capital of the province Gelderland in the east Netherlands, located on the north bank of the Rhine River, about 60 mi (100 km) east of Rotterdam. A major river port with shipyards and a large tin refinery, Arnhem produces textiles, furniture, leather goods, and synthetic fibers. The city was seriously damaged in September 1944, when it was the site of one of the largest Allied paratroop landings in World War II.

**Arnica**, genus of plants of which the flowers and rootstock are used for medicinal purposes. The horizontal, dark-brown, branched rootstock of the arnica sends up a slightly hairy simple or tightly branched stem that reaches a height of 1-2 ft (30-61 cm). The basal leaves are oblong-ovate with short stems.

**Arnold, Benedict** (1741-1801), general and traitor in the American Revolution. He fought outstandingly for the American cause at Ticonderoga (1775) and Saratoga (1777) and in 1778 received command of Philadelphia. In 1780 Arnold assumed the command of West Point and with John André plotted its surrender to the British in revenge for past criticisms. André's capture forced Arnold to flee to the British side, and in 1781 he went into exile in London.
*See also:* Revolutionary War in America.

**Arnold, Henry "Hap" Harley** (1886- 1950), pioneer aviator and U.S. Air Force general who helped build U.S. air power and develop the Air Force as a unified separate service. Arnold held several early flying records, became chief of the U.S. Army Air Corps (1938), headed the Army Air Forces in World War II, and was made general of the Army (1944), a title later changed to general of the Air Force.

**Arnold, Matthew** (1822-88), English poet and literary critic. His poetry, as represented by *Empedocles on Etna* (1852) and *New Poems* (1867), is mainly introspective, though Arnold also achieved a classical impersonality. Both in his poetry and in his criticism—*Culture and Anarchy* (1869), *Literature* *and Dogma* (1873)—Arnold showed a keen awareness of the changing cultural climate of his time.

**Arnold of Brescia** (c.1100-50), Italian religious reformer and political activist who strongly opposed the temporal power of the pope. He was a supporter of Peter Abelard, with whom he was condemned at the Council of Sens in 1140. In 1147 Arnold, a great orator, became leader of the rebellion that had suppressed papal authority in Rome and replaced it by a republic. On the collapse of the republic, Arnold fled to Campania but was captured, delivered to the pope by Emperor Frederick Barbarossa, and executed as a heretic.

**Arno River**, river in central Italy, about 150 mi (241 km) long. Its source lies in the Apennine Mountains, from which it flows through the city of Florence, emptying into the Ligurian Sea below Pisa. Much of its valley is a fertile plain where olives and grapes are grown.

**Arpád**, dynasty of Hungarian rulers founded by Arpád (c.840-907), around whose life countless heroic legends are woven. In 890 he became chief of the Magyars and 6 years later led the conquest of Hungary and proceeded to lay the foundations for a strong, centralized state. His successors ruled as dukes of Hungary and replaced the predominantly nomadic Magyar culture by one based on agriculture and firm central rule.

**Arp, Jean**, or **Hans** (1887-1966), French sculptor, painter, and poet. Briefly associated with the expressionist art movement Der Blaue Reiter, he was a cofounder of Dada in Zürich (1916). He was also one of the best known exponents of the surrealist movement. Starting in the 1930s he created sculptures and reliefs notable for their elemental purity and strength.
*See also:* Dada; Surrealism.

**Arraignment**, appearance of a person in a court of law to plead guilty or not guilty to legal charges. Before or after entering this plea, the defendant may also enter various motions in his or her own behalf, such as requesting a change of venue (moving the place where the trial is to be held) or a continuance (allowing more time to prepare the case), and the defendant can even challenge the validity of the arrest and trial. If the defendant is not yet represented by a lawyer, the court may appoint one.

**Arrau, Claudio** (1903-91), Chilean pianist. A child prodigy, he was noted throughout his long career mainly for his performances of the Romantic composers, such as Brahms.

**Arrest**, taking into custody of a person believed to have committed a crime. Most often an arrest is made by police or other law-enforcing officer on the strength of a warrant issued by a court and supported by evidence indicating that the named person or persons have probably committed a crime. As a general rule, and in most states, arrests may be made without a warrant only when the arresting officer has evidence that a felony (serious crime) has been committed; and on the basis of suspicious behavior, even when there is no evidence of an actual felony. A private person may sometimes make a "citizen's arrest" for a crime he or she sees committed.

**Arrhythmia,** irregularity in rhythm of the heartbeat, either in time or force. Arrhythmias are often extra heartbeats that cause no serious problems, although sometimes the heart rhythm can become dangerously slow or fast or is disruptive to heart function.

**Arrow** *See:* Archery.

**Arrow, Kenneth Joseph** (1921-  ), U.S. economist, former professor at Harvard and adviser on economic affairs to the U.S. government. In 1972 he won the Nobel Prize in economic science.

**Arrowroot,** plant (genus *Maranta*) native to warm, humid regions of the Western Hemisphere; also, form of starch from the rhizomes (underground stems) of the arrowroot plant and various other tropical plants. Easily digested, arrowroot is valued as a food for children and people with delicate stomachs, and is used as a thickening agent in sauces.

**Arsenic,** chemical element, symbol As; for physical constants see Periodic Table. Arsenic has been known since ancient times. Elemental arsenic was first described by Albertus Magnus in the 13th century. Sometimes found native, it occurs widely in the form of arsenides, from which the element is obtained as a byproduct. Arsenic is a soft and brittle gray element with a metallic luster which sublimes without melting; several other allotropic forms have been reported. The metal conducts electricity moderately well. Arsenic is used in bronzing, hardening, and improving the sphericity of metal shot, and in pyrotechnics. Compounds of arsenic are used as agricultural insecticides and poisons. Arsenic in high purity is used as a doping agent in solid-state devices. Gallium arsenide is used as a laser material to convert electricity directly into coherent light. Arsenic and its compounds are poisonous.

**Artagnan, Charles d'** (1620-73), French soldier whose name was immortalized by the swashbuckling character d'Artagnan in Alexandre Dumas's *The Three Musketeers.* The real d'Artagnan served bravely in the armies of Louis XIII and Louis XIV and rose to the rank of brigadier general before his death at the siege of Maastricht.

**Art and the arts,** skill of making or doing. The term can be used to define useful arts (beautiful objects that have functional value), decorative arts (beautiful objects that exist for their own sake), liberal arts (the study of humanities), applied arts (such as architecture), language arts (the related skills of reading, writing, speaking, and spelling), and graphic arts (such as printmaking and bookmaking). However, the term *art* is most often used to describe the fine arts, which consist of painting, sculpture, literature, dance, music, and film. Works of art can be classified as verbal (literature) or nonverbal (musical composition and visual design). Mixed arts, a combination of 2 or more basic arts, include dance, drama, and film. Theories of art which attempt to define its meaning, explain its effects, assess its worth, set guidelines for its execution, or provide a historical or social context for its interpretation have existed since the ancient Greeks and continue to be a subject of discussion among artists, scholars, and critics.

**Art deco**, style of design popular in the United States and Europe from the late 1920s through the 1930s. In its emphasis on geometrical shapes and simplified lines, art deco represented a radical reaction to the ornateness of Victorian design. The style was applied in architecture, interior decoration, furnituremaking, and the design of a wide range of objects from locomotives to salt-and-pepper shakers. Prime examples are the Chrysler Building and the interior of Radio City Music Hall in New York City.

**Artemis**, in Greek mythology, virgin goddess of the hunt. Apollo's twin, the daughter of Zeus and Leto, Artemis is usually pictured carrying a bow and arrows or a torch. She presided over wild animals and is primarily known as the goddess of the hunt. Although Artemis was a stern protector of chastity, she also watched over women in childbirth. She was worshipped as goddess of the waters; fruit, grain, and domestic animals were sacrificed to her at harvest time. Artemis is also sometimes known as the moon goddess, probably through identification with the huntress Diana, Roman goddess of the moon.

**Arteriosclerosis**, generic term for disease of the arteries in which their walls become thickened and rigid, and blood flow is hindered, often resulting in heart disease or stroke. The most common form of arteriosclerosis is atherosclerosis, in which fatty deposits accumulate on the artery walls, which then tend to harden. Research indicates that there probably is a connection between atherosclerosis and a bacterium (Chlamydia pneumoniae). This bacterium allegedly accelerates the accumulation of fat in the artery and might be responsible for the development of small wounds in the artery walls. *See also:* Artery.

**Artery**, blood vessel that carries blood away from the heart to other parts of the body. The two main arteries are the pulmonary artery and the aorta. The pulmonary artery carries blood from the right side of the heart to the lungs to be reoxygenated; the aorta, the main arterial vessel, carries oxygen-enriched blood to the body from the left side of the heart. The main arteries are quite large, the aorta being about the width of a garden hose (about 1 in/2.5 cm in diameter). Major arteries branch from the aorta to supply each limb and organ, dividing repeatedly down to the arterioles, which in turn supply the capillaries, located in body tissue. The structure of artery walls accounts for their strength and elasticity and makes them well suited to resisting the stress of the pulsating flow of blood. *See also:* Arteriosclerosis.

**Artesian well**, well in which water rises under hydrostatic pressure above the level of the aquifer (water-bearing layer of rock) in which it has been confined. True artesian wells (named for the French province of Artois, where they were first constructed) flow without assistance. *See also:* Ground water.

**Arthritis**, inflammation of a joint, usually accompanied by pain and frequently by changes in structure. The two most widespread arthritic disorders, osteoarthritis and rheumatoid arthritis, are usually chronic problems for which there is no cure, though modern medicine can now do a good deal to control them. Two or three times more women than men are affected by

osteoarthritis, and women have the most serious form. rheumatoid arthritis, three times as often.
*See also:* Joint.

**Arthropod**, largest and most diverse phylum of the animal kingdom, containing insects, millipedes, centipedes, crustacea, arachnida, and king crabs. Arthropods are characterized by a segmented exoskeleton (external skeleton) with joined limbs that is shed at intervals, the animal emerging in a new, soft exoskeleton that has developed beneath; often this molting is followed by rapid growth. Molting may cease on attainment of adulthood, but many crustacea molt periodically throughout their lives.

**Arthroscopy**, technique used to visualize the interior of a joint. Using a fiber-optic endoscope (arthroscope) inserted into the joint through a small incision, a doctor can perform a thorough examination and certain surgical operations. Arthroscopy is most commonly used to treat torn cartilage in the knee, although arthroscopic procedures of the shoulder, elbow, and hip are also common. The low morbidity associated with this procedure makes it useful in a variety of joint disorders as an adjunct to diagnosis, to determine prognosis, and as a treatment.

**Arthur, Chester Alan** (1830-86), 21st president of the United States. Arthur was vice president under James A. Garfield and became president on Garfield's assassination. Probably his most important accomplishment as president was his support for reforms in the federal civil service system.
*Lawyer.* Arthur was the son of a Baptist minister and schoolteacher from Northern Ireland. He graduated from Union College in Schenectady, N.Y. in 1847 and taught school while studying law. In 1853 he joined a New York City law office and was admitted to the bar the following year. Arthur soon gained a reputation as a progressive attorney in two important civil rights cases.
Arthur opened his law firm in 1856 and became active in Republican party politics in New York State. During the Civil War he was given several honorary posts on the Republican governor's military staff.
*Politician.* Arthur returned to his law practice in 1863, and remained active in politics. President Ulysses Grant appointed him customs collector for the Port of New York in 1871. The customs house was notorious for being staffed with political appointees who paid part of their salaries into the party treasury.

---

**Chester Alan Arthur**

21st U.S. president

| | |
|---|---|
| Born: | Fairfield, Vermont; October 5, 1830 |
| Term: | September 1881 - March 1885 |
| Vice President: | None (Arthur succeeded to the presidency on the death of President James A. Garfield) |
| Political Party: | Republican |
| Spouse: | Ellen Lewis Herndon Arthur |
| Children: | 2 |
| Died: | New York City; November 18, 1886 |

While Arthur performed his official duties conscientiously, he made little effort to change the system of rewarding party workers with government jobs. In July 1878 President Rutherford B. Hayes, seeking to reduce procedures at the customs house, had Arthur removed from his post. Two years later the Republican party chose Arthur as its candidate for vice president, with James A. Garfield running for president.

*President.* Garfield and Arthur won the election of 1880, but Garfield's term as president was brief. He was shot by a disappointed office-seeker, Charles J. Guiteau, on July 2, 1881, and died on September 19. Arthur was sworn in as president the following day.

The assassination led to a widespread demand for a new system of civil service appointments. To the surprise of most people, Arthur strongly supported the proposed reforms. He signed into law the Pendleton Civil Service Act in January 1883. This law opened the way to the eventual elimination of the worst excesses of the spoils system in national politics. Arthur sought renomination at the Republican convention of 1884, but he was defeated on the fourth ballot by James G. Blaine. After leaving the presidency, he resumed his law practice in New York City, where he died less than 2 years later.

**Arthur, King,** legendary British king, subject of tales and poems dating back to the 7th century. Although there are many variations of the story, which probably arose out of Irish heroic folktales, all of these have certain common elements: Arthur wins recognition as king by pulling a sword (Excalibur) from a stone; he reigns from his castle at Camelot; his Knights of the Round Table, including such heroes as Lancelot and Tristram, engage in heroic quests and illicit sexual unions.

**Artichoke** (*Cynara scolymus*), tall, thistlelike perennial plant of the composite family; also, its globe-shaped flower bud, the heart and spiny bracts of which are eaten as a vegetable. Native to the Mediterranean region, the artichoke is grown commercially in warm regions of the U.S.

*See also:* Jerusalem artichoke.

**Articles of Confederation,** first written constitutional structure for the United States, drafted in 1776-77, but ratified by 13 states only in 1781. The Articles established a weak national government based on a Congress, dependent on the states for funds and for executive functions. "Sovereignty, freedom, and independence" remained vested with the separate states, and there were no federal courts. The shortcomings of the Articles were recognized when the Constitutional Convention of 1787 abandoned them in favor of the present United States Constitution, which was ratified in 1789.

*See also:* Congress of the Confederation; Constitution of the United States; Continental Congress.

**Articles of War,** code adopted in 1775 by the Continental Congress to guide administration of justice and discipline in the Continental Army. The articles were based on British Army Code. Revised many times, they were replaced in 1950 by the Uniform Code of Military Justice.

**Artificial insemination,** introduction of sperm into the vagina by means other than copulation. The technique, widely used for breeding livestock as it produces many offspring from 1 selected male, has a limited use in treating human impotence and sterility. In humans, the procedure is timed to coincide with the woman's ovulation. If she has a regular 28-day menstrual cycle, insemination should be performed as many as 3 times between the 10th and the 14th days of the cycle.

**Artificial intelligence** (AI), use of computers to perform functions normally associated with human intelligence, such as reasoning, learning, and self-improvement. The question of whether it is possible to develop machines that genuinely "think" in the same sense that humans do is one of the most controversial issues in the computer sciences.

**Artificial limb,** device to replace missing hands, feet, arms, or legs. Prosthetics, the branch of medicine dealing with artificial limbs, has developed rapidly since World War I. Prosthetic devices are now complex mechanisms made of materials such as aluminum alloys, rubber, and plastics. Some of them are capable of mimicking the use of human limbs to a considerable extent.

**Artificial organ,** mechanical device designed to assume the functions of an organ of the body, particularly during surgical procedures. The 3 most commonly used artificial organs are the heart-lung machine, the artificial kidney, and (since 1985) the artificial heart, still in an experimental stage.

**Artificial sweetener,** synthetic substance, usually saccharin, aspartame, or acesulfame-K, used in place of sucrose (table sugar) to sweeten food and beverages. The U.S. Food and Drug Administration regulates the use of artificial sweeteners and has banned some of them as possible cancer risks.

**Artificial turf,** grasslike product of nylon or other synthetic material used to carpet athletic playing fields and also used in outdoor landscaping. It came into widespread use during the 1960s.

**Artigas, José Gervasio** (1764-1850), Uruguayan military leader who championed the cause of national independence. He joined the 1810 Argentine revolt against Spanish rule but later fought against both Portuguese and Argentine troops. He was forced into exile after Brazil occupied Montevideo in 1820. An independent Uruguay was achieved only in 1828.

**Artillery,** once the term for all military machinery, now applied to guns too heavy to be carried by one or two soldiers. Modern artillery had its origins in the 14th century, when weapons using gunpowder were first developed. Its use became more important as equipment became more mobile, accurate, and effective. World War II saw the development of antitank and antiaircraft guns and the first effective use of rockets. The most modern artillery is often made of light, tough alloys, and targeting systems draw on laser and radar technology.

**Art nouveau,** late 19th-century art movement that influenced decorative styles throughout the West. Its themes were exotic or decadent, its characteristic line sinuous and highly ornamental. The movement aimed to reunite art and life, and so to produce everyday objects of beauty. Some notable architecture, furniture, jewelry, and book designs were produced in this style. The graphic arts were much affected by art nouveau, as seen in the work of Aubrey Beardsley. Other notable artists were the painter Gustav Klimt, the architects Antonio Gaudi and Victor Horta, and applied artists Louis Comfort Tiffany and René Lalique.

**Aruba** (pop. 70,000), island off the Venezuelan coast, part of the Netherlands Antilles, about 19 mi (30.6 km) long and 4 mi (6.4 km) wide. Its capital is Oranjestad. The chief industry is the refining of crude oil imported from Venezuela. Other important aspects of the economy are tourism and banking. On Jan. 1, 1986, Aruba became a semi-independent state. However, contributions made by the Dutch government are still necessary.

**Arum**, common name of certain plants of the Araceae family, including lily, philodendron, and elephant's ear.

**Aryan** (Sanskrit, "noble" or "ruler"), name originally applied to peoples who invaded the Indus Valley in India about 1500 B C As a linguistic term, Aryan applies to speakers of Indo-European languages. As a racial category—used by the Nazis to designate Germans and other North Europeans—the term has no valid basis and has been discredited as an instrument of bigotry.

**Asafetida**, foul-smelling substance extracted from the roots of an Asian herb. Asafetida has long had a mystical significance and was often used in magical ceremonies or worn as an amulet to keep away evil spirits. It was also once used in medicine as a sedative. The plant belongs to the carrot family (Umbelliferae).

**Asante** *See:* Ashanti.

**Asbestos**, name for various fibrous minerals, such as chrysotile, used as noncombustible material. Canada and the USSR are the chief producers. It can be spun to make fireproof fabrics or molded to make tiles, bricks, and automobile brake linings. If inhaled, asbestos particles cause lung cancer and asbestosis, a serious lung disease.

**Asbury, Francis** (1745-1816), first Methodist bishop in the United States, elected 1784. Born in England, he came to the United States in 1771 as a missionary and played a major role in the spread of Methodism. *See also:* Methodists.

**Asbury Park** (pop. 17,015), Atlantic Coast resort in eastern New Jersey, founded in 1871 as a religious meeting place and incorporated as a city in 1897. It is known primarily as a convention center and summer resort. It is also the birthplace of rock star Bruce Springsteen.

**ASCAP** *See:* American Society of Composers, Authors and Publishers.

**Ascension, The,** in Christian belief, the bodily ascent of Jesus Christ into heaven on the 40th day after his resurrection. Ascension Day is a major Christian festival.
*See also:* Jesus Christ.

**Asceticism,** self-denial or self-mortification in the interest of heightening spiritual powers. The term was first used by the ancient Greeks to describe the discipline of athletic training, but was later applied by Stoicists to the conquest of the body and its   desires as a means to spiritual awareness. The practice is an essential means of escape from matter in Hindu and Buddhist belief
*See also:* Stoicism.

**Asch, Sholem** (1880-1957), Yiddish novelist and playwright. Born in Poland, he spent most of his life in the United States. His many books deal with Jewish life in both countries and with the relationship between Judaism and Christianity.

**ASCII,** acronym for American Standard Code for Information Interchange, the character code used for representing information by most non-IBM equipment.
*See also:* Computer.

**Asclepius,** in Greek mythology, the god of healing, who became so skilled that he attempted to resurrect the dead, thus angering Zeus, who struck him dead with a thunderbolt. The medical profession has adopted his symbol, a staff entwined by a snake.

**Ascorbic acid** *See:* Vitamin.

**Asexual reproduction** *See:* Reproduction.

**Asgard,** or Aesir, in Norse mythology, the realm of the gods. It contained many halls and palaces; chief of these was Valhalla, where Odin entertained warriors killed in battle. The only entry to Asgard was by the rainbow bridge called Bifrost.

**Ash,** tree or shrub (genus *fraxinus*) of the olive family. The hard, elastic wood of the white ash (*F. americana*) is used for items like mallets and baseball bats; that of the blue ash (*F. quadrangulata*) for barrel hoops, furniture veneers, and baskets.

**Ashanti,** or Asante, region of central Ghana, in West Africa, inhabited by the people of the same name. From the 17th century to 1902, when Britain militarily took over the region, the powerful Ashanti Confederacy linked several kingdoms under one chief. The symbol of their unity was the sacred Golden Stool.

**Ashbery, John** (1927-), U.S. poet of unconventional style, whose poems are experimental, fragmentary, and dreamlike. Associated with the poets of the "New York School," Ashbery is also an art critic. His *Self-Portrait in a Convex Mirror* won the Pulitzer Prize for poetry in 1975. Other works include *Some Trees* (1956), *The Tennis Court Oath* (1962), and *A Wave* (1984).

**Ashcan School**, or "The Eight," name given to a group of painters in New York City, formed in 1908, because they painted everyday aspects of city life. The Eight—Arthur Davies, William Glackens, Ernest Lawson, George Luks, Maurice Prendergast, Everett Shinn, Robert Henri, and John Sloan—differed in many ways but were united in their dislike of academicism. They were instrumental in organizing the Armory Show in New York in 1913, which introduced modern European art to the American public.

**Ashcroft, Dame Peggy** (1907-91), British stage actress. She is best known for her roles in *Dear Brutus*, *Othello*, *The School for Scandal*, and *The Merchant of Venice*.

**Ashe, Arthur** (1943-93), U.S. tennis player. As a student at UCLA, he won the NCAA singles and doubles titles (1966). He became the first African-American (and the first U.S. player since 1955) to win the U.S. Men's National Singles Championship (1968). He won the Australian Open (1970) and the men's singles title at Wimbledon (1975). Since 1983 he served as nonplaying captain of the U.S. Davis Cup team. He also wrote *A Hard Road to Glory: a History of the African American Athletes*.
In 1992 he founded the Ashe Foundation to fight AIDS. He was infected with this disease while being given a blood transfusion.

**Asheville** (pop. 174,821), city and resort in the Appalachian Mountains, western North Carolina, seat of Buncombe County, near the Great Smoky Mountains National Park and the Blue Ridge Parkway. Asheville is a processing center for a rich agricultural region. Local industries produce textiles, leather goods, and wood products. Founded in 1794 and chartered as a city in 1883, it is the birthplace of the writer Thomas Wolfe and is described in his novels.

**Ashkenazim**, Jews whose medieval ancestors lived in Germany. Persecution drove them to spread throughout central and eastern Europe and, in the 19th and 20th centuries, overseas, notably to the United States. Their ritual and Hebrew pronunciation differ from those of Sephardim (Jews originally from Spain and Portugal). Most of the Jews in the United States and the majority of the world's Jews are Ashkenazim.

**Ashland** (pop. 27,064), city in northern Kentucky on the Ohio River, the seat of Boyd County. It lies in a region of coal, natural gas, and oil deposits and is an important center for iron, steel, and petroleum. The city was settled in 1815 and incorporated in 1870.

**Ashton, Sir Frederick** (1906-88), British dancer and choreographer. Among his influential works are *Façade* (1931) and *La Fille Mal Gardée* (1960). He was director of the Royal Ballet from 1963 to 1970.

**Ashurbanipal**, or Assurbanipal (d. 626? B.C.), last of the great kings of Assyria, ruled 669-633 B.C. over an empire that included Babylonia, Syria, and Palestine. Though troubled by numerous revolts, his reign was prosper-

ous. He established the library of cuneiform tablets in Nineveh, discovered in the 1840s.
*See also:* Babylonia and Assyria.

**Ash Wednesday,** 40th weekday before Easter Sunday and the first day of the Christian fast of Lent. The name derives from the early practice of sprinkling penitents with ashes. Today the ash of burnt palms is used to mark the sign of the cross on the foreheads of believers.

**Asia,** world's largest continent, more than 17,139,000 sq mi/44,390,000 sq km (nearly 1/3 of the earth's land), with about 3.1 billion people (more than 60% of the world population). It extends from the Arctic Ocean to the Indian Ocean, and from the Pacific Ocean to the Mediterranean. Its traditional border with Europe is formed by the Ural Mountains. Asia is separated from Africa by the Red Sea and the Suez Canal. The combined land mass of Europe and Asia is sometimes treated as a single continent, Eurasia
Asia is a continent of physical contrast, with Mt. Everest (29,028 ft/8,848 m), the world's highest mountain, and the Dead Sea (1,292 ft/394 m below sea level). At its heart is the system of mountain chains and high plateaus that includes the Karakoram Range, Himalayas, Kunlun Shan, Tien Shan, Altai Mountains, Hindu Kush, and Sulaiman Range. The major rivers include the Ob and its tributary, the Irtysh, the Yenisey, and the Lena, all flowing to the Arctic Ocean; the Indus (Pakistan), Ganges (India and Bangladesh), and Brahmaputra (China and India); and the Yellow and Yangtze rivers (China). Lake Baikal (Russian Federation) is the largest freshwater lake. Deserts include the Gobi Desert in Mongolia and the Great Sandy Desert of Arabia. The cultural regions of the continent are East Asia (China, Korea, Japan), South Asia (India, Pakistan, Sri Lanka), Southeast Asia (Malaysia, Indonesia, etc.), and the Middle East.
The countries of Asia are Afghanistan, Armenia, Azerbaijan, Bahrain, Bangladesh, Bhutan, Brunei, Burma, Byelorussia, China, Cyprus, part of Egypt, Georgia, India, part of Indonesia, Iran, Iraq, Israel, Japan, Jordan, Kampuchea, Kazakhstan, Kirghizstan, Kuwait, Laos, Lebanon, Malaysia, Maldives, Mongolia, Nepal, North Korea, Oman, Pakistan, Philippines, Qatar, Russian Federation, Saudi Arabia, Singapore, South Korea, Sri Lanka, Syria, Tadjikistan, Taiwan, Thailand, part of Turkey, Turkmenistan, United Arab Emirates, Uzbekistan, Vietnam, and the Republic of Yemen.

**Asia Minor,** peninsula in southwestern Asia including most of modern Turkey, mountainous and surrounded on 3 sides by the Black and Mediterranean seas, bounded on the east by the upper Euphrates River. After the destruction of the Hittite empire c.1200 B C., the land was occupied successively by the Medes, Persians, Greeks, and Romans. In the 5th century of the present era it passed to the Byzantine emperors. It was settled by Turks beginning in the 13th century and became part of the Ottoman Empire in the fifteenth. The modern Turkish state was founded in 1923.

**Asimov, Isaac** (1920-92), prolific (almost 400 books) U.S. author, biochemist, and educator, known for his science fiction works, including the *Foundation* trilogy (1951-53, 1982) and *The Gods Themselves* (1972), as well as for his many popular works on various fields of science and general knowledge.

**Asmara** (pop. 275,400), capital of Eritrea. The city is situated on a plateau about 7,000 ft (2,134 m) above sea level and has road and rail connections to the interior and to the Red Sea port of Massawa, about 40 mi (64 km) away. Industrial centre with production of textiles, soap and food. Seized by Italy in 1889, the town became the administrative seat of the colony of Eritrea in 1900. Awarded to Ethiopia by the UN in 1952, Eritrea became a province in 1962. From the 1970s the Eritrean guerillas waged a war of independence and the control of Asmara has been contested. When Asmara was captured by the Eritreans in the early 1990s independence was on its way and formally achieved in 1993.

**Asoka** (d.232 B C), third emperor of the Maurya dynasty of India, whose acceptance of Buddhism as the official religion of his vast empire contributed to that faith's predominance in Asia. He was said to have been so repelled by a particularly bloody victory of his troops over what is now Orissa that he turned to nonviolence and the Buddhist way of righteousness, and sent missionaries into Burma, Ceylon (Sri Lanka), Syria, Greece, and Egypt. *See also:* Buddhism.

**Asp**, Egyptian cobra (*Naja haja*) of the family Elapidae, an extremely poisonous snake up to 7 ft (2 m) in length. Considered sacred in ancient Egypt, it was, according to legend, the snake that killed Cleopatra. The name is also applied to several species of vipers. *See also:* Cobra.

**Asparagus**, garden vegetable (*Asparagus officinalis*) of the lily family, a perennial plant cultivated for its tender stalks. A well-tended asparagus bed may yield heavy crops for as long as 20 years. The main asparagus-growing areas in the U.S. are California and New Jersey. One variety of asparagus is grown for its attractive foliage alone.

**Aspartame** *See:* Artificial sweetener.

**Aspasia** (5th century B C), learned woman from Miletus, mistress of the Athenian statesman Pericles, by whom she had a son, Pericles the Younger. Her house was the literary and social gathering place for intellectual Athenians. She was the target of many spiteful attacks, mainly by conservatives who did not dare confront Pericles himself. Pericles was compelled to defend her against a charge of "impiety" in 432 B C.

**Aspen** (pop. 3,678), town in south-central Colorado and seat of Pitkin County. In the late 19th century, Aspen (originally Ute City) was a flourishing silver-mining town, but its prosperity declined when ore deposits were exhausted. Located in the Rockies, at an altitude of 8,000 ft (2,438 m), it has become a year-round resort, with world-famous skiing facilities and a noted summer cultural festival.

**Aspen**, deciduous tree of the poplar genus widely distributed in north temperate regions, commercially valued as a source of pulp and matches. The best known varieties in the U.S. and Canada are the large-toothed aspen (*Populus grandidentata*) and the quaking aspen (*P. tremuloides*), a smaller tree with broad, delicate foliage that trembles with the slightest breeze.

**Asphalt,** tough black material made of heavy hydrocarbons and used in road paving, roofing, and canal and reservoir lining. Although natural deposits are still used, asphalt is now obtained mainly from petroleum refinery residues.

**Asphodel,** perennial herbaceous plant (genera *Asphodelus* and *Asphodeline*) of the lily family, with white or yellow flowers along the stalk. The yellow asphodel, or Jacob's rod, is often cultivated as an ornamental plant. Native to southern Europe and India, the asphodel was considered the flower of Hades by the ancient Greeks.

**Asphyxiation,** complex of symptoms resulting from a lack of oxygen or excess of carbon dioxide in the lungs. The commonest causes are drowning, suffocation or strangulation, inhalation of poisonous gases, and the obstruction of the larynx, trachea, or bronchi (as in severe cases of croup and asthma).

**Aspidistra,** perennial plant (*Aspidistra lurida*) of the lily family, with sturdy leaves, once a widely grown houseplant. Native to China, Java, and Japan, aspidistras bear small blue flowers close to the ground and have particularly attractive foliage.

**Aspirin,** or acetylsalicylic acid, effective painkiller that reduces fever and inflammation. It is useful in treating headache, minor fever, menstruation pain, rheumatic fever, inflammatory arthritis, and may help in the prevention of thrombosis (blood clots). Possible side effects include gastrointestinal irritation and hemorrhage.

**Asquith, Herbert Henry, 1st Earl of Oxford and Asquith** (1852-1928), English prime minister, 1908-16. His term as head of the Liberal Party was one of great activity and political reform, but his leadership foundered in Dec. 1916 over his conduct of World War I, coupled with the chaos brought about by the Easter Rising in Ireland. He resigned in favor of the rival Liberal leader, David Lloyd George.

**Assad, Hafez al-** (1930-), president of Syria since 1971. As minister of defense and member of the moderate wing of the Baath party, he led a coup that later made him president. A steadfast foe of Israel, Assad has supported various factions of the Palestine Liberation Organization. In 1976 he sent Syrian troops to Lebanon, where they have intervened actively in the civil war, holding power in much of the country. Assad opposed the Camp David peace treaty between Egypt and Israel. A member of the Alawi sect of Islam, Assad rules dictatorially over a population that is mostly Sunni Muslim. In the early 1990s Assad attempted to ameliorate the country's relationship with western countries, especially the United States. Assad was willing to cooperate in the Middle East peace proces.
*See also:* Persian Gulf War; Syria.

**Assam** (pop. 22,414,300), state in India located in the extreme northeast of the country and connected to the rest of India by West Bengal. To the north it is bordered by Tibet and Bhutan and to the east by Burma. The rugged land is drained by the Brahmaputra River. The climate is subtropical and rainfall varies from 70 in (178 cm) to more than 400 in (1,016 cm) per year. Tea is the main commercial product, and about 90% of the population is engaged in agriculture. Assamese is one of the official languages of India.

**Assault and battery**, any threatening physical act that reasonably causes another person to fear bodily harm or offensive contact. If there is actual contact, the crime is called battery. One may have assault without battery, but any case of battery necessarily includes assault. Assault and battery may be either a felony or a misdemeanor, depending on the degree of seriousness.

**Assaying**, method of chemical analysis used to determine the presence, absence, or quantity of a particular component of ores or alloys, used since the 2nd millennium B.C In modern assaying, the sample is fused with a flux containing lead oxide. This produces a lead button containing the material being sought (such as gold or silver), which is heated in oxygen to oxidize the lead and other impurities. This leaves a bead of the metal sought, which is then weighed.

**Assembler**, computer program that converts symbolic code into binary object (machine) code for execution.
*See also:* Computer.

**Assemblies of God**, largest of the Protestant Pentecostal denominations in the United States. It was organized as a separate entity in 1914 and has about 2 million members.
*See also:* Pentecostalism.

**Assembling**, in computer terminology, automatic process by which a computer converts a symbolic-language program into a machine language, usually on an instruction-by-instruction basis.
*See also:* Assembler; Computer.

**Assembly language**, hardware-dependent symbolic language used in computers, usually characterized by a one-to-one correspondence of its statements with machine-language instructions.
*See also:* Computer.

**Assembly line**, production line of equipment, machinery, and workers along which successive operations are performed until the final product is complete. The modern assembly line, largely a result of innovations by Henry Ford in the automotive industry, also employs automation (machines run by machines).
*See also:* Mass production.

**Assessment**, value of property (most commonly homes, shops, and offices) for purposes of taxation, or the process of determining this value. The tax rate is generally stated as so many dollars per thousand dollars of assessed valuation. The term also refers to a demand made by a corporation for extra funds from its stockholders.

**Assignment**, in law, transfer of rights, especially intangible property rights: insurance policies, certificates of corporate shares, and rights to monies due or to become due. In bankruptcy, a debtor's assets may be assigned to a trustee for distribution among the creditors.

**Assimilation,** the process by which food is appropriated as nourishment for the body, following digestion and absorption. The food is converted into living tissues by the cells.
*See also:* Cell; Digestive system.

**Assiniboia,** 2 former, distinct districts of Canada, one formed by the Hudson's Bay Company around the Red River in 1835, incorporated in Manitoba (1870), the other, a section of the Northwest Territories (1882-1905), in the southern portion of present-day Alberta and Saskatchewan.

**Assiniboine,** Sioux tribe of the North American plains who left the Yanktonai Sioux to spread out from Canada across the northwestern United States. A nomadic people who lived primarily by hunting, they were greatly weakened by the extinction of the   buffalo as a result of European settlements, and were placed on reservations in 1884.

**Assisi, Francis of** *See:* Francis of Assisi, Saint.

**Associated Press (AP),** oldest and one of the largest U.S. news agencies (gatherers and distributors of news). Founded in 1848 by 6 New York City newspapers, it now has offices worldwide. The AP is a nonprofit organization financed by subscriptions from member newspapers, periodicals, and broadcasting stations.

**Association,** in psychology, mental linking of one item with others, by similarity, contiguity, opposition, or other principles. In association tests, subjects are presented with a word and asked to respond either with a specifically related word, such as a rhyme or an antonym, or with the first word that comes to mind.
*See also:* Learning.

**Associationism,** psychological school holding that the sole mechanism of human learning consists in the permanent association in the intellect of impressions that have been repeatedly presented to the senses. Originating in the philosophy of John Locke and developed through the work of John Gay, David Hartley, James and John Stuart Mill, and Alexander Bain, the "association of ideas" was the dominant thesis in British psychology for 200 years.

**Assumption of the Virgin,** Roman Catholic belief (declared as official dogma by Pope Pius XII in 1950) that the Virgin Mary was "assumed into heaven body and soul" at the end of her life. Assumption Day is celebrated Aug. 15.

**Assurbanipal** *See:* Ashurbanipal.

**Assyria** *See:* Babylonia and Assyria.

**Astaire, Fred** (Frederick Austerlitz; 1899-1988), U.S. dancer, choreographer, and actor. First in partnership onstage with his sister Adele and later with Ginger Rogers in such films as *Top Hat* (1935) and *Swing Time* (1936), he became one of the most popular dancers and musical comedy stars, renowned for his originality and perfection. Later films, with other partners, included *Holiday Inn* (1942), *The Band Wagon* (1953), and *Funny Face* (1957).

**Astarte**, Phoenician goddess of love and fertility, corresponding to Babylonian Ishtar and Greek Aphrodite. In Syrian art Astarte is frequently represented with two curled ram's horns on her head.

**Astatine**, chemical element, symbol At; for physical constants see Periodic Table. Astatine was synthesized in 1940 by Corson, MacKenzie, and Segré at the University of California by bombarding bismuth with alpha particles. Minute quantities of astatine exist in nature as isotopes produced from uranium and thorium reacting with naturally produced neutrons. Astatine is radioactive and belongs to the halogen group of elements. It behaves chemically very much like them and is reported to be more metallic than iodine. The longest-lived isotope, astatine-210, has a half-life of 8.1 hours. Twenty-eight isotopes of astatine are known.

**Aster** (genus *Aster*), also known as Michaelmas or Christmas daisy, perennial plant with blue, purple, white, or red flowers that bloom in autumn. The China aster (*Callistephus chinensis*), in the same family, produces bigger, almost chrysanthemum-like flowers in bright colors.

**Asteria**, in Greek mythology, daughter of Coeus, the Titan, and mother of Hecate. Courted by Zeus in the form of an eagle, she threw herself into the sea, where she was changed into an island, later called Delos.

**Asteroid**, planetoid, or minor planet of irregular shape, orbiting the sun. Ranging in diameter from a few feet (1 m) to Ceres's 470 mi (750 km), most (some 50,000 that are too small to yield to diameter measurements) lie in the asteroid belt between the orbits of Mars and Jupiter, their total mass estimated to be 0.001 that of the earth. Ceres was the first to be discovered (1801 by Giuseppe Piazzi), and Vesta is the only one visible to the naked eye. The Apollo asteroids have highly elliptical, earth-approaching orbits, and may have caused several of earth's meteorite craters. The Trojan asteroids share the orbit of the planet Jupiter.

**Asthenosphere**, the worldwide "soft layer" underlying the rigid lithosphere, located some 43.5-155 mi (70-250 km) below the earth's surface. Considered part of the upper mantle, the zone is characterized by low seismic velocities, suggesting that it may be partially molten. In plate tectonic theory, rigid slablike plates of the lithosphere move over the asthenosphere.

**Asthma**, reversible obstruction of the airways that compromises the respiratory system. Asthma attacks are typically accompanied, by coughing and wheezing. Asthma is a chronic disorder that can be triggered by exposure to certain allergens or in response to physical or emotional stress. Therapy includes the use of steroids and bronchodilators.
*See also:* Allergy; Bronchitis.

**Astigmatism,** defect of vision caused by irregular shaping in the cornea or lens. In astigmatism, light rays do not converge evenly, some focusing behind the retina, some before it, others on it. It can be corrected by glasses or contact lenses.
*See also:* Eye.

**Aston, Francis William** (1877-1945), British physicist and chemist. At the Cavendish Laboratory, Cambridge, Aston accomplished the first artificial separation of isotopes. He was awarded the Nobel Prize for chemistry in 1922, chiefly for devising the mass spectrograph to study isotopes.

**Astor,** name of a prominent U.S. family involved in fur trading, real estate, and finance, as well as in U.S. and British politics. **John Jacob Astor** (1763-1848), arrived in Baltimore from Waldorf, Germany, began as a baker's boy, became a fur trader and real estate investor, and eventually amassed the fortune of the Astors. **William Backhouse Astor** (1792-1875), John Jacob's son, doubled the family's wealth. His son, **John Jacob IV** (1864-1912), an inventor and science fiction writer, died in the sinking of the *Titanic.* **William Waldorf, 1st Viscount Astor** (1848-1919), John Jacob's great-grandson, was a financier who moved to England, where he was made baron and later viscount. **Nancy Witcher (Langhorne) Astor, Viscountess Astor** (1879-1964) was the first woman to serve in the British Parliament,  as Conservative member for Plymouth.

**Astrakhan** (pop. 510,000), capital of Astrakhan Oblast in the RF. A port on the Caspian Sea at the   mouth of the Volga River, Astrakhan   handles trade in oil, fish, grain, and wood.

**Astringent,** substance that causes the organic tissues and canals of the body to contract, thereby checking or diminishing excessive discharges.

**Astroarcheology** *See:* Archeoastronomy.

**Astrolabe,** astronomical instrument dating from ancient times, used to measure the altitude and movements of celestial bodies. Before the introduction of the sextant, it served as a navigational aid.
*See also:* Sextant.

**Astrology,** system of beliefs based on the theory that movements of celestial bodies influence human events, which can therefore be predicted. The key factor in Western astrology is the position of the stars and planets, described relative to the 12 divisions of the zodiac, at the moment of an individual's birth.
*See also:* Zodiac.

**Astronaut,** term for U.S. test pilot or scientist chosen by NASA to crew space flights. Alan B. Shepard, Jr., made the first suborbital flight in 1961. John Glenn, Jr., orbited the earth in 1962, and Edwin E. Aldrin, Jr., and Neil Armstrong landed on the moon in 1969.

**Astronautics,** or astronautical engineering, scientific study of the principles of space flight, including astrodynamics, space communications, propulsion theory, astrobiology, astrogeology, and the design analysis of spacecraft.

**Astronomy,** study of the planets, stars, and galaxies. To most early astronomers, the earth appeared to be surrounded by a sphere that contained the stars. The high point of early astronomy was the work of the Greeks. Pythagoras (6th century B.C.), who imagined the sun, moon, and planets positioned on transparent spheres that moved along with the sphere of stars, introduced the notion of "the music of the spheres." Hipparchus (2nd century B.C.) compiled—without a telescope—an accurate catalog of 850 stars; his system of magnitude ratings is the basis for the one used today. Ptolemy (2nd century A.D.) laid out a geocentric scheme of the universe, with the earth at the center, that was regarded as gospel for 1,500 years. In 1543, the Polish mathematician Nicholas Copernicus challenged Ptolemy's theory with the idea that the sun is stationary, with everything else circling around it. In 1609, the Italian Galileo Galilei made his own telescope and confirmed Copernicus's heliocentric theory. At the same time, the German mathematician Johannes Kepler finally discredited the geocentric theory. In the late 17th century English mathematician Isaac Newton formulated laws of motion to explain why objects move as they do, how the planets stay in orbit, and why their orbits are elliptical.

Nineteenth-century astronomers analyzed the composition of stars and wondered what causes them to burn. In the early 20th century, Albert Einstein announced his theory that mass and energy are equivalent, and the idea of nuclear power was introduced. It is now known that the sun produces energy by nuclear fusion.

The branch of astronomy called cosmology seeks to find out how the universe originated. One clue discovered in the 1930s by Edwin Hubble resulted in the idea of an expanding universe and the possibility that it started off with a giant explosion—the big bang theory. An opposing idea, promoted by Fred Hoyle, the steady state theory, holds that the universe remains stable because new matter is created to fill the gaps created as galaxies expand. Space exploration and new techniques (advances in radio astronomy, and methods based on gamma, ultraviolet, and X rays) continue to expand our knowledge of the universe.

*See also:* Cosmology.

**Astrophysics,** science dealing with the physical laws governing the nature of celestial objects and events, enabling astronomers to formulate theories of stellar evolution and cosmology.

*See also:* Astronomy; Cosmology.

**Asturias, Miguel Ángel** (1899-1974), Guatemalan writer and diplomat. He won the Lenin Peace Prize in 1966 and the Nobel Prize for literature in 1967. His books *The Cyclone* (1950) and *The Green Pope* (1954) attack the exploitation of Guatemalan Indians.

**Asunción** (pop. 456,000), capital and largest city of Paraguay. Situated on the Paraguay River, Asunción is the main port and the industrial, transportation, and administrative center of the country. Founded in 1537 by Spanish explorers searching for a short route to Peru, Asunción was the rival of

Buenos Aires until the 18th century when it was weakened by conflict between the Jesuits and their enemies.

**Aswan High Dam**, one of the world's largest dams, built on the Nile River in Egypt (1960-70), located 4 mi (6.4 km) south of the 1902 Aswan dam. The dam's hydroelectric generating station has a capacity of 10 billion kwh, and Lake Nasser, formed by the dam, has enough water to irrigate more than 7 million acres of farmland.

**Asylum**, sanctuary or place of refuge; an institution for receiving and maintaining persons suffering certain physical or mental diseases or defects.

**Asyut** (pop. 2,223,000), city in the eastern central region of Egypt, on the left bank of the Nile, about 250 mi (402 km) south of Cairo. A commercial and industrial center producing textiles, pottery, and ivory and wood carvings, Asyut is also the educational center of the Upper Nile Valley; its schools and institutions include the University of Asyut and the Technical and Trade School. A large community of Coptic Christians lives in the city. Asyut Barrage controls the flow of the Nile and provides water for the irrigation of Middle Egypt.

**Atacama Desert**, arid plateau extending from central Chile to southern Ecuador, some 600 mi (966 km) long and 2,000 ft (610 m) high. One of the driest regions on earth, it is a major source of nitrates and copper.

**Atahualpa** (1500-33), last Inca emperor of Peru. After holding power only in Quito, Atahualpa deposed his half brother Huascar as heir of the Inca kingdom. In 1532 the Spanish conquistadors under Francisco Pizarro executed Atahualpa for refusing to accept Christianity.
*See also:* Inca.

**Atalanta**, in Greek mythology, beautiful, swift-footed huntress who promised to marry any suitor who outran her, but to kill any she could beat. She lost to (and married) Hippomenes, who, helped by the goddess Aphrodite, had dropped 3 golden apples that Atalanta paused to pick up.

**Atatürk, Kemal** (Mustafa Kemal; (1881-1938), founder of modern Turkey. An army officer who gained prominence during World War I, Atatürk headed a provisional government in Ankara that opposed the Allied regime in Istanbul established after the collapse of the Ottoman Empire. In 1923 he won European recognition of the new Turkish republic. His secular regime replaced the political power of Islam and modernized the Turkish economy.

**Atavism**, inheritance by an individual organism of characteristics not shown by its parental generation. Once thought to be throwbacks to an ancestral form, atavisms are now known to be primarily the result of the random appearance of recessive traits, though they may result also from aberrations in the development of the embryo or from disease.

**Ataxia**, impaired muscular coordination resulting in unsteady gait, difficulty in fine movements, and speech disorders. Usually caused by damage to the cerebellum or the spinal cord, ataxia occurs with multiple sclerosis, syphilis, and brain tumors.

**Atchison,** city in northeastern Kansas, on the Missouri River. It became a trade and travel center for the opening West as a river port, Pony Express Station, and eastern terminus for the Atchison, Topeka & Santa Fe Railroad.

**Atchison, David Rice** (1807-86), U.S. Senator and proslavery leader of the Missouri Democratic Party. He served in the Missouri State legislature (1834-38) and was appointed to the U.S. Senate in 1843.

**Athabasca,** river and lake in northern Alberta and Saskatchewan, Canada. The river rises in Jasper National Park and flows to the 3,120 sq mi (8,080 sq km) lake.

**Athanasius, Saint** (c.297-373), early Christian theologian and Greek Father of the Church. Athanasius was elected archbishop of Alexandria in 328. He was banished to Trèves (Trier) in 335 by the emperor Constantine for his refusal to compromise with Arianism, but was restored by Constantius in 338. His writings include *On the Incarnation, Five Books Against Arius,* and *Life of St. Anthony.*

**Atharva-Veda** *See:* Vedas.

**Atheism,** denial of the existence of God, distinguished from agnosticism, which holds that the existence of God cannot be proved or disproved but does not necessarily take any position on belief.
*See also:* Agnosticism.

**Athena** (Pallas Athena), in Greek mythology, goddess of wisdom, war, and peace, who sprang fully grown from the head of Zeus. She was a patron of agriculture, arts, and the crafts of civilization. The Romans identified her with Minerva.

**Athens** (pop. 748,100), capital and largest city of Greece, in east central Greece. The center of ancient Greek civilization, Athens reached its political peak after the Persian wars (499-449 B C ). Athens lost its supremacy to Sparta in the Peloponnesian War (431-404 B C ) and later became a subject of Macedonia and then of Rome. Modern Athens, including the Aegean port of Piraeus, is the administrative, political, cultural, and economic center of Greece.

**Atherosclerosis** *See:* Arteriosclerosis.

**Athlete's foot,** popular name for a fungus infection of any area of the skin of the feet or toes, causing inflammation and itching. The fungus thrives in a warm, humid environment.
*See also:* Ringworm.

**Athlone, Alexander Augustus Frederick William Alfred George Cambridge, 1st Earl of** (1874-1957), British army officer and member of the royal family. After a military career during the Boer War and World War I, he was governor general of the Union of South Africa (1923-31) and governor general of Canada (1940- 46).

**Atlanta** (pop. 394,900), capital and largest city of Georgia, seat of Fulton County. Founded in 1837 as the terminus of the Western and Atlantic Railroad, Atlanta was burned by Union forces under General William Sherman during the Civil War in 1864. It was rapidly rebuilt and is today the major commercial and financial center of the South Atlantic states. The city has more than 20 colleges and universities.
*See also:* Georgia.

**Atlanta, Battle of** *See:* Civil War, U.S.

**Atlantic Charter**, declaration of common objectives signed by U.S. President F. D. Roosevelt and British Prime Minister Winston Churchill on Aug. 14, 1941, before the United States entered World War II. It affirmed the determination of the 2 governments not to extend their territories and to promote human rights.

**Atlantic City** (pop. 40,200), seaside resort and convention center in southeast New Jersey. Its famous Boardwalk (built 1870) is lined by hotels, restaurants, casinos, and Convention Hall.

**Atlantic Intracoastal Waterway**, shallow, sheltered water route extending 1,134 mi (1,825 km) along the Atlantic seaboard from Norfolk, Va., to Key West, Fla., and serving pleasure craft and light shipping.

**Atlantic Ocean**, world's second-largest ocean (c.31.8 million sq mi/82.3 million sq km), separating the Americas from Europe and Africa. The North Atlantic carries the greatest proportion of the world's shipping, and about half of the world's fish come from the area.

**Atlantic Provinces**, the 4 Canadian provinces of Newfoundland, New Brunswick, Nova Scotia, and Prince Edward Island, the last 3 of which are sometimes called the Maritime Provinces. Comprising about 5 percent of the area of Canada, these provinces have been a fishing center since the late 1400s. Service industries, increasingly important during the 1900s, are now the leading economic activity. The majority of inhabitants are of English, Irish, Scottish, or Welsh descent.

**Atlantic States**, those states of the U.S. south of New England bordering on the Atlantic Ocean or closely relying on it economically. New York, New Jersey, and Pennsylvania are Middle Atlantic states. Maryland, Delaware, Virginia, North Carolina, South Carolina, Georgia, and Florida, are South Atlantic states, West Virginia occasionally considered to be part of this group as well.

**Atlantis**, in Greek mythology, an island in the western sea (Atlantic Ocean?). Plato described it as an advanced civilization destroyed by volcanic eruptions and earthquakes. The legend has fascinated humanity since antiquity, and many have searched for the lost island. Some scholars identify Atlantis with the Mediterranean island of Thera (also called Santorini), a center of ancient Cretan civilization devastated by volcanic eruptions in 1625 B.C.

**Atlas**, in Greek mythology, a titan. After the titans were defeated by the Olympians, he was condemned to carry the sky on his shoulders for eternity.

**Atlas Mountains**, mountain system of northwest Africa. The highest peak, 13,671 ft (4,167 m), is Mount Toubkal in southwestern Morocco. The Atlas mountains are  rich in coal, oil, iron ore, and phosphates.

**Atmosphere**, spheroidal envelope of gas and vapor surrounding a planet, retained by gravity. The composition of the earth's atmosphere and most of its physical properties vary with altitude. About 75% of the total mass of the atmosphere and 90% of its water vapor are contained in the troposphere, the lowest zone, which extends from the earth's surface to an altitude of about 5 mi (8 km) at the poles and 10 mi (16 km) at the equator. The stratosphere, where the ozone layer filters out the sun's ultraviolet radiation, extends from the troposphere to about 30 mi (50 km); the mesosphere ranges from there to about 50 mi (80 km); the ionosphere, containing electrically charged particles that reflect radio signals, goes to about 400 mi (640 km); finally, the exosphere merges into the interplanetary medium. Overall, the atmosphere is about 78% nitrogen by volume. Other major components include oxygen (21%), argon (0.93%), and carbon dioxide (0.03%).

**Atoll**, low-lying oval or circular coral reef, enclosing a lagoon, most prevalent in the western Pacific Ocean. Examples are the Maldive Islands, Whitsunday Island, and the Bikini Atoll.
*See also:* Coral.

**Atom**, classically, one of the minute, indivisible, homogeneous particles of which physical objects are composed; in 20th-century science, the name given to a relatively stable package of matter that is itself made up of at least 2 subatomic particles, and that defines an element. Every atom consists of a tiny nucleus (containing positively charged protons and electrically neutral neutrons) with which a number of negatively charged electrons are associated. The much smaller electrons occupy a hierarchy of orbitals that represent the atom's electronic energy levels and fill most of the space taken up by the atom. The number of protons in the nucleus of an atom (the atomic number, $Z$) defines the chemical element of which the atom is an example. In an isolated neutral atom the number of electrons equals the atomic number, but an electrically charged ion of the same atom has either a surfeit or a deficit of electrons. The number of neutrons in the nucleus (the neutron number, $N$) can vary among different atoms of the same element. Atoms with the same number of protons but different numbers of neutrons are called isotopes of the element in question. Most stable isotopes have slightly more neutrons than protons.Although the nucleus is very small, it contains nearly all the mass of the atom—protons and neutrons having very similar masses, the mass of the electron (about 0.05% of the proton mass) being almost negligible. The mass of an atom is roughly equal to the total number of its protons and neutrons. This number, $Z + N$, is known as the mass number of the atom, $A$, the mass of a proton being counted as 1. In equations representing nuclear reactions, the atomic number of an atom is often written as a subscript preceding the chemical symbol for the element, and the mass number as a superscript following it. Thus an atomic nucleus with a mass number 16 and containing 8 protons belongs to an atom of oxygen-16, written $_8O^{16}$. The average of the mass numbers of the various naturally occurring isotopes of an element, weighted according to their relative abundance, gives the chemical atomic weight of the element. Subatomic particles fired into atomic nuclei can cause nuclear reactions that give rise either to new isotopes of the original element or to atoms of a different element. Such nuclear reactions emit alpha particles, or beta rays, sometimes accompanied by gamma rays.

**Atomic bomb** *See:* Nuclear bomb.

**Atomic clock**, precise electric device for measuring time, indirectly controlled by atomic or molecular vibration.

**Atomic energy** *See:* Nuclear energy; Fission; Nuclear energy.

**Atomic fusion** *See:* Fusion; Nuclear energy.

**Atomic number** *See:* Atom.

**Atomic particle** *See:* Atom.

**Atomic reactor** *See:* Nuclear reactor.

**Atomic theory** *See:* Atom.

**Atomic weight**, mean of the masses of all the various isotopes of a given element. Atomic weight is normally given in atomic mass units; an atomic mass unit is defined as 1/12 of the mass of an atom of carbon-12.
*See also:* Atom; Periodic table.

**Atom smasher** *See:* Particle accelerator.

**Atonement**, in Christian theology, reconciliation of humanity with God through the sacrificial death of Christ. In Jewish theology, one day of the year is designated as the Day of Atonement (*Yom Kippur*).

**Atreus,**, in Greek mythology, king of Mycenae and the father of Agamemnon and Menelaus. His brother, Thyestes, seduced Atreus's wife, Aërope, and attempted to seize the throne of Mycenae. Atreus, pretending to forgive his brother, invited him to a banquet at which he served Thyestes the bodies of his 2 sons.

**Atrium**, unroofed or partially roofed interior court of a Roman house, with rooms extending around it; also, entrance court of early Christian churches.

**Atrophy** (Greek, "not nourished"), decrease in size and function or wasting away of any organ, tissue, or part of the body as a result of disease, malnutrition, decreased work, or normal processes of growth or body function. Among the types of atrophy are acute yellow atrophy, massive necrosis of the liver associated with severe infection; toxemia of pregnancy or ingested poisons; and progressive muscular atrophy, a motor neuron disease characterized by loss of power and wasting in the arms and legs.

**Atropine**, crystalline alkaloid contained in plants such as jimsonweed and deadly nightshade (belladonna), used in many gastrointestinal and ophthalmic preparations. Its chief use is as an antispasmodic to relax smooth muscles.
*See also:* Belladonna.

**Atsina** *See:* Gros Ventre.

**Attachment**, seizure of property by legal process, to prevent a defendant from disposing of disputed property before trial, and to guarantee payment of any judgment against him or her.

**Attainder**, loss of civil rights (strictly, rights of ownership and disposition of property) by someone outlawed or sentenced to death. Attainder has been almost universally abolished except in cases of treason.

**Attar**, fragrant, essential oil, often made from various species of roses, that forms a valuable perfume.

**Attila** (A D. 406?-453), king of the Huns, who claimed domination from the Alps and the Baltic to the Caspian Sea. From 441 to 450 he ravaged the Eastern Roman Empire as far as Constantinople, and invaded Gaul in 451, this expedition earning him the title Scourge of God. He was defeated by the Romans, and subsequently invaded Italy (452), but retired without attacking Rome, apparently due to lack of supplies and sickness among his troops. He died of overindulgence at his wedding feast.
*See also:* Hun.

**Attlee, Clement Richard, 1st Earl** (1883-1967), British politician and prime minister (1945-51). Attlee led the Labour party from 1935 and served in Winston Churchill's wartime coalition cabinet before becoming prime minister. During his administration he instituted a broad program of social reforms, including the National Health Service, and nationalized many industries and the Bank of England. Also during his administration, independence was granted to India, Burma, Pakistan, Palestine, and Ceylon.

**Attorney**, one who is legally appointed in the place of another as an agent to transact any business for him or her; especially a lawyer.

**Attorney general**, chief law officer of a nation (in Canada also called minister of justice). The U.S. attorney general heads the Department of Justice, is a member of the president's cabinet, enforces federal laws, and advises the president on legal questions. Attorneys general in individual states and Canada perform similar functions.
*See also:* Justice, Department of.

**Attucks, Crispus** (c.1723-70), U.S. patriot of African and Native American parentage who was the first of 5 men to die in the Boston Massacre. It is historic irony that one of the first persons to die in the cause of American

independence was an individual whose personal rights were not secure at the time of his death.
*See also:* Boston Massacre.

**Atwood, Margaret** (1939-   ), Canadian poet and novelist. Atwood gained prominence with a collection of poetry, *The Circle Game* (1966). Among her other works are *Bluebeard's Egg* (1983), a collection of short stories, and the novels *Surfacing* (1972), *Lady Oracle* (1976), *The Handmaid's Tale* (1985), and *Cat's Eye* (1989).

**Auckland** (pop. 889,200), chief port, largest city, naval base, and industrial center of New Zealand, capital of Auckland province on North Island. Founded in 1840, Auckland was New Zealand's capital until 1865, when the government was transferred to Wellington. Important industries include shipbuilding, oil refining, food processing, and automobile manufacturing. The city's War Memorial Museum contains one of the finest collections of Maori art in the world.

**Auckland Islands**, group of uninhabited islands, of volcanic origin, lying in the southern Pacific Ocean about 200 mi (320 km) south of New Zealand. They were used as a whaling station during the early 19th century. The islands are controlled by New Zealand.

**Auden, W(ystan) H(ugh)** (1907-73), Anglo-American poet and major influence in 20th century literature. In the 1930s, when he also collaborated with Christopher Isherwood on verse plays (*The Dog Beneath the Skin*, *The Ascent of F6*, and *On the Frontier*), his poetry probed pre-World War II European culture. In 1939 Auden moved to the United States, where he became a citizen in 1946. His later work, which delves into religion, psychology, and politics, includes *The Double Man* (1941), *The Age of Anxiety* (1947, Pulitzer Prize), *The Shield of Achilles* (1955), and *About the House*. He also wrote opera librettos and literary criticism.

**Audiology**, science of hearing; particularly, the study of hearing disorders and rehabilitation of individuals with hearing defects. Audiologists determine whether a person has a hearing deficiency by identifying and measuring hearing function loss and assessing the patient's ability to communicate. Corrective treatment may involve a hearing aid, learning to read lips, or improvement of listening skills.

**Audit**, in accounting, examination of accounts or dealings with money or property, performed by persons not involved in the preparation of the accounts.
*See also:* Accounting.

**Audubon, John James** (1785-1851), U.S. artist and ornithologist famous for his paintings of North American birds, reproduced in *Birds of America* (1827-38). He collaborated with the Scottish naturalist William MacGillivray on an accompanying text, *Ornithological Biography* (1831-39).

**Auerbach, Red** (Arnold Auerbach; 1917- ), U.S. basketball coach who led the Boston Celtics to 9 championships in 10 years (1957; 1959-66). He retired in 1966 after having won 1,037 professional games.

**Augsburg** (pop. 258,300), capital of the administrative district of Swabia in Bavaria, Germany, on the Lech River about 35 mi (56 km) from Munich. Situated on the site of a Roman colony founded by Emperor Augustus (late 1st century B C ), it became a free imperial city (1276) and flourished as an important trade center. Augsburg lost much in power and prestige during the Thirty Years War (1618-48) and eventually was annexed by Bavaria (1806). Today it is an important commercial and rail center for south Germany. Its medieval inner quarter includes the late Gothic church of St. Ulrich and the Renaissance-style Rathaus.
*See also:* Augsburg Confession.

**Augsburg Confession**, statement of Lutheran beliefs presented to the Diet of Augsburg on June 25, 1530. The Confession, largely the work of Philip Melanchthon, was an attempt to reconcile Luther's reforms with Roman Catholicism. It was rejected by Emperor Charles V, which sealed the break between the Lutherans and Rome.
*See also:* Luther, Martin.

**Augur**, in ancient Rome, official who derived signs (auguries) concerning future events from the flight or other actions of birds, certain appearances in quadrupeds, lightning, or other unusual occurrences. In an elaborate ceremony, the augur would choose a spot with a clear view to wait for any signs—from thunder in the skies to the squeak of a mouse—that might indicate the "will of the gods." No important business of state could be initiated without first consulting such a diviner.

**Augusta** (pop. 23,000), capital of Maine and seat of Kennebec County on the Kennebec River. Among its products are textiles, shoes, paper, and foodstuffs. A Plymouth Colony trading post was established on the site in 1628, and the town grew up around Fort Western, its first permanent structure, built in 1754. Augusta became the state capital in 1831 and was incorporated in 1849.
*See also:* Maine.

**Augusta** (pop. 396,809), city in eastern Georgia on the Savannah River, seat of Richmond County. Founded as a trading post by James Oglethorpe in 1736, it was the scene of fighting during the Revolutionary War and was an important Confederate ordnance center during the Civil War. Today Augusta, a popular winter resort, houses diversified industries, the University of Georgia School of Medicine, and Woodrow Wilson's boyhood home.

**Augustan Age** *See:* Augustus; England; English literature; Latin literature.

**Augustine, Saint** (A D 354-430), bishop of Hippo, church father. Though raised as a Christian by his mother, St. Monica, in northern Africa, he embraced Manichaeism while in school at Carthage. Moving to Rome (383), he was influenced by Neoplatonism, but it was in Milan, where he met St. Ambrose, bishop of the city, that he was baptized a Christian (387) and took the vows of priesthood (391). In 396 he became bishop of Hippo (northern Africa). Generally acknowledged by Christians as the father of theology, he wrote many books, including the autobiographical *Confessions* and *De Civitate Dei* (*The City of God*), containing the great defense against paganism and the Christian philosophy of history. His feast day is Aug. 28.

**Augustine, Saint** (d. A D 604), Italian missionary and first archbishop of Canterbury (from 601). A Benedictine monk, he was sent to England by Pope Gregory the Great to convert the populace and bring the Celtic Church under Rome's control. He was given support by King Ethelbert of Kent. His feast day is May 27 (May 26 in England and Wales).

**Augustus** (63 B C-A D 14), honorific title given in 27 B C to Gaius Julius Caesar Octavianus, adopted great-nephew and heir of Julius Caesar. With Lepidus and Marc Antony he formed a triumvirate that avenged his great-uncle's murder by defeating and destroying the main conspirators, at Philippi (42 B.C.). The deposition of Lepidus (36 B C) and the suicide of Antony after his defeat at Actium (31 B C) left Augustus sole master of the Roman world. After the ravages of 50 years of civil war, he used his power to institute religious, legal, and administrative reforms and to promote literature, the arts, and agriculture. While nominally restoring the Republic, his control of the state's finances and armed forces made him the sole ruler. He is accounted first Roman emperor (Latin, *imperator*, "commander"). He was succeeded by his stepson Tiberius. The month of August is named for him.
*See also:* Antony, Marc; Cleopatra; Caesar, (Gaius) Julius.

**Auk**, marine diving bird of the family Alcidae, including razorbills, puffins, and guillemots. Of the 22 species (including the extinct great auk) the smallest is the dovekie, or little auk (*Plautus alle*), which is about the size of a robin (lengths of other species are 6-30 in/15-76 cm). Auks, who seldom leave the water except to nest, usually breed in colonies, sometimes millions of individuals, and nest on high ledges or in burrows.
*See also:* Guillemot; Murre; Puffin.

**Aurelius, Marcus** *See:* Marcus Aurelius.

**Aurora**, display of colored lights and shimmering forms seen at night, most frequently during the equinoxes, in regions of high latitude. The aurora borealis, or northern lights, can be seen in northern Scandinavia, Canada, and Alaska, and the aurora australis, or southern lights, are seen on the borders of Antarctica in the Southern Hemisphere. Fast-moving electrons from the sun are attracted to the earth's magnetic poles, where they collide with oxygen and nitrogen ions in the ionosphere, causing them to give off energy in the form of light. The aurora most frequently appears following a major solar flare; the occurrence and intensity of the aurora is also related to the 11-year sunspot cycle.

**Auschwitz**, present-day Oswiecim in Poland, site of the infamous Nazi concentration camp in World War II where some 4 million inmates, mostly Jews, were murdered. The camp was opened in 1940 and run by Rudolf Hoess for 3 years. Its huge gas chambers were responsible for most deaths.

**Austen, Jane** (1775-1817), English novelist. Daughter of a clergyman, her novels, including *Sense and Sensibility* (1811), *Pride and Prejudice* (1813), and *Emma* (1816), vividly portray the provinciality of the English middle class of her time with ironic insight and vivid characterizations. She ultimately gave up writing, discouraged by her inability to find a publisher. Her novels were published many years after she wrote them; 2 were published posthumously. Today she is considered one of the greatest novelists in the English language, and her work is an inspiration and model for many writers.

**Austerlitz** (pop. 5,000), town in Moravia in the southern part of the Czech Republic. Currently an agricultural center, on Dec. 2, 1805 it was the site where Napoleon's army defeated the combined forces of Emperor Francis I of Austria and Tsar Alexander I of Russia in the "Battle of the Three Emperors," the beginning of Napoleon's mastery in Europe.
*See also:* Napoleon I.

**Austin** (pop. 492,300), capital of Texas and seat of Travis County on the Colorado River in south-central Texas. Founded in 1839 as Waterloo, it served as the capital of the Republic of Texas 1840-42 and was renamed in honor of Stephen F. Austin. It became state capital in 1870. Austin has seen great industrial development since the 1930s, currently is the site of extensive scientific and electronic research, and is also the center of an important agricultural, ranching, dairy, and poultry region.
*See also:* Texas.

**Austin, Stephen Fuller** (1793-1836), U.S. pioneer statesman, "Father of Texas." Upon bringing 300 families to Texas (1821), he was made the settlement's administrator. Between 1822 and 1830 he presented Texan demands for autonomy to the Mexican government, and was imprisoned for it. On his release in 1835, he joined the Texan rebellion against Mexico, and in 1836 was appointed secretary of state of the Republic of Texas.

**Australia**, world's largest island and smallest continent, with a total area of 2,966,151 sq mi (7,682,000 sq km). It is the only continent occupied by a single nation, the Commonwealth of Australia, a federal union comprising 6 states (the island of Tasmania, Queensland, New South Wales, Victoria, South Australia, Western Australia), the Northern Territory, Jefferson Bay Territory and the Australian Capital Territory (Canberra).
*Land and climate.* Geologists believe that 120 million years ago Australia was part of a vast land mass that included India, Arabia, and parts of Africa and South America. Later land bridges to Australia were destroyed by geological upheavals, leaving the continent completely isolated. This isolation accounts for the development of various species of animal life peculiar to Australia. For example, the pouched mammals (marsupials) are found mainly in Australia and neighboring islands. Australia is the world's flattest continent. Approximately 75% of its area is covered by a plateau rarely higher than 1,500 ft (4,600 m) The outstanding physical feature of the continent is the Great Western Plateau, most of which is desert or semi-arid scrub country. The Great Barrier Reef, a mass of coral reefs and islands, extends for 1,250 mi (2,012 km) along its east coast. Australia has a moderate-warm climate, ususally dry and sunny.

## Australia

| | |
|---|---|
| Capital: | Canberra |
| Area: | 2,966,151 sq mi |
| | (7,682,000 sq km) |
| Population: | 18,623,000 |
| Language: | English |
| Government: | Parliamentary monar chy in the British Commonwealth |
| Independent: | 1901 |
| Head of gov.: | Prime minister |
| Per capita: | U.S. $18,720 |

**People.** Australia has a low population density, with about 17 million people living in a country almost as large as the United States. The people of Australia are mainly of European (particularly British) origin (95%), Asian immigrants (4%), or Aboriginals and others (1%). Most of the population is concentrated in the coastal cities, of which the largest is Sydney. The majority belongs to the Roman Catholic Church (26%) or to the Anglican Church (24%). Asians and Aboriginals have their own religions. The official language is English.

**Economy.** The Australian export products wheat, sugar, and wool are an important part of the world market. Australia is also an important exporter of raw materials.

**History.** Visited by the Dutch in the early 1600s, Australia was claimed for Britain by Capt. James Cook (1770). New South Wales, the first area settled, began as a penal colony (1788). But free settlement began in 1816, and no convicts were sent to Australia after 1840. The gold rushes (1851, 1892) brought more people to Australia, and in 1901 the 6 self-governing colonies formed an independent commonwealth. In the late 1990s, demands for more Aboriginal rights increased.

**Australian Aborigines**, earliest native inhabitants of Australia, racially distinguished by dark hair, dark skin, medium stature, broad noses, and narrow heads. Before European encroachment in the 18th and 19th centuries, they lived by well-organized nomadic food-gathering and hunting. Aborigines were enfranchised in 1962. The Australian government has attempted to integrate them into the European population, but they still face discrimination.

**Australian Desert**, comprises 3 deserts that cover about one-third of Australia's western and central area. They are the Great Sandy Desert, about 160,000 sq mi (414,000 sq km); the Gibson Desert, 120,000 sq mi (311,000 sq km); and the Great Victoria Desert, 130,000 sq mi (337,000 sq km).

**Austral Islands**, group of islands of volcanic origin in the South Pacific, south of Tahiti. They have a combined area of about 70 sq mi (180 sq km). The largest of the island are Rurutu and Tubuai.

**Austria**

| | |
|---|---|
| Capital: | Vienna |
| Area: | 32,377 sq mi |
| | (83,855 sq km) |
| Population: | 8,134,000 |
| Language: | German |
| Government: | Federal republic |
| Independent: | Republic since 1918 |
| Head of gov.: | Chancellor (chosen |
| | by the President) |
| Per capita: | U.S. $26,890 |
| Mon. unit: | 1Schilling (S) = |
| | 100 groschen |

**Australopithecus**, or "southern ape," a genus of hominids whose fossilized bones, discovered in South Africa in 1924, date back about 3 million years. Australopithecines stood erect at about 4-5 ft (120-150 cm) and walked on 2 legs without the help of their arms. Their teeth were more human than apelike, their brains about one-third those of humans in size.

**Austria**, federal republic in central Europe divided into 9 provinces: Vienna, Lower Austria, Burgenland, Upper Austria, Salzburg, Styria, Carinthia, Tyrol, and Vorarlberg.
*Land.* There are 4 geographic regions: the Austrian Alps to the West, including the country's highest mountain, Grossglockner (12,457 ft/3,797 m); the North Alpine foreland, a plateau cut by fertile valleys between the Danube and the Alps; the Austrian granite plateau, north of the Danube; and the Eastern lowlands, where the capital, Vienna, stands.
*People.* About 98% of today's Austrians are Germans ethnically and linguistically, although there are considerable differences in dialect among the provinces. About 75,000 Austrians speak Croatian, Slovene, Hungarian, or Czech only, or speak German only as a second language. The largest minority group are the Croatians, who mainly live in Burgenland. Austria's cultural contributions have been noteworthy. In the 19th century Vienna was a world center for musicians and composers. Wolfgang Amadeus Mozart, Franz Joseph Haydn, Franz Schubert, Anton Bruckner, and Gustav Mahler were all Austrians, while Ludwig van Beethoven, Johann Strauss, and Franz Lehar spent most of their lives in Vienna. Sigmund Freud, the father of psychoanalysis, studied and practiced in Vienna, along with many other psychologists.
*Economy.* Austrian farm crops include sugar beets, potatoes, grains, grapes, fruits, tobacco, flax, and hemp; wines and beers are produced in quantity. Almost 40% of the country is forested, so wood and paper are important products. Iron ore is the primary mineral resource, but there are also deposits of lead, magnesium, copper, salt, zinc, aluminum, silver, and gypsum. Vienna, Graz, and Linz are the chief industrial centers. Tourism has helped to stimulate economic growth in recent years.
*History.* Inhabited from prehistoric times, settled by the Celts, and subsequently part of the Roman Empire, starting in the third century A.D. Austria

was devastated by invading Vandals, Goths, Alemanni, Huns, and Avars. In 788 Charlemagne conquered Austria. The Babenberg family inherited it in 976 and retained it as duchy until 1246. In 1247 the Habsburgs acquired Austria, which became a central part of their empire until 1918. By the Treaty of Versailles, independent states (Czechoslovakia, Hungary, and Yugoslavia) were created from the old empire, while Austria itself became a republic. In 1938 Austria was annexed by Hitler's Third Reich, regaining independence following the Allied victory in 1945. When Austria joined the European Union in 1995, this step ended the country's neutral position, maintained since World War II.

**Austria-Hungary**, empire formed by the union of the Kingdom of Hungary and the Austrian Empire in 1867. It was the assassination of the Archduke Francis Ferdinand, heir to the empire's throne, in 1914, by one of the many nationalist groups seeking independence that led directly to World War I. The empire, which was allied with Germany, ceased to exist at the end of World War I, and its lands were divided among the East European nations.

**Authoritarianism**, political philosophy based on the principle of total submission of the population to a leader or elite group that is not constitutionally responsible to the people.

**Autism**, impairment in the perception of and response to environmental stimuli, accompanied by absorption in self-centered mental activity. In infantile autism, the development of speech is delayed; ritualistic behavior is usual and may include abnormal routines; resistance to change, attachment to odd objects, and stereotyped patterns of play are the norm. The capacity for abstract or symbolic thought and for imaginative play is diminished. Treatment is experimental, and performance has been found to be better on tasks involving rote memory than on those requiring symbolic or linguistic skills.

**Autocracy**, form of government in which an individual or group has absolute power, as in Russia under the tsars and France under Louis XIV.

**Autogiro**, or **autogyro** rotary-wing aircraft that uses a conventional propeller to provide forward motion and an unpowered horizontal rotor for lift. Though it cannot hover or land vertically, current technology permits almost vertical takeoffs.

**Automatic frequency control** (AFC), circuit used in electronic devices such as radio, television, and radar to help maintain and control the frequency. The AFC circuit corrects frequency drifts (e.g., from a particular radio station) by producing a voltage that automatically reverses the drift and holds it on frequency.

**Automatic pilot** *See:* Gyropilot.

**Automation**, automatically controlled operation of an apparatus, process, or system by mechanical or electronic devices (often computers) that replace constant human observation, effort, and decision.

**Automobile**, small, 4-wheeled vehicle that carries passengers. The 4 major components of an automobile are its power plant, drive system, control system, and body.

*Power plant.* Almost all automobiles are powered by internal combustion engines, usually with 4-8 cylinders attached to a crankshaft. In the internal combustion engine, gasoline from the fuel tank is mixed with air in the carburetor and fed to the cylinders. The highly explosive mixture is ignited by the spark plugs and, as it explodes, expands rapidly. The piston within the cylinder is forced downward, turning the crankshaft. The heavy metal flywheel attached to one end of the crankshaft moves the piston back up the cylinder to its original position. The order in which the spark plugs fire is controlled by the distributor. In most engines, the gasoline vapor simply enters the cylinder through a valve at the beginning of the downstroke, but some automobiles have fuel-injection systems that greatly increase efficiency.

*Drive system.* In most cars, the drive is supplied by the rear wheels. The motion of the crankshaft must therefore be transmitted by a driveshaft to the rear axle, where a system of cogs turns the wheels. The rotation of the crankshaft is transmitted to the driveshaft by the clutch, which consists of 2 circular plates, one attached to the driveshaft, the other to the crankshaft. When the plates are in contact, both rotate. When one plate is drawn back, the crankshaft rotates without affecting the driveshaft, and the engine can "turn over" without moving the car. Gears alter the number of turns required from the engine to achieve a single turn of the drive wheels. The gear box also makes reverse movement possible. When cars are equipped with automatic transmission, manual control of the gears or clutch is not required.

*The controls.* Steering is controlled by a steering wheel, attached to horizontal track rods between the two front wheels. The movement of these rods turns the wheels. In heavy cars, power steering uses hydraulic pressure to assist the driver in turning the wheel. The pedal-operated brake system uses either the pressure of brake shoes against brake drums attached to the wheels or the more efficient disk brakes. The handbrake, which clamps onto the driveshaft or one set of wheels, is used as an emergency brake or for parking. The gas pedal is connected to the carburetor and controls the amount of gasoline vapor that enters the cylinders of the engine. The greater the quantity of vapor, the more powerful the explosion and the greater the speed of the automobile.

*Body.* The chassis of the car is the large steel frame that supports the engine and the control and running mechanisms. It may be a solid piece of stamped metal or a series of metal parts welded together. In cars that do not have a chassis, the body may simply be the framework that links the mechanical parts. The weight of the car is supported at the front and rear axles by metal springs, or sometimes by a hydraulic mechanism, to absorb shocks transmitted from the road and ensure a smooth ride.

**Automobile Association, American** (AAA), U.S.-based travel organization. Consisting of more than 800 travel agencies and 65 clubs, it has a membership of 25 million motorists throughout the United States and Canada. Among its various services are emergency road assistance, insurance, trip planning, and public education on automobile and traffic safety. The AAA was founded in 1902 and has its headquarters in Falls Church, VA.

**Automobile racing,** sport in which specially designed or adapted motor vehicles race indoor or outdoor courses. Dating from 1894 in France, races include the Grand Prix (worldwide series culminating in world-champion driver), stock car (special equipment on standard vehicles), midget car, sports car, and drag (acceleration competition). Major U.S. races include the Indianapolis 500 and the Daytona 500 (a stock-car race).

**Automobile Workers, United** *See:* United Automobile Workers.

**Autonomic nervous system,** certain sections of the brain, spinal cord, and nerve pathways that govern the activity of a number of organs, making them function largely independently of conscious control. The autonomic nervous system regulates the organs of the chest (heart and lungs), the abdomen (stomach, intestine, liver, etc.), the pelvis, and many other organs and tissues of the body, including the blood vessels and skin. By contrast, the somatic nervous system comprises those parts of the brain, spinal cord, and nerve pathways that respond to the external environment, and are under voluntary control. The autonomic nervous system governs the processes that serve to maintain the individual and the species: metabolism, growth, reproduction, respiration, nutrition and digestion, the functioning of the heart and blood vessels, the excretion of waste products, temperature control, etc. An intricate system of nuclei and nerve pathways in the brain regulates the workings of the various organs. In the hypothalamus lie dozens of nuclei and pathways that exert a controlling influence over such basic life functions as eating and drinking behavior, temperature regulation, and the percentage of sugars, fats, and water in the blood. The autonomic nervous system is also involved in emotional response. Emotions can give rise to quickening of the heartbeat, changes in breathing patterns, increased secretion of gastric acid in the stomach, and alterations in the secretory pattern of the gallbladder. Malfunction of the autonomic nervous system can easily lead to serious disturbances in the functioning of an organ. Often a stomach ache is caused by the malfunction of one of the subsystems of the autonomic nervous system. The autonomic nervous system can be divided into the sympathetic and the parasympathetic systems, which in general produce opposite effects on various organs.
*See also:* Nervous system.

**Autopsy,** examination of the external structures and internal organs of a dead body for the purpose of determining the cause of death or for studying the damage done by disease; also called necropsy or postmortem examination. The law requires that every cause of death be verified by a physician or by a coroner's jury. If the cause of death is known, the death certificate is signed and no autopsy is needed, but if authorities are uncertain of the conditions leading to death, such as in a suicide or homicide, an autopsy may be indicated.

**Auxin,** any of several organic compounds that act as plant hormones to promote cell growth.

**Avant-garde,** term referring to those who experiment with new and original art forms. Used originally to describe a military unit that led the rest of the troops, *avant-garde* was first given its modern meaning by the French socialist Henri de Saint-Simon in 1825. During the 19th century, the avant-garde notion of art as a tool of social reform gave way to the idea of "art for art's sake," leading to the Dadaist and Surrealist movements of the early 20th century. Important avant-garde artists include U.S. composer John Cage (1912-92) and French painter Marcel Duchamp (1887-1968).

**Average**, number that is typical of a group of numbers or quantities. The 3 kinds of averages—mean, median, and mode—have different statistical significance. The mean is derived by taking the sum of a group of quantities and dividing it by the number of quantities. The median divides a sampling in half; there are the same number of items above and below it. The mode is the most frequently occurring number in a group.

**Averroës** (Ibn-Rushd; 1126-98), Spanish-Arabian philosopher, commentator on Aristotle and Plato who exerted a great influence on the development of Latin scholastic philosophy. For him, the source of philosophic truth was reason, not faith, though he believed there was no conflict between the two.

**Aviation**, term referring to all aspects of building and flying aircraft. Aviation has not only changed the face of long-distance travel, but affected medical accessibility, farming practices, and the way nations wage war. The aviation industry, which includes the manufacture of aircraft and the operations of airlines, involves the work of millions of engineers, mechanics, pilots and air traffic controllers, as well as many governmental agencies. The world's first successful airplane flight was made by Wilbur and Orville Wright in 1903. Within a few years Europe and the United States had several small airplane-producing factories. Interested in developing their own air forces, various governments around the world began to purchase airplanes for military purposes. The first solo, nonstop flight across the Atlantic Ocean was accomplished by Charles Lindbergh on May 21, 1927. Amelia Earhart was the first person to fly solo from Hawaii to California in 1935. The use of commercial airplanes in the late 1930s assured the growth of aviation as an industry. The jet airliner, developed in the 1950s, gave the industry a further boost. Because of the rapid growth of civil aviation, more effective government regulation was needed. In 1958, various governmental agencies combined to form the Federal Aviation Agency (FAA), which was responsible for establishing and enforcing air traffic procedures and controls.

**Avicenna** (Ibn-Sina; 980-1037), Persian physician and philosopher. Of his prolific writings on theology, logic, metaphysics, and mathematics, his greatest is considered to be *The Canon of Medicine*, which remained a standard medical text in Europe until the Renaissance.

**Avignon** (pop. 91,500), French city on the east bank of the Rhône River in southern France, capital of Vaucluse department. During the "Babylonian Exile" (1309-78) Avignon was the papal seat. From 1378 to 1417, the city was the home of the "antipopes," rivals to the popes in Rome.

**Avila Camacho, Manuel** (1897-1955), Mexican soldier and statesman. As Mexico's president (1940- 46), he supported the U.S. and promoted Latin American opposition to the Axis powers.
*See also:* Mexico.

**Avocado** (*Persea americana*), tropical evergreen tree native to the United States, Mexico, and the West Indies. The fruit, also called avocado or alligator pear, has a dark green or purple rind, bright green flesh rich in protein, vitamins, iron, and oil, and a large central seed. Avocados are also grown as house plants.

**Avocet**, any of several long-legged wading birds (genus *Recurvirostra*). One species flourishes in Europe, Asia, and Africa. It uses its long curving beak to sweep the water in search of the small aquatic animals on which it feeds. It has black-and-white plumage. The related American avocet has a pinkish head and breast.

**Avoirdupois**, English system of weight in which 1 lb contains 16 oz, in contrast to troy weight, another English system, in which 1 lb equals 12 oz. In the United States, commodities are generally weighed in avoirdupois. Most other countries use the metric system, to which Britain is gradually converting.
*See also:* Weights and measures.

**Avon**, name of 2 British rivers. The longer, the Upper Avon, arises in Northamptonshire and flows 96 mi (154 km) past Warwick and Stratford-upon-Avon to join the Severn at Tewkesbury. Stratford-upon-Avon was the birthplace of William Shakespeare.

**AWOL (Absent Without Leave)** *See:* Desertion.

**Axiom**, any general statement accepted as true without proof as the basis for building a logical system of other statements that are proven. These proven statements are called theorems. The axioms of a system need not be self-evident, but they must be consistent with one another.
*See also:* Geometry.

**Axis Powers**, countries allied with Nazi Germany before or during World War II. The Rome-Berlin Axis, a diplomatic agreement between Hitler and Mussolini, was formed in 1936 and reinforced by the Italian-German military pact of 1939. Japan joined the pact in 1940, and other countries followed: Hungary, Bulgaria, Romania, Slovakia, and Croatia. The Axis Powers were defeated by the Allies (or Allied Powers), led by the United States, Britain, and the Soviet Union.
*See also:* World War II.

**Azalea**, number of species of a shrub (genus *Rhododendron*), cultivated principally for ornamental purposes. Best known in the United States are the pinxter (*R. nudiflorum*), the flame azalea (*R. calendulacea*), and the rhodera (*R. canadense*).
*See also:* Heath.

**Azazel**, evil spirit thought by the early Hebrews to inhabit the wilderness. On the Day of Atonement, a goat would be sent out to the Azazel bearing the discarded sins of the people; hence the word *scapegoat*.

## Azerbaijan

| | |
|---|---|
| Capital: | Bakoe |
| Area: | 33,400 sq mi |
| | (86,600 sq km) |
| Population: | 7,856,000 |
| Language: | Azerbaijani |
| Government: | Republic |
| Independent: | 1991 |
| Head of gov.: | Prime minister |
| Per capita: | U.S.$480 |
| Mon. unit: | 1 Azerbaijan manat= |
| | 100 gepik |

**Azerbaijan**, or Azerbaidjan, independent country on the westcoast of the Caspian Sea, bordered by Russia, Armenia and Iran. The capital and chief port is Baku, and Kirovabad and Sumgait are important cities.

*Land and climate*. The republic consists mainly of lowlands surrounded by the Kura River and its tributary, the Araks, which forms the border with Iran. Near the Caspian coast is a fertile plain with an abundant water supply. Tea, citrus fruits, tobacco, and rice are produced there. Further inland the climate is arid, but extensive irrigation makes cultivation possible.

*People*. The majority of the inhabitants are Azerbaijanis. The most important minority group consists of Armenians. Most Azerbaijanis are Muslims. The official language is Azerbaijani.

*Economy*. Cotton and sheep are the basis of a large textile industry. The region is rich in minerals, notably oil and natural gas from the long-established Baku oilfields; it is one of the oldest oil-producing areas in the world. The Caucasian hills provide iron ore.

*History*. Settled by Medes as part of the Persian Empire, it was periodically dominated by Romans, Arabs, Mongols, and Turks, returning to Persia in the 16th century. The Russian Tsar Alexander I annexed northern Azerbaijan in 1813. An independent republic was formed in 1918, but was conquered by the Soviets in 1920. In 1991 Azerbaijan regained its independence and joined the Commonwealth of Independent States. Relations with Russia remained tensed. The economic outlook seems favourable because of the large oil and gas supplies.

*See also:* Union of Soviet Socialist Republics.

**Azimuth**, in navigation and astronomy, the angular distance, measured from 0 to 360°, along the horizon eastward from an observer's north point to the point of intersection of the horizon and a great circle passing through the observer's zenith and a star or planet.

**Azimuth circle** *See:* Navigation.

**Azores** (pop. 252,200), 9 mountainous islands in the North Atlantic about 900 mi (1,448 km) west of Portugal. São Miguel is the largest and most populated. Colonized and under Portuguese rule since the mid-15th century, the islands enjoy considerable autonomy.

**Azov, Sea of,** arm of the Black Sea in southwest RF, joined to that sea by the Strait of Kerch. Maximum depth is only 50 ft (15 m); length is 200 mi (322 km), maximum width 80 mi (129 km). The Don River flows into the eastern end of the sea, known as the Gulf of Taganrog.

**Aztec Ruins National Monument,** site in northwestern New Mexico on the Animas River containing the excavated ruins of a 12th-century Pueblo Indian town. Mistaken for Aztec by European American settlers, the ruins include a 500-room building and many Pueblo artifacts. The monument was established in 1923.

**Aztecs,** pre-Columbian natives of Central Mexico, traditionally thought to have migrated from Aztlán in the north to the Valley of Mexico. A warrior tribe, they took over the cities of the Toltecs, from whom they also derived part of their culture. The Aztec empire consisted of a confederation of 3 city states, Tenochtitlán (the capital, site of present-day Mexico City), Tlacopan, and Texcoco. The empire expanded under the rule of Montezuma I, and eventually extended to present day Guatemala. Montezuma I would die defending Tenochtitlán. Religious belief contributed greatly to Aztec political and social structure. The 2 chief gods were Huitzilopochtli, god of war and the sun, and Quetzalcoatl, god of learning. Human victims were sacrificed to these and other gods. The Aztecs were superb artisans, working in gold, silver, and copper and creating fine pottery and mosaics. They are famed for their lavishly decorated temples, such as those at Tenochtitlán, Tula, Cuicuilco, Xochicalco, and Cholula. The arrival of the conquistador Hernán Cortés (1519) heralded the destruction and collapse of the Aztec empire.
*See also:* Mexico.

**Azurite,** blue-colored crystalline mineral once used to make artist's pigment but now mainly used in jewelry. The crystals consist of copper carbonate and water and commonly occur near the surfaces of copper mines. Large deposits of azurite are found at Chessy, near Lyons in France, in Southwest Africa, and in smaller deposits in the western United States (Arizona, Utah).

---

# B

**B,** second letter of the English alphabet, can be traced back to ancient Semitic roots. The letter is believed to derive from the Maobite Stone hieroglyph, found in the present state of Jordan, dating from the 9th century B.C. The Hebrew letter *beth*, meaning "house," and the Greek *beta* both come from this form. The Latin is virtually the same as the Greek, and it is this latter which is still used today. The lowercase *b*, a variant in which the upper loop has disappeared through the speed of writing, appeared in the Roman period.

**Baal** (Semitic, "lord" or "owner"), ancient Middle East fertility god. Canaanite tablets dating from 2500 B.C. represent him combating Mot, god of drought and sterility. In Babylonia, Baal was known as Bel, and in Phoenicia as Melkart. In the Old Testament the name is used pejoratively, the cult of Baal having been denounced by the Hebrew prophets.

**Ba'al Shem Tov** (Israel ben Eliezer; 1700?-60), Jewish teacher and founder of the religious movement Hasidism. Ba'al Shem Tov (Hebrew: "Master of the Good Name") was considered by his followers a miracle healer. He advocated the joyous worship of God in all activities, opposing fasting and other forms of self-denial. Hasidism is now practiced by some Jews in Europe, Israel, and the United States.
*See also:* Hasidism.

**Babar** (1483-1530), also spelled Babur or Baber, Turkish prince who founded the Mogul empire in India. A descendant of Genghis Khan and Tamerlane, Babar ruled 1526-30. He defeated the forces of the Afghan sultan near Delhi and went on to conquer most of northern India.
*See also:* Akbar.

**Babbage, Charles** (1792-1871), British mathematician and inventor who devoted much labor and expense to an unsuccessful attempt to devise a mechanical calculator, his so-called "analytical engine." With J. Herschel and G. Peacock, he introduced the Leibnizian "d" notation for calculus into British mathematical use in place of the less flexible "dot" notation devised by Sir Isaac Newton.

**Babbitt, Irving** (1865-1933), U.S. scholar and noted opponent of Romanticism. He led the New Humanism movement in literary criticism, which stressed classical reason and restraint. His works include *The New Laokoön* (1910) and *On Being Creative* (1932).

**Babbler,** any of a large and varied group of birds of the Muscicapidae family found mainly in Africa, southern Asia, and Australia. Named for their loud, repeated calls, babblers are sometimes called babbling thrushes or chatterers.

**Babel, Isaak Emanuilovich** (1894-1941?), Russian short-story writer best known for his collections *Odessa Tales* (1923-24) and *Red Cavalry* (1926), the former describing Jewish life in the Ukraine, the latter his service with the Red Army during the Russian civil war (1918-20). Arrested in 1939, he died in a Siberian prison camp.

**Babel, Tower of,** in the Old Testament, a tower erected to reach heaven. God punished the builders for their presumption by making them speak many mutually unintelligible languages.
*See also:* Old Testament.

**Babirussa** (*Babirussa babirussa*), wild hog of Indonesia, about 27 in (69 cm) tall and weighing about 128 lb (58 kg). The males are notable for their long tusks. A docile, night-hunting member of the pig family, it forages for fruits and vegetables in the soil near rivers and swamps.

**Babi Yar,** ravine near Kiev, in the Ukraine. On Sept. 29 and 30, 1941, German SS troops executed and buried more than 33,000 Soviet Jews who

had been brought to the ravine on a promise of resettlement. In "Babi Yar" (1962) the Russian poet Yevgeni Yevtushenko indicted the Soviet leadership for failing to commemorate the massacre or to honor its victims.
*See also:* Holocaust.

**Baboon,** large primate monkey of the African savannas (genus *Papio*), distinguished by long muzzle and great strength. Baboons move in groups of 20 to 150 individuals. They are highly aggressive omnivores with a complex social structure. Their bodies are covered with unusually long hair, except for parts of the face and the buttocks, which may be brightly colored.
*See also:* Mandrill; Monkey.

**Baby,** infant, newborn, neonate. Babies are classified as premature, full-term, or postmature, depending on their gestational age (i.e. whether they are born early, on time, or late). Premature babies often have medical problems.

**Baby boom,** steep increase in the U.S. birthrate following World War II. During 1946-64, 76 million people were born, accounting for nearly one-third of the U.S. population in 1980; in the 1970s, the birthrate dropped.

**Babylon,** capital of the ancient kingdom of Babylonia, between the Tigris and Euphrates rivers (Babylon, "gate of the god"), about 55 mi (88.5 km) south of modern Baghdad. The reign of Nebuchadnezzar II (d.  562 B C) marked the height of Babylonian splendor. The city's Hanging Gardens were one of the Seven Wonders of the World. Cyrus of Persia captured Babylon in 538 B.C
*See also:* Hammurabi; Nebuchadnezzar.

**Babylonia and Assyria,** ancient kingdoms of the Middle East in Mesopotamia, the fertile valley of the Tigris and Euphrates rivers. Assyria was in northern Mesopotamia, while Babylonia lay to the south. The Tigris-Euphrates Valley, along with the Nile, the Indus, and the Yellow rivers, was one of the cradles of world civilization. Agriculture and the raising of livestock may have begun in Mesopotamia earlier than anywhere else, about 8000-7000 B C. The first urban economy was also established in Mesopotamia.
About 3000 B.C the Sumerian civilization began to emerge in southern Babylonia. The Sumerians built an irrigation system and invented cuneiform writing. Sumer was composed of the independent and frequently hostile city-states of Lagash, Ur (where the biblical Abraham was born), Kish, Erech, and Umma. Northern Babylonia was conquered by a Semitic people from the west around 2500 B C and the kingdom of Akkad emerged. Its founder, Sargon (c.  2306-2250), conquered Sumer areas to the east and west, a policy of expansion that was continued by his successors. Sumerian civilization survived for a time under the kings of Ur, under whom the earliest known code of laws was compiled and work started on the great ziggurat, a tiered pyramid-shaped temple.
Meanwhile an Amorite dynasty established itself in Akkad and made the town of Babylon its chief center. Southern Mesopotamia came to be called Babylonia. The sixth king of this dynasty, Hammurabi (c.  1792-1750), was an able ruler who organized his territories on imperial lines. Hammurabi's

famous code divided the people into 3 classes (citizens, commoners, and slaves), and contained laws on property, inheritance, marriage, and the family. Punishments for criminal offenses were usually severe, and increased with the status of the victim. About 1594 a Hittite army sacked Babylon, and the country was conquered by the Kassites, who ruled for more than 400 years, adopting Babylonian culture. By 1171 a native Babylonian dynasty had taken over, but its authority was uncertain. The 11th and 10th centuries B C saw the influx of Aramaean tribes from the west and Chaldean infiltration along the Persian Gulf.

The Middle Assyrian Empire began to emerge as a great military power in the 14th century B C, reaching the height of its power around 1100. A period of decline followed, but a new Assyrian Empire rose in the 9th and 8th centuries B.C. Babylonia, Syria, and Israel fell to Assyrian arms; even Egypt was for a time under Assyrian rule. Sennacherib (705-682) made Nineveh his capital and transformed it into one of the most splendid cities of the time. During his reign Babylon revolted (689) and he destroyed the city and its inhabitants, but Babylon was in part restored by his successor, Esarhaddon. The last great king of Assyria was Ashurbanipal (669-627?). An able general like his predecessors, he was also a devoted patron of the arts and literature. Some 25,000 tablets from the large library he assembled are now in the British Museum, London. During this period Assyria was the most powerful nation in the Middle East, but after Ashurbanipal's death it suddenly began to collapse. There was widespread revolt, and in 612 the Chaldeans of Babylonia, in alliance with the Scythians and Medes, captured and destroyed Nineveh. The last Assyrian forces were destroyed in 609.

The Assyrians decorated their buildings with glazed bricks and wall paintings. During the height of the empire the palace walls were covered with great stone reliefs that give a vivid impression of life of the time. Other remains include great statues of winged bulls and lions with human heads that once guarded the palaces.

*The Neo-Babylonian Empire.* After many years as a subject state of the Assyrian Empire, Babylonia recovered its independence under the Chaldean king Nabopolassar (626 B C.). He devoted most of his reign to the destruction of Assyria, and after the fall of Nineveh brought the southern part of the empire, including Syria, Palestine, and part of southern Persia, under his control, despite the opposition of Egypt. This new Babylonian Empire, which was to enjoy immense power and prosperity, was consolidated by his son Nebuchadnezzar II (605-562).

Nebuchadnezzar continued the war against Egypt. Meanwhile, Tyre and Judah revolted. He twice captured Jerusalem, and on the second occasion (587) destroyed the city and deported most of the inhabitants of Judah to captivity in Babylon. Tyre surrendered after a siege lasting 13 years. Nebuchadnezzar made Babylon one of the most magnificent cities of ancient times. It was girdled by massive outer and inner walls with numerous gates, including the gate of Ishtar, which opened on to the great processional way that led to the temple of Marduk. The terraced Hanging Gardens overlooking the Euphrates River were one of the seven wonders of the ancient world and formed part of the imposing palace. Assassination and civil war followed his death, but prosperity returned under Nabonidus and his son Belshazzar. In 539 B.C. the ambitious Cyrus II, king of the Medes and Persians, invaded Babylonia. The Book of Daniel tells how Belshazzar was warned of the final disaster by the "writing on the wall" that mysteriously appeared during a feast the evening before Babylon fell. Babylonia now became a province of the Persian Empire, and Babylon the provincial administrative center.

Knowledge of Babylonian life comes largely from the thousands of clay cuneiform tablets that have been found at various sites, including legal and commercial records, literary and historical texts, and treatises on magic and astrology. The ancient Babylonians based their number system on 60. They separated the day into 12 double hours and the year into 12 months of 30 days each. They were the first to divide the circle into 360 degrees and the minute into 60 seconds. Their system was able to express fractions and squares and cube roots. The later Babylonians were noted astronomers, and the Chaldean priests could predict eclipses of the sun and moon.

Midway between the civilizations of the Indus and the Nile, the Babylonians acted as the great cultural intermediaries of the ancient world. Because Mesopotamia lacked such raw materials as metals, stone, and wood, the Babylonians became great merchants, trading as far as Armenia and the Red Sea. The Chaldeans, like the Assyrians before them, brought the area of the Near East known as the Fertile Crescent together under one rule, creating the first cosmopolitan society of peoples of many cultures and languages.
*See also:* Hammurabi; Nebuchadnezzar.

**Babylonian Captivity**, in Israeli history, period from the fall of Jerusalem to the Babylonians (586 B C.) to the reconstruction of new Jewish Palestinian state (after 538 B.C ).

**Baby's breath**, or babies' breath, garden plant (*Gypsophila paniculata*), known for branched clusters of tiny white or pink flowers. Most are perennials; annuals are grown from seed. Ranging from 2 to 3 ft (61 to 90 cm) in height, baby's breath is frequently used in floral bouquets.
*See also:* Pink.

**Bacchus**, in Roman mythology, god of wine and revelry. The festivals in his honor, called *bacchanalia*, became orgies of drink and sex and were banned in 186 B C
*See also:* Dionysus.

**Bach, Carl Philipp Emanuel** (1714-88), German composer and musician, known as the "Hamburg Bach"; one of the sons of Johann Sebastian Bach. His *Essay on the True Art of Playing Keyboard Instruments* (1753) is still considered a valid guide to keyboard technique. From 1740 until his death he was court musician and harpsichordist to Frederick the Great.

**Bach, Johann Christian** (1735-82), German composer and musician, often known as the "English Bach"; youngest son of Johann Sebastian Bach. He spent many years in Italy, where he angered his family by converting to Catholicism and writing operas. He spent the last 20 years of his life in London, where he was music master to King George III.

**Bach, Johann Sebastian** (1685-1750), German composer. He composed preludes, passacaglias, toccatas, and fugues for the organ, perfecting the art of polyphony. The 48 preludes and fugues he wrote for the keyboard, published collectively as *The Well-Tempered Clavier*, are particularly renowned. Bach wrote much music for other solo instruments, notably the

cello, as well as a number of concertos and orchestral suites. He also wrote hundreds of church cantatas. Among his religious compositions are the *St. John Passion*, the *Mass in B Minor*, and the *Christmas Oratorio*. His music is seen as the crowning achievement of the Baroque Age.
*See also:* Baroque; Cantata.

**Bachelor's button**, common name for several annual plants bearing small, button-shaped flowers. The cornflower is the best known.

**Bachelor's degree** *See:* Degree, academic.

**Backbone** *See:* Spine; Vertebrate.

**Back swimmer** *See:* Water bug.

**Bacon, Francis** (1561-1626), English philosopher and statesman who held various posts, finally becoming lord chancellor to James I in 1618. In 1621 he was banished from office for taking bribes and spent his last years writing. His most important contribution to philosophy was his advocacy of induction, the process of reasoning from the particular to the general, building theories on the basis of observed fact rather than making predictions from immutable general propositions. In this he was one of the founders of modern experimental science. His philosophical works were compiled in *Instauratio Magna* (1620).

**Bacon, Francis** (1909-92), English painter. His unique style expresses the isolation and horror of the human condition, through distorted figures often conveying panic and menace.

**Bacon, Nathaniel** (1647-76), leader of a popular uprising in Virginia (1676) called Bacon's Rebellion. Governor William Berkeley was driven from Jamestown by the rebels, who objected to his failure to defend European settlements from Native Americans. Bacon's death from malaria ended the revolt.
*See also:* Bacon's Rebellion.

**Bacon, Roger** (c.1214-92), English Franciscan and scholastic philosopher renowned for his interest in science and his observation of natural phenomena. He is sometimes credited with many precocious discoveries (of the microscope, for example), but there is great doubt about the truth of these claims.

**Bacon's Rebellion**, uprising in colonial Virginia, 1676, led by planter Nathaniel Bacon against the governor, Sir William Berkeley. Bacon led unauthorized forces against the Native Americans. Though denounced as a traitor, he briefly controlled the Jamestown colony. The civil war between his and Berkeley's forces ended shortly after Bacon's death from malaria.

**Bacteria**, unicellular (one-celled) microorganisms of the class Schizomycetes, existing either as free-living organisms or as parasites. Bacteria may be divided into 3 groups: aerobes, which require atmospheric oxygen to live; anaerobes, which cannot live when exposed to it; and facultative anaerobes,

which can live with or without it. They also come in 3 main shapes: rod, round, and spiral, called bacillus, coccus, and spirillum respectively. Generally a bacterium has an exterior cell wall within which a membrane encloses the soft *cytoplasm*, where enzymes digest and assimilate food. The DNA in which genetic information is encoded is in a portion of the cytoplasm, but unlike that of most other cells, is not separately enclosed in a nucleus. Bacteria reproduce asexually, by fission (*mitosis*), with each cell dividing evenly in two. In certain bacteria DNA is also sometimes transferred between 2 cells (*conjugation*). Bacteria cause many different chemical reactions in their hosts. Some aid in digestion and after processes within animals, and others break down dead plant and animal material in soil to provide nutrients for new growth. Bacteria that cause disease are called pathogens.
*See also:* Bacteriology; Cell; Leeuwenhoek, Anton van.

**Bacteriological warfare** *See:* Chemical and biological warfare.

**Bacteriology,** science that deals with the characteristics and activities of bacteria, as related to medicine, industry, and agriculture. Bacteria were discovered in 1676 by Anton van Leeuwenhoek. Modern techniques of study began to arise around 1870, with the use of stains and the discovery of methods of growing bacteria in laboratory dishes. Much pioneering work was done by Louis Pasteur and Robert Koch.
*See also:* Antibiotic; Bacteria; Immunity.

**Bactria,** ancient Greek kingdom in central Asia, lying between the Hindu Kush Mountains and the Amu Darya River, in what is now Afghanistan and Russian Turkestan. Bactria became part of the Persian Empire and fell to Alexander the Great in 330 B C. It became independent in 256 B.C. but fell 150 years later.

**Bad Aachen** *See:* Aachen.

**Baden-Baden** (pop. 48,700), city and spa in the German state of Baden-Württemberg. It is situated at the edge of the Black Forest in the Rhine Valley, and is famous for its warm mineral springs.

**Baden-Powell, Agnes** *See:* Girl Scouts and Girl Guides; Baden-Powell, Robert Stephenson Smyth, Lord.

**Baden-Powell, Robert Stephenson Smyth, Lord** (1857-1941), British army officer and founder of the Boy Scouts (1908) and Girl Guides (1910). His sister, Agnes Baden-Powell, was cofounder of the Girl Scouts. His published works include *Scouting for Boys* (1908) and *Girl Guiding* (1917).
*See also:* Boy Scouts.

**Badger,** any of several medium-size (about 30 lb/13.6 kg), omnivorous, burrowing mammals of the weasel family Mustelidae, distributed throughout Eurasia, North America, and parts of Indonesia. Badgers are almost always nocturnal.

**Badlands,** region of southwestern South Dakota, about 100 miles (160 km) long and 40 miles (64 km) wide, characterized by an almost total lack of

vegetation. Heavily eroded by wind and water, the area shows rugged hills, gullied slopes, steep buttes, fluted pinnacles, and layers of multicolored shales and sandstones. The term "badlands" is also applied to similar regions in western North Dakota, eastern Arizona, northwestern Nebraska, and northern Wyoming.
*See also:* South Dakota.

**Badlands National Park**, some 243,302 acres (98,461 hectares) of badlands in southwestern South Dakota. It comprises barren ravines, ridges of multi-colored shale, fossiled sandstone, and wildlife. A national monument since 1929, the area was renamed a national park in 1978.

**Badminton**, game played by 2 or 4 persons using lightweight rackets and a shuttlecock or bird (a feathered ball made of cork or rubber), which is hit back and forth over a 5-foot high net that divides the court at the center. Each player "serves" by hitting the shuttlecock over the net to an opponent, who must return it before it hits the ground. The game, which probably originated in India, was introduced in the United States in the late 19th century.

**Baeck, Leo** (1873-1956), German rabbi and theologian of Reform Judaism. Baeck survived the Theresienstadt concentration camp. His *Essence of Judaism* (1905) interpreted Judaism as a religion devoid of mythology and concerned with the personal duty.

**Baekeland, Leo Hendrik** (1863-1944), Belgian-born chemist who, after emigrating to the United States in 1889, devised Velox photographic printing paper (selling the process to Eastman in 1899) and discovered Bakelite, the first modern synthetic plastic.

**Baer, Karl Ernst von** (1792-1876), German founder of comparative embryology. He discovered the notochord and the mammalian egg in the ovary.

**Baez, Joan** (1941-    ), U.S. singer of folk ballads and popular songs, known for her clear, expressive voice and her involvement in social and political action. Baez achieved widespread fame during the height of the Vietnam War as a performer of protest songs.

**Baffin, William** (c.    1584-1622), English navigator and Arctic explorer. As pilot on a vessel seeking the Northwest Passage, he is credited with the discovery of Baffin Bay (1616). Baffin Island is named after him.

**Baffin Island**, world's fifth-largest island, between Greenland and Canada, part of Canada's Northwest Territories, a rugged, glaciated tract 183,810 sq mi (477,906 sq km) in area with a mountain range along its east coast. The largely Eskimo population lives by fishing, trading, and whaling.
*See also:* Baffin, William.

**Baganda** *See:* Ganda.

**Baghdad** (pop. 4,000,000), capital and largest city of Iraq, on both banks of the Tigris River, at a point where the Tigris is only 25 mi (40 km) from the Euphrates. Founded 762 A.D., the city became the center of Arab and Muslim

**Bahamas**

| | |
|---|---|
| Capital: | Nassau |
| Area: | 5,382 sq mi |
| | (13,939 sq km) |
| Population: | 280,000 |
| Language: | English |
| Government: | Parlementary monar- |
| | chy |
| Independent: | 1973 |
| Head of gov.: | Prime minister |
| Per capita: | U.S. $11,940 |
| Mon. unit: | 1 Bahamian dollar = |
| | 100 cents |

civilization during its golden age, in the 9th and 10th centuries. In 1258 the city was sacked by the Mongols, and in 1638 it became part of the Ottoman Empire. In 1921 it became the capital of the newly formed kingdom of Iraq. After World War II Baghdad developed into a modern metropolis. The city is a shipping and industrial center and has an international airport. During the Gulf War the city was damaged by allied bombing.
*See also:* Iraq; Persian Gulf War.

**Bagpipe**, musical wind instrument in which air is blown into a leather bag and then forced out through musical pipes. The melody is played on one or two pipes (the chanters), while drone pipes sound bass tones. The bagpipe originated in Asia but is best known as Scotland's national instrument.

**Baguio** (pop. 119,000), mountain resort city in Luzon in the Philippines. Baguio was developed as a modern city by William Howard Taft, then U.S. governor of the Philippines, when the country was under U.S. rule in the early 1900s. Nearly destroyed during World War II, the city was later rebuilt and is now an important gold-mining center.
*See also:* Philippines.

**Baha'i faith**, religion founded by the Persian Mirza Husain Ali Nuri (1817-92), known as Baha Ullah ("Glory of God"). The Baha'is believe in the unity of all religions and the equality of men and women. They advocate world government. The faith It has a worldwide following; its international center is in Haifa, Israel.

**Bahamas**, nation of some 700 subtropical islands and more than 2,000 islets, or cays, extending about 600 mi (970 km) from the coast of Florida, southeast toward Haiti. Nassau is the capital. The economy is based on tourism, fishing, and the export of wood products, cement, salt, and crayfish. Colonized by Britain in the 1640s, the islands became an independent state in the British Commonwealth in 1973. The Bahamas are a tax haven.
*See also:* Nassau.

**Baha Ullah** (Mirza Husain Ali Nuri; 1817-92), Persian religious leader. A disciple of Babism, a sect that split off from Islam in 1848, he was exiled to Turkey by the Persian government in 1863. In that year he proclaimed himself the Promised One awaited by the Babists. He later founded the Baha'i faith, authoring its basic text, *Kitabi Ikan*, or *Book of Certitude*.
*See also:* Baha'i faith.

**Bahrain**, independent Arab emirate consisting of Bahrain Island and a number of smaller islands, in the Persian Gulf between the Saudi Arabian coast and the Qatar peninsula. The capital is Manama. The country has a desert climate, and the economy is based on oil drilling and refining. A trading center in ancient times, Bahrain became an emirate (monarchy) in 1783 and fell under British control in 1861. It attained independence in 1971. Since the oil supply is slowly becoming exhausted, Bahrain is now developing the industrial sector and the services sector.
*See also:* Arab League; Manama.

**Bail**, money or property security deposited to obtain a prisoner's freedom of movement, pledging that he or she will appear before the court when called.

**Bailey, Liberty Hyde** (1858-1954), U.S. botanist and educator whose studies of cultivated plants linked the practice of horticulture to the science of botany. He established (1888) the country's first horticulture laboratory at what is now Michigan State University. As a professor of botany and horticulture (1888-1903), and later as dean of the College of Agriculture at Cornell University (1904-13), he pioneered agricultural education in the United States. His *Cyclopedia of American Horticulture* (1900-02) was considered a major reference work.

**Bailey Bridge**, strong temporary or semi-permanent bridge constructed by a method suggested in 1941 by Sir Donald Bailey, then chief designer at the Royal Engineers Experimental Bridging Establishment in England. It consists of a series of mass-produced, lightweight girders that can be easily bolted together to produce the required length or to reinforce one another.

| Bahrain | |
|---|---|
| Capital: | Manama |
| Area: | 267 sq mi |
| | (691 sq km) |
| Population: | 616.000 |
| Language: | Arabic |
| Government: | Absolute monarchy |
| Independent: | 1971 |
| Head of gov.: | Prime Minister |
| Per capita: | U.S. $7,840 |
| Mon. unit: | 1 Bahrain dinar = |
| | 1,000 fils |

Its immense flexibility and ease of construction made it immediately successful, particularly for military use. During World War II over 4,000 were built in Europe.

**Baily's Beads,** named for Francis Baily (1774-1844), the apparent fragmentation of the thin crescent of the sun just before totality in a solar eclipse, caused by sunlight shining through mountains at the edge of the lunar disk. *See also:* Eclipse.

**Baja California,** or Lower California, 761-mi (1,220-km) dry, mountainous peninsula in northwest Mexico. Separating the Pacific Ocean from the Gulf of California, it is 30-150 mi (48-241 km) wide. It is divided into the state of Baja California in the north and the territory of Baja California Sur in the south.

**Baker, George** *See:* Divine, Father.

**Baker, Howard Henry, Jr.** (1925-    ), U.S. political leader. He was the senior Republican on the Senate committee investigating the Watergate affair and was elected minority leader of the Senate in 1977. He became majority leader in 1981 and was White House chief of staff under Pres. Ronald Reagan in 1987 and 1988.

**Baker, James Addison, III** (1930-    ), U.S. secretary of state under President George Bush (1989-92). A lawyer from Texas, Baker was appointed secretary of commerce in 1975 by President Gerald R. Ford. He served as President Ronald Reagan's chief of staff (1981-85) and later secretary of the treasury (1985-88). He managed the 1988 and 1992 presidential campaign of Bush.
*See also*: Bush, George Herbert Walker.

**Baker, Josephine** (1906-75), U.S. born, French black singer and dancer of international fame. She was a film and stage artist, philanthropist, and social campaigner.

**Baking soda** *See:* Soda.

**Bakke case,** suit brought by Allan Bakke in 1974 against the University of California claiming that the institution's affirmative-action program had wrongfully denied him admission to medical school solely because he was white. On June 28, 1978, the U.S. Supreme Court ruled 5 to 4 in Bakke's favor, declaring that strict racial quotas to determine university admission are unconstitutional.

**Baku** (pop. 1,500,000), capital of Azerbaijan. On the southwest shore of the Apsheron peninsula in the Caspian Sea, Baku is an oil refining center as well as an important port, industrial center, and railroad center.
*See also:* Azerbaijan.

**Balaklava,** seaport village in the Crimean region, southwestern part of the former USSR, and site of the Crimean War battle (Oct. 25, 1854) commemorated by Alfred Lord Tennyson's "The Charge of the Light Brigade" (1854). *See also:* Crimean War.

**Balalaika,** usually 3-stringed musical instrument of ancient Slavic origin used in Russian and East European folk music. It has a triangular body and long fretted neck. Its six sizes may be combined in ensemble playing.

**Balance,** instrument for weighing; usually a bar with 2 matched pans suspended from each end, which pivots on a central point as weights are placed in the pans. If the weights are equal, the force of gravity on them is equal, and the balance swings level. *See also:* Scale, weighing.

**Balance of nature,** concept of nature as a network of relationships and interdependencies between animals and plants, all of which support and control each other in a stable and unchanging equilibrium. The concept has been greatly modified since it was first suggested in the latter half of the 19th and early 20th centuries. It is now recognized that although a degree of balance does exist, it is a highly dynamic and unstable state. The main reason for this is that animals and plants depend not only on each other but on such external factors as climate and availability of food. Where food supplies are plentiful and the range of forms of life is large, a community may achieve a fairly high degree of stability. But where the "food web" is simple, as in the northern tundras, there may be insufficient control mechanisms to prevent the periodic explosions of population that cause, for example, the self-destructive mass migration of lemmings. Many natural communities that were once stable have become unstable or have been destroyed by industry, agriculture, and disposal of sewage. Pesticides may kill beneficial insect parasites and thus lead to an uncontrollable increase in the pest population in succeeding years. Pesticides may also become concentrated in the bodies of predators at the top of the food chain. The death of hawks and owls from pesticides allows the population of rodent pests to increase. A small alteration in the balance of nature may produce unexpected consequences in some other part of the community.

**Balance of payments,** relation between payments in and out of a country. The figures that make up the balance of payments include trading (imports and exports), invisible earnings (insurance and banking), and capital movements (investment overseas or money from abroad). A country that persistently shows a deficit may have to devalue its currency, borrow money, or adopt strict economies. A country with a large surplus is pressured by inflation.

**Balance of power,** system of international relations wherein nations alter their alliances to other nations so no single nation dominates. Sincer World War II, the United States and the former Soviet Union have emerged as superpowers, but Japan and China may, by virtue of size and military-industrial potential, demand a radically altered balance of power. *See also:* International relations.

**Balanchine, George** (George Melitonovich Balanchivadze; 1904-83), Russian-born choreographer, founder of the School of American Ballet (1934).

He worked with Sergei Diaghilev in France in the 1920s and came to the United States in 1934. In 1948 he became artistic director of the New York City Ballet.
*See also:* Ballet.

**Balboa, Vasco Núñez de** (c.1475-1519), Spanish conquistador credited as first European discoverer of the Pacific Ocean. In 1510 he cofounded one of the first lasting European settlements on the American mainland, Antigua in Panama. Encouraged by Native American tales of a wealthy kingdom on "the other sea," in 1513 he led an expedition across the isthmus, saw the Pacific, and claimed it and all its coasts for Spain. He was later charged with treason and executed.
*See also:* Pacific Ocean.

**Balch, Emily Greene** (1867-1961), U.S. sociologist, economist, and humanitarian; joint winner of the 1946 Nobel Peace Prize. Cofounder of the Women's International League for Peace and Freedom, she was its secretary 1919-22 and 1934-35 and its honorary president from 1936.

**Bald cypress**, common name for a family (Taxodiaceae) of evergreens with wood cones and needlelike or scalelike leaves. The common bald cypress (*Taxodium distichum*), the state tree of Louisiana, is prized for its wood and may be found in swamps and wetlands of the United States, from Texas to New Jersey.

**Bald eagle** (*Haliaetus leucocephalus*), only native North American eagle, national bird of the United States since 1782. About 3 ft (90 cm) long, with a wingspan that may reach 7 ft (2 m), it is black, with white feathers on neck, tail, and head. A member of the hawk family, it preys on fish and is protected as an endangered species in all states.

**Baldness**, or alopecia, lack or loss of hair, usually from the scalp, due to disease of hair follicles. Pattern baldness is an inherited tendency, often starting when a man is in his 20s. It is found in about 40% of the male population. Alopecia areata is a disease of unknown cause producing usually temporary patchy baldness, though it may be total. Prolonged fever, lupus erythematosus, ringworm, certain drugs, and poisons may lead to temporary baldness.

**Baldpate** *See:* Wigeon.

**Baldwin, James** (1924-87), African-American novelist, essayist, and playwright much of whose work deals with racial themes. His novel *Go Tell It on the Mountain* (1953) was based on his Harlem adolescence, while *Another Country* (1962) deals with sexual and racial identity. His best-known essays are collected in *Notes of a Native Son* (1955) and *The Fire Next Time* (1963). His book, *The Evidence of Things Not Seen*, about the Atlanta child murders (1985) is one of his most controversial works.

**Baldwin, Matthias William** (1795-1866), U.S. inventor and philanthropist. *Old Ironsides*, his early locomotive (1830s), was the first of more than 1,500 locomotives designed and manufactured by Baldwin and his Baldwin Locomotive Works. His other inventions included processes for plating gold and for printing patterns on cloth. An abolitionist, he supported education for black children and founded the Franklin Institute.

**Baldwin, Robert** (1804-58), Canadian statesman; leader, with Louis LaFontaine, of the "Great Ministry" (1847-51). He later worked for improved relations between English and French Canadians.

**Baldwin, Stanley** (1867-1947), British Conservative politician, 3 times prime minister (1923-24, 1924-29, 1935-37). He led the breaking of the General Strike of 1926 and was criticized for underestimating the dangers of the rise of fascism in Europe.

**Balearic Islands,** Mediterranean archipelago off eastern Spain, under Spanish rule since 1349. The largest are Majorca, Minorca, and Ibiza. Products include grapes, olives, and citrus fruit.
*See also:* Majorca.

**Baleen** *See:* Whale.

**Balfour, Arthur James Balfour, 1st Earl of** (1848-1930), British statesman best known as author of the Balfour Declaration. He was a Conservative member of parliament 1874-1911; prime minister, 1902-05; and foreign secretary 1916-19.
*See also:* Balfour Declaration.

**Balfour Declaration,** statement of British policy issued in 1917 by Foreign Secretary Arthur Balfour. It stated British support for a Jewish national home in Palestine without prejudice to the rights of the non-Jewish population.

**Bali,** volcanic island and province of South Indonesia, 2,171 sq mi (5,623 sq km). It is a lush, densely populated island. Industries include food processing, tourism, and handicrafts. The largely Hindu Balinese are famous for dancing, music, and decorative arts.

**Baline, Israel** *See:* Berlin, Irving.

**Balkan Peninsula,** mountainous land area in southeastern Europe, south of the Danube and Sava rivers, surrounded by the Adriatic, Ionian, Mediterranean, Aegean, and Black seas. It contains the nations of Bulgaria, Albania, Greece, European Turkey, and most of former Yugoslavia.

**Balkan Wars,** 2 wars in which the Ottoman Empire lost almost all its European territory. In the first war (1912-13) Serbia, Bulgaria, Greece, and Montenegro conquered all of Turkey's European possessions except Constantinople. In the second war (1913) Bulgaria attacked Serbia, but was itself attacked by Rumania, Greece, and Turkey. In the ensuing Treaty of Bucharest (Aug. 1913) Bulgaria lost territory to each of its enemies.

**Ballad,** verse narrative, often meant to be sung, usually describing an event. Traditionally ballads celebrated folk heroes or related popular romances; they were developed by European minstrels in the Middle Ages. Romantic writers, such as Sir Walter Scott, William Wordsworth, and Samuel Taylor Coleridge, adapted the form. In modern popular music the term is used loosely to apply to any kind of sentimental song, but the United States has also produced ballads of the traditional type, ranging from the anonymous "Frankie and Johnny" to the work of Bob Dylan and Joan Baez.

**Ballade,** verse of three 8-line stanzas concluding with a 4-line summary. The French poet François Villon (1431-63?) and the English poet Geoffrey Chaucer (c.1340-1400) used this form, which originated in 14th-century France.

**Ball bearing** *See:* Bearing.

**Ballet,** form of solo and ensemble dance meant for the stage. Ballet evolved from court entertainments of Renaissance Italy, where training in graceful movement was considered essential to a courtier's education. These entertainments were introduced into France by Catherine dé Medici, wife of King Henry II. In the courts of later kings, ballet became firmly established as an aristocratic pastime, and the kings themselves were skilled dancers. King Louis XIV established the first professional ballet school, the Royal Academy of Music and Dance, in 1661. Charles Louis (Pierre) Beauchamp, balletmaster of the Academy, originated the 5 basic foot positions and turnout of the feet that are still fundamental to ballet technique. Early-18th-century ballet was an adjunct to opera. By mid-18th century self-contained pantomime ballets began to appear, and virtuoso dancers modified their costumes to allow more freedom of movement. Jean Georges Noverre helped establish ballet as an integral art form in which plot, music, decoration, and dance were fused into an artistic whole. The 19th-century romantic movement introduced a new emphasis on lightness and grace. Ballerinas began to dance on their toes and adopted the short, full-skirted tutu. The center of European ballet shifted to Russia with the appointment of the French dancer Marius Petipa as balletmaster of the Imperial Ballet in the 1850s. Petipa brought new standards of technical perfection, and his use of Russian folk themes and music gave ballet a wider support among the public. With his assistant Lev Ivanov, he created such classical ballets as *Swan Lake*, *The Nutcracker*, and *The Sleeping Beauty*.

In 1907 the visit of the U.S. dancer Isadora Duncan to St. Petersburg spurred the Russian choreographer Michel Fokine to create a new, modern ballet. Fokine joined with the Russian impresario Sergei Diaghilev to form the Russian Ballet, which opened in Paris in 1909. Diaghilev's company included some of the greatest dancers in the history of ballet: Vaslav Nijinsky, Anna Pavlova, Léonide Massine, and George Balanchine. Many of these dancers went on to found new ballet companies, thus extending Diaghilev's influence throughout the world of the dance. For the Russian Ballet Fokine created *Les Sylphides*, *The Firebird*, and *Rite of Spring*. From 1909 until his death, Diaghilev was the most important figure in European ballet. England's first permanent ballet company, the Vic Wells (later Sadler's Wells), was formed in 1930. Renamed the Royal Ballet in 1957, it is noted for the choreography of Frederick Ashton, and featured dancers Margot Fonteyn and Rudolph Nureyev. After the Revolution, the Russian Ballet was devoted to experimental works on political and social themes, but then returned to the classical models of Petipa. Russian dancers are acknowledged masters of the traditional style. In the United States, contemporary ballet has evolved into a distinctive form combining the modern dance of Jerome Robbins, Martha Graham, and Ruth St. Denis with the tradition of the classical ballet as adapted by Massine and Balanchine. The Ballet Theater, established in 1940, encouraged the work of new U.S. composers and choreographers, and George Balanchine's New York City Ballet has continued to add new and unorthodox works to the repertoire. Professional ballet companies have been established throughout the United States, and the popular tours U.S. companies have undertaken abroad have made this country among the most vital and influential in the dance world. Canada also has several major professional companies: Royal Winnipeg Ballet, National Ballet of Canada (Toronto), and Les Grands Ballets Canadiens (Montreal).

*See also:* Ailey, Alvin; Balanchine, George; Baryshnikov, Mikhail; Diaghilev, Sergei Pavlovich; Pavlova, Anna; Dance; Nijinsky, Vaslav.

**Ballistic missile** *See:* Guided missile.

**Ballistic Missile Early Warning System** *See:* Radar.

**Ballistics**, science dealing with projectiles, traditionally divided into 3 parts: interior ballistics, relating to the progress of the projectile before it is released from the launching device; exterior ballistics, relating to the free flight of the projectile; and terminal ballistics, relating to the behavior of the projectile upon impact, at the end of its trajectory.

**Balloon**, nonpowered, nonrigid, lighter-than-air craft consisting of a bulbous envelope that holds the lifting medium and a payload-carrying basket, or "gondola," suspended below. Balloons may be captive (secured to the ground by a cable) or free-flying. Lift may be provided by a gas such as hydrogen or nonflammable helium or by heated air. Balloons are used in science (weather forecasting and astronomy), as well as for recreational purposes.

*See also:* Zeppelin, Ferdinand von.

**Ballot**, method of registering a vote. It can be a pre-printed list of people running for office or of issues to be decided by a popular vote (referendum). In the United States, about 50% of the elections are held in a closed booth with a printed ballot mounted on a voting machine. The other type of balloting involves voters checking off their choices and depositing their ballots into a sealed box. After voting is over, the ballots are counted and the highest vote-getters are determined to be the winners.

*See also:* Voting.

**Balm**, any of various fragrant herbs of the mint family (genera *Melissa* or *Monarda*). Used in medicinal teas and wine drinks in ancient Greece and Asia, balm is now widely used as a scent in perfume and as a food and drink flavoring.

*See also:* Balm of Gilead.

**Balm of Gilead**, liquid resinous balsam derived from an evergreen tree (*Commiphora meccanesis*). The balsam had medicinal uses in ancient times. By extension, balm of Gilead may refer to anything that soothes or heals.

**Balsa**, or corkwood, tropical U.S. tree (*Ochroma lagopus*), known for its extremely light wood. Ecuador is a large producer of balsa wood, which is an effective insulating material and is also popular for making model airplanes and boats.

**Balsam**, aromatic resinous substance produced by certain plants and trees. Balsam is used in medicines, ointments, chewing gum, varnish, and perfumes.

**Balsam fir** (*Abies balsamea*), evergreen tree of the pine family, found in the northeastern United States and throughout much of Canada. The balsam fir makes a popular Christmas tree; its bark produces a resin called Canada balsam.

**Balsam poplar** *See:* Poplar.

**Baltic Sea**, arm of the Atlantic Ocean, extending into northern Europe. Its 163,000 sq mi (422,170 sq km) are surrounded by Sweden, Finland, Estonia, Latvia, Lithuania, RF, Poland, Germany, and Denmark. It is linked to the North Sea by the Skagerrak, Kattegat, and Oresund straits.

**Baltic States**, Baltic coast republics of Estonia, Latvia, and Lithuania. They became independent in 1917 but were annexed by the USSR in 1940. In the late 1980s, separatist nationalist movements aimed at restoring sovereignty, this was achieved in 1991.
*See also:* Estonia; Latvia; Lithuania.

**Baltimore** (pop. 726,100), largest city in Maryland, on the Patapsco River near Chesapeake Bay. The seventh-largest city in the United States, it is one of the nation's busiest ports, an important road, rail, and air transportation hub, and a leading manufacturing center with metallurgical, electronic, and food- processing industries.
*See also:* Maryland.

**Baltimore, Lord**, collective title of 6 members of the Calvert family, founders of the colony of Maryland. **George Calvert** (1580?-1632) was granted the proprietorship of what became Maryland by Charles I of England in 1632, but died before the charter was signed. The charter rights passed to George's son **Celilius Calvert** (1605?-75), who founded the colony of Maryland in 1632. In 1691, Maryland became a royal colony, but in 1715 the Crown returned the charter to the Calverts.

**Baltimore oriole** (*Icterus galbula*), North American songbird about 18 in (20 cm) long, with a wingspan of about 12 in (30 cm). Males are black and bright orange; females and young are olive, yellow, and brownish. "Baltimore oriole" is now a popular term for the northern oriole because it is no longer considered a separate species but a subspecies.

**Balzac, Honoré de** (1799-1850), French novelist noted for social observation and sweeping vision. *The Human Comedy*, his greatest work, is a collection of novels and stories that offer a comprehensive portrait of French society. Written over a period of two decades, its best-known novels are *Père Goriot* (1835) and *Cousin Bette* (1847).

**Bamako** (pop. 801,500), capital of Mali, located on the Niger River in West Africa. Bamako is a trade center linked by rail to Dakar, Senegal, on the Atlantic Ocean. Factories manufacture food, textiles, and metal goods. A former French colony, Mali became independent in 1960.
*See also:* Mali.

**Bamboo,** woody plant (genus *Bambusa*) with hollow stems found in Asia, Africa, Australia, and the southern United States. Some species grow to 120 ft (27 m). In Asia the young shoots are a major foodstuff, while mature stems are used in building houses and furniture. Amorphous silica from stems is used as a catalyst in some chemical processes.

**Banana,** edible fruit of a large (30-ft/9-m) perennial herb that reaches maturity within 15 months from planting. Main areas of commercial cultivation are in tropical Asia, South America, and the West Indies. Only female flowers produce the banana fruit, and each plant bears fruit only once.

**Banaras** *See:* Varanasi.

**Bancroft, George** (1800-91), U.S. historian and statesman. As secretary of the navy (1845-46), he helped develop the U.S. Naval Academy at Annapolis. His 10-volume *History of the United States* (1834-74) became a standard work, though it was later criticized for its strong nationalistic bias.
*See also:* United States Naval Academy.

**Banda, Hastings Kamuzu** (1906-97), African nationalist leader, first prime minister (1964-66) and president of Malawi (from 1966-94). As leader of the Nyasaland nationalists and head of the Malawi Congress party (from 1960), he sought dissolution of the Federation of Rhodesia and Nyasaland. Following his defeat at the 1994 presidential elections he stepped down.
*See also:* Malawi.

**Bandaranaike, Sirimavo Ratwatte Dias** (1916-   ), prime minister of Sri Lanka and the world's first woman premier. After the assassination of her husband, Prime Minister Solomon Bandaranaike, in 1959, she led his Sri Lanka Freedom party to victory in 1960, continuing his pro-Buddhist and pro-Sinhalese policies. She lost office in 1965 but returned in 1970 with a landslide victory for her left-oriented coalition. Conservatives defeated her in 1977.
*See also:* Sri Lanka.

**Bandicoots,** any of several genera of marsupials of the family Peramelidae found in Oceania, roughly rabbit-sized with tapering snouts. There are considerable reproductive differences from other marsupials, and their fossil history is problematic, so that their relationship to other marsupials is not fully understood.

**Bandung** (pop. 2,056,900), capital city of West Java province, Indonesia. The third-largest city in the country, Bandung is an important industrial, educational, and tourist center.

**Baneberry**, several herbaceous plants with poisonous red, white, or black berries. Two species known as cohosh are native to the United States. Native Americans used them as emetics and cathartics.

**Banff** (pop. 5,200), resort town in Alberta, Canada. Situated in the Bow River Valley of the Rocky Mountains at 4,538 ft (1,383 m) altitude, its attractions are hot springs, skiing, and an abundance of wildlife.

**Banff National Park**, oldest park in Canada, established in 1885, located on the eastern slopes of the Rocky Mountains in southwestern Alberta. The 2,564-sq-mi (6,640-sq-km) park is characterized by glaciers, deep valleys, and mountains. There are also dense forests, alpine meadows, and many animals, including bighorn sheep, bear, and deer.

Bangalore (pop. 2,600,000), capital city of Karnataka state, south central India. A major industrial city, it manufactures soap, telephones, machine tools, pharmaceuticals, and aircraft, along with cotton textiles and hand-loomed silk.

**Bangkok** (pop. 5,876,000), capital city of Thailand. Situated on the Chao Phraya River, about 25 mi (40 km) inland from the Gulf of Siam, Bangkok is Thailand's main port. About three-fourths of Thailand's foreign trade passes through Bangkok; principal exports include rice, teak, rubber, tin, gold, and silver. The city is also a famous jewelry trading center. In addition, almost all of Thailand's higher education institutions are located in Bangkok. Among its numerous Buddhist temples (wats) is the Wat Phra Keo, located within the Grand Palace and containing the famed "Emerald Buddha," carved from jasper.
*See also:* Thailand.

**Bangladesh**, People's Republic of Bangladesh, republic in the northeast of the Indian subcontinent, on the Bay of Bengal; formerly East Pakistan. Bangladesh is a low-lying land centered on the alluvial Ganges-Brahmaputra Delta. A tropical monsoon climate prevails, and because of heavy rains and severe cyclones, most of the country is subject to flooding. Overpopulation accentuates periodic famines and epidemics among the mainly Muslim Bengalis who constitute the great majority of the population. Bangladesh produces a large portion of the world's jute; tea is the other main cash crop, and sugarcane is also grown. Rice and wheat are the major subsistence crops. Natural gas is the only important mineral resource, and manufacturing is largely limited to the proceessing of raw materials. The region was created as East Pakistan (Pakistan's eastern province) in 1947. The province sought greater independence, but West Pakistan refused autonomy and troops crushed large-scale opposition in the ensuing civil war (March-Dec. 1971). Guerrilla fighting continued, Bengalis exiled in India proclaimed a Bengali republic, and Indian invasion forces overran the West Pakistani forces. A Bangladesh

## Bangladesh

| | |
|---|---|
| Capital: | Dhaka |
| Area: | 55,598 sq mi |
| | (143,998 sq km) |
| Population: | 127,567,000 |
| Language: | Bengali |
| Government: | Republic |
| Independent: | 1971 |
| Head of gov.: | President |
| Per capita: | U.S. $240 |
| Mon. unit: | 1 Bangladesh taka = |
| | 100 paisa |

government was established in Dhaka in Dec. 1971. At the end of the 1990s Bangladesh was still one of the poorest countries in the world.

**Bangor** (pop. 88,745), port city of southern Maine, at the convergence of the Penobscot and Kenduskeag rivers. Bangor is the gateway to northern and eastern Maine's resort and lumber areas and a regional commercial center producing shoes, paper, and electronic equipment.

**Bangui** (pop. 451,700), capital city of the Central African Republic. On the Ubangi River, it is being developed as a tourist center for the country's wildlife preserves.
*See also:* Central African Republic.

**Banjarmasin**, **Banjermasin**, or **Bandjarmasin** (pop. 480,700), capital of South Kalimantan province in Indonesia, located on an island between the Barito and Martapura rivers in southeastern Borneo. Exports include oil, diamonds, and lumber.

**Banjo**, stringed musical instrument with a long fretted neck and a circular frame covered by a skin resonator. Its 4 to 9 strings are played by plucking. The banjo originated among slaves in North America and may have been derived from West African instruments. It became popular in 19th-century minstrel shows, in early jazz bands, and in folk music.

**Banjul** (pop. 44,200), capital of Gambia in West Africa, located on St. Mary's Island where the Gambia River flows into the Atlantic Ocean. It is Gambia's only large city, its chief port and economic center. Exports include peanuts, clothing, and farm machinery. It was founded in 1816 (as Bathurst) as a British base for eliminating the slave trade. Gambia gained independence in 1965, and the city was renamed Banjul in 1973.
*See also:* Gambia.

**Bankhead, Tallulah Brockman** (1903-68), U.S. actress in plays and films. A rebel from a distinguished Southern family who made her stage debut at 16, she established herself in such plays as *Rain* (1935) and *The Little Foxes*

(1939), and in films such as *Lifeboat* (1944). Her deep, cynical voice and flamboyant personality made her a successful comedienne on radio and television.

**Bank holiday,** day on which banks are legally closed. In England, such days are fixed annual public holidays. In U.S. history, the term refers to the 4-day period in March 1933 when President Franklin D. Roosevelt ordered all banks closed to halt panic and to assess their financial condition. More than 1,900 banks had collapsed since the beginning of the Depression in 1929.

**Banking,** business of dealing with money and credit transactions. The services offered by banks fall into 4 categories: safe storage, interest-bearing deposit facilities, money transfer, and loans. The nature of safe storage has changed now that most money is held in the form of bank deposits rather than gold or silver coin. Bank branches keep cash available for customers. Most banks also have safe-deposit boxes for storing valuables other than cash. The second basic service arises from the first. Since money given to a bank for safekeeping effectively amounts to a loan to the bank, the bank pays interest on it. Rates vary, depending in part on how much notice the bank requires for withdrawals. The third category of bank services, transfer of money, is carried out mainly by means of checks and credit cards. In making out checks customers authorize the bank to transfer a specified sum from their own account to someone else's (or to pay them in cash). After the check has been handed in or mailed to the bank by the payee (the person to whom the money is to be paid) it is returned to the bank of the person who has writen the check (the payor) through the clearing system run countrywide by the Federal Reserve. Credit cards, in widespread use since about 1970, allow the purchase of services and goods even in places where the bearer is not well known enough to be able to use a check. The final category of bank services, lending to customers, is the most highly developed.

Although basic services are the same from one bank to another all around the world, the details and, in particular, the manner in which they are offered vary considerably. In the United States, state-chartered savings banks and state- or federally-chartered savings and loan associations originally only handled savings deposits and home mortgages, while commercial banks offered checking and a wide range of loans. Recently, however, the distinctions between these institutions have been blurred. In 1913 the Federal Reserve System was set up to strengthen the U.S. banking system. Bank failures in 1933 led to the setting up of the Federal Deposit Insurance Corporation. Since 1974 the banking industry in the United States has suffered from government regulations, increased competition in financial services, and risky investments in real estate, Third World countries, and leveraged buyouts. This has resulted in the collapse of hundreds of banks in 1990 and 1991. As a result, the government has had to face great strain on its bank insurance fund. Banking and the financial services industry are now in a state of transition and restructuring to meet the financial demands of the 21st century.

**Bank of Canada,** central bank of Canada. It controls the amount of money available to other banks in the country. By regulating the money supply, the central bank can make sure that a stable economy and a balanced rate of growth are maintained. The central bank also issues all Canadian bank notes.

It was incorporated in 1934, and, although managed by an independent governor and board of directors, it is owned by the Canadian government. The headquarters are in Ottawa.

**Bank of England,** central bank of the English government founded in 1694 by an Act of Parliament and Royal Charter. In 1946 it was nationalized and its stock was passed to the British Treasury. It advises the government on financial and economic conditions, facilitates the payment of government debt, services the foreign exchange markets, issues bank notes, and administers foreign exchange control.

**Bank of the United States,** name of 2 central banks established in the early years of the United States. In 1791 Alexander Hamilton created the first bank of the United States, chartered by Congress for 20 years. It held government deposits and had some control over the issue of paper currency and the extension of credit. But its constitutionality was questioned, and it was so strongly opposed by agrarian interests and the state banks that its charter was not renewed. A second central bank was chartered for 20 years in 1816 to help finance debts of the War of 1812, but its charter renewal was vetoed by President Andrew Jackson.

**Bankruptcy,** legal status of a debtor whom the courts have declared unable to pay debts. Bankruptcy is regulated by federal laws that provide for an orderly adjustment when a person or business becomes insolvent. A person or business with more debts than assets and no means of meeting debt payment may declare bankruptcy. The interest of both creditors and debtor are given consideration by the court. The Constitution gives Congress the power to establish "uniform Laws on the subject of Bankruptcies throughout the United States" (Article I, Section 8). The first bankruptcy act was passed by Congress in 1800, patterned on English law. The act on which current law is based was passed in 1898. Bankruptcy may be voluntary (filed by the debtor) or involuntary (filed by creditors). When a petition of bankruptcy is filed, the court assumes control over the assets of the debtor. A custodian or trustee is appointed to oversee the debtor's property to protect it from loss. This trustee has legal ownership of all assets of the bankrupt estate except those exempt under local law. The property of the debtor must be sold and the proceeds distributed to creditors on a percentage basis. The debtor is then legally discharged from all previous obligations.

**Banneker, Benjamin** (1731-1806), U.S. mathematician and astronomer, notable as the first African American to gain distinction in science. He was the author of many celebrated astronomical almanacs (1791-1802).

**Bannister, Sir Roger Gilbert** (1929-    ), British athlete, the first man to run a mile in less than 4 minutes, on May 6, 1954, in Oxford. His time was 3 min 59.4 sec.

**Bannock,** tribe of Native American hunters who lived in what is now eastern Idaho and western Wyoming. In 1878 some 1,500 Bannocks and Paiutes, dissatisfied with living conditions in their reservations, participated in the last Native American uprising in the Northwest.

**Bannockburn,** battlefield named for a village in Stirlingshire, central Scotland. Here, in 1314, Scottish forces under Robert the Bruce routed the numerically superior English army of King Edward II, assuring the throne of Scotland for Bruce and ending English rule over Scotland for a period. *See also:* Bruce, Robert the.

**Bantam,** any of a variety of small domestic fowl, often miniatures of larger breeds.

**Banting, Sir Frederick Grant** (1891-1941), Canadian physiologist who, with C.H. Best, first isolated the hormone insulin from the pancreas of dogs (1921), thus providing a major breakthrough in the treatment of diabetes. For this he shared the 1923 Nobel Prize in physiology or medicine with J.J.R. Macleod, who developed the experimental facilities.
*See also:* Insulin.

**Bantu,** linguistic group of central, east, and south Africa. Bantu languages include Swahili and Zulu. The term is often used in South Africa to denote black Africans.

**Bañuelos, Romana Acosta** (1925-     ), U.S. treasurer (1971-74) under President Nixon, first Mexican-American woman to hold high government office. She began her business career in 1949 with a small tortilla stand and built it into a $5 million food company. She was the founder (1964) of the first U.S. bank owned and operated by a Mexican American, the Pan American Bank of East Los Angeles. In 1969 she established a Mexican-American student scholarship.

**Banyan tree,** sacred tree (*Ficus bengalensis*) of India, related to the fig. It grows up to 100 ft (30 m) high, and its branches send down aerial roots that form new trunks on reaching the soil. An individual tree can thus become a dense thicket of intertwined stems and secondary trunks covering an acre or more.

**Baobab** (*Adansonia digitata*), tree of tropical Africa and India with a remarkably thick trunk, reaching 30 ft (10 m) in diameter. The related Australian species is sometimes called the bottle tree for its unusual shape. The branches bear dense masses of leaves, used for medicine and condiments, white flowers, and an edible gourdlike fruit, the juice of which is made into a beverage. The bark is used to make rope, cloth, and paper, and the hollowed trunks are used for dwellings.

**Bao Dai** (1913-97), Vietnamese emperor during the French colonial period. He was the last emperor of Annam (1926-45), until overthrown by the Viet Minh. He was later made head of state of a unified Vietnam (1949-55) created by the French in a final bid to retain Indochina, but he was forced into exile. *See also:* Vietnam.

**Baptism,** rite of initiation into the Christian church. Some churches consider the ceremony the first step to salvation, as a symbolic purification of water. Others regard baptism as a confirmation of salvation through Christ.
*See also:* Christianity; John the Baptist, Saint; Roman Catholic Church.

**Baptists**, members of a Protestant denomination who hold that baptism is for believers only, not simply those born into the faith. Baptism, often at age 12, is by immersion. Total world membership is said to be more than 31 million, most of whom live in the United States, where they constitute the largest Protestant group. Individual churches have considerable autonomy. There is no single Baptist creed; beliefs range from fundamentalist to modernist. The evangelistic and revivalist tradition emphasizes the influence of the laity as well as ministers. The church originated with John Smyth, the leader of a group of English religious dissenters who sought refuge in Holland around 1608. The first U.S. church was founded in Providence, R.I. in 1639, by Roger Williams, and the new denomination evolved independently among the variety of Puritan dissenters. Williams later left the faith to follow his own religious vision. John Clarke in Newport, R.I. and Shubal Stearns in North Carolina were also important early leaders. The Baptist evangelical tradition began during the Great Awakening, an 18th-century U.S. religious revival, and Baptist converts spread westward along the expanding frontiers. In the 19th century the Baptists founded more than 100 colleges and universities. By 1845 the denomination had become particularly influential in the Midwest and the South. In that year a great split occurred over the slavery issue, creating Northern and Southern Baptists. After the Civil War, black churches developed an independent grouping, the National Baptist Convention of America (1880). In 1915 a dispute within that membership created another major group, the National Baptist Convention, USA, Inc. In 1950 the interracial Northern Baptists formed the American Baptist Convention. The Southern Baptist Convention now includes churches beyond the borders of the historic South. U.S. Baptists are active in the World Council of Churches through the Baptist World Alliance, which was founded in 1905.
*See also:* Protestantism.

**Bar**, professional association of lawyers. Attorneys must be admitted to the bar before they can practice law in the United States. The American Bar Association, with over 90,000 members, helps to maintain the standards of the legal profession and is consulted by government on legal matters and judicial appointments.
*See also:* American Bar Association; Law.

**Barabbas**, man described in the New Testament as a bandit condemned to crucifixion at the same time as Jesus. The Roman governor Pontius Pilate agreed to spare one prisoner, and a palace crowd chose Barabbas instead of Jesus.
*See also:* New Testament.

**Baraka, Imamu Amiri** (LeRoi Jones; 1934- ), African-American author and political activist whose plays, especially *Dutchman* (1964), express revulsion at the oppression of black people in white society.

**Barbados**, densely populated small island in the Caribbean; a parliamentary state, part of the British Commonwealth.
About 21 mi (34 km) long and 14 mi (22.5 km) wide, Barbados lies surrounded by coral reefs 250 mi (400 km) northeast of Venezuela. Bridgetown is the capital and chief business center. Carlisle Bay on the southwest

## Barbados

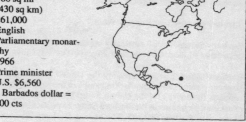

| | |
|---|---|
| Capital: | Bridgetown |
| Area: | 166 sq mi |
| | (430 sq km) |
| Population: | 261,000 |
| Language: | English |
| Government: | Parliamentary monarchy |
| Independent: | 1966 |
| Head of gov.: | Prime minister |
| Per capita: | U.S. $6,560 |
| Mon. unit: | 1 Barbados dollar = 100 cts |

coast is the only harbor. The island has no real mountains and no rivers, and water supply is from artesian wells. The mild climate makes Barbados a popular resort, but it lies in a zone of tropical storms, and destructive hurricanes are not uncommon. The soil is fertile and the whole island is cultivated. Sugarcane, introduced in the 17th century, is still the main crop, though efforts are being made to diversify agriculture and to establish light industry. Chief exports are sugar, molasses, and rum. Nearly 90% of the very dense population is of African descent. Emigrants, mainly to other West Indian islands, are numerous, and money sent home forms a useful part of the economy, which is based on the tourist sector.

Barbados was claimed by the British in 1605 and remained a colony for more than 300 years. The representative assembly was established in 1639, giving the island one of the oldest constitutions in the Commonwealth. Slavery was abolished in 1834, and full adult suffrage was granted in 1950. In 1966 the island gained independence and was admitted to the United Nations. The language is English, the Anglican church is established, and the general outlook is much influenced by a traditional image of England, though many details of life reflect historical and family links with North America.

**Barbarian**, term originally used by ancient Greeks to denote any non-Greek-speaking people. As Greek culture spread with the conquests of Alexander the Great in Asia and the subsequent expansion of the Roman Empire in Europe, the word came to refer to peoples who lived beyond the borders of the Empire and therefore outside Greco-Roman civilization. It then took on a pejorative meaning and now refers to anyone considered uncivilized, primitive, or unsophisticated.
*See also:* Goths; Hun; Vandals.

**Barbarossa** (Khayr ad-Din; c.1483-1546), Turkish naval commander of the western Mediterranean. As high admiral of the Turkish fleet he captured Tunis and Algiers in 1518 and brought the Barbary states under Turkish sovereignty. In 1533 and 1544 he defeated Italian fleets and raided towns in Greece, Italy, France, and Spain.

**Barbarossa** *See:* Frederick.

**Barbary ape**, small tailless monkey (*Macaca sylvana*) of Algeria, Morocco, and Gibraltar. There is a legend that the British will lose the Rock of Gibraltar when its small colony of Barbary apes departs.

**Barbary Coast** *See:* Barbary States.

**Barbary pirates** *See:* Barbary Wars.

**Barbary States**, term historically applied to countries along the Mediterranean coast of North Africa, now Algeria, Tunisia, Libya, and Morocco.

**Barbary Wars**, 2 wars waged by the United States against African states. Barbary pirates had been attacking ships in the Mediterranean since the 16th century. In May 1801, the United States blockaded Tripoli in opposition to exorbitant payments to the Barbary States to protect its shipping. The United States won the war in 1805. The second Barbary War was fought in 1815 with Algiers. Treaties ending piracy were signed with Algiers, Tunis, and Tripoli.

**Barbel** *See:* Catfish.

**Barber, Samuel** (1910-1981), U.S. composer. Initially, he composed in a late romantic style. His music is generally tonal. Major works include two symphonies, *Adagio for Strings* (1936), and the cycle *Knoxville: Summer of 1915* (1947) for soprano and orchestra. He also wrote the operas *Vanessa* (1956) and *Anthony and Cleopatra* (1966), the latter commissioned to open the new Metropolitan Opera House in New York.

**Barberry**, any of several mostly evergreen, usually spiny shrubs (genus *Berberis*) having globular yellow flowers and red berries. The sour berries of the common barberry make excellent preserves, and the bark yields a yellow dye used in leather manufacture.
*See also:* May apple; Oregon grape.

**Barbirolli, Sir John** (1899-1970), English cellist and conductor, famous for his interpretations of compositions by Sibelius and other late romantics. After conducting the New York Philharmonic Orchestra (1937-42), he began a lifelong association with the Halle Orchestra in Manchester, England, and conducted the Houston Symphony Orchestra (1961-67).

**Barbiturate**, any of a group of drugs, derived from bituric acid, that act as sedatives, anesthetics, or anticonvulsants in the central nervous system by depressing nerve cell activity. Widely prescribed in the past for insomnia, their use is now discouraged because of high rates of addiction and the danger of overdose. Phenobarbital is used in the treatment of convulsions. Overdoses of barbiturates cause the deep and rapid onset of coma and can be fatal, especially when combined with alcohol.
*See also:* Drug.

**Barbizon school**, informal group of French painters of natural and rural subjects, active c.1830-70, who frequented the village of Barbizon, near Paris. It included Théodore Rousseau, Narciso Diaz de la Peña, Jean-Baptise

Corot, Jean François Millet, Jules Dupré, Constant Troyon, and Charles Daubigny.

**Barbuda,** island in the West Indies (62 sq mi/160 sq km), located north of the Windward group and southeast of Puerto Rico. Antigua and Barbuda form an independent nation within the Leeward Islands. Barbuda's main product is sea-island cotton.

**Barcarole,** or barcarolle (from Italian for "boat"), traditional boat song or musical composition of the 18th or 19th century written in that style. Barcaroles were originally sung by gondoliers in Venice. Many European composers, including Frédéric Chopin, adapted the style for their own works. Sung or played primarily in 6/8 time, barcaroles were composed as opera arias and instrumental pieces for pianos, orchestras, and choruses.

**Barcelona** (pop. 1,643,500), Spain's largest seaport and second largest city after Madrid. It is situated on the Mediterranean coast, in northeastern Spain, on a broad plain dotted with hills, between the Besos and Llobregat rivers. Barcelona's wide range of industries includes shipbuilding, metalworking, food processing, the manufacture of chemicals, textiles (including silk), leather goods, and glass. Agricultural commodities such as wine, olive oil, and cork are exported, and raw materials such as coal, grain, and textile fibers pass through its port. The city was founded in the 3rd century B.C. by Carthaginians. It flourished in the Middle Ages as an economic center. In 1137 it united with Aragon. Except for two brief periods of French rule (1640, 1808-14), Barcelona has been under Spanish rule ever since. Among the city's principal landmarks are the cathedral (begun 1298, completed 1498) and the Church of the Holy Family, by Antonio Gaudi, begun in 1882 and still unfinished. The center of Catalan nationalism in modern times, Barcelona was the stronghold of left-wing politics and Republican allegiance in the Spanish Civil War. It was the host city for the 1992 Summer Olympic Games.
*See also:* Spain.

**Bar code,** identifying code consisting of dark and light bars, designed to be read by an optical viewer. The bar code contains information about a particular product and is used primarily for inventory control.

**Bard,** ancient Celtic minstrel. First written of around 200 B.C., the early bards were educated poets who wielded political power in Wales, Scotland, and Ireland. Through the Middle Ages they mainly composed eulogies to their noble patrons.

**Bardeen, John** (1908-91), U.S. physicist noted for his studies of transistors and superconductors. He shared the 1956 Nobel Prize for physics with W. H. Brattain and W. Shockley, doing much of the research in solid-state physics that led to the development of transistorized electronic equipment. In 1972 he became the first person to win a second Nobel Prize in the same field, sharing the award with L.P. Cooper and J.R. Schrieffer for the development of their theory of superconductivity.
*See also:* Superconductivity.

**Barenboim, Daniel** (1942-    ), Argentine-born Israeli pianist and conductor known for his musical interpretations of Beethoven. He made his debut at the age of 7 in Buenos Aires. From 1975 to 1989 he was music director of the Orchestre de Paris.

**Barents, Willem** (c.1550-97), Dutch navigator, for whom the Barents Sea is named. He made 3 voyages to the Arctic in search of a northeast passage to Asia.

**Barents Sea**, shallow arm of the Arctic Ocean north of Norway and European Russia, bounded by Svalbard (Spitsbergen) to the northwest, Franz Josef Land to the north, and Novaya Zemlya to the east. The southwestern portion is warmed by the North Atlantic Drift and remains ice-free in winter; on its southwestern coast lies the former Soviet port of Murmansk.
*See also:* Barents, Willem.

**Barge dog** *See:* Schipperke.

**Bar Harbor** (pop. 4,120), village on Mount Desert Island, eastern Maine, on the Atlantic Ocean. First settled in 1763, Bar Harbor is a popular resort near the Acadia National Park.
*See also:* Maine.

**Bari** (ancient Barium; pop. 342,100), southern Italian port on the Adriatic Sea, capital of Bari province and of the Apulia region. The city is an important agricultural, commercial, and industrial center and also has a university. Bari is the site of the Fiera del Levante, an annual trade fair highlighting the city's role as center for commercial exchanges with the Balkan countries and the Middle East. In the old quarter are the cathedral, the Church of St. Nicola (begun 1087), and the 13th-century castle of Frederick II.
*See also:* Italy.

**Barite** *See:* Barium.

**Barium**, chemical element, symbol Ba; for physical constants see Periodic Table. Barium, a soft, silvery white metal, was discovered by Sir Humphrey Davy in 1808. In nature it is found chiefly as *barite* or *heavy spar* (sulfate) or *witherite* (carbonate). Barium is produced by electrolysis of its chloride and is easily oxidized. Barium sulfate (*blanc fixe*) has good covering power and does not darken in the presence of sulfides. It is used in pigments and as a filler in paper, as well as in X-ray diagnostic work and glassmaking. Other compounds of barium are used in fireworks and rat poison. Soluble barium compounds are poisonous.

**Bark**, outer covering of the stems and branches of woody plants. The protective outer bark usually consists of cork, while the inner bark contains food-conducting phloem and the reproductive cells of the cork cambium. Bark is usually formed in annual rings, the outer layers bursting and splitting with each new growth. Bark helps to protect the tree from extremes of climate and from various pests and diseases. Some varieties of bark have medicinal uses, others are sources of textile fibers and dyes.

**Bark beetle** *See:* Dutch elm disease.

**Barkley, Alben William** (1877-1956), vice president of the United States (1949-53), under Harry Truman. A Democrat from Kentucky, Barkley served in the House of Representatives (1913-27) and the Senate (1927-49). He returned to the Senate in 1954.

**Barlach, Ernst** (1870-1938), German expressionist sculptor, graphic artist, and playwright whose figures in bronze and wood show Gothic and cubist influences. Barlach also produced many woodcuts and lithographs, some of them to illustrate his own writings. His war memorials and other works earned him fame in the 1920s, although he fell into disfavor under Hitler and his works were removed from museums.
*See also:* Gothic art and architecture.

**Barley**, adaptable and hardy cereal plants (*Hordeum vulgare* and *Hordeum distichon*), of the grass family, cultivated since ancient times. The former USSR was the largest producer, with Canada and the United States following. Over half of the world's crop is used for animal feed, and 10% is turned into malt.

**Bar mitzvah**, Jewish religious ceremony marking a boy's entrance into the adult community, traditionally performed at the age of 13. The initiate is usually called upon to read part of the weekly portion of the Pentateuch or the Prophets in the synagogue. The equivalent for girls, the bas (or bat) mitzvah, was established in 20th-century Reform and Conservative Judaism.
*See also:* Judaism.

**Barnacle**, marine crustacea of the subclass Cirripedia. The shell consists primarily of calcium carbonate. Adults attach themselves to solid surfaces (even the bodies of other sea animals) and trap plankton by means of feathery organs known as cirri. There are some 1,000 species.

**Barnacle goose** (*Branta leucopsis*), bird that breeds in the Arctic and winters in northern Europe and occasionally North America.

**Barnard, Christiaan Neethling**(1922-   ), South African surgeon who performed the first successful human heart transplant in Dec. 1967. His autobiography *One Life* was published in 1970.

**Barnard, Edward Emerson** (1857-1923), U.S. astronomer who discovered Amalthea, the fifth satellite of Jupiter (1892). In 1916 he discovered Barnard's star, a red dwarf only 6 light-years from the earth, with the largest known proper motion.
*See also:* Jupiter.

**Barnard, Frederick Augustus Porter** (1809-89), president of Columbia College (1864-89), which he helped transform into a great university; and advocate of higher education for women. Barnard College (founded 1889) bears his name.

**Barnard, Henry** (1811-1900), U.S. educator. Instrumental in the creation of the U.S. Office of Education and first U.S. commissioner of education (1867-70), he edited and published the *American Journal of Education* (31 vol., 1855- 81).

**Barnburners**, radical, antislavery faction of the New York State Democratic Party in the 1840s. When the 1847 State Democratic convention defeated their resolution opposing the extension of slavery into the western territories, the Barnburners left the party and later joined with the Free Soil Party, of which Martin van Buren was the unsuccessful presidential candidate in 1848. The Barnburners then disbanded, but in the 1850s many members joined the new, antislavery Republican Party.
*See also:* Free Soil Party.

**Barnes, Djuna** (1892-1982), U.S. poet, playwright, and novelist. Her works include a collection of stories and poems entitled *A Book* (1923) and the novels *Ryder* (1928) and *Nightwood* (1936).

**Barnhart, Clarence Lewis** (1900-     ), U.S. lexicographer, editor of the *American College Dictionary* (1947), the *New Century Cyclopedia of Names* (1954), and *The World Book Dictionary* (1963). He was influenced by the linguist Leonard Bloomfield and the educational psychologist Edward Lee Thorndike.
*See also:* Thorndike, Edward Lee.

**Barn owl**, common white owl (*Tyto alba*) useful as a destroyer of rodents. It grows to a length of about 18 in (46 cm), with a white face and cinnamon-dappled white breast. It nests in cliffs, hollow trees, and buildings. Its piercing scream is probably responsible for many tales of "haunted houses."

**Barn swallow** (*Hirundo rustica*), common North American bird. The upper parts of the wings and head are a metallic blue, the throat is chestnut brown, and the breast is white. Barn swallows eat insects harmful to crops.

**Barnum, P(hineas) T(aylor)** (1810-91), U.S. impresario, showman, and publicist. The hoaxes, freaks, and curiosities exhibited in his American Museum (founded 1841) in New York included the original Siamese twins and General Tom Thumb. In 1871 he opened his famous traveling circus, which in 1881 merged with James A. Bailey's show to become Barnum and Bailey's "Greatest Show on Earth." Today there is a Barnum Museum in Bridgeport, Conn., the city of his birth.
*See also:* Circus.

**Barometer**, instrument for measuring air pressure, used in weather forecasting and for determining altitude. Most commonly encountered is the aneroid barometer, in which the effect of the air in compressing a thin corrugated metal box is amplified mechanically and read off on a scale.
*See also:* Altimeter.

**Baron**, title of nobility in Europe, indicating a powerful man, especially a business magnate.

**Baroque**, European style of art and architecture, and by extension, music, that flourished from the early 17th to the mid-18th century. The style in art emphasized dramatic lighting, emotional portrayal of subjects, and the illusion of depth. The direct simplicity, apparent realism, and revolutionary painting technique of the Italian artist Michelangelo Caravaggio (1573-1610) helped to spread baroque art throughout Europe. The same effects were adapted to sculpture, as seen in the works of Giovanni Lorenzo Bernini (1598-1680), whose *Ecstasy of St. Theresa* (1646) has a softness and fluidity typical of the style. From Rome baroque art spread to Naples with Luca Giordano (1632-1705) and to Venice with Giovanni Piazetta (1683-1754) and Giovanni Battista Tiepolo (1696-1770). Outside Italy the baroque was modified by national tastes and traditions. In Holland, where life was dominated by a prosperous Protestant middle class, religious and mythological subjects gave way to portraits, still lifes, interior scenes, and landscapes. Frans Hals (1580-1666), Rembrandt van Rijn (1606-69), and Jan Vermeer (1632-1675) explored techniques of light effects. In Flanders, high baroque art was epitomized in the art of Peter Paul Rubens (1577-1640). In France Caravaggio's influence can be seen in the works of Georges de la Tour (1593-1652), Louis le Nain (1593-1648), and Nicolas Poussin (1594-1665). After 1680 the impact of Rubens, who was employed at the French court, is evident. In Spain important painters of the Baroque included the court painter Diego Rodriguez de Silva y Velazquez (1599-1660) and Bartolome Esteban Murillo (1617-1682).

Music of the early Baroque was characterized by simplicity; the florid style often identified as baroque did not appear in music until around 1700. The period began around 1600 in Italy with the invention of opera, originally an attempt to reproduce the declamation of classical Greek drama, best exemplified in the music of Claudio Monteverdi (1567-1643). The Baroque also saw the cultivation of virtuoso instrumental writing and the development of the concerto by Antonio Vivaldi (c.1675-1741) and others in Italy. In France, Jean Baptiste Lully (1632-87) composed orchestral ballet music; in England, Henry Purcell (c.1659-95) wrote theater works and George Frideric Handel (1685-1759), oratorios. In Germany, church composer and organ and harpsichord virtuoso Johann Sebastian Bach (1685-1750) perfected the fugue.

**Barquisimeto** (pop. 785,300), capital of Lara state in northwestern Venezuela, about 220 mi (354 km) southwest of Caracas, founded in 1552. It is the commercial and agricultural center of central and western Venezuela.

**Barr, Alfred Hamilton, Jr.** (1901-81), U.S. art historian. Barr directed New York's Museum of Modern Art, 1929-43, organizing some of the most important shows in the history of modern art. He wrote three contemporary classics: *Cubism and Abstract Art* (1936), *Picasso* (1946), and *Matisse* (1951).

**Barracuda**, predatory fish (family Sphyraenidae) found in warm seas. Barracudas have elongated, cigar-shaped bodies, long snouts, and sharp teeth. They strike automatically at any gleaming object.

**Barras, Paul François Jean Nicolas, Vicomte de** (1755-1829), French revolutionary. At first a Jacobin, in favor of Louis XVI's execution, he later became the most powerful member of the Directory (the revolutionary

government) and aided Napoleon's rise to power. He was exiled after Napoleon's coup d'état of Brumaire (1799).
*See also:* French language.

**Barrault, Jean-Louis** (1910-94), French actor, director, producer, and mime. He was with the Comédie Française 1940-46 and directed the Théâtre de France 1959-68. His most famous film role was that of the mime in *Les Enfants du Paradis* (1944).

**Barrett, Elizabeth** *See:* Browning, Elizabeth Barrett.

**Barrie, Sir James Matthew** (1860-1937), Scottish playwright and novelist best known for *Peter Pan* (1904), his play about a boy who will not grow up. His works—including *The Admirable Crichton* (1902), *What Every Woman Knows* (1908), and *Dear Brutus* (1917)—range in tone from whimsy and sentimentality to satire and pathos.

**Barrier reef** *See:* Coral; Great Barrier Reef.

**Barrios, Justo Rufino** (1835-85), president of Guatemala from 1873 until his death in 1885. A dictator, Barrios dreamed of a united Central America. He died in El Salvador fighting to achieve that goal by force.
*See also:* Guatemala.

**Barron, James** (1769-1851), U.S. Navy Commodore. In 1807, Barron was ordered by a British frigate to surrender several sailors suspected of being British deserters. After being fired upon and suffering casualties, he surrendered the suspects and was court-martialed and suspended for 5 years.

**Barrow, Point**, northernmost point on the North American continent, at the tip of Point Barrow Peninsula on the Arctic coast of Alaska, named for Sir John Barrow, 19th-century British geographer. The city of Barrow lies some 12 mi (19 km) south.

**Barry, John** (1745-1803), Irish-born naval hero of the American Revolutionary War, often called "Father of the American Navy." Commander of the frigate *Lexington*, he captured the first British warship taken in combat by a regularly commissioned American cruiser.
*See also:* Revolutionary War in America.

**Barry, Philip** (1896-1949), U.S. playwright, best known for popular drawing room comedies such as *Holiday* (1928) and *The Philadelphia Story* (1939).

**Barrymore**, name of a noted Anglo-American theatrical family. The father was the British actor Herbert Blythe (1847-1905), who adopted the stage name **Maurice Barrymore** and came to the United States in 1875, marrying actress Georgina Drew. **Lionel Barrymore** (1878-1954), their eldest child, became an outstanding stage, radio, and film actor, continuing to perform even after arthritis had confined him to a wheelchair. **Ethel Barrymore** (1879-1959), famous for her style and wit, gave many distinctive performances on stage and screen, winning an Academy Award for her supporting role in *None But the Lonely Heart* (1944). **John Barrymore** (1882-1942) was a distinguished interpreter of Shakespearean roles, particularly *Richard III* (1920) and *Hamlet* (1922). Later he became a popular and flamboyant film actor, nicknamed "the great profile." His children **Diana Barrymore** (1921-60) and **John Barrymore, Jr.** (1932-    ) also became actors.

**Barter,** exchange of goods or services instead of money. Many primitive economies work on this system, and barter agreements are still common in international trade. During acute inflation when the value of money changes daily, a barter system may work better.

**Barth, John** (1930-    ), U.S. novelist known for his ironic style and use of comic and elaborate allegory. His best-known works include *The Sot-Weed Factor* (1960) and *Giles Goat-Boy* (1966). Other novels include *Sabbatical* (1982) and *The Tidewater Tales* (1987).

**Barth, Karl** (1886-1968), Swiss theologian, one of the most influential voices of 20th-century Protestantism. He taught in Germany 1921-35, was expelled by the Nazis, and spent the rest of his life in Basel. In his "crisis theology," Barth stressed revelation and grace and reemphasized the principles of the Reformation, initiating a movement away from theological "liberalism."
*See also:* Protestantism.

**Barthelme, Donald** (1931-89), U.S. short-story writer and novelist noted for his innovative techniques and surrealistic style. His works include the novels *Snow White* (1967) and *The Dead Father* (1975); the children's book *The Slightly Irregular Fire Engine or the Hithering Thithering Djinn* (1971), for which he won a National Book Award; and *Sixty Stories* (1981).

**Barthes, Roland** (1915-80), French philosopher, literary critic, and theorist of semiology. His works include *Writing Degree Zero* (1953), *Mythologies* (1957), *A Lover's Discourse* (1978), and his autobiography, *Roland Barthes* (1975).

**Bartholdi, Frédéric Auguste** (1834-1904), French sculptor, creator of the Statue of Liberty. His other monumental works include *Lion of Belfort* at Belfort, France.

**Bartholomew, Saint**, one of the 12 apostles. According to tradition, he preached the Gospel in Asia Minor and India and was martyred in Armenia.
*See also:* Apostles.

**Bartlett, John** (1820-1905), U.S. editor and publisher, best known for his *Familiar Quotations*, which has gone through more than a dozen editions since its first appearance in 1855.

**Bartlett, Josiah** (1729-95), U.S. politician, and a signer of the Declaration of Independence. Bartlett served in the second Continental Congress (1775-76 and 1778-79) and was later chief justice (1788-90) and governor (1790-94) of New Hampshire.
*See also:* Continental Congress.

**Bartlett, Robert Abram** (1875-1946), arctic explorer who commanded the *Roosevelt* for Robert E. Perry's 1905-09 expedition. In 1913 he led his own expedition. Bartlett explored Alaska in 1925, served the U.S. government during World War II, and wrote several books.

**Bartók, Béla** (1881-1945), Hungarian composer, one of the major figures of 20th- century music, also a virtuoso concert pianist and teacher at the Budapest Academy of Music (1907-34). In 1940 he emigrated to the United States. His work owes much to the rhythmic and melodic vitality of Eastern European folk music, on which he was an authority. Bartók's major works include his six string quartets (1908-39), *Music for Strings, Percussion*, and *Celesta* (1936), and *Concerto for Orchestra* (1943).

**Barton, Clara** (1821-1912), founder of the American Red Cross (1881) and its first president (until 1904). She began a lifetime of relief work by organizing care and supplies for the wounded in the Civil War. On a trip to Europe (1869-73) she became involved in the activities of the International Red Cross, working behind German lines in the Franco-Prussian War. She was later influential in extending the range of the organization's relief work. *See also:* Red Cross.

**Bartram,** 2 American naturalists, father and son. **John Bartram** (1699-1777) planted America's first botanical garden at Kingessing, Pa., in 1728. **William Bartram** (1739-1823), famous for his book *Travels* (1791), based on his trips with his father in the southeast United States, inspired Wordsworth and Coleridge.

**Baruch, Bernard Mannes** (1870-1965), U.S. financier and presidential economic adviser. He was chairman of the War Industries Board in World War I, adviser to F. D. Roosevelt in World War II, and U.S. delegate to the UN Atomic Energy Commission in the 1950s, proposing the "Baruch Plan" for international control of atomic energy.

**Barye, Antoine Louis** (1796-1875), French painter and sculptor who specialized in animal statues. His artwork is noted for its attention to detail. Barye also painted realistic landscapes.

**Baryon,** in particle physics, largest class of elemental particles, including protons, neutrons, and hyperons, also called "heavy particles" because of their relatively high mass.
*See also:* Atom.

**Baryshnikov, Mikhail** (1948-    ), Soviet-born U.S. dancer and choreographer. He was a soloist with the Kirov Ballet, Leningrad, from 1966 until 1974, when he defected to the West, joining the American Ballet Theatre and appearing there and with other companies in modern and classical ballets. He served as director of the American Ballet Theatre 1980-89. In Philadelphia he began his own company (the White Oak Dance Project).

**Barytes** *See:* Barium.

**Basalt**, dense rock formed by the solidification of lava. It underlies ocean floors and is the basis of most oceanic islands. Frequently dark in color, its main constituents are labradorite feldspar and pyroxene. Basalt strata usually consist of hexagonal columns produced by crystallization of the molten lava during a slow cooling process, as seen in the Palisades along the Hudson River, the Devil's Postpile National Monument, Calif., and the Giant's Causeway in Ireland.

**Base**, in chemistry, complement of an acid. Bases are often defined as substances that react with acids to form salts, or as substances that give rise to hydroxyl ($OH^-$) in aqueous solutions.
*See also:* Chemistry.

**Baseball**, outdoor team sport which derives its name from the 4 bases on the playing field. Called the "national pastime" in the United States, it is also popular in Japan, Latin America, and Canada. Invented, according to legend, by Abner Doubleday in Cooperstown, N.Y. in 1839, it appears rather to have evolved from the game of rounders which was played by New England colonists. Popular with Union troops during the Civil War, it was played nationally by the late 1880s.

Baseball is played on a large field between 2 opposing teams each consisting of 9 players: a pitcher, a catcher, 4 infielders, and 3 outfielders. The field consists of the infield, outfield, and foul territory. The infield is square, with a base at each corner—home plate, first, second, and third base. The foul lines extend from home plate past first base on one side and past third on the other, separating fair (infield and outfield) from foul territory. The pitcher's mound stands near the center of the infield. The outfield is the large area between the infield and the walls or fences farthest from home plate. While one team positions itself in the field, the other team bats. The pitcher, standing on the pitcher's mound, throws the small, hard ball (about 9 in/23 cm in circumference) over home plate, within an area between the batter's knees and shoulders (the strike zone)—sometimes at speeds over 90 mph (145 kmph). The batter attempts to hit the ball with the bat, a long rounded piece of wood or metal up to 42 in (107 cm) long and 2.75 in (7 cm) in diameter. A pitch outside of the strike zone is called a ball; 4 balls pitched to the batter allow the batter to "walk" to first base. A pitch counts as a strike if the batter fails to swing at a good pitch, swings and misses, or hits the ball foul (except when there are already 2 strikes); 3 strikes and a batter is out. If the ball is hit into fair territory, the batter runs to first base. The batter is out if the ball is caught without a bounce (fly), if it is thrown to first base before the batter gets there, or if the batter is "tagged" with the ball by a fielder. As new batters walk or get hits, earlier batters move around the bases. A batter reaching home plate scores a run. When 3 batters are out, the teams switch position. When each team has had a turn at bat, an inning is complete. A team wins by scoring the most runs within 9 innings. In the case of a tie, extra innings are added.

Players in the field wear padded leather gloves to catch the ball. All players wear shoes with spiked soles so they can start and stop quickly. Batters wear plastic batting helmets to avoid injuries. Catchers wear metal face masks, padded chest protectors, and shin guards. Most major league games have 4 umpires (game officials). The home plate umpire decides whether a pitch is a ball or a strike as well as whether runners attempting to reach home plate are safe or out. The other umpires rule on plays near as well as in the outfield. There are 2 major baseball leagues; the American League (founded 1900), with 14 teams, and the National League (founded 1876), with 12. The teams in each league are divided into Eastern and Western Divisions. These teams play a 162-game schedule between April and September. The 2 divisional champions in each league meet in a playoff after the regular season, and the first team to win 4 games in each playoff is the league champion. The American and National League champions then play in the World Series. The first team to win 4 games in this series wins the world championship. In addition to major and minor leagues, the game is played in amateur leagues and college and high school associations, as well as by neighborhood teams of all age groups. Originally restricted to boys, baseball is now played by girls as well.

**Basel** (pop. 174,600), second largest city in Switzerland, capital of the half-canton of Basel Stadt. The city is Switzerland's only river port, located on the Rhine, its major trans-European railhead, and one of its most important commercial, industrial, and financial centers. Situated at the junction of the French and German borders, Basel is a key distribution center for raw materials and manufactured products between northern and central Europe. The most important industries are chemical, electrical, and machine engineering.
Founded by the Romans, Basel joined the Swiss confederation as a canton in 1501. It later became the center of the Protestant Reformation, Luther's writings being printed here. The city's ancient cathedral (founded 1019) housed the great ecumenical council of 1431-48, and Erasmus is buried there. Switzerland's oldest university, founded in 1459, is in Basel.
*See also:* Switzerland.

**Basenji,** breed of dog, first bred in central Africa. The Basenji has short silky hair, pointed ears, and a wrinkled forehead. It weighs 22-24 lb (10-11 kg), and does not bark.
    **BASIC,** Beginner's All-purpose Symbolic Instruction Code, easy-to-use, algebraic programming language developed at Dartmouth College in 1967 by John Kemeny and Thomas Kurtz. BASIC has a small repertory of commands and simple statement formats. For this reason, BASIC is widely used in programming instructions, personal computing, and business and industry.

**Basie, Count** (William Basie; 1904-84), U.S. jazz pianist, composer, and bandleader. Count Basie's big band, which included some of the outstanding jazz musicians of the time, brought the ragged rhythm and improvisational verve of jazz into the smooth swing era of the late 1930s and 1940s.

**Basil,** annual aromatic herb of the mint family, native to Asia, whose leaves are used in cooking and in the preparation of Chartreuse liqueur. The most popular kinds are known as sweet basil (*Ocimum basilicum*).

**Basilica,** in its earliest usage, large public building of ancient Rome of characteristic rectangular layout, with a central area (nave) separated by rows of columns from 2 flanking side aisles with high windows. At one or both ends was a semicircular or polygonal apse. This design was adopted as a basic pattern for Christian churches from the time of Constantine (4th century A.D.). The term "basilica" is also a canonical title for certain important Roman Catholic churches.

**Basil the Great, Saint** (c.330-379), one of the great Fathers of the Eastern Church, bishop of Caesarea, a founder of Greek monasticism and author of the *Longer* and *Shorter Rules* for monastic life.

**Baskerville, John** (1706-75), English printer and type designer, whose elegant Baskerville type was the ancestor and inspiration of the "modern" group of typefaces. He took great care in all aspects of his craft and produced many handsome editions.

**Basketball**, popular indoor team sport in the United States, the object of which is to score points by propelling a leather ball through a basket (hoop and net). Two baskets, 18 in (46 cm) in diameter and 10 ft (3 m) from the floor, are fixed on two backboards situated at either end of a court, the maximum dimensions of which are 94 x 50 ft (29 x 15 m). Basketball is played between 2 teams, each of 12 players and a coach, with 5 players from each team allowed on court at any one time (2 forwards, 2 guards, and a center, who is usually the tallest player on the team). The coach calls timeouts, advising the team on tactics and substituting players on the "bench" for players who are tired, injured, off their stride, or disqualified. The ball is moved by *passing* from one player to another or by an individual player *dribbling* (bouncing) it, never by kicking or by carrying it more than one and a half steps. In addition to game violations involving illegal moves with the ball, there are *personal fouls*, involving bodily contact or unsportsmanlike conduct. Five fouls disqualify a player from the game. Basketball is a fast-moving game played within a relatively confined space. The game is split into 2 or 4 equal periods of play, with the actual playing time for the whole game varying between 32 minutes and one hour depending upon the level and whether U.S. or international rules govern the game. The World Congress of the International Federation of Basketball approved several modifications to the rules of the game as of the 1984-85 season, including a 3-point basket for distance shots.

Originated by Dr. James A. Naismith in 1891, the game caught on rapidly, and in 1894 the YMCA collaborated with the Amateur Athletic Union in administering the new sport. In 1898 teams from New York, Brooklyn, Philadelphia, and Southern New Jersey formed the first professional league. International interest in basketball was first kindled by an exhibition game played at the 1904 Olympic Games in St. Louis, Missouri. The rules had been translated into 30 languages by 1913, when it was estimated that as many as 20 million people were playing the game throughout the world. The universities of Pennsylvania and Yale were the first to play college basketball, and in 1908 the National Collegiate Athletic Association was formed, establishing rules governing play in both colleges and secondary schools. The game was once dominated by New York's Celtics (1915-28), the all-black New York Renaissance (1923-40s), and the all-black Harlem Globetrotters (formed 1928). Like the original New York Celtics, the Globetrotters became an exhibition team.

Top-level college basketball was first brought to large audiences when Ned Irish, a sportswriter, convinced the promoters of athletic events at Madison Square Garden in New York that basketball could draw large crowds in a metropolitan sports arena. The National Collegiate Athletic Association championships began in 1939. A Stanford player, Hank Luisetti, demonstrated his *jump shot* to Eastern players during the late 1930s, and adoption of this shot caused the game to become much faster, with scores rocketing to the 70s and 80s. Despite many new rules designed to arrest this trend, scores have continued to rise as players become both taller and more proficient. The fast break and the technique of screening (blocking) to set up plays, backed up by tall centers to take the rebounds and other offensive tactics, have been countered by the use of player-to-player and zone defense. In 1949, the professional National Basketball League (formed in 1937) merged with the Basketball Association of America (organized in 1946). However, it was not until the 1970s that the NBA, expanded and after a merger with the new American Basketball Association (1967), became the solid crowd-drawing equivalent of professional leagues in other sports. Basketball is played in more countries than any other team ball game, and remains among the most popular player/spectator sports in the United States.

**Basket Makers,** prehistoric Native American culture flourishing in the Southwest more than 2,000 years ago. An agricultural people, the Basket Makers were the earliest members of a large group called the Anasazi. They developed a multi-storied dwelling called a pueblo; after about 700 A.D., the Anasazi were called the Pueblo.
*See also:* Pueblo.

**Basket making,** popular handicraft dating back to prehistoric times. It uses flexible materials to make utensils, primarily for the preparation, transportation, or storage of food. Two kinds of material are used to make baskets: hard material including grasses, leaves, and wood, and soft material including cotton, wool, and jute fiber. Two different strands are woven together to produce the basket: the warp strand runs vertically, the weft horizontally.

**Baskin, Leonard** (1922-   ), U.S. graphic artist and sculptor. His work includes the prints *Mid-Century Monster* and *The Poet Laureate* and the sculpture *Man with a Dead Bird.* Since 1953 he has taught at Smith College, Mass., where he founded the Gehenna Press, noted for fine typography.

**Basking shark** (*Cetorhinus maximus*), one of the largest living sharks, reaching a length of 45 ft (14 m). Found chiefly in temperate waters, the basking shark feeds only on plankton. The liver, a valuable source of oil, may account for a tenth of the total weight of the fish and provides the buoyancy that enables the shark to bask, motionless, on the surface.
*See also:* Shark.

**Bas mitzvah** *See:* Bar mitzvah.

**Basov, Nikolai Gennadievich** (1922-   ), Russian physicist who, with his colleague Alexander Prokhorov, stated the principles of using molecular energy to amplify radio waves. They shared the 1964 Nobel Prize in physics with the U.S. physicist Charles H. Townes.

**Basques,** people of unique language and culture living mainly in the vicinity of the Pyrennees Mountains (about 100,000 in southwestern France and 600,000 in northeastern Spain). Research into their blood groups indicates a long separation from other Europeans. After the Spanish Civil War, in which many Basques fought against General Franco, an effort was made to subdue the region. A surge of Basque nationalism in recent years was marked by the assassination of Admiral Luis Blanco by the Basque resistance movement ETA in 1973. In 1980 the Basques were given limited political self-determination by Spain by allowing the 3 Basque regions of Spain a parliament and some control over police, education, taxes, and other administrative procedures.

**Basra** (pop. 620,000), city and major port in Iraq, situated on the Shatt-al-Arab River, about 75 mi (120 km) from the Persian Gulf. The actual port is the suburb of Al'Ashr, the old town of Basra being 2 mi (3 km) away. The third part of Basra is the modern port of Ma'quil, 4 mi (6 km) above Ashr and accessible to seagoing vessels. Oil is exported through the pipeline terminus at Fao, about 4 mi (6 km) downstream, where there is also a refinery. The other main industry is the packing and export of dates. Under the rule of the Abbasid family in the 8th century, and until its conquest by the Mongols in the 13th century, Basra was a center of Arabic culture noted for its mosques and library. The city was heavily damaged during the war with Iran in the 1980s and during the Gulf War (1991).
*See also:* Iraq.

**Bas relief** *See:* Relief.

**Bass,** fish of the Serranidae and Centrarchidae families. In Europe the name usually refers to saltwater fish of the family Serranidae, popular as game fish and food. Most of them grow to 2 ft (60 cm) or more, and the giant sea bass found in tropical waters may exceed 7 ft (2 m). The European bass is common around the Mediterranean and Atlantic coasts, but related species are found in shallow tropical waters and in fresh water. In the United States and Canada, the name is applied to freshwater fish of the Centrarchidae family. The black bass, one of the most popular of game fishes, is found in lakes and streams of eastern North America. Sunfish, the smaller members of the family, are often found in aquariums. Other North American freshwater bass are spotted bass, rock bass, grass bass, largemouth bass, smallmouth bass, and silver bass.

**Bass,** or double bass, largest instrument of the violin family. Its form is less standardized than the other string instruments, but it usually stands about 6 ft (2 m) high and has 4 strings 42 in (108 cm) long and tuned in fourths. To increase its range a fifth low string is sometimes added. The strings are made of thick copper wire or steel cable. They are played with a bow.

**Bassae,** site of one of the best-preserved temples of classical Greece, located near the ancient city of Phigalia in Arcadia. The temple of Apollo at Bassae was built at the end of the 5th century B C and its architect may have been Ictinus, builder of the Parthenon.

**Bass, Sam** (1851-78), U.S. outlaw, the "Robin Hood" of Texas. He rode the West, first with the Joel Collins gang and then with one of his own. He died of gunshot wounds.

**Bass drum** *See:* Drum.

**Basse-Terre** (pop. 14,300), capital city of the French department of Guadeloupe in the Antilles islands in the Caribbean. Settled by the French in 1643, Basse-Terre is a transportation center exporting bananas, coffee, cocoa, and sugar.
*See also:* Guadeloupe.

**Basset hound**, short-legged, long, heavy-bodied, long-eared dog. Averaging 12-14 in (30-36 cm) in height and 45-60 lb (20-27 kg) in weight, the basset is a scent hound originally bred for hunting by the abbots of St. Hubert in France.

**Bassoon,** musical instrument, bass of the woodwind family, an 8-ft (2.4-m) conical tube bent double, with a double-reed mouthpiece, 8 holes, 20-22 keys, and a range of 3.5 octaves. Irrational key placement and an unstable pitch make it difficult to play.

**Basswood**, or linden, tree (genus *Tilia*) of the linden family that grows to 120 ft (37 m) in height and 3.5 ft (107 cm) in diameter. The basswood tree is valued for ornamentation and shade as well as for its soft wood and tough bark.

**Bastille**, fortress in Paris built c.1370, destroyed during the French Revolution. It was first used to house political prisoners by Cardinal Richelieu, in the 17th century, but was almost empty by the time of the Revolution. It remained a symbol of oppression, however, and its capture on July 14, 1789, was the first act of the Revolution. Bastille Day, July 14, is a French national holiday.
*See also:* French Revolution.

**Bastogne** (pop. 12,500), small town on the Ardennes plateau in southeast Belgium. During the Battle of the Bulge, the German counteroffensive of 1944 in World War II, an American division under Gen. Anthony McAuliffe was surrounded here for some weeks before the Germans were driven back.
*See also:* World War II.

**Bat,** nocturnal mammal, the only mammal capable of flight, a member of the order Chiroptera. There are almost 1,000 species of bats, accounting for about one-seventh of mammalian species. Bats generally live in caves, trees, roofs, and other enclosures, hanging upside down to sleep. Most are insectivorous (insect-eating), but some are vegetarian and yet others carnivorous—the 3 species of the family Desmodontidae are blood suckers, preying on birds and mammals. There are a few historical inaccuracies concerning the bat. It is not blind, it does not get tangled in hair, and it is not really aggressive. In fact, bats perform an important job by consuming insects and by depositing guano (manure), which can be used as fertilizer. Bats navigate their travel using high-frequency noises which they produce while in flight.

These sounds create echoes that allow the animal to determine distance and direction, a method of navigation known as echolocation.

**Bataan Peninsula**, province of southwestern Luzon, the Philippines. A mountainous jungle region historically known as the last stronghold of U.S. and Philippine troops who held out 3 months against Japanese forces in 1942, during World War II. The prisoners were sent on a "death march" to a prison camp.
*See also:* Philippines; World War II.

**Bates, Katharine Lee** (1859-1929), U.S. author, best known for writing the lyrics of "America the Beautiful." She was a professor of English at Wellesley College and wrote children's literature.

**Bateson, Gregory** (1904-80), British-born U.S. anthropologist, best known for his study of New Guinea, *Naven* (1936; rev. 1958), and *Ecology of Mind* (1972). He wrote *Balinese Character* (1943) with his wife, Margaret Mead.

**Batfish**, beautifully colored marine fish of the family Ogcocephalidae, found in the Indian and Pacific oceans. Its highly compressed, almost circular body and long fins give it the appearance of a bat when swimming.

**Bath** (pop. 84,200), city in southwest England, on the River Avon near Bristol. Bath was founded by the Romans, who were attracted by the mineral hot springs there. In the 1700s Bath became a resort for English high society. During World War II many government services were moved there.

**Bath, Order of the**, British honor, established by George I in 1725 (supposedly based on an order founded in 1399). There are two divisions, military and civil, with three classes in each: knight grand cross (G.C.B.), knight commander (K.C.B.), and companion (C.B.).

**Baths and bathing**, historically, primarily religious, social, or pleasurable functions more often than hygienic ones. The Egyptians, Assyrians, and Greeks all used baths, but the Romans developed bathing as a central social habit, constructing elaborate public buildings, often ornately decorated and of enormous size. A Roman bath contained several rooms for disrobing, exercise, and entertainment, as well as bathing. Men and women bathed at separate times, except for one brief period in the 1st century A.D. The baths were tended by slaves. After the fall of the Roman Empire bathing declined in popularity in Europe, though it did survive as a part of monastic routine, in Jewish ritual, and in Muslim countries. In Russia and Turkey the steam bath became popular. The crusaders brought steam bathing back with them from the Middle East, but an association with immorality caused it to fall into disrepute. In the 18th century it became fashionable to spend a season at a watering-place, such as Bath, England, but only 19th-century research into hygiene made a virtue of bathing, often with primitive and usually portable cold baths at schools and institutions. Only after World War I did plumbing and bathtub production allow the bath to become a permanent installation in the home.

**Bathsheba**, in the Bible, wife of King David and mother of Solomon. David married Bathsheba after arranging the death of her husband, Uriah the Hittite (2 Samuel 11, 12; 1 Kings 1-20).
*See also:* Bible.

**Bathyscaph**, submersible deep-sea research vessel, invented by Auguste Piccard in the late 1940s, comprising a small, spherical, pressurized passenger cabin suspended beneath a cigar-shaped flotation hull. Before dives most of the flotation tanks in the hull are filled with gasoline, the rest with air. For dives, the air is vented and seawater takes its place; seawater is allowed to enter the gasoline-filled tanks from the bottom, compressing the gasoline and increasing the density of the vessel. To begin descent, iron ballast is jettisoned. As the vessel rises, the gasoline expands, expelling water from the flotation tanks, thus lightening the vessel further and accelerating the ascent. Battery-powered motors provide the vessel with a degree of submarine mobility.

**Batik**, dyeing technique in which the portions of material not to be colored are covered with wax before the fabric is dipped into dye. After the dye is dry, the wax is removed by boiling and, if necessary, the procedure is repeated for each new dye. It is an ancient Indonesian technique, introduced into Europe by Dutch traders and now also used in Africa. Imperfections caused by the breaking or melting of the wax surface are responsible for much of the accidental effect that gives batik work its character.

**Batista y Zaldívar, Fulgencio** (1901-73), Cuban military dictator. Becoming army chief of staff after the overthrow of the Machado government in 1933, he appointed and deposed presidents at will. He was himself president 1940-44, and took the title permanently in 1952. After his overthrow by Fidel Castro in 1959 he lived in exile in Spain.
*See also:* Cuba.

**Bat mitzvah** *See:* Bar mitzvah.

**Baton Rouge** (pop. 245,800), capital of Louisiana, situated on the Mississippi River. A deepwater port and regional trade center, the city also has major oil refineries and petrochemical and aluminum factories. Founded by the French in 1719, Baton Rouge was later transferred to the British and was occupied by the Spanish from 1779. U.S.-born citizens rebelled against Spanish rule and established their independence at the battle of Baton Rouge on Sept. 23, 1810. Acquired by the United States in 1815, the city was incorporated in 1817 and became the state capital in 1849. Louisiana State University and Agricultural and Mechanical College and Southern University are both located there.
*See also:* Louisiana.

**Battenberg**, name of princely family of Germany. **Prince Alexander of Battenberg** (1857-93) was prince of Bulgaria 1879-86. **Prince (Louis) Alexander of Battenberg** became a British subject, joined the Royal Navy, married the granddaughter of Queen Victoria, and changed his name to Mountbatten in 1917.

**Battering ram,** ancient war machine used to break down walls and doors. Used by the Assyrians and by Alexander the Great, it was made of a beam of heavy timber with a metal tip and survived as a weapon until the 1400s, when it was replaced by the cannon.

**Battery,** device for converting internally stored chemical energy into direct-current electricity. The term is also applied to various other electricity sources, including the solar cell and the nuclear cell, but is usually taken to exclude the fuel cell, which requires the continuous input of a chemical fuel for operation.
*See also:* Electric circuit; Fuel cell.

**Battle Creek** (pop. 135,982), city in southern Michigan, famous as a health and sports center. John Harvey Kellogg, associated with the breakfast cereal company that bears his name, was a principal founder of the Battle Creek Health Center. The city is the world's leading producer of breakfast cereal and also produces automobile parts, electrical equipment, and machinery.
*See also:* Michigan.

**Battleford** (pop. 3,800), historic town in Saskatchewan, Canada, now a grain depot, manufacturing town, and site of the Battleford Historic Park and Fred Light Museum. Battleford was the capital of the Northwest Territories (1876-83) and of the district of Saskatchewan (1882-1905).
*See also:* Saskatchewan.

**Battle Hymn of the Republic,** U.S. patriotic song, unofficial hymn of Union troops in the Civil War. Written in 1861 by Julia Ward Howe and sung to the tune of "John Brown's Body," it later became a Protestant hymn and a protest marching song.
*See also:* Howe, Samuel and Julia.

**Battle of,** Battles are listed under the key word, as in *Antietam, Battle of.*

**Battleship,** historically the largest of conventionally armed warships. Aircraft carriers superseded them during World War II as the largest fighting ships afloat. The largest battleship now is the USS *New Jersey*, with a full-load displacement of 59,000 tons (59,100 metric tons) and an overall length of 887 ft (309 m). The USS *Massachusetts* is now a floating marine museum in Fall River, MA.

**Batu Khan** (d. 1255 A.D.), Mongol conqueror of Russia, grandson of Genghis Khan. He ruled the westernmost part of the Mongol Empire and threatened eastern Europe from 1235 to 1242. He founded the khanate of the Golden Horde that ruled southern Russia for 200 years, isolating it from western European developments.
*See also:* Mongol Empire.

**Baud,** in computer technology, one bit per second. In general, the rate at which data is transmitted.
*See also:* Computer.

**Baudelaire, Charles Pierre** (1821-67), French poet and critic, forerunner of the Symbolists. The poems in *Les Fleurs du Mal* (*The Flowers of Evil*, 1857), with their probing of even the most bizarre sensations, outraged public opinion and led to the poet's being tried for obscenity. His later prose poems were posthumously published in *Le Spleen de Paris* (1869). He was also a critic of music and fine art, and was renowned for his translations of Edgar Allen Poe.

**Baudot, Emile** *See:* Telegraph.

**Baudouin** (1930-93), fifth king of the Belgians. He spent World War II with his family in Nazi internment, and succeeded his father, King Leopold III, who abdicated in 1951. In 1960 Baudouin proclaimed Congolese independence. He married a Spanish noblewoman, now Queen Fabiola. Succeeded by his brother Albert.
*See also:* Belgium.

**Bauhaus,** school of design and architecture in the 20th century. Founded by Walter Gropius in 1919 at Weimar, Germany, its teachers included some of the leading artists of the time. Gropius's ideal of uniting form with function is now a universal canon of design, and the dictum "less is more" has influenced much U.S. design. The Bauhaus left Weimar in 1925 and was installed in new premises designed by Gropius in Dessau in 1927. The school was closed by the Nazis in 1933. Bauhaus teachers Gropius, Lyonel Feininger, and Ludwig Mies van der Rohe later moved to the United States.
*See also:* Gropius, Walter.

**Baum, Lyman Frank** (1856-1919), U.S. children's writer, author of 14 Oz books, including *The Wonderful Wizard of Oz* (1900), a tale of a girl carried by a cyclone to a land of adventure. The 1939 film adaptation became a motion-picture classic.

**Baumfree, Isabella** *See:* Truth, Sojourner.

**Bausch,** name of U.S. family involved in the optical industry. **John Jacob Bausch** (1830-1926) founded Bausch and Lomb Optical Company in 1853. His 3 sons joined the company in 1875.

**Bauxite,** ore consisting of hydrated aluminum oxide, usually with iron oxide; the main source of aluminum. It is a claylike, amorphous material formed by the weathering of silicate rocks, especially under tropical conditions. Bauxite is used as a lining for furnaces, and is an ingredient in some quick-setting cements. Leading bauxite-producing countries include Jamaica, Australia, the former USSR, Suriname, Guyana, France, and the United States.
*See also:* Aluminum.

**Bavaria** (German: *Bayern*), southwest state in Germany. Its area is 27,239 sq mi (70,549 sq km) and its population exceeds 12 million. Munich is the capital and administrative center, and the site of most of the state's industry. Forestry and agriculture are also important in Bavaria. The region's borders have often changed, and it has seen many rulers, including the Romans in the 6th century B.C. and Charlemagne in the 9th century A.D. Bavaria became

a kingdom in 1805 and a part of Germany in 1871. Following World War I it was a short-lived republic and then part of Germany again. After World War II Bavaria was part of West Germany.
*See also:* Germany.

**Bavarian Succession, War of the** *See:* Succession wars.

**Bay,** inlet of water formed along the coastline of an ocean or lake. Examples include Hudson Bay, and the Bay of Bengal.

**Bayard,** family name of politicians, statesmen, and U.S. senators from Delaware. **James Asheton Bayard** (1767-1815) served in the U.S. House of Representatives from 1797 to 1803 and as a U.S. senator from 1805 to 1813. His two sons, **Richard Henry** (1796-1868) and **James Asheton** (1799-1880), and his grandson, **Thomas Francis** (1828-98), also represented Delaware in the U.S. Senate. Thomas Francis Bayard served as secretary of state from 1885 to 1889 and was U.S. ambassador to Britain from 1893 to 1897. His son, also named **Thomas Francis** (1868-1942), served in the U.S. Senate in the 1920s.

**Bayberry** (Myricaceae), any of a family of trees and shrubs found in temperate and subtropical climates. The North American bayberry shrub (*Myrica pennsylvanica*) is found along the eastern coast from North Carolina to Nova Scotia. The waxy fruit of some species is used to make candles, scented soaps, sealing wax, and cosmetics.

**Bay Colony** *See:* Massachusetts.

**Baylor, Elgin** (1934- ), U.S. basketball player and coach. Baylor, a 6 ft 5 in (196 cm) forward, played on the Los Angeles (formerly Minneapolis) Lakers of the National Basketball Association (NBA) from 1958 to 1971 and is considered one of the best all-around players in history. His achievements include being named NBA Rookie of the Year (1958-59), and scoring 71 points in a game (1960). Baylor was head coach for the New Orleans Jazz (1976-1979), and is director of basketball operations for the Los Angeles Clippers (1986- ).

**Bay of Bengal,** wide arm of the Indian Ocean between India and Ceylon on the west, and Burma on the east. In the north, along the coast of Bangladesh, the sea is shallow because vast quantities of silt are brought down by the rivers. Further south the depth increases to a maximum of 13,020 ft (3,968 m). The winds and surface sea currents vary with the prevailing monsoon: clockwise with the northeast monsoon and counterclockwise with the southwest monsoon. In October particularly, at the change of monsoon, very severe storms occur. The important rivers flowing into the bay are the Ganges, Brahmaputra, Godavari, Kistna, and Cauvery.
*See also:* Indian Ocean.

**Bay of Biscay,** section of the Atlantic Ocean adjoining northern Spain and part of the west coast of France. The name is a corruption of "Vizcaya," the term used by the Basques, an ethnic group populating northern Spain and southern France.
*See also:* Atlantic Ocean.

**Bay of Fundy**, funnel-shaped inlet of the Atlantic Ocean between New Brunswick and Nova Scotia in Canada. It is known for having the highest tides in the world, reaching up to 50 ft (15 m) in some parts.
*See also:* Atlantic Ocean.

**Bay of Pigs**, English name for Bahia de Cochinos (southwestern Cuba), scene of an abortive invasion of Cuba on April 17, 1961. The invaders were Cubans who had fled to the United States after Fidel Castro seized power. Although U.S. citizens were not directly involved, the CIA helped plan the invasion. The invasion was a political disaster for President Kennedy, who had approved the operation.

**Bayonet**, stabbing or thrusting weapon that may be fitted at the muzzle of a rifle without preventing normal firing. Usually consisting of a straight tapering blade, but sometimes a sabre or cutlass, it is used in close combat.

**Bayonne** (pop. 65,000), city and port in New Jersey, about 7 mi (11 km) southwest of New York City. Located on a penninsula between Newark Bay and New York Bay, it is a busy commercial port with 9 mi (14 km) of docks and large oil refineries. Other industries include the manufacture of chemicals, textiles, and electronic instruments.
*See also:* New Jersey.

**Bayou**, shallow, slow-moving creek or water channel running into a lake or a river. The word is Louisiana French, probably derived from the Choctaw (Native American) *bayuk*.

**Bay Psalm Book**, *The Whole Booke of Psalmes Faithfully Translated into English Metre*, first book printed in colonial America. Published in Cambridge, Mass., in 1640 as a hymnal for the Massachusetts Bay Colony, it was the work of Richard Mather, John Eliot, and Thomas Weld, and was printed by Stephen Day.

**Bayreuth** (pop. 70,900), industrial city in northeastern Bavaria, Germany. It is famous as the last home of Richard Wagner and as the site of his opera house, the Festspielhaus. The Bayreuth festivals, held each summer since 1876, feature Wagner's music.
*See also:* Wagner, Richard.

**Bazooka**, portable rocket launcher constructed from a smooth-bore steel tube 5 ft (1.5 m) long and open at both ends. Two people operate it: The midpoint of the tube rests on the shoulder of one person, who aims and fires the weapon while the other person loads the rockets.

**BBC** *See:* British Broadcasting Corporation.

**B.C.**, "Before Christ" in the Christian (and now generally Western) system for dating events, developed by the monk Dionysius Exiguus and based on the time he believed Christ to have been born. The year of Christ's birth is considered the year 1, and the higher the number, the earlier the event. The year 100 B.C., for instance, was the year before 99 B.C. Events in the years after the birth of Christ are designated A.D. (for the Latin *Anno Domini*, "in the year of our Lord"). The expressions B.C E. ("Before the Common Era") and C.E. ("Common Era") are also used.

**BCG,** bacillus Calmette-Guérin, a vaccine used to immunize against tuberculosis.

**Beach, Amy** (1867-1944), U.S. composer. Her *Gaelic Symphony* (1896) was the first symphony by a U.S. woman. She wrote over 150 works, including a piano concerto (1900), a string quartet (1929), and a one-act opera, *Cabildo* (1932).

**Beach, Sylvia** (1887-1962), U.S. expatriate bookstore owner whose Paris shop, Shakespeare & Co., was the center of expatriate literary life in Paris during the interwar period. James Joyce, Ernest Hemingway, and other important writers were frequent visitors. Beach published Joyce's *Ulysses* (1922).

**Beach plum,** wild shrub (*Prunus maritima*) of the rose family, found along the eastern coast of the United States from Virginia to Maine. It produces an edible fruit, resembling a small plum, used in sauces, preserves, jellies, and pies.

**Beacon,** originally a warning sign or signal, for example, a fire kindled at a prominent point on the coast to warn of the approach of hostile fleets.

**Beaconsfield, Earl of** *See:* Disraeli, Benjamin.

**Beaded lizard** (*Heloderma horridum*), poisonous lizard found in Mexico, close relative of the Gila monster. It is slow-moving, with small bead-like scales and markings of alternate black and pink-orange rings, and has hooked, grooved teeth. Glands along the inside of the lower lip secrete poison.

**Beads,** term derived from the Saxon word *biddan,* meaning to pray. Primitive beads were made of seeds, pierced shells, teeth, and stone; later materials ranged from semiprecious stones to gold and silver. Beads have been used by humans since before history. Magical properties were assigned to them, such as the promotion of fertility and the ability to guard against evil spirits. They were often exported over vast distances by explorers for trade.

**Beagle,** small, short-legged hound originally bred for hunting hares. There are 2 breads of beagle in the United States. The larger growes up to 15 in (38 cm) tall, the smaller up to 13 in (33 cm). Beagles weigh from 20 to 40 lb (9-18 kg).

**Beagle,** *See:* Darwin, Charles Robert.

**Beaked whale,** any of various medium-sized toothed whales whose snouts are narrow and pointed. They feed mainly on cuttlefish and generally have 2 or 4 teeth protruding from the lower jaw. There are 15 species living in all seas.

**Bean,** any plant of the pulse family (especially genus *Phaseolus*), also called legumes, cultivated for its edible seeds, immature pods, or shoots. The high protein content of beans, and especially of soybeans, make them a staple item in the diets of many peoples as well as an important animal feed. Soybeans are also used for a growing range of industrial products including adhesives, plastics, and firefighting foam.

**Bean, Roy** (1825?-1903), U.S. justice of the peace who called himself "the only law west of the Pecos." After an early life that included arrest, jailbreak, and proprietorship of tent saloons, he settled in western Texas, where he built a combination store, saloon, and pool hall, and held court as justice and coroner. His decisions were more notable for six-gun drama and humor than legal sagacity.

**Bean beetle,** insect (*Epilachna varivestis*) of the order of beetles (Coleoptera), and the ladybug family (Coccinellidae). A serious pest to bean plants in Mexico, the bean beetle was accidentally introduced into Alabama around 1920, and later spread through the central and eastern United States and southern Canada.

**Bean curd** *See:* Tofu.

**Bear,** large mammal (family Ursidae), usually omnivorous, characterized by heavy build, thick limbs, small tail, and small ears. All have coarse thick hair which is, with the exception of the polar bear, dark in color. Species include the brown bear, the North American black bear, the spectacled bear, the Asiatic black bear, the sun bear, and the sloth bear. The Kodiak, a brown bear, is the largest, up to 9 ft (2.7 m) tall and 1,600 lb (730 kg).

**Beard, Charles and Mary,** U.S. authors and historians who coauthored seven books, the best-known being *The Rise of American Civilization* (2 vols, 1927) and its sequels. **Charles Austin Beard** (1874-1948) taught history and political science at Columbia University from 1904 to 1917, when he resigned to protest U.S. participation in World War I. The author of more than 70 books, his most controversial was *An Economic Interpretation of the Constitution* (1913), in which he argued that the U.S. Constitution reflected the economic interests of its authors. **Mary Ritter Beard** (1876-1958), an author and leader of the women's rights movement, focused on the historical role of women.

**Beard, Daniel Carter** (1850-1941), painter, illustrator, and organizer of the Boy Scouts of America. As National Scout Commissioner (1910-41), he gave the movement its distinctly American character, based on Indian and pioneer lore.
*See also:* Boy Scouts.

**Bearded collie,** breed of dog distinguished by a beardlike growth of hair around its mouth. Bred in Scotland as a sheep and cattle herder, the bearded collie is a popular farm pet. It stands 20-25 in (51-56 cm) tall and weighs about 60 lb (27 kg).

**Beardsley, Aubrey Vincent** (1872-98), English illustrator and author. By 1894 Beardsley had become art editor of the *Yellow Book* magazine and a prolific artist. His graphic style was one of sharp black-and-white contrasts, with flowing lines and detailed patterning; his subject matter—for instance, Oscar Wilde's *Salomé*, or Aristophanes' *Lysistrata*—tended toward the decadent or erotic.

**Beardtongue**, any of a genus (*Pentstemon*) of tubular flowers containing five stamens. The flower derives its name from the fifth stamen, whose strands of yellow filament give a beardlike appearance. These flowers are native to North America and are widespread in the United States.

**Bear Flag Republic**, republic declared in 1846 by U.S. settlers in Sacramento Valley, Cal., who rejected Mexican rule. The explorer John C. Fremont aided the insurgents, but the republic collapsed after the outbreak of the Mexican War in May 1846. In 1848 California ceded to the U.S.
*See also:* Mexican War.

**Bearing**, device to minimize friction and provide support and guidance for the moving parts of a machine. There are 2 main types of bearings—plain or journal bearings, and ball or roller bearings. In the plain bearing, a sheath lined with a special metal is clamped around a turning or sliding axle or journal. Plain bearings are used in engines and industrial machines. In roller or ball bearings, small round balls or rollers are placed between the journal and the housing of the bearing case. Contact is made only at points (ball bearings) or along thin lines (roller bearings), thus reducing friction to a minimum. Ball bearings are used mainly with revolving axles such as those of cars. Roller bearings are used to carry heavy loads at relatively slow speeds. Bearings were first used in Egypt to move blocks of stone from quarries to build palaces and pyramids.

**Bears and bulls**, popular terms for stock and commodity investors of opposing views of market prospects. Bulls believe that stock prices will rise, bears that they will fall. Bulls therefore buy, where bears seek to sell, either to prevent a loss or to buy back at lower prices. Rising stock values are therefore referred to as a bullish market, while falling ones constitute a bearish market.
*See also:* Commodity exchange.

**Beat generation**, U.S. literary movement of the 1950s, exemplified by Jack Kerouac's *On the Road* (1956), the adventures of the original social dropout, Allen Ginsberg's long poem *Howl*, and work by such poets as Lawrence Ferlinghetti and Gregory Corso, and by novelist William S. Burroughs. The movement, a protest against complacent middle-class values, was short-lived, but influenced artistic experiments for the next 15 years.
*See also:* Kerouac, Jack.

**Beatitudes**, in the New Testament, 8 blessings pronounced by Jesus as a prologue to the Sermon on the Mount (Matthew 5:3-10), in which he calls "blessed" those who are poor in spirit, the meek, those who mourn, those

who seek after holiness, the merciful, the pure in heart, the peacemakers, and those who suffer persecution for righteousness' sake.
*See also:* New Testament.

**Beatles**, English rock music group that dominated popular music in the 1960s. Guitarists and composers **John Lennon** (1940-80), **Paul McCartney** (1942-  ), and **George Harrison** (1943-  ), and drummer **Ringo Starr** (Richard Starkey; 1940-  ), won fame in Britain with their recording "Please Please Me" (1963). The 1964 song "I Want to Hold Your Hand" introduced them to the United States, where their concerts became scenes of mass adulation. *Revolver* (1966) and *Sgt. Pepper's Lonely Hearts Club Band* (1967) are ranked among their finest albums. The group disbanded in 1970. John Lennon's murder by a demented fan in New York City (December 1980) caused mourning around the world. In 1995, the other three members launched a new single "Free as a Bird", using a demo tape with John Lennon's voice.
*See also:* Lennon, John; McCartney, (James) Paul.

**Beaton, Sir Cecil Walter Hardy** (1904-80), English photographer and designer, known for his royal portraits, collections such as *Cecil Beaton's Scrapbook* (1937), and set and costume designs for shows and films such as *My Fair Lady* (stage, 1956; motion picture, 1964).

**Beatrix** (1938-  ), queen of the Netherlands (1980-  ), following the abdication of her mother, Juliana.
*See also:* Netherlands.

**Beauchamp, Kathleen** *See:* Mansfield, Katherine.

**Beaufort scale**, scale from 0 to 12 used to measure the force of wind. An 8 on the scale signifies a gale and a 12 a hurricane.
*See also:* Wind.

**Beauharnais, Joséphine de** (1763-1814), first wife of Napoleon I and empress of France. Her first husband, General Alexandre, Vicomte de Beauharnais, was guillotined in the Reign of Terror. Their son, Eugène de Beauharnais (1781-1824), was made viceroy of Italy by Napoleon. He distinguished himself in campaigns against Austria and Russia.

**Beaumarchais, Pierre Augustin Caron** (1732-99), French dramatist and variously an artist, litigant, and political agent. His best-known plays, *The Barber of Seville* (1775) and *The Marriage of Figaro* (1784), the basis of operas by Rossini and Mozart, ridiculed the established order and the nobility. He was instrumental in furnishing the Americans with arms and money at the outbreak of their Revolution.

**Beaumont** (pop. 361,226), city and major oil-refining center in east Texas, seat of Jefferson County. Beaumont was the first petroleum boom town in the United States, expanding rapidly after the first gusher, in 1901.
*See also:* Texas.

**Beaumont, Francis** (1584-1616), English Jacobean playwright. He is best known for his collaborations with John Fletcher, although Beaumont is probably the sole author of *The Woman Hater* (1607) and *The Knight of the Burning Pestle* (1607?). Beaumont and Fletcher's works include *Philaster* (1608), *The Maid's Tragedy* (1609), and *A King and No King* (1611).
*See also:* Fletcher, John.

**Beaumont, William** (1785-1853), U.S. army physician noted for his research on the human digestive system. He treated a trapper with a gunshot stomach wound; when the abdomen wouldn't close, Beaumont conducted experiments over several years to analyze the digestive process.
*See also:* Digestive system.

**Beauregard, Pierre Gustave Toutant de** (1818-93), Confederate general of the U.S. Civil War. In 1861 Beauregard commanded the attack on Fort Sumter, S.C., which opened the war. He distinguished himself at the First Battle of Bull Run, shared command at Shiloh, and held off Union naval attacks on Charleston. Joining General Joseph E. Johnston, he fell back to the Carolinas in the face of Sherman's Georgia campaign, and remained there until the end of the war.
*See also:* Civil War, U.S.

**Beauvoir, Simone de** (1908-86), French writer and a leading exponent of Existentialism and the role of women in politics and intellectual life. Her best-known works are *The Second Sex* (1953) and *The Mandarins* (1956). She also wrote an autobiographical trilogy, and a moving account of her mother's death, *A Very Easy Death* (1966). Jean-Paul Sartre was her close associate.
*See also:* Existentialism.

**Beaver**, large rodent (family Castoridae), weighing up to 100 lb (45 kg) or over, of northern lands. Beavers have thick, furry waterproof coats, powerful, web-footed hindlegs, and small forelimbs with dexterous, sensitive paws. Although lissencephalic (smooth-brained), they are the most intelligent rodents, building dams and lodges (domes up to 23 ft/7 m in diameter, in which they live) from logs and mud. They use their powerful incisor teeth to fell trees and gnaw logs into shape. Their large, heavy tails are used on land for balance and in the water as rudders. Their respiratory system enables them to remain underwater for up to 15 minutes.

**Beaverbrook, William Maxwell Aitken, 1st Baron** (1879-1964), Canadian-born British newspaper owner and Conservative cabinet minister under Winston Churchill. Among his mass-circulation newspapers were the *Daily Express*, *Sunday Express*, and *Evening Standard*.

**Bebel, August** (1840-1913), leading German socialist and cofounder of the Social Democratic Party (1869). A strong antimilitarist and fighter for women's rights, his *Women and Socialism* was published in 1879.

**Bebop** *See:* Jazz.

**Becker, Boris** (1967- ), German tennis player. He was the youngest winner of the men's singles title at Wimbledon (1985) and he won it again the following year. In 1988 he helped West Germany win its first Davis Cup, while winning the Masters and World Championship the same year. In 1989 he won his third Wimbledon title. Among other victories were the U.S. Open in 1989, the Masters tournament (1992), and the Australian Open in 1991 and 1996.

**Becket, Saint Thomas à** (1118?-70), martyr and archbishop of Canterbury. He first served as chancellor under Henry II, becoming a close friend. In 1162 he was appointed archbishop of Canterbury. After years of dissension with the king, in 1170 he was murdered in the cathedral of Canterbury by four knights inspired by some rash words of the king.

**Beckett, Samuel Barclay** (1906-89), Irish dramatist and novelist, resident in France from 1937. His work, much of it written in French, deals with habit, boredom, and suffering, and is deeply pessimistic. His novels include *Murphy* (1938) and the trilogy, *Molloy, Malone Dies,* and *The Unnameable* (1951-53). Among his plays are *Waiting for Godot* (1952) and *Happy Days* (1961). Beckett won the 1969 Nobel Prize for literature.

**Beckwourth, James Pierson** (1798-1867?), African-American pioneer, rancher, fur-trader, and Army scout, discoverer of Beckworth Pass through the Sierra Nevada Mountains around 1850. The pass opened a direct route to California's Sacramento Valley. Believed to have been born a slave in Fredericksburg, Virginia, Beckworth grew up in St. Louis and participated in trading expeditions to the Rocky Mountains, where he encountered and lived with the Crow tribe from 1826 to 1837.

**Becquerel, Antoine Henri** (1852-1908), French physicist, discoverer of natural radioactivity in uranium (1896). He shared the 1903 Nobel Prize for physics with Pierre and Marie Curie.
*See also:* Radioactivity.

**Bedbug,** blood-sucking insect of the order Hemiptera (bugs), family Cimicidae. Parasites on warm-blooded animals, bedbugs are about one-quarter in (6mm) long and may survive for a year without feeding.

**Bede, Saint** (673?-735), known as The Venerable Bede, Anglo-Saxon monk and scholar. His *Ecclesiastical History of the English Nation*, written in Latin, is a major source for the early history of England.

**Bedford, Gunning, Jr.** (1747-1812), U.S. lawyer, statesman, and signer of the Constitution. Bedford attended the Constitutional Convention as a delegate from Delaware and played a major part in the drafting and ratification of the Constitution. He was appointed judge of the U.S. District Court for Delaware by George Washington in 1789.

**Bedlington terrier,** long-legged, fleecy-coated breed of terrier first bred in Bedlington, England, in the 19th century. It stands about 16 in (41 cm) tall and weighs 22-24 lb (10-11 kg), and was bred to fight badgers.

**Bedloe's Island** *See:* Liberty Island.

**Bedouin,** nomadic peoples of the Middle East and North Africa, especially the Syrian, Arabian, and Sahara deserts. Many bedouins have adopted non-nomadic life styles as a result of 20th-century development.

**Bed sore,** ulceration of the skin on the back of a person who is bedridden. Pressure of the bed against the skin first restricts the blood supply and then, by friction, breaks down the tissues into an ulcer (sore).

**Bedstraw,** any of a group of wild plants (genus *Galium*) found in damp woods and swamps. They have slender, square stems and fine needle-shaped leaves arranged in whorls of four to eight. The clustered flowers may be white, brown, yellow, or green. The name is derived from their former use as mattress stuffing.

**Bee,** any of about 20,000 species of flying insects of the superfamily Apoidae. Bees cross-pollinate plants and convert nectar into honey. Social bees (honeybees and bumblebees) live in complex societies of 10,000-50,000 members. Headed by the queen (who lays up to 2,000 eggs a day), the colony also includes female workers, who collect pollen and build cells, and fertile male bees, or drones.
*See also:* Beeswax; Honey; Pollen; Bumblebee.

**Beebe, Charles William** (1877-1962), U.S. naturalist best remembered for his record 3,028 ft (923 m) descent into the ocean off Bermuda in a bathysphere in 1934.

**Beech,** common name for a family (Fagaceae) of deciduous forest trees indigenous to the Northern Hemisphere. Featuring thin, smooth gray bark, oval leaves, and edible nuts, beech trees may grow up to 100 ft (305 m) high. The European beech is ornamental; the American beech is used for furniture and flooring.

**Beecham, Sir Thomas** (1879-1961), English conductor, founder of the London Philharmonic and the Royal Philharmonic orchestras.

**Beecher, Catharine Esther** (1800-78), U.S. educator and advocate of higher education for women. Beecher established seminaries for women in Hartford and Cincinnati. She originated the discipline of home economics and pioneered calisthenics for girls. Beecher was opposed to women's suffrage, believing that women should devote their lives to being homemakers and that the purpose of their education was to prepare them for this role.

**Beecher, Henry Ward** (1813-87), U.S. clergyman, orator, lecturer, author, and abolitionist. The preacher of Plymouth Congregational Church (1847-87) in Brooklyn, N.Y., he was an advocate of women's suffrage and of the theory of evolution.

**Beecher, Lyman** (1775-1863), U.S. clergyman and liberal theologian who helped found the American Bible Society (1816); father of Harriet Beecher

Stowe. Beecher's sermons against slavery and intemperance made him one of the most influential orators of his time.

**Bee-eater,** any of various species of insect-eating birds (family Meropidae) living mainly in tropical Africa and Asia. They range in length from 6 to 14 in (15-36 cm), are usually green and yellow, and have long curved beaks.

**Beef,** the flesh of mature cattle slaughtered for food. Leading beef consuming and exporting countries include the United States, Argentina, Australia, Canada, and New Zealand.

**Bee fly,** insect of the family Bombyliidae that closely resembles a bee but has only one pair of wings and no stinger.

**Beefwood,** pine-like tree (*Casuarina equisetifolia*) native to Australia and commonly found in warm climates around the world. It thrives in sandy soil, grows to 50 ft (15 m), and is prized for its dense, hard wood.

**Beekeeping,** practice of cultivating bees dating back over 7,000 years. In prehistoric times, people and animals collected honey from the nests of wild bees. Today the main value of the domestic honey bee is the pollination of crops.

**Beelzebub,** in the Bible, one of the names for the devil.

**Beer,** alcoholic beverage known since ancient times, made by fermenting cereals. Ale, stout, porter, and lager are varieties of beer. Today beer is produced worldwide but the beers of Germany and Holland are especially popular. In the United States the average beer consumption per person is over 20 gallons a year. The alcohol content of beer can range from 2 to 6%.

**Beerbohm, Sir Max** (1872-1956), English critic, satirist, and caricaturist best known for his caustic but benign characterizations of eminent Victorian and Edwardian figures, his satirical novel about Oxford, *Zuleika Dobson* (1911), and his parody *A Christmas Garland* (1912).

**Beers, Clifford Whittingham** (1876-1943), founder of the U.S. mental health movement. His autobiographical *A Mind That Found Itself* (1908), an account of his three years in a mental institution, informed the public of the abuses and injustices inflicted on the mentally ill.

**Beersheba** (pop. 112,600), chief city of the Negev Desert in southern Israel, 45 mi (72 km) southwest of Jerusalem. The city was closely associated with the biblical patriarchs Abraham and Isaac. After almost 2,000 years of somnolent existence, Beersheba was rebuilt by the Turks in the late 19th century. Since 1948 it has grown into a major industrial, trading, and transportation center.

**Beeswax,** yellow secretion of the glands on the abdomen of worker bees, who use it to make honeycombs. After the honey is removed, the honeycomb is melted in boiling water to yield the beeswax, which is used in such products as candles, chewing gum, cosmetics, and polishes.

**Beet** (*Beta vulgaris*), biennial or annual root vegetable. Red beets are edible; white-rooted sugar beets provide about one-third of the world's sugar supply; spinach beets, or chard, are used as herbs, and mangel-wurzel for fodder.

**Beethoven, Ludwig van** (1770-1827), German composer, recognized worldwide as one of history's greatest musicians. His progressive deafness, total by the time he reached his late 40s, never interfered with his creativity. Beethoven's work may be divided into 3 periods. During the first, ending about 1802, he was still influenced by Haydn and Mozart. The middle period, ending about 1816, was his most productive. His individual style was developed in such works as the Third (*Eroica*) and Fifth symphonies, the Fifth Piano Concerto (*Emperor*), the *Kreutzer* Violin Sonata, and his only opera, *Fidelio*. His later, more intense works include the Ninth (Choral) Symphony, the *Missa Solemnis* (Mass in D), and the late string quartets, including the Great Fugue.

**Beetle**, any of the more than 250,000 species of the insect order Coleoptera. Beetles are found worldwide except in oceans and have evolved adaptations to nearly all extremes of climate and environment. Beetle eggs hatch into soft, usually wormlike, larvae known as grubs. These grow and metamorphose into pupae, which are soft but resemble adult beetles in form. Pupae often live underground while they develop into adults. Adult beetles range from 1/32 in (1 mm) to over 6.5 in (16 m) in length. Their hard, protective wing cases enclose the fragile flight wings. Beetles are generally plant eaters. Many beetles, such as weevils and leaf beetles, are serious pests to crops, eating seeds or boring into roots and stems. Ladybugs are helpful to humans, feeding on other insect pests.

**Beggar-tick**, or stick-tight, flowering plant of genus *Bidens* of the composite family, named for the hairy, barbed seeds of its yellow flowers, which adhere to clothing or animal fur. The name is often applied to the tick trefoil, a plant of a different family (Leguminosae) but with similar barbed seeds.

**Beggarweed**, tall (6 ft/1.8 m), fast-growing, flowering plant (*Desmodium tortuosum*), native to the West Indies and now found in many warm climates. Beggarweed is commonly cultivated as a natural fertilizer; its roots are a source of nitrogen-fixing bacteria.

**Begin, Menachem** (1913-92), Israeli prime minister, 1977-83. Begin was active in the Zionist Movement's effort to create a Jewish state in the 1930s and 1940s. He was a member and leader (1944-48) of the Irgon Zvai Leumi, an organization that fought for the creation of Israel. He fought in the Arab-Israeli war of 1948. He was elected to the Knesset (parliament) in 1948, with Israel's independence, and was an opposition leader for most of the next 30 years, pressing Israel's claim to the West Bank of the Jordan River and refusing to consider sovereignty for the Palestinians. Begin signed a peace treaty with Egypt in 1979; in 1978 he shared the Nobel Peace Prize with Egyptian President Anwar Sadat. In 1982 Begin launched a much criticized invasion of Lebanon intended to destroy command and military units of the Palestinian Liberation Organization (PLO). Israeli forces succeeded in driving out the PLO but also occupied West Beirut, a move that was very unpopular in Israel and abroad. Israeli forces were accused of allowing the

massacre of Palestinian civilians in refugee camps during their occupation. The Israelis withdrew most of their forces between 1983 and 1985. Since this event Begin remained in almost total, self-imposed seclusion and made rare public statements.
*See also:* Israel.

**Begonia**, common name for a family (Begoniaceae) of perennial plants with about 900 species. Mostly succulent herbs, native to tropical regions, they are cultivated in houses and gardens for their colorful foliage.

**Behan, Brendan** (1922-64), Irish playwright and author, noted for his vivid ribaldry and satire. His works *The Quare Fellow* (1956), the autobiographical *Borstal Boy* (1958), and *The Hostage* (1959) deal largely with his experiences in the Irish Republican Army and his subsequent imprisonment.

**Behavioral sciences**, sciences dealing with human behavior, individually or socially, as opposed to their physiological makeup. The term embraces anthropology, psychology, and sociology.
*See also:* Anthropology; Psychology; Sociology.

**Behaviorism**, school of psychology that studies behavior exclusively in terms of objective observations of reactions to environmental stimuli. Originating with Pavlov's animal experiments in conditioned reflexes, behaviorism in human psychology was introduced by J.B. Watson and championed by B.F. Skinner.
*See also:* Pavlov, Ivan Petrovich; Watson, John Broadus; Skinner, B.F.

**Behavior therapy**, methods for changing undesirable habits through learning,

**Behn, Aphra** (1640-89), dramatist, novelist, and poet, first professional female author in England. Her plays *The Rover* (1677) and *The Forced Marriage* (1670) and her novel *Oroonoko* (1688) show technical ingenuity and wit.

**Behrens, Peter** (1868-1940), German architect who pioneered a mode of functional design suited to industrial technology. His most influential work was the AEG turbine factory in Berlin (1908-09). He influenced Le Corbusier, Gropius, and Mies van der Rohe.

**Behrman, Samuel Nathaniel** (1893-1973), U.S. dramatist noted for his comedies of manners, including *Biography* (1932) and *No Time for Comedy* (1939). He also wrote film scripts and a biography of satirist Max Beerbohm (1960).

**Beiderbecke, Bix** (Leon Bismarck Beiderbecke; 1903-31), U.S. jazz musician. An accomplished pianist and brilliant cornetist, he joined the renowned Paul Whiteman band in 1928. Despite his early death through alcoholism and general ill health, he was a major innovator in the development of jazz.
*See also:* Jazz.

**Beijing** (formerly Peking; pop. 7,000,000), capital of the People's Republic of China, lying within the Hebei province, but administered directly by the central government. It is the political, commercial, cultural, and communications center of the country, and embraces a massive industrial complex. The city's rectangular layout was the work of Kublai Khan in the 13th century, and its splendors were described by Marco Polo. It became the permanent capital of China in 1421. Its occupation by French and British troops from 1860 was a contributing cause of the Boxer Rebellion (1900). In 1928 Peking (renamed Peiping) was superseded by Nanking (Nanjing), but regained its capital status and its name with the Communist victory under Mao Zedong in 1949. Beijing has two historic districts: the Inner City, enclosing the Imperial Palace and the Forbidden City, and the Outer City. In mid-1989 a massacre of demonstrators in Beijing's Tiananmen Square signaled the difficulty of China's democracy movement in the face of totalitarian authority.
*See also:* China.

**Beirut** (pop. 700,000), capital city and chief port of the Republic of Lebanon, situated on the Mediterranean Sea. During early Roman times the city became famous as a center of learning. The Arabs conquered the city in A.D. 635. In 1110 it was captured by the Crusaders, who held it for two centuries. It eventually became part of the Ottoman Empire. During World War I it came under French rule and was proclaimed the capital of Lebanon in 1920. Beirut has excellent railroad connections with other nearby cities, which have enlarged the region served by its harbor. Growth of the city during the 20th century was rapid until the Lebanese civil war of 1975-76 between Muslims and Christians caused severe damage and ended Beirut's success as a financial center and tourist resort. Much of the city was left in ruins following a siege by Israeli forces in 1982, which brought about the expulsion of thousands of PLO guerrillas.

**Béjart, Maurice** (1927-    ), French dancer and choreographer. He danced with various companies in Europe and organized his own company in 1954. The Ballet of the 20th Century in Brussels, Belgium, which he has directed since 1959, has an international reputation.
*See also:* Ballet.

**Bekesy, Georg von** (1899-1972), Hungarian-born U.S. scientist who was awarded the 1961 Nobel Prize for medicine for research into the mechanism of the inner ear. A senior research fellow at Harvard University since 1947, he made discoveries about the physical mechanisms of hearing, particularly with respect to discrimination of pitch.
*See also:* Ear.

**Belafonte, Harry** (1927-    ), U.S. singer and actor best known for his interpretations of West Indian calypso folksongs. Belafonte is also active in many human rights causes.

**Belasco, David** (1853-1931), U.S. playwright and theatrical producer; famous for mounting spectacular New York productions, with lavishly detailed sets, to promote newly discovered stars.

**Belém** (pop. 758,100), capital of the state of Pará in northern Brazil. Situated on the Pará River, about 90 mi (145 km) from the Atlantic coast, Belém is the commercial center of the mouth of the Amazon River basin. Among its industries are tourism, rubber, timber, cacao, and Brazil nuts.
*See also:* Brazil.

**Belfast** (pop. 300,000), seaport and capital of Northern Ireland, located at the mouth of the Lagan River, an inlet of the Irish Sea. The town was populated by about 2,000 English settlers in 1613, became a county borough in 1898, and was made capital of Northern Ireland in 1920. By the end of the 18th century Belfast had become the export center for the Irish linen trade and for the developing cotton industry. The city was long known for shipbuilding, but that industry has recently declined in importance. Although newer industries, including an aircraft factory, have been established, unemployment in the area is still the highest in the United Kingdom. For the past century, Belfast has been the scene of violent conflict between the Protestant majority and Catholic minority and, recently, of guerrilla fighting between the Irish Republican Army and British troops.
*See also:* Ireland.

**Belgian Congo** *See:* Zaïre.

**Belgium**, kingdom of northwestern Europe, bordered to the west by France, to the east by Luxembourg and Germany, and to the north by the Netherlands. Belgium is one of Europe's most densely populated countries.
*Land and climate.* The region called Flanders borders the North Sea and is mostly flat plain with sandy beaches; further inland, the country is intensively cultivated, and is drained by the Leie, Schelde, and Dender rivers. Central Belgium consists of a low plateau that is also a rich agricultural area. At the southern end of this plateau is the Sambre-Meuse valley, the main industrial and coal-mining region. About 25% of all Belgians live in this area of only 800 sq mi (2,000 sq km). The country has a generally temperate climate.
*People.* Belgium is linguistically, culturally, and politically divided. A line running from east to west, just south of Brussels, divides the Flemish-speaking Flemings in the north from the French-speaking Walloons in the south. Both languages are in official use.
*Economy.* Belgium is not rich in natural resources, except for the coal deposits of the Sambre-Meuse valley and the Kempenland region. Its high standard of living derives from successful manufacturing industries, which account for 30% of the gross national product. The chief commodities include textiles, glass, chemicals, metal and machine goods, and diamonds; Antwerp is one of the world's leading diamond centers. Brussels (the capital), Bruges, and Mechelen are noted for lace. Belgium's numerous small farms provide about 80% of the country's food needs. Belgium's excellent system of transportation, including fine inland waterways and well-equipped ports at Antwerp and Ghent, facilitate the foreign trade that has made the country prosperous.
*History.* The kingdom emerged in the 1830s, when it seceded from the Netherlands, and in 1839 Belgium was recognized as a perpetually neutral sovereign state. In 1914 the Germans invaded and occupied the country for the next 4 years. In May 1940 Germany again violated Belgian neutrality,

**Belgium**

| | |
|---|---|
| Capital: | Brussels |
| Area: | 11,783 sq mi |
| | (30,518 sq km) |
| Population: | 10,174,000 |
| Language: | Dutch, French, German |
| Government: | Federal state with |
| | constitutional monarchy |
| Independent: | 1830 |
| Head of gov.: | Prime minister |
| Per capita: | U.S. $24,710 |
| Mon. unit: | 1 Belgian franc = |
| | 100 centimes |

invading Belgium, the Netherlands, and Luxembourg simultaneously. Belgian forces capitulated in June 1940, but Belgian resistance forces fought alongside the Allies until the country was liberated in 1944. Belgium was a founding member of the United Nations in 1945 and a founding member of the North Atlantic Treaty Organization (NATO) in 1950. It also helped to establish the European Economic Community (EEC), which was to become part of the European Community (EC), with headquarters in Brussels. After 1995 several large-scale vice scandals and political scandals took place in Belgium.
*See also:* Brussels.

**Belgrade** (pop. 1,087,900), capital and largest city of Yugoslavia, a port and industrial center at the junction of the Danube and Sava rivers. Important products include metals, chemicals, and textiles. Held in turn by the Romans, Byzantines, Bulgars, Serbs, and Ottoman Turks, the city became Yugoslavia's capital after World War I and kept it's status after the disintegration of former Yugoslavia in 1991. Belgrade is known for its beautiful parks, churches, and museums.
*See also:* Yugoslavia.

**Belisarius** (c.505-565 A D ), Byzantine general under Justinian I. He crushed the Vandals in North Africa and the Ostrogoths in Italy, taking Rome in 536. In 559 Belisarius was called from retirement to repel the Huns and Slavs from the gates of Constantinople.
*See also:* Byzantine Empire; Justinian I.

**Belize** (British Honduras until 1973), independent nation since 1981, on the subtropical Caribbean coast of Central America, bordered by Mexico on the north and Guatemala on the southwest. The country is densely forested. The population consists of Creoles (of mixed African and European origin), descendants of the Carib and Maya tribes, and a small minority of Europeans. Most people live on the coast. Citrus fruits, bananas, and sugarcane are the mainstay of the export-oriented economy. Fishing and livestock industries are being developed. European settlement began in the 17th century, and in the 18th century African slaves were brought in to cut mahogany. The

**Belize**

Capital: Belmopan
Area: 8,867 sq mi
(22,965 sq km)
Population: 230,160
Language: English
Government: Constitutional monarchy
Independent: 1981
Head of gov.: Prime minister
Per capita: U.S. $2,630
Mon. unit: 1 Belizean dollar = 100 cents

country became a British colony in 1862 and achieved internal self-government in 1964. Disputes with Guatemala concerning the latter's claim that it had inherited Belize from Spain delayed the proclamation of independence until 1981. In the 1990s, the smuggling of narcotics and the tensions between Hispanic immigrants and the black creole population were the most important problems.

**Belize City** (pop. 45,100), largest city and former capital of Belize, a country on the Caribbean coast. Though its proximity to the sea earned Belize City a reputation as a chief seaport, it also makes the city especially susceptible to hurricanes. Following a devastating hurricane in 1961 that destroyed the city, killed hundreds, and left thousands homeless, the capital was moved from Belize City inland to Belmopan, the current capital. For over 300 years, Belize City has been world renowned for its shipping of mahogany and logwood. The city also ships rosewood, cedar, coconuts, maize, bananas, and sugar. The British first settled Belize City in the 1600s. Now about 1 in 4 Belize citizens live in Belize City.

**Bell**, metal instrument rung by a metal clapper inside. Most bells are cup-shaped, with the bottom edges tapering outward, but as musical instruments they can be pipes of varying lengths (chimes) that create different tones when struck. Bells originated in China in the 800s B.C and were introduced to Europe in the 6th century A.D. Commonly associated with churches, where they were rung to summon people to worship, bells have also signalled emergencies or momentous events such as the independence movements in the United States and Mexico.
*See also:* Big Ben; Liberty Bell.

**Bell, Alexander Graham** (1847-1922), Scottish-born U.S. scientist and educator who invented the telephone (1876), the wax-cylinder phonograph, and various aids for teaching the deaf. He also founded the Bell Telephone Company.
*See also:* Telephone.

**Bella Coola**, tribe of Native Americans in western Canada near the North Pacific coast. The 600 Bella Coola still living reside near Queen Charlotte Sound, British Columbia, in a village on the Bella Coola River. Though they speak English and have lifestyles similar to their Canadian neighbors, they maintain their cultural heritage, lavishing gifts on guests at frequent ceremonial feasts (potlatches) and electing a band council to administer and govern the tribe. The ancestors of modern Bella Coola were successful fishermen (particularly of salmon) and woodworkers for centuries.

**Belladonna**, or deadly nightshade (*Atropa belladonna*), poisonous herbaceous plant of the nightshade family whose dried leaves and roots produce a crude drug of the same name. Various medicinal alkaloids, such as the muscle relaxant atropine, are produced by refining belladonna.

**Bell, John** (1797-1869), "Tennessee Bell," presidential candidate of the Constitutional Union Party (1860) who lost to Lincoln on the eve of the U.S. Civil War. As representative (1827-41) and senator (1847-59), he led a conservative group of antisecessionist southerners.

**Bellamy, Edward** (1850-98), U.S. author. His Utopian *Looking Backward 2000-1877* (1888) pictured a benevolent state socialism with worker-ownership and made him famous. His other novels include *Miss Ludington's Sister* (1884) and *Equality* (1897), a sequel to *Looking Backward.*

**Bellarmine, Saint Robert Francis Romulus** (1542-1621), theologian known for his opposition to Protestant Reformation doctrines. An Italian Jesuit, Saint Bellarmine was regarded by the Roman Catholic church as a key defender of the church's rights in an age when royal absolutism reigned. In 1560, he joined the Jesuit order. He became a cardinal (1599) and then archbishop of Capua (1602). A theology professor at the University of Louvain, Bellarmine was a prolific author. He was passionate about helping the poor, and gave all his money to those less fortunate, dying a pauper. Bellarmine was canonized in 1930. His feast day is May 17.
*See also:* Roman Catholic Church.

**Bellbird**, common name for a number of bird species whose songs resemble ringing bells. The *campañero* of the South American tropical rain forest is a well-known white bellbird.

**Belleau Wood, Battle of** (June 6-25, 1918), part of the World War I second battle of the Marne in which a brigade of U.S. Marines, with French support, halted five German divisions. In 1923 the battlefield was dedicated as a memorial to the American dead.
*See also:* World War I.

**Bellerophon**, Greek mythological hero. Bellerophon tamed the winged horse Pegasus to aid him in the tasks set by King Iobates. He attempted to reach Olympus on his mount, but Pegasus, stung by a gadfly sent by Zeus, threw him, and Bellerophon was crippled and blinded.
*See also:* Mythology.

**Bellflower**, or bluebell, any of several species of annual, biennial, and perennial plants producing bell-shaped flowers, ranging from a few inches to more than 6 ft (1.8 m) tall, found in temperate and subtropical areas.

**Bellini**, family of Early Renaissance Venetian painters. **Jacopo** (c.1400-1470) evolved a much-imitated compositional technique of depicting small figures in vast, detailed architectural settings. **Gentile** (1429-1507), his elder son, is noted for his realistic portraits and his use of perspective to give a sense of spatial depth. **Giovanni** (1430-1516), the younger son, is considered the greatest Early Renaissance Venetian painter, famous for his use of light and color. His pupils, Titian and Giorgione, continued and developed his style.
*See also:* Renaissance.

**Bellini, Vincenzo** (1801-35), Italian opera composer of the bel canto school. His most popular works today are his last 3: *La Sonnambula* (1831), *Norma* (1831), and *I Puritani* (1835).
*See also:* Opera.

**Belloc, (Joseph Pierre) Hilaire** (1870-1953), French-born English poet, essayist, and historian. An ardent Roman Catholic polemicist, his first well-known work was *The Bad Child's Book of Beasts* (1896).

**Bellow, Saul** (1915-    ), Canadian-born U.S. novelist noted for his narrative skill and his studies of Jewish-American life. His best-known books are *The Adventures of Augie March* (1953) and *Herzog* (1964). Other novels include *Dangling Man* (1944), *Henderson the Rain King* (1959), *Humboldt's Gift* (1975), *The Dean's December* (1982), *More Die of Heartbreak* (1987), and *The Actual* (1992). He won the 1976 Nobel Prize in literature.

**Bellows, George Wesley** (1882-1925), U.S. painter and lithographer, early 20th century "realist" who remained aloof from modern European influences and was influential in reviving U.S. lithography. His painting of New York City include *Forty-Two kids* and *Stage at Sharkey's.*
*See also:* Lithography.

**Bell's palsy**, nerve disorder that causes paralysis of one side of the face. Thought to be due to a virus infection, Bell's palsy occurs most often in young men. It begins suddenly with a dull ache behind the jaw and weakened facial muscles. The paralyzed muscles usually begin to recover within ten days or so.

**Belmopan** (pop. 4,000), capital city of Belize, a country on the Caribbean coast. Belmopan, the capital since 1970, is a new city built approximately 50 mi (80 km) inland from Belize City, the former capital, which was plagued by devastating hurricanes. Many of the buildings in Belmopan are adorned with ancient Mayan designs. The country's most modern hospital and many government buildings are located in the city.
*See also:* Belize.

**Belo Horizonte** (pop. 1,443,000), city in Brazil, about 220 mi (354 km) north of Rio de Janeiro. It is a fast-growing city, with heavy industry and

secondary products including furniture, textiles, and footwear. The capital of Minas Gerais state, Belo Horizonte was built in 1895-97 as Brazil's first planned city. It is a center of culture and tourism.
*See also:* Brazil.

**Belorussia** *See:* Byelorussia.

**Belsen,** German village in Lower Saxony, site of the infamous Nazi concentration camp called Bergen-Belsen, where over 115,000 people, mostly Jews, were killed.
*See also:* Holocaust.

**Beluga,** or white whale, small (13 ft/4 m) whale (*Delphinapterus leucas*) living in northern seas and prized for its skin. The sturgeon, largest Russian freshwater fish, source of caviar, is also called beluga.

**Bemelmans, Ludwig** (1898-1962), Austrian-American writer and illustrator of *Hansi* (1934), *My War with the United States* (1937), *Madeline* (1939), and other satiric and children's stories.

**Bemis, Samuel Flagg** (1891-1973), U.S. historian. A Yale professor (1935-60) and an expert on U.S. diplomatic history, his books include *A Diplomatic History of the United States* (1936) and 2 Pulitzer Prize-winning works, *Pinckney's Treaty* (1926) and *John Quincy Adams and the Foundations of American Foreign Policy* (1950).

**Benares** *See:* Varanasi.

**Benavente y Martínez, Jacinto** (1866-1954), Spanish playwright. He wrote and staged 172 comedies and helped establish the modern theater in Spain. He was awarded the 1922 Nobel Prize for literature for such popular plays as *The Bonds of Interest* (1907) and *La Malquerida* (1913).

**Ben Bella, Ahmed** (1918-    ), Algerian revolutionary who helped plan the 1954 anti-French revolt. After the post-independence power struggle, Ben Bella became president in 1962. He was ousted during Col. Houari Boumedienne's 1965 coup. He was imprisoned until 1979 and returned from exile in 1990.
*See also:* Algeria.

**Benchley, Robert Charles** (1889-1945), U.S. writer, drama critic of *Life* (1920-29) and *The New Yorker* (1929-40). He is best known for his short humorous pieces, published in several collections—*My Ten Years in a Quandary* (1936), *Benchley Beside Himself* (1943)—and such satirical short films as—*The Treasurer's Report* (1928). His grandson, Peter Benchley (1928-    ), wrote the best-selling novel *Jaws* (1975).

**Bendix, Vincent** (1882-1945), U.S. mechanical engineer and industrialist who developed and mass-produced a 4-wheel brake system for automobiles and devised a practicable self-starter. He also had interests in aviation, and the Bendix Aviation Corporation manufactured radio and radar equipment.
*See also:* Automobile.

**Bends,** also known as caisson disease or decompression sickness, dangerous physiological reaction resulting from a rapid decrease in atmospheric pressure that may release nitrogen bubbles into the body. These can obstruct small blood vessels, collect in the joints, and damage the nervous system. Symptoms involve painful joints and muscles, convulsions, double vision, and paralysis. Divers, airplane pilots, and others working in compressed-air situations are the usual victims.

**Benedict XV** (Giacomo Della Chiesa; 1854-1922), Roman Catholic pope during the outbreak of World War I. Benedict was elected pope in 1914, 3 months after he was made a cardinal. His reign was punctuated by World War I and a conflict with Italy regarding Italian troops that were occupying Rome. Though Benedict tried to maintain and encourage strict neutrality, his papacy was plagued with war problems. The Allies eventually excluded him from peace negotiations. After the war, Benedict encouraged international reconciliation and endorsed the founding of the League of Nations. In 1917, he was credited with the issuance of the Code of Canon Law, a compilation of comprehensive church laws.

**Benedict, Ruth Fulton** (1887-1948), U.S. cultural anthropologist whose extensive fieldwork helped illustrate the theory of cultural relativism—what is considered deviant in one culture may be normal in another. Her classic work was *Patterns of Culture* (1934).
*See also:* Anthropology.

**Benedictine Orders,** the "Black Monks," order of monks and nuns following the rule of St. Benedict of Nursia. They believe in a combination of prayer, choral office, study, and manual labor under an abbot's supervision.
*See also:* Benedict of Nursia, Saint.

**Benedict of Nursia, Saint** (c.480-547), father of Western monasticism, whose "rule" set the pattern of monastic life from the mid-7th century. He founded the first Benedictine monastery at Monte Cassino.
*See also:* Benedictine Orders.

**Benelux,** customs union formed by Belgium, the Netherlands, and Luxembourg, in 1948. "Benelux" is often used collectively for the countries themselves.

**Benes, Eduard** (1884-1948), co-founder, with Thomás Masaryk, of the Czechoslovak Republic. He held the posts of foreign minister (1918-35), prime minister (1921-22), president (1935-38 and 1946-48), and head of the government-in-exile (1940-45). His appeals to Great Britain and France in 1938 failed to prevent Hitler's occupation of the Sudetenland. He died after the 1948 Communist coup.
*See also:* Czechoslovakia.

**Benét, Steven Vincent** (1898-1943), U.S. poet, novelist, and short story writer, whose works center on U.S. history and tradition. His epic poems *John Brown's Body* (1928) and *Western Star* (1943) won Pulitzer Prizes. Among his most famous short stories is "The Devil and Daniel Webster" (1937).

**Bengal,** region including Bangladesh and northeastern India on the Bay of Bengal. Its chief city, Calcutta, was capital of British India 1833-1912, and it was an autonomous province from 1935 until the partition of India in 1947. At that time the western part became West Bengal State of India. The eastern part became a province of Pakistan, and in 1971, the independent nation of Bangladesh.

**Bengal, Bay of** *See:* Bay of Bengal.

**Benghazi** (pop. 368,000), seaport and second largest city of Libya. It is situated in northeastern Libya on the Gulf of Sidra about 600 mi (966 km) east of the capital, Tripoli. Benghazi markets and exports the products of a rich agricultural region: wool, grains, citrus fruits, dates, and olives. There is also considerable tuna and sponge fishing. Benghazi was the scene of fighting (changing hands several times) during World War II.
*See also:* Libya.

**Ben-Gurion, David** (David Grün; 1886-1973), Polish-born Israeli states-man and first prime minister of Israel. After World War I, he helped to found the Haganah, the underground Jewish army, and the Histadrut, the General Federation of Jewish Labor (1920). He became leader of the Mapai Labor Party (1930) and the World Zionist Organization (1935). As prime minister (1949-53 and 1955-63) he helped to mold the state of Israel.
*See also:* Israel.

**Ben-Hur** *See:* Wallace, Lew.

**Benin** (formerly Dahomey), republic in West Africa, flanked by Togo in the west, Burkina Faso (formerly Upper Volta) in the northwest, Niger in the north, Nigeria in the east, and the Gulf of Guinea in the south.
*People.* The population is concentrated in the south coastal region, where Cotonou, a major port city and commercial center, and Porto-Novo, the capital, are located. There are 4 major tribes: the Fon, Adja, and Yoruba in the south and the Bariba in the northeast and central regions. There is a small European community, mostly French.
*Economy.* Benin is one of the world's poorer countries. Its economy is principally agricultural with most people engaged in subsistence farming. The major cash crop is the oil palm. Other exports include hides and skins, cotton, peanuts, and coffee. Benin's position as a transit point for Nigeria and land-locked Niger has provided the impetus for an expanding transport sector. Manufacturing presently accounts for less than 13% of the country's economy.
*History.* The independent Fon Kingdom of Dahomey emerged in the 17th century and engaged in profitable trade with the Portuguese. Known as the Slave Coast, Dahomey became one of the main slave exporting regions of West Africa. King Gezo (1818-58) raided the Yoruba for slaves and extended Dahomey's northern boundaries with the aid of its famous women soldiers. By 1850 the slave trade was declining and in 1851 the French established a trading station at Cotonou. By 1894 the French conquered the kingdom and in 1904 merged Dahomey into French West Africa. In 1960, after more than 50 years as a French colony, Dahomey became an independent republic and joined the United Nations. Plagued by economic and political instability,

**Benin**

| | |
|---|---|
| Capital: | Porto-Novo |
| Area: | 43,450 sq mi |
| | (112,622 sq km) |
| Population: | 6,200 |
| Language: | French |
| Government: | Presidential republic |
| Independent: | 1960 |
| Head of gov.: | President |
| Per capita: | U.S. $370 |
| Mon. unit: | 1 CFA franc = |
| | 100 centimes |

Dahomey witnessed a series of takéovers after independence. The first president, Herbert Maga, was toppled from power in 1963. Rivalry between President Sourow-Migan Apithy and the prime minister resulted in a coup in 1965. Following a series of unstable regimes, a 3-man Presidential Council was established in 1970 only to be overthrown by Maj. Mathiew Kerekou in 1972. In 1975 Dahomey was renamed and became the People's Republic of Benin. As a result of the socio-economic crisis in the late 1980s Kerekou was forced to introduce economic and political liberalization measures and was replaced by Nicephore Soglo in 1991. In 1996 Kerekou returned to power.

**Benjamin, Judah Philip** (1811-84), West Indian-born U.S. politician and lawyer, called the "brains of the Confederacy." As U.S. senator from Louisiana (1853-61), he was an able advocate of the Southern cause. After secession, his friend Jefferson Davis appointed him attorney general, secretary of war, and finally secretary of state (1862-65) in the Confederate government. On the collapse of the Confederacy Benjamin fled to England, where he became a successful barrister.
*See also:* Civil War, U.S.

**Bennett, Arnold** (1867-1931), English novelist, journalist, and playwright. He is famous for his novels set in the potteries of Staffordshire: *Anna of the Five Towns* (1902), *The Old Wives' Tale* (1908), and *These Twain* (1916). He was influenced by Zola's naturalism.

**Bennett, Floyd** (1890-1928), U.S. aviator who piloted Richard Byrd on the first flight over the North Pole (May 9, 1926).

**Bennett, James Gordon** (1795-1872), Scottish-born U.S. newspaper publisher and editor, pioneer of modern news reporting. In 1835 he launched the sensationalist *New York Herald*, the first to print stock market items and use the telegraph. His son, James Gordon Bennett (1841-1918), sent H. M. Stanley to find David Livingston (1869) and founded the *New York Evening Telegram* (1869) and the *Paris Herald* (1887).

**Bennett, Richard Bedford** (1870-1945), prime minister of Canada (1930-35) and leader of the Conservative Party. He was created a viscount in 1941.

**Bennington,** town in southwestern Vermont, about 35 mi (56 km) northeast of Albany, N.Y. In 1777, during the Revolutionary War, the Green Mountain Boys defeated the British troops under General John Burgoyne in an important battle at Bennington. A granite monument just outside the town commemorates this action. Other historical landmarks are the first schoolhouse in Vermont, William Lloyd Garrison's printing shop, and several colonial buildings. The town has a historical museum. Bennington is now a manufacturing town, producing clothing, plastics, pottery, and precision machinery.

**Benny, Jack** (Benjamin Kubelsky; 1894-1974), U.S. comedian. Benny was known for his radio and television routines about the hilarious experiences of a miserly man. He was 17 when he made his show business debut playing violin in vaudeville shows. More than 20 films and an 18-year radio career followed. In 1950, Benny made his first television appearance using the themes that made him famous—stinginess, condemning quiet stares, and his violin playing.

**Bent, William** (1809-1869), U.S. fur trader and pioneer, the first permanent white resident in Colorado. He formed Bent, St. Vrain & Company, a trading firm in the upper Arkansas valley, and ran Bent's Fort, a famous trading post.

**Bent grass,** popular name for some grasses (genus *Agrostis*) of Europe, North America, and North Africa, widely grown for pasture cover and for hay. In the United States one widely grown species is redtop (*A. albot*). Some kinds of bent grass are suitable for lawns and golf greens.

**Bentham, Jeremy** (1748-1832), English philosopher, economist, and jurist, founder of Utilitarianism, a social philosophy whose aim was to achieve "the greatest happiness of the greatest number." His major work was *An Introduction to the Principles of Morals and Legislation* (1789). Bentham's ideas were influential in legal reform in the 19th century and in the thinking of John Stuart Mill and David Ricardo.
*See also:* Utilitarianism.

**Bentley, Eric** (1916-    ), British-born U.S. drama critic and university professor. He wrote *The Playwright as Thinker* (1946) and *What Is Theatre?* (1956). Through his translations and theater work he introduced Brecht's and Pirandello's plays to the English-speaking world.

**Benton, Thomas Hart** (1782-1858), U.S. statesman; great uncle of the painter Thomas Hart Benton. He represented Missouri in the U.S. Senate for 30 years (1821-51), championing the development of the West and opposing the extension of slavery. He also opposed the Mexican War. After leaving the Senate, he served one term (1853-55) in the House of Representatives.

**Benton, Thomas Hart** (1889-1975), U.S. painter; greatnephew of Senator Thomas Hart Benton. He was a leader of the influential 1930s regionalist school of painting, devoted to depicting the life of rural America as in his *Threshing Wheat*.

**Bentonite**, type of fine-grained clay that greatly increases in volume when saturated with water. It is found in rocks formed from volcanic ash. Bentonite is used in ceramics, paper manufacture, and the sealing of dams and oil wells.

**Bentsen, Lloyd Millard, Jr.** (1921-    ), U.S. Senator. As a Texas Democrat, he served 3 terms in the U.S. House of Representatives (1949-55) and won election to the U.S. Senate (1970), defeating George Bush. In 1988 he was the running mate of unsuccessful Democratic presidential candidate Michael Dukakis. Bentsen won reelection to the Senate.

**Benz, Karl** (1844-1929), German engineer believed to have built the first automobile (1885) with an internal combustion engine. His earliest autos had tricycle carriages and electric ignitions. His company merged with Daimler in 1926, and Daimler-Benz became the manufacturer of the Mercedes-Benz. *See also:* Automobile.

**Benzedrine**, U.S. trade name of a drug containing amphetamine.

**Benzene**, colorless, flammable, toxic liquid hydrocarbon ($C_6H_6$) produced from petroleum and from coal gas and coal tar. Benzene is used in the manufacture of plastics and as a fuel in some engines. *See also:* Aniline; Faraday, Michael.

**Benzine**, flammable liquid distilled from petroleum. Clear, colorless, and lighter than kerosene, benzine is a volatile mixture consisting primarily of aliphatic hydrocarbons. Benzine is often used as a drycleaning solvent, motor fuel, and to dissolve fats and oils. Benzine boils between 95° and 175F° (35°-79°C). *See also:* Petroleum.

**Benzocaine**, crystalline ester, used as a local anesthetic, usually in an ointment or in lozenges. It reduces pain or itching in minor wounds. *See also:* Anesthesia.

**Benzol** *See:* Benzene.

**Ben-Zvi, Itzhak** (1884-1963), Russian-born second president of Israel (1952-63). Active in Jewish self-defense groups in Palestine from 1907, in 1929 he founded the National Council of Palestine Jews.

**Benzyl alcohol** (also called phenylcarbinol $C_6H_5CH_2OH$), colorless, aromatic alcohol found in the oils of many flowers. Ephedrine and adrenaline are derived from it. Benzyl alcohol is widely used in the perfume industry, in pharmaceuticals, and as a solvent in cellulose lacquers.

**Beograd** *See:* Belgrade.

**Beothuk**, tribe of Native Americans that once lived on the island of Newfoundland and spoke Bethukian, an independent language. Hunters by trade, the Beothuk were most likely the first people encountered by early European settlers. They had a reputation as skilled canoeists and accomplished hunters and fishermen. In 1497 the Beothuk tribe consisted of nearly 500 people, but their numbers diminished until they became extinct in 1829.

**Beowulf**, anonymous heroic epic poem, probably composed in the 8th century, the greatest extant poem in Old English. Using elements of Germanic legend, it is set in Scandinavia and recounts the hero Beowulf's victories over the monster Grendel and Grendel's mother, his battle with a dragon, and his death and burial.
*See also:* English literature.

**Berbers**, several culturally distinct North African peoples, usually Muslim, who speak the Hamitic Berber language or any of its main dialects. They live mainly in Algeria, Libya, Morocco, and Tunisia. Most are farmers or nomadic herders, but some are oasis-dwellers.

**Berchtesgaden** (pop. 8,300), small Alpine resort town in southeastern Bavaria. Nearby, Adolf Hitler built the Berghof, his fortified chalet retreat.

**Berdyayev, Nikolai Aleksandrovich** (1874-1948), Russian religious philosopher. A Marxist in his youth, he later turned to Christianity and created a highly individual Christian existentialism. Expelled from the USSR in 1922, he settled in Paris.

**Berg, Alban** (1885-1935), Austrian composer of expressive 12-tone music. A pupil of Schoenberg, he adopted his technique in such works as his violin concerto (1935) and his operas, *Wozzeck* (1925), and the unfinished opera *Lulu*.

**Bergamot** (*Citrus bergamia*), fruit whose rind yields an oil used in perfumes and essences. Related to the orange, it is pear-shaped, pale-yellow or green in color, and has fragrant green pulp.

**Bergen** (pop. 218,100), seaport and second largest city in Norway, situated on the southwest coast on the By Fjord. From the 14th to the 16th centuries it was the northernmost member of the Hanseatic League. Several buildings from this period survive, most notably the Tyskebyggen (German House), now a museum. The central districts of the city have been destroyed by fire several times, notably in 1702, 1855, and 1916.
Modern architects have used the "open plan" to create wide streets and many parks. Bergen is a major commercial and communications center for western Norway. Its shipping industry is the third largest in the country. Processing and canning of fish, shipbuilding, paper manufacture, and metalworking are its important modern industries. Bergen was the birthplace of the composer Edvard Grieg. Playwright Henrik Ibsen was manager of the National Theater there (1851-57).
*See also:* Norway.

**Bergen-Belsen** *See:* Belsen.

**Bergerac, Cyrano de** *See:* Cyrano de Bergerac, Savinien de.

**Berger, Victor Louis** (1860-1929), first Socialist member of U.S. Congress (1911-13, 1918, 1919). Born in Austria, Berger founded and led the American Socialist Party. In World War I he was sentenced to 20 years' imprisonment for aiding the enemy, but was freed on appeal and returned to Congress (1923-29).

**Bergman, Ingmar** (1918-   ), Swedish film and stage director, producer, and writer. He combines realism with imaginative symbolism to explore themes such as good and evil, love, old age, and death. Motion pictures include *The Seventh Seal* (1956), *Wild Strawberries* (1957), *Persona* (1965), *Cries and Whispers* (1972), and *Fanny and Alexander* (1982).

**Bergman, Ingrid** (1917-84), Swedish stage and screen actress. In 1936 she came to the attention of Hollywood with the film *A Woman's Face*. She went to the United States in 1939 and soon became a star. Her fresh style was shown to advantage in such films as *Intermezzo* (1939), *Gaslight* (1944), for which she won an Academy Award, and *Notorious* (1946). In 1950 her love affair with the Italian director Roberto Rossellini led to her ostracism from Hollywood. She married and later divorced Rossellini, returning to the United States with the film *Anastasia* (1956), for which she won a second Academy Award. Returning to the stage in the 1960s, Bergman was acclaimed for her performances in Turgenev's *A Month in the Country* in London and Eugene O'Neill's *More Stately Mansions* on Broadway.

**Bergson, Henri-Louis** (1859-1941), French philosopher. He viewed the world as containing a life-force (*élan vital*) in constant conflict with matter. Evolution, he wrote, is creative process energized by the *élan vital*, and time he saw not as a unit of measurement but as the duration of life experience. Bergson was awarded the Nobel Prize for literature in 1927.

**Beriberi**, disease caused by lack of vitamin $B_1$ (thiamine). Beriberi leaves the nerves and heart impaired. Treatment involves thiamine replacement.

**Bering, Vitus Jonassen** (1681-1741), Danish explorer. Sailing in the service of Russia, he explored northeast Siberia (in the 1720s) and Alaska (1741). The Bering Sea and the Bering Strait are named for him.

**Bering Sea**, extreme northern arm of the North Pacific Ocean, 885,000 sq mi (2,292,150 sq km) in area, bounded by East Siberia, Alaska, and the Aleutian Islands. It contains Nunivak Island, St. Lawrence Island, and the Komandorskiye Islands (former USSR). The international dateline crosses it diagonally.
*See also:* Bering, Vitus Jonassen.

**Bering Sea Controversy**, Anglo-American dispute in 1886. When indiscriminate slaughter by various nations threatened seal herds in the U.S.-owned Pribilof Islands in the Bering Sea, the United States seized three Canadian ships (1886) and claimed dominion over the Bering Sea (1889). Britain objected, and in 1893 an arbitration tribunal declared the sea international.
*See also:* Pribilof Islands.

**Bering Strait**, sea-channel linking the Arctic Ocean with the Bering Sea and separating Siberia from Alaska. The channel is shallow and 55 mi (90 km) wide, covered with drift-ice from November to June.
*See also:* Bering, Vitus Jonassen.

**Berkeley** (pop. 102,724), California city on the east side of San Francisco Bay. Berkeley is the home of several renowned schools including the University of California's main campus. Incorporated in 1878, the city is named after George Berkeley, a bishop and philosopher. Its major industries include printing and chemical, equipment, and metal manufacturing. During the Vietnam War Berkeley was the site of major antiwar protests.
*See also:* California.

**Berkeley, Busby** (1895-1976), U.S. choreographer and film director who revolutionized the staging of musical production numbers in Hollywood films. He introduced lavish settings, revolving platforms, and giant staircases upon which hundreds of extras performed in such extravaganzas as *42nd Street* (1933), *Gold Diggers of 1933*, and *The Gang's All Here* (1942).

**Berkeley, George** (1685-1753), Irish philosopher and bishop who, rejecting the views of Locke, argued that the apparent existence of material reality was merely a projection of the mind of God.
*See also:* Idealism.

**Berkeley, Sir William** (1606-77), royal governor of Virginia, 1642-52 and 1660-77. His inability to deal with Native American frontier attacks led to Bacon's Rebellion (1676). Berkeley's harsh treatment of the rebels led to his recall to England.
*See also:* Bacon's Rebellion.

**Berkelium**, chemical element, symbol Bk; for physical constants see Periodic Table. Berkelium was discovered in Berkeley, Calif., in 1949 by S.G. Thompson, Albert Ghiorso, and Glenn Seaborg. It was synthesized initially by bombarding americium-241 with helium ions. It is produced from plutonium by multiple neutron capture in a high-flux nuclear reactor. Berkelium is a metallic element and a member of the actinide series. Several compounds of berkelium have been made, and its chemistry is analogous to that of curium. Berkelium-247 is the longest-lived isotope. It is an alpha-emitter with a half-life of 1,400 years. Ten isotopes of the element are known.

**Berkman, Alexander** (1870-1936), Polish-born U.S. anarchist. During a steel strike, he tried to assassinate the Carnegie Steel Co. head, Henry C. Frick (1892). He served 14 years' imprisonment. In 1917 he was imprisoned for draft obstruction, then deported to Russia in 1919.
*See also:* Anarchism.

**Berle, Milton** (Milton Berlinger; 1908-   ), U.S. comedian. Nicknamed "Uncle Miltie" and "Mr. Television," Berle had successful careers in vaudeville, motion pictures, stage musicals, and radio before becoming host of the "Texaco Star Theatre" on NBC (1948). For the next 6 years, his comedy show was the most frequently watched program on television and he is credited with popularizing the new medium.

**Berlin** (pop. 3,438,000), capital city of Germany located in the eastern part of the country on the Spree and Havel rivers. It covers 341 sq mi (883 sq km) and is at the center of a network of railroads and waterways. It was the capital of Germany from 1871-1945. After World War II, it was divided into East Berlin (which became the capital of the communist state of East Germany) and West Berlin (a state of West Germany). In August 1961 East Germany erected the Berlin Wall to separate the 2 parts of the city. On October 3, 1990, divided Berlin was officially reunited as East Germany ceased its independent existence and became part of a unified German state.The new German government appointed Berlin as the new capital city in 1991. The full transition to Berlin will take until the early 2000s.
*See also:* Germany.

**Berlin, Congress of,** international meeting of Russia, Turkey, and major European powers held in 1878 under the leadership of Otto von Bismarck to settle problems created by the 1877-78 Russo-Turkish War. The resultant Treaty of Berlin redrew boundaries in eastern Europe, generally to the advantage of Great Britain and Austria-Hungary.
*See also:* Bismarck, Prince Otto von.

**Berlin Airlift,** operation by the United Kingdom and the United States to fly essential supplies into West Berlin during the Russian land and water blockade (1948- 49). Its 250,000 flights and 2 million tons of supplies cost $224 million.
*See also:* Cold War.

**Berlin, Irving** (Israel Baline; 1888-1989), U.S. songwriter. He wrote over 900 popular songs, including "Alexander's Ragtime Band" (1911), "God Bless America" (1918), and "White Christmas" (1942). His film scores include *Top Hat* (1935), *Annie Get Your Gun* (1946), and *Call Me Madam* (1950).

**Berliner, Emile** (1851-1929), inventor who contributed to early telephone and phonograph developments. A year following Alexander Graham Bell's invention of the telephone, Berliner developed a powerful transmitter that enhanced the telephone receiver. He also created the flat phonograph disc, or record, and a process that employed a needle moving horizontally, thus minimizing distortion of Thomas Edison's earlier method. Berliner later produced a method for mass-duplication of records from one master disc. Born in Hanover, Germany, Berliner moved to the United States in 1870.
*See also:* Phonograph; Telephone.

**Berlin Wall,** wall 26 mi (42 km) long built in 1961 dividing East and West Berlin. Before 1961, many people fled East Germany by crossing from East to West Berlin. The wall halted this emigration. Between 1961 and 1989 over 70 East Germans were killed attempting to get past the Berlin Wall. In November 1989 the wall began to be dismantled after demonstrations for political reform erupted in East Germany.
*See also:* Berlin; Cold War.

**Berlioz, Louis-Hector** (1803-69), French romantic composer of dramatic, descriptive works. Major works include his *Symphonie Fantastique* (1830),

*Requiem* (1837), the choral symphony *Romeo and Juliet* (1838-39), the oratorio *The Childhood of Christ* (1850-54), and the operas *Benvenuto Cellini* (1838), and *The Trojans* (1856-59).

**Bermuda,** British colony comprising about 150 coral islands of which 20 are inhabited, lying in the North Atlantic Ocean, 580 miles (933 km) east of North Carolina. The main island is Bermuda Island, with the capital, Hamilton. The climate is warm and the vegetation lush and tropical. Bermuda's first British colonists arrived in 1609. Some 60% of present inhabitants are descendants of African slaves, and the rest are mainly British. The economy depends on tourism and 2 U.S. military bases.

**Bermuda Triangle,** area of the Atlantic Ocean roughly bounded by Bermuda, the Greater Antilles, and the southeastern coast of the United States, in which many ships and planes are said to have vanished. Though supernatural causes have been proposed to explain the allegedly mysterious disappearances, there is no evidence of any unusual phenomena in the area at all.

**Bern,** or Berne (pop. 138,600), capital city of Switzerland and of Bern canton. It lies on the Aare River in German-speaking west-central Switzerland. It is an important commercial, industrial, and cultural center and the headquarters of some major international communications organizations. Bern was founded in 1191 and retains many old buildings.
*See also:* Switzerland.

**Bernadette, Saint** (Marie-Bernarde Soubirous; 1844-79), French peasant girl who claimed to have had 18 visions of the Virgin Mary in a Lourdes grotto in 1858. The grotto became a shrine, and she was beatified (1925) and canonized (1933). Her feast day is Feb. 18 in France, April 16 elsewhere.
*See also:* Lourdes.

**Bernadotte, Jean Baptiste Jules** (1763-1844), French general who founded Sweden's present royal dynasty. One of Napoleon's marshals (1804), he was elected Swedish crown prince in 1810. He fought Napoleon at Leipzig (1813) and ruled Sweden and Norway as Charles XIV (1818-44).
*See also:* Sweden.

**Bernard, Claude** (1813-78), French physiologist, one of the founders of experimental medicine. He studied the digestive process and the function of glycogen in the liver, and in 1851 he reported the existence of the vasomotor nerves.
*See also:* Digestive system.

**Bernard of Clairvaux, Saint** (1090?-1153), French theologian and mystic who was the abbot of a Cistercian monastery and inspired the Second Crusade. Founder of the Clairvaux Abbey in 1115, he was adviser to popes, kings, and bishops and was instrumental in Abelard's condemnation (1140). He was canonized in 1174.
*See also:* Crusades.

**Bernese mountain dog**, Swiss breed of large, powerful dog. They have long black hair with russet brown spots on the legs and face and white feet and chests. The dogs typically weigh from 50-75 lbs (23-34 kg) and stand 21-27 in (53-69 cm) tall at the shoulders. Romans originally brought the breed to Switzerland more than 2,000 years ago.

**Bernhardt, Sarah** (Henriette Rosine Bernard; 1844-1923), French actress. Renowned for her great emotional power, she was the leading performer in classical French theater, appearing in roles created by Victorien Sardou and Edmond Rostand, among others. She made several triumphant worldwide tours.

**Bernier, Joseph Elzéar** (1852-1934), Canadian explorer renowned for his arctic voyages. Bernier staked Canada's claim to all the North American arctic islands, captained a dozen voyages to the arctic, and journeyed around the world several times.

**Bernini, Giovanni Lorenzo** (1598-1680), Italian sculptor and architect who gave Rome many of its characteristic baroque features. He designed the tomb of Pope Urban VIII, the canopy over the high altar in St. Peter's, the Piazza S. Pietro, the fountain *Four Rivers* in the Piazza Navona, and the statue *St. Teresa in Ecstasy*.
*See also:* Baroque.

**Bernoulli's principle**, theorem of aerodynamics stating that the pressure of a moving gas will be lowest where its speed is highest, or that a moving fluid conserves energy. The theorem, named after Swiss mathematician Daniel Bernoulli (1700-82), explains how airplane wings create lift. Because the air flow is faster across the wing's curved top surface than across its flat underside, air pressure is greater under the wing than over, creating lift.
*See also:* Aerodynamics; Hydraulics.

**Bernstein, Carl** *See:* Watergate.

**Bernstein, Leonard** (1918-1990), U.S. conductor and composer, best known for his musical *West Side Story* (1957). He rose to fame as conductor of the New York Philharmonic Orchestra (1958-69). His varied works include the symphony *The Age of Anxiety* (1949), the musical *On The Town* (1944), and *The Mass* (1971).

**Berra, Yogi** (Lawrence Peter Berra; 1925-   ), U.S. baseball player for the New York Yankees, 1946-63. He holds the record for World Series games played (75) and greatest number of series hits (71). He won the American League's Most Valuable Player Award in 1951, 1954, and 1955.

**Berrigan, Daniel and Philip** (1922-   ) and (1924-   ), Roman Catholic priests in the pacifist "Catonsville Nine" group. In 1969, as a Vietnam War protest, the group broke into the Selective Service Office at Catonsville, Md., and poured oxblood over records and files. The Berrigans were convicted and given 3-year sentences; in 1972 Philip was tried on conspiracy charges but acquitted. In 1981 they were convicted of burglary and conspiracy after they broke into a General Electric plant and damaged 2 nuclear-missile nose cones.

**Berry, Chuck** (Charles Edward Anderson Berry; 1926-   ), U.S. rock and roll singer, songwriter, and guitarist. An influential pioneer of rock and roll music, Berry gained notoriety with white audiences and shaped blues rock and roll into his own big-beat and melodic patterned style that later influenced the Beatles and the Rolling Stones. His lyrics, loaded with ironies, spoke about the importance of rock and roll and the value of youth. Born in St. Louis, Mo., Berry played the guitar as a teenager and had his first big hit, "Maybellene," in 1955. Other hits followed: "Johnny B. Goode," "Roll Over Beethoven," "Sweet Little Sixteen," "My Ding-A-Ling," and "Rock and Roll Music."

**Berryman, John** (1914-72), U.S. poet, active from the 1930s. His reputation was solidified by the long poem *Homage to Mistress Bradstreet* (1956). Berryman's later work, distinguished by its black ironies and linguistic innovation, includes *His Toy, His Dream, His Rest* (1968) and *Dream Songs* (1969). He committed suicide, throwing himself off a bridge in Minneapolis.

**Bertillon, Alphonse** (1853-1914), French criminologist who devised a system for identifying criminals based on the body measurements. The system was adopted by the French police in 1888 and used until fingerprints became a method of identification.

**Bertolucci, Bernardo** (1940- ), Italian filmmaker known for such films as *The Conformist* (1970), *Last Tango in Paris* (1972), *La Luna* (1979), *Tragedy of a Ridiculous Man* (1981), *The Last Emperor* (1985), *The Sheltering Sky* (1990), *Little Buddha* (1993), and *Stealing Beauty* (1995). is films are often controversial and provocative.

**Beryl**, beryllium and aluminum silicate ($Be_3AP_2Si_6O_{18}$), the most common ore of beryllium. It is a transparent or translucent mineral found mainly as hexagonal crystals in granite rocks. The gem emerald is a dark green beryl containing a small amount of chromium; aquamarine is a blue-green variety of beryl. The finest varieties are found in Brazil, Sri Lanka, Siberia, and New England.
*See also:* Aquamarine; Beryllium.

**Beryllium**, chemical element, symbol Be; for physical constants see Periodic Table. Beryllium was isolated as a free metal by Friedrich Wöhler and Antoine Bussy in 1828. *Beryl* (beryllium aluminum silicate) is the commercial source of the element. The element is prepared by the reduction of beryllium fluoride with magnesium metal. Beryllium is one of the lightest and strongest of all metals and greatly increases the strength of other metals when used in alloys.
Beryllium copper is extensively used for springs, electrical contacts, and nonsparking tools. Beryllium is used as a moderator in nuclear reactors. It is also used in gyroscopes, computer parts, and inertial guidance instruments. Beryllium and its salts are toxic and should be handled with the greatest of care.

**Berzelius, Jöns Jakob, Baron** (1779-1848), Swedish chemist who determined the atomic weights of nearly 40 elements before 1818, discovered cerium (1803), selenium (1818), and thorium (1829), introduced the terms *protein, isomerism,* and *catalysis,* and devised the modern method of writing chemical formulas (1813).

**Besant, Annie (Wood)** (1847-1933), British theosophist and social reformer. Besant joined the Fabian Society and was an early advocate of birth control. She became international president of the Theosophical Society (1907-33) and championed independence for India, becoming president of the Indian National Congress (1917). She published many theosophical works.
*See also:* Fabian Society.

**Bessarabia**, historic region of southeastern Europe, northwest of the Black Sea, between the Dniester and Danube rivers. After various Russo-Turkish conflicts it was ceded to Russia in 1812. After the Crimean War it passed to Moldavia (1856) but was regained by Russia (1878). Romania controlled it almost continuously from 1918 to 1944, when it joined the USSR. In 1991 it became part of independent Moldavia and Ukraine.

**Bessel, Friedrich Wilhelm** (1784-1846), astronomer and mathematician. Born in Germany, Bessel made the first authentic measurement of a star's distance from the earth, also called a parallax. This discovery allowed astronomers to document the earth's movement. Bessel also established a class of mathematical functions known as Bessel functions.
*See also:* Parallax.

**Bessemer process**, process of making steel from pig iron. The pig iron is loaded into a specially designed furnace or Bessemer converter. A continuous blast of compressed air is forced through the molten metal to oxidize impurities, which are burned off or form slag. The result is molten steel. Since the 1950s, a modification of the Bessemer process, the basic oxygen process, has been in use. The Bessemer process was developed by the British inventor Sir Henry Bessemer (1813-98).
*See also:* Steel.

**Best, Charles Herbert** (1899-1978), Canadian physiologist. As a medical student at the University of Toronto, he and several colleagues isolated the hormone insulin from the pancreas and developed it as a treatment for diabetes (1921). Best's other discoveries include histaminase for the treatment of allergies, the blood-clotting agent heparin, and the vitamin choline.
*See also:* Insulin.

**Beta-blocker**, drug that affects the transmission of signals at beta-receptors, parts of the sympathetic nervous system located in the heart, lungs, kidneys, and blood vessels. Beta-blockers (or beta-adrenergic blocking agents) interfere with the stimulation of the beta-receptors. They thereby lower blood pressure and heart rate. They are used in the treatment of hypertension and cardiac arrrhythmia.
*See also:* Drug.

**Betancourt, Rómulo** (1908-81), president of Venezuela (1945-47 and 1957-63) and founder of the left-wing Acción Democrática Party (1935). Betancourt spent 1948-58 in exile after a military coup. He survived an assassination attempt in 1960.
*See also:* Venezuela.

**Beta particle**, one of the particles that can be emitted by a radioactive atomic nucleus. Most are high-speed electrons, with a mass off about $^1/_{1837}$ and a negative charge. More rarely, a beta particle can be positively charged (positron). The emission of an electron entails the change of a neutron into a proton within the nucleus. The emission of a positron is similarly associated with the change of a proton into a neutron.
*See also:* Radioactivity.

**Betatron**, apparatus designed to accelerate electrons to high velocities. Electrons are injected into a ring-shaped vacuum tube where an electromagnet running on alternating current creates a magnetic field whose polarity changes at short intervals. The electrons are accelerated around the ring by the changing magnetic field. Large betatrons can accelerate particles to energies of several hundred million electron volts.
*See also:* Particle accelerator.

**Betel**, preparation made with the seeds of the betel palm. A masticatory, betel has been chewed as a stimulant by southern Asians and eastern Africans since ancient times. Betel is made by combining slices of the betel nut seeds with lime paste and other flavorings and spreading it on a betel pepper leaf. It is then rolled and chewed.

**Betelgeuse**, or Alpha Orionis, second brightest star in the constellation Orion. The name was given to it by Arab astronomers (*bayt al-jawzaa*, "house of twins" in Arabic). Betelgeuse is a regular variable first magnitude red giant with a diameter up to 420 times that of the sun. It is about 500 light-years from Earth.
*See also:* Orion.

**Bethe, Hans Albrecht** (1906-    ), German-born U.S. theoretical physicist who proposed the nuclear carbon cycle to account for the sun's energy output (1938). During World War II he worked on the Manhattan Project. He was awarded the 1967 Nobel Prize in physics for his work on the source of stellar energy.

**Bethesda** (pop. 62,936), city in Montgomery County, central Maryland, a residential suburb of Washington, D.C. The U.S. Naval Medical Center is located here, as are several noted medical research centers and institutes, including the National Cancer Institute.
*See also:* Maryland.

**Bethlehem** (pop. 71,428), city in eastern Pennsylvania, 50 mi (80 km) northwest of Philadelphia, on the Lehigh River. Bethlehem was founded in 1741 by refugees from Moravia and Bohemia seeking religious freedom. The Moravian Brethren maintain a theological seminary and chapel (1803). The city is largely supported by the Bethlehem Steel Company. Bethlehem's

cultural fame rests upon its patronage of music; it is the home of the Bach Choir and the annual Bach Festival.
*See also:* Pennsylvania.

**Bethlehem** (Hebrew: *Bayt Lahm*; pop. 16,300), town in Israeli-occupied West Bank, 6 mi (9.7 km) south of Jerusalem, and sacred to Jews, Christians, and Muslims. According to the Bible, it is the city where David was annointed by Samuel and the birthplace of Jesus; the traditional tomb of Rachel is outside the town. A basilica built by the Emperor Constantine over the Grotto of the Nativity (326-333) and rebuilt by Justinian I now forms the Church of the Nativity, a major attraction for tourists and pilgrims. Long contested by Christians and Muslims, it was taken by Israel during the 1967 Six-Day War.
*See also:* Jesus Christ; West Bank.

**Bethune, Mary McLeod** (1875-1955), African-American educator and civil rights activist. She founded the Daytona Normal and Industrial Institute for Negro Girls (1904), now called Bethune-Cookman College, and was Director of Negro Affairs in the National Youth Administration (1936-44) as well as President F.D. Roosevelt's special adviser on minority affairs.

**Bethune, Norman** (1890-1930), Canadian physician who achieved national hero status in China in 1938 for the establishment of hospitals and medical schools, and for his role as chief medical officer of the Chinese Communist Army. Bethune also achieved fame for his contribution to medicine through experiments in lung surgery and for the invention of medical instruments. He was also active in the Spanish Civil War in 1936, where he created the first mobile blood transfusion operation.

**Betjeman, Sir John** (1906-84), English poet laureate and architectural conservationist, often called a lyrical satirist. His works include *New Bats* in *Old Belfries* (1945), *Selected Poems* (1948), *Collected Poems* (1958), and *Victorian and Edwardian Architecture in London* (1969).

**Bettelheim, Bruno** (1903-90), Austrian-born U.S. psychologist who drew on his personal experience as an inmate of Nazi concentration camps to write his famous article, "Individual and Mass Behavior in Extreme Situations" (1943). His subsequent work mainly concerned the treatment of autistic and disturbed children.

**Better business bureau,** consumer protection organization such as exists in nearly 200 cities in the United States, Canada, and Israel. Better business bureaus answer telephone calls and written complaints from business customers who feel they have been treated unfairly. Complaints are investigated and corrective actions are recommended if the business is at fault. In cases where corrective action is not taken, the bureau can report the case to the appropriate federal agency.

**Betts v. Brady** *See:* Gideon v. Wainwright.

**Bevatron,** in physics, a 6 or more billion electron volt accelerator of protons and other atomic particles.
*See also:* Particle accelerator.

**Beveridge, William Henry** (1879-1963), British economist and social planner, director of London School of Economics (1919-37). In *Social Insurance and Allied Services* (1942), he proposed a social security system that became law. Beveridge became a knight in 1919 and a baron in 1946.

**Beverly Hills** (pop. 31,971), residential city in southern California, completely surrounded by Los Angeles. Formerly a Spanish ranch, it is now the home of wealthy film and television stars. The town extends into the foothills of the Santa Monica Mountains.
*See also:* California.

**Bhagavad-Gita** (*Song of God*), anonymous Sanskrit poem dating from c.200 B C., incorporated into the Mahabharata epic, a classic work of Hinduism. It consists of a dialogue in 700 verses between Prince Arjuna and the god Krishna. The dialogue, held on the eve of a battle, covers many aspects of Hindu religious thought.
*See also:* Hinduism; Vishnu.

**Bhopal** (pop. c. 1,062,700), capital of Madhya Pradesh in central India. On December 3, 1984, a deadly cloud of toxic gas leaked from a Union Carbide plant, killing some 2,000 people and injuring about 200,000 others for the worst industrial accident in history. The Indian government filed lawsuits in the U.S. and in India, charging Union Carbide with negligence. Union Carbide offered a $350-million settlement over a period of 30 years, which the Indian government refused. The U.S. courts rejected the suit in 1986, but in 1989 the Indian Supreme Court ordered Union Carbide to pay $470 million in damages, which seemed to close the matter although many in India still felt the assessment was too low.
*See also:* India.

**Bhutan**, kingdom on the southern slopes of the eastern Himalayas, between Tibet on the north and Bangladesh and India on the south. It is extremely mountainous, falling from 24,000 ft (7,315 m) on the northern border to 600 ft (183 m) on the frontier with India.

| Bhutan | |
|---|---|
| Capital: | Thimphu |
| Area: | 18,150 sq mi (47,000 sq km) |
| Population: | 1,908,000 |
| Language: | Dzongkha |
| Government: | Constitutional monarchy |
| Independent: | 1949 |
| Head of gov.: | Monarch |
| Per capita: | U.S. $420 |
| Mon. unit: | 1 Ngultrum = 100 chetrum |

Agriculture, limited to a few areas, is backward; terraced rice cultivation might be extended, but the cultivators lack capital. Corn, potatoes, wheat, millet, and buckwheat are grown. Fine handicrafts include wood carving, basketry, and swords and daggers with elaborately chased silver engravings. The country is slowly changing from an isolated barter system into a transitional market economy. Buddhism of the Tibetan Mahayana type mingles with propitiation of spirits.

**Bhutto, Benazir** (1953-    ), prime minister of Pakistan (1988-90, 1993- ). She was the first female leader of an Islamic nation. Bhutto, a graduate of both Harvard and Oxford universities, went into exile in 1984, returned to Pakistan after 2 years, and headed the Pakistan People's Party (PPP), which her father, Zulfikan Ali Bhutto, founded. She was removed from power by political and military opponents in 1990 and reinstalled in 1993. *See also:* Pakistan.

**Bhutto, Zulfikar Ali** (1928-79), president and prime minister of Pakistan (1971-77); father of Benazir Bhutto. He held several government posts under President Mohammad Ayub Khan, but became one of his leading opponents and was imprisoned (1968-69). He was deposed by Mohammad Zia ul-Haq in a military coup and executed 2 years later. *See also:* Pakistan.

**Biafra**, name assumed by Nigeria's Eastern Region during its attempted secession (1967-70). Under the leadership of Colonel Ojukwu, the Ibo people of the Eastern Region declared their independence in May 1967, and the civil war, for which both sides had been preparing for some time, broke out. Outnumbered and outgunned, the Biafrans suffered heavy losses, with large numbers dying from starvation, before their final surrender. The former breakaway region was divided to form the East-Central, River, and South-Eastern states. *See also:* Nigeria.

**Bialik, Chaim Nachman** (1873-1934), one of the greatest of modern Hebrew poets and novelists. Born in the Ukraine, he settled in Palestine in 1924. His poetry gave fiery expression to Jewish national aspirations. His publishing business in Odessa was a significant force in the revival of Hebrew language and literature.

**Bible**, name of the sacred writings of the Christian religion. The word "bible" is derived from the Greek *biblia*, meaning "books." A collection of writings gathered into books, the Bible consists of two main parts, the Old Testament and the New Testament. The Old Testament, written in Hebrew and Aramaic centuries before the birth of Christ, is the Christian name for the Jewish Bible. It comprises 39 books, of which the most important are the five books of the Law (Pentateuch), the Jewish Torah: Genesis, Exodus, Leviticus, Numbers, and Deuteronomy. These are followed by the books of the Prophets (Joshua, Judges, the two books of Samuel, the twelve minor prophets, and others). Finally, the Writings (Hagiographa) include Esther, Job, Psalms, Proverbs, Ecclesiastes, the Song of Songs, Lamentations, and Daniel. The New Testament, the specifically Christian part of the Bible, was written in Greek in the first 2 centuries after Christ. Of its 27 books, the 4 Gospels—of Matthew,

Mark, Luke, and John—occupy the hallowed central position. These describe aspects of the life and teachings of Jesus. The remaining 23 books consist of a selection of early Christian writings that were definitively selected as canonical in the 4th century A.D.. The English translation of the Bible in widest use is the King James version (1611). In Christian doctrine, the Bible is written under the guidance of God and contains the moral and historical bases of the Christian view of the world.
*See also:* Christianity.

**Bibliothèque nationale**, national library in Paris, France. Also a depository (a library that stores copies of most printed works, especially government documents), the Bibliothèque nationale is one of the largest libraries in Europe. Known more as a government archive than a public library, this expansive facility houses about 20 million printed volumes as well as numerous magazines, manuscripts, maps, engravings, coins, and medals. Many of the collections and manuscripts were once part of royal libraries.

**Bicameral legislature** *See:* Legislature.

**Bicarbonate of soda** ($NaHCO_3$), sodium bicarbonate, or baking soda, chemical compound used to relieve stomach acidity. It is also used in baking powder and fire extinguishers.

**Bichat, Marie François Xavier** (1771-1802), French anatomist and pathologist, founder of histology, the study of the small-scale structure of tissue. Although working without the microscope, Bichat distinguished 21 types of elementary tissues of which the organs of the body are composed.

**Bicuspid** *See:* Teeth.

**Bicycle**, 2-wheeled vehicle propelled by pedals. In the late-18th century, a device called a célérifère was demonstrated in Paris by Count Mède de Sivrac. By the early 19th century, an improved model, called a draisine, had been developed, with handlebars and a saddle. The design was further improved by Kirkpatrick MacMillan, a Scottish blacksmith, who introduced treadles that the rider moved back and forth to provide power to the rear wheels. The use of rotary pedals was incorporated by the Frenchman Ernest Michaux in his vélocipède. Popular in the 1870s was the "penny-farthing," which had a large front wheel and a much smaller rear wheel. The first bicycle with a chain-drive powering the rear wheel was made in England in 1885. Pneumatic tires were introduced soon after, and the bicycles of the 1890s were similar to those of today. Subsequent improvements include the use of gear-changing systems.

**Bicycle racing**, popular sport in many countries, especially in Europe. Races may take place on a special track or on open roads. Track events, which range from 140-500 m (459-1,640 ft), exercise the cyclists' tactical skills as well as testing their strength and endurance. Road races cover 50 mi (80 km) to several thousand miles. The most famous event is the Tour de France, an annual international competition that covers about 2,500 mi (4,000 km) and lasts three weeks.

**Biddle, Nicholas** (1786-1844), president of the second Bank of the United States (1823-36). He made it the country's first authoritative central bank, but President Andrew Jackson vetoed renewal of the bank's charter.
*See also:* Bank of the United States.

**Bieber, Owen Frederick** (1929- ), president of the United Automobile Workers (UAW). The UAW, founded as a labor union in 1935, has been tainted with struggles since its beginning. Bieber, elected in 1983, is the first UAW president not involved in the union's early disputes. He initiated successful compromises between UAW and automobile manufacturers. A progressive leader, Bieber emphasized job security over pay increases and leveraged UAW interests by encouraging numerous local strikes rather than a national walkout. Bieber became a director of the Chrysler Corporation in 1984.
*See also:* United Automobile Workers.

**Biedermeier,** utilitarian middle-class style of furniture popular in Germany from about 1810 to 1850.

**Bienville, Jean Baptiste le Moyne, Sieur de** (1680-1768), French explorer and naval officer who founded New Orleans. Born in Canada, he helped to colonize French Louisiana, which he governed at various periods between 1701 and 1743.
*See also:* New Orleans.

**Bierce, Ambrose Gwinett** (1842-1914?), U.S. short-story writer and satirical journalist. His works include *In the Midst of Life* (1891), *Can Such Things Be?* (1893), and *The Devil's Dictionary* (1906), a compilation of sarcastic definitions. An adventurer, he distinguished himself in the Union army during the Civil War. He disappeared without trace during the Mexican Revolution of 1913-14.

**Bierstadt, Albert** (1830-1902), German-born U.S. landscape painter famous for his large, realistic Western scenes, including *Sierra Nevada* and *The Settlement of California.*

**Bifocals** *See:* Glasses.

**Bigamy,** in law, felony or misdemeanor of being married to 2 persons simultaneously. Ignorance of the fact that the first marriage is still valid is not an acceptable defense in most courts.

**Big and Little Dippers,** 2 constellations that each resemble a water dipper. The Big Dipper, located in the constellation of Ursa Major (the Great Bear), has 7 stars that are often used as reference points to find other stars. The Little Dipper, a smaller, similar grouping of stars, is fainter except for the North Star, which lies at the end of the Little Dipper's handle. The Little Dipper forms most of the constellation of Ursa Minor, the Little Bear.
*See also:* Constellation.

**Big bang,** theory that all the matter and energy of the universe was concentrated in a compact, infinitely small volume that exploded some 15 to 20

billion years ago, giving rise to the present universe, still expanding from the initial explosion. The big bang theory is the most widely accepted cosmological theory today.
*See also:* Cosmology.

**Big Ben**, popular name for the tower clock of the Houses of Parliament in London. It is named for Sir Benjamin Hall, the commissioner of works at the time of its installation in 1856. The bell of the clock weighs 13 tons.

**Big Bend National Park**, tract of mountains and desert on the Texas border with Mexico, in the Big Bend of the Rio Grande River. The park, which covers over 700,000 acres (283,500 hectares), was established in 1944 and is the last great expanse of wild land left in Texas.

Big Five, the 5 permanent members of the UN Security Council: China, France, Great Britain, Russia, and the United States. Each of these countries has the right to veto Security Council resolutions.
*See also:* United Nations.

**Bighorn**, Rocky Mountain sheep (*Ovis canadensis*) inhabiting the higher mountain ranges of the western United States from New Mexico and southern California northward. The large horns of the male form a full circle; those of the female are smaller and upright. The bighorn stands about 3 ft (1 m) high at the shoulder.

**Bighorn Mountains**, range of the eastern Rocky Mountains, mainly in northern Wyoming, but extending into Montana east of the Bighorn River. The highest point is Cloud Peak (13,165 ft/4,013 m).
*See also:* Rocky Mountains.

**Bighorn River**, river in the Wind River Canyon in Wyoming and flowing through Montana, where it joins the Yellowstone River. Much of its 335 mi (539 km) course runs through deep canyons. Dams and reservoirs provide irrigation, flood control, and hydroelectric power.

**Bignonia**, any of several hundred species of plants of the Bignoniaceae family, native to warmer parts of the Americas. They usually have creeping or climbing stems and may reach the top of even the highest trees. One of the best known in the United States is the cross vine, which has orange-red, trumpet-shaped flowers.
*See also:* Calabash.

**Bihzad, Kamal ad-Din** (1450-1537), Persian miniature painter, famous for illustrating manuscripts such as *Timur Namah*, *Gulistan*, and *Khamsa*. His paintings of battle scenes and nature scenes were admired throughout the world.

**Bikini**, atoll in the Marshall Islands in the central Pacific Ocean. It was the site of U.S. nuclear bomb tests in the 1940s and 1950s. Inhabitants evacuated during the tests began to return in the early 1970s, but the island was again declared uninhabitable because of dangerously high radiation levels in 1978.
*See also:* Marshall Islands.

**Bilbao** (pop. 369,800), major seaport in northern Spain and former capital of a once autonomous Basque region. The town is built on both sides of the Nervión River, 8 mi (13 km) from the Bay of Biscay. The banks of the Nervión below the city are lined with shipyards, blast furnaces, and factories, for Bilbao is one of Spain's leading centers of heavy industry. The good harbor and rail connections have helped make the city the most important port on Spain's Atlantic coast. Iron ore, lead ore, and steel products rank high among its exports. Also important are wine, olive oil, and canned fish. The 14th-century city on the right bank has provisions for drainage, ventilation, and orderly pedestrian traffic that were advanced for their time.
*See also:* Spain.

**Bile**, yellow or greenish fluid secreted by the liver which aids in digestion and absorption, particularly of fatty foods. It contains water, lecithin, cholesterol, bile salts, and the pigments bilirubin and biliverdin. When needed, it is discharged through the common bile duct into the small intestine, where it breaks down fats and enables them to be absorbed through the intestinal wall. Bile is also a route of excretion for cholesterol and various drugs.
*See also:* Digestive system.

**Bilharziasis** *See:* Schistosomiasis.

**Bilirubin** *See:* Bile; Jaundice.

**Bill**, term for various written documents in politics, law, banking, commerce, and so forth. In politics, it is the draft of a statute submitted to the legislature for debate and eventual adoption as law. In the courtroom it was formerly applied to the written statement of a plaintiff's case, now usually referred to as a writ or statement of claim. Bills of attainder, passed by the English parliament and some American colonial legislatures, meted out penalties for certain political crimes but were later abolished as unconstitutional. In the commercial field, a bill of sale is a document transferring ownership of goods or property, sometimes used to secure a debt. In international trade, a bill of lading is a receipt given by a public carrier, agreeing to convey goods to a stated destination. In banking, a bill of exchange is a negotiable document, guaranteeing payment by the drawer to the payee, a form of promissory note or check. A bill of health is a document given to a ship's captain by a local authority, signifying absence of infectious or contagious disease on board.

**Billiards**, any of several indoor games in which balls set on a felt-covered rectangular table with cushioned edges are struck by the end of a long tapering stick (the cue). Billiards was popular in France and England as early as the 14th century. In most forms of the game, the table has 6 pockets, one in each corner and one midway along each of the longer sides. The object is to sink balls into the pockets by playing one ball off another or, in games played without pockets, to hit the balls against each other successively. *Carom billiards* and *English billiards* feature 2 white cue balls and 1 red ball. *Snooker* has 1 white cue ball, 15 red balls, and 6 balls of other colors. *Pool* (or pocket billiards), as played in the United States, has 1 white cue ball and 15 numbered colored balls and is the country's most popular billiard game.

**Billings** (pop. 113,419), largest city in Montana, seat of Yellowstone County, located in the south central part of the state. Billings was founded in 1882 during construction of the Northern Pacific Railroad and became a shipping and fur trading center. Major industries today include oil and sugar refining, meat packing, and flour milling.
*See also:* Montana.

**Billings, William** (1746-1800), first professional composer and musician born in the American colonies. He was noted for his simple, lively styles in hymns, psalms, and anthems.

**Bill of exchange,** negotiable instrument used in commerce that is drawn up and signed by one person to direct another person to pay a certain sum of money at a certain time to the bearer or to the party named on the bill. Parties involved in this transaction are frequently banks and businesses; the bill is a convenient means of transferring funds.

**Bill of rights,** constitutional document that defines the rights of a people, safeguarding them against undue governmental interference. In the United States these rights and safeguards are embodied in the first 10 amendments to the Constitution. After the American Revolution there was great popular demand for constitutionally defined rights to limit the power of the new government. Bills of rights were drafted in 8 states between 1776 and 1781, but when the Constitution was drawn up in 1787 no such bill was included, and ratification by the states lagged until promises were made that a bill of rights would be added. When the first Congress met in 1789, James Madison presented one containing 12 amendments, 10 of which were accepted. On Dec. 15, 1791, Secretary of State Thomas Jefferson proclaimed the Federal Bill of Rights in full force. The bill guarantees freedom of speech, of the press, and of religion. It protects against arbitrary searches and self-incrimination. It sets out proper procedures for trials, giving to all the right to trial by jury and to cross-examination of witnesses. In addition to these rights, the 5th Amendment provides that no person shall "be deprived of life, liberty, or property, without due process of law." Between 1798 and 1971, the states ratified 16 additional amendments to the Constitution.
*See also:* Constitution of the United States.

**Billy the Kid** (William H. Bonney; 1859-81), U.S. outlaw. Notorious in New Mexico as a cattle thief, he was sentenced to hang. In 1878 he escaped from jail by killing 2 guards, and was tracked down and killed by Sheriff Pat Garrett.

**Biloxi** (pop. 197,125), second largest city in Mississippi, a summer and winter resort located on the southern coast along the Gulf of Mexico. Fishing and boat building are major industries. The name Biloxi comes from the Sioux word for "first people." French Old Biloxi, founded 1699, was the first European settlement in the lower Mississippi Valley.
*See also:* Mississippi.

**Bimetallism,** economic term for the use of 2 metals (usually gold and silver) to back a country's currency, making every coin and bill in circulation related to a definite value of both gold and silver. Nearly all countries now use currency based only on gold (monometallism).

**Binary numbers**, system of designating numbers using only the digits 0 and 1, widely employed in digital computers. Each digit in the binary system represents a successive power of 2, just as digits in the decimal system represent successive powers of 10. For example, in the binary system, the number 110 represents: $(1 \times 2^2) + (1 \times 2^1) + (0 \times 2^0)$, which equals (in the decimal system) $4 + 2 + 0$, or 6. While this system may appear cumbersome, it is easily adaptable to electronic circuits, where the 2 digits (0 and 1) can be represented by the 2 states of a switch: open or closed.

**Binary star**, or double star, pair of stars that orbit around their common center of gravity. Though some binaries can be observed separately without a telescope, in most cases the stars are so close together that they appear to be a single star. A great number of binaries are too close to be seen separately by even the most powerful optical telescopes and are detected by studying the spectral lines of the stars.
*See also:* Black hole; Nova; Pulsar.

**Bindweed**, common name for a weedy plant (genus *Convolvulus*) of the morning-glory family, Convolvulaceae. Bindweeds have long twining stems, arrow-shaped leaves, and white or pink funnel-shaped flowers that often open only in the morning.
*See also:* Morning-glory.

**Binet, Alfred** (1857-1911), French psychologist who pioneered methods of mental testing. He collaborated with Théodore Simon in devising the Binet-Simon tests, widely used to estimate intelligence.
*See also:* Intelligence quotient; Psychology.

**Bing, Sir Rudolf** (1902-    ), Austrian-born British opera impresario. An opera administrator in Germany, he emigrated to Britain when the Nazis came to power, headed the Glyndebourne Opera (1935-49), and helped organize the Edinburgh Festival (1947). As general manager of New York's Metropolitan Opera (1950-72), he introduced black singers and presided over the company's move to Lincoln Center.
*See also:* Opera.

**Bingham, George Caleb** (1811-79), U.S. genre painter noted for his mid-western river scenes, such as *Fur Traders Descending the Missouri* (1845) and *Raftsmen Playing Cards* (1846). He also treated political subjects with warmth and humor, as in *Canvassing for a Vote* (1851), He served in the Missouri state legislature in 1848, and later held other state offices.

**Binoculars**, optical instrument consisting of a pair of compact telescopes mounted side by side. Since both eyes are used, the magnified image of distant objects appears to be in 3 dimensions. The magnifying power of a pair of binoculars and the diameter of the object lens (front lens) are engraved on the instrument. Binoculars marked 10 x 50, for example, will make objects appear 10 times closer and have object lenses that are 50 mm (about 6 in) in diameter. Binoculars can be adjusted to focus the image, to move the two telescopes nearer or farther apart to fit the eyes, and to remove double images.

**Biochemistry,** study of the substances occurring in living organisms and the reactions in which they are involved. It is a science on the border between biology and organic chemistry. The main constituents of living matter are water, carbohydrates, lipids, and proteins. The total chemical activity of the organism is known as its metabolism. Landmarks in biochemistry include the synthesis of urea by Friedrich Wöhler (1828), the pioneering research of Von Liebig, Pasteur, and Bernard, and, more recently, the elucidation of the structure of DNA by James Watson and Francis Crick (1953).
*See also:* Biology; Chemistry.

**Biofeedback,** method of electronically monitoring various specific biological functions, such as blood pressure, with the aim of helping a person gain greater control of otherwise unconscious physiological processes. Biofeedback techniques have been used with some success in the treatment of hypertension, chronic headaches, epilepsy, and other disorders.

**Biogenesis,** origin and evolution of living forms. The law of biogenesis is the principle that all living organisms are derived from a parent or parents.
*See also:* Reproduction.

**Biological clock,** mechanism that controls the rhythm of various activities of plants and animals. Some activities, such as mating, migration, and hibernation, have a yearly cycle; others, chiefly reproductive functions (including human menstruation), follow the lunar month. But the majority have a period of roughly 24 hours, called the circadian rhythm. Although related to the day/night cycle, circadian rhythms are not directly controlled by it. Many organisms in unvarying environments will continue to show 24-hour rhythms, but the pattern can be changed and the clock "reset." In December 1997 a human clock gene "rigui" was discovered, named after the ancient Chinese sundial.

**Biological warfare,** war waged with microorganisms and their toxins against people, animals, and plants. The United States, USSR, Great Britain, and more than 100 other countries signed an agreement in 1972 to prohibit the development, production, and stockpiling of biological weapons.

**Biology,** science of living things. The most important subdivisions of biology are zoology, the study of animals, and botany, the study of plants. Advances in scientific knowledge have led to an increase in the number of fields of biological study. Some biologists study subdivisions of the animal and plant kingdoms: entomology (the study of insects), mycology (fungi), paleontology (fossils), and microbiology (microorganisms). The they were mainly interested in anatomy, still an important field of study. As early biologists accumulated information about plants and animals, they noticed that some closely resembled others. Such observations were the basis for a system of classification. The Swedish naturalist Carolus Linnaeus devised a method of classifying living things, called taxonomy, in which each plant and animal is assigned a unique name. Physiology is the study of the workings of organs and how they are affected by disease. The study of diseases themselves is called pathology. Biology is also connected with other scientific disciplines. Biochemistry is the application of chemistry to biology, and biophysics is the application of physics to biology. The study of animal behavior often employs the techniques of psychology. Molecular biology studies biological processes at the level of the molecule. The study of genetics, dealing with heredity, has become increasingly important. Genetic engineering is now making possible the production of substances by means of intervention in genetic processes.

**Bioluminescence**, the production of nonthermal light by living organisms, such as fireflies, many marine animals, bacteria, and fungi. The effect is an example of chemiluminescence. In some cases its utility to the organism is not apparent, though in others its use is clear: In the firefly, the abdomen of the female glows, enabling the male to find her; similarly, luminescence enables many deep-sea fish to locate each other or to attract their prey. The glow in a ship's wake at night is due to luminescent microorganisms.

**Biome**, major ecological unit that is relatively stable, widespread, and well-defined. An example would be a savanna, a tropical grassland with a characteristic range of interlocking plant and animal forms.
*See also:* Ecology.

**Biomedical engineering**, application of principles of engineering to biology and medicine, usually involving collaboration between engineers and biological scientists. There are a number of specialty areas in the field. Bioinstrumentation is the use of electronic measuring devices to monitor, diagnose, and treat diseases; biomechanics is the study of effects of various forces on the body, such as gravity. The development of appropriate materials that can be implanted inside the human body is the province of biomaterials, and systems physiology aims at an integrated understanding of living organisms. Clinical engineering involves the development of computer instruments in hospitals, and rehabilitation engineering develops devices and procedures to expand the capabilities of disabled people.

**Bionics**, science of designing artificial systems that apply the principles that govern the functioning of living organisms. These may be simple imitations of nature or systems that embody laws learned from nature. An example of the latter would be radar, inspired by the echolocation systems of bats.

**Biophysics**, branch of biology in which the methods and principles of physics are applied to the study of living things. It has grown up in the 20th century alongside the development of electronics. Its tools include the electroencephalograph and the electron microscope. Its techniques include those of spectroscopy and X-ray diffraction. Its field of study deals with such questions as nerve transmission, bioluminescence, and materials transfer in respiration and secretion.
*See also:* Biology; Physics.

**Biosphere**, the part of the earth inhabited by living things. It forms a thin layer around the earth, including air, water, and land.

**Biosynthesis,** biochemical reactions by which living cells build complex molecules from simple ones.
*See also:* Biochemistry; Cell.

**Biotechnology,** industrial application of biological knowledge, in particular through the alteration of genes, called genetic engineering. Alteration of genes has been used to create new drugs, chemicals, and animal growth hormones, as well as therapies to repair genetic defects. Ethical and safety concerns about the uses of genetic engineering have generated many legal and moral conflicts in recent years.
*See also:* Genetic engineering.

**Biotite** *See:* Mica.

**Birch,** name for various deciduous trees and shrubs of the family Betulaceae, characterized by their smooth, white outer bark, which sometimes peels off in layers. The heart-shaped leaves have saw-tooth edges. Birch grows widely in the cooler parts of the Northern Hemisphere. The close-grained timber is used for furniture, the bark for tanning and thatching. Among the best-known species are the paper birch of North America, used by Native Americans to make canoes and tents; the silver birch, a native of Europe, widely used in the USSR for roofing material, containers, and in processing leather; and the yellow birch, which makes up some 75% of the American harvest of birchwood.

**Bird,** animal adapted for flight and unique in its body covering of feathers. There are more than 8,500 species. Birds are warm-blooded descendants of reptiles of the dinosaur group. They developed feathers from scales (still evident on their legs) and became two-legged as their forelimbs became wings. Their teeth disappeared, replaced by a horny bill used for feeding and performing complicated tasks, such as nest-building. The bird's body has been adapted for flight. The feathers, an efficient and light body covering, streamline the body and extend the flight surfaces: wings and tail. The skeleton is light, and the bones are hollow. Large breast muscles provide power for flight. The heaviest flying bird is the trumpeter swan of North America, which can weigh up to 38 lb (17 kg). At the other end of the scale, the bee hummingbird is about 2.5 in (6 cm) long and weighs 1/10 oz (3 g). Flightless birds can be much larger. The ostrich stands up to 8 ft (2 1/2 m) and can weigh 300 lb (136 kg). Flightless birds are mainly adapted for running or swimming. Runners have strong legs, like the ostrich; swimmers have wings that are modified as flippers, as in penguins. But some flying birds are also powerful runners, or swimmers. All birds reproduce by laying eggs that must be kept warm for correct development.
In 1997 fossils were found in Patagonia, which belonged to a previously unknown dinosaur variety (IUnenlagia comahuensis). Scientists put that this variety is the missing link between birds and dinosaurs. In 1998 scientists presented the *Rahona ostromi*, a primitive bird with claws that resemble those of carnivorous dinosaurs.

**Bird, Larry** (1956- ), U.S. basketball player. Known for his excellence in all phases of the game, he is considered one of the best players of all time. The 6-ft 9-in (206-cm) forward joined the Boston Celtics of the National Basketball Association (NBA) in 1979 and was named the NBA Rookie of the Year. Bird's other achievements include winning 6 NBA Most Valuable Player (MVP) awards—3 regular season (1984, 85, 86), 2 playoff (1984, 85), and 1 All-Star (1982)—and leading the Boston Celtics to 3 NBA Championships (1981, 84, 86).

**Bird of paradise**, any of more than 40 species of brilliantly colored, plumed birds of the family Paradiseidae, found in eastern Australia, the Moluccas, and New Guinea.

**Bird of paradise**, plant (*Strelitzia reginae*) named for the colorful bird which its flowers resemble. Native to South Africa, this perennial herb grows to a height of 3 to 4 ft (0.9 to 1.2m) and has long-stalked leaves. Several showy flowers, with orange sepals and blue-purple petals, rise from each of the boat-shaped bracts that tip the flowering stalks.

**Birdseye, Clarence** (1886-1956), U.S. inventor and industrialist who, having observed during fur-trading expeditions to Labrador (1912-16) that many foods keep indefinitely if frozen, developed a process for freezing food. In 1924 he founded General Foods to market frozen produce.
*See also:* Food, frozen.

**Birmingham** (pop. 1,009,100), second-largest city in England, about 200 mi (161 km) northwest of London. Birmingham is known as the steel city, producing everything from pins to automobiles. In ancient times a Saxon settlement existed in this area, and by 1166 the site had become a busy market village trading in small metal goods made in nearby Staffordshire, where iron and coal were plentiful. By the late 16th century the population was manufacturing metal products, from swords and cutlery to guns, buckles, jewelry, and plate. In the 17th century Birmingham became a center for scientific ideas and innovation in industry. Scientists and inventors established the Lunar Society there, its members including James Watt, Matthew Boulton, and Joseph Priestley. By 1800 Birmingham was one of the major industrial towns in Britain, but its rapid growth caused deplorable living and working conditions, resulting in riots (1839). The modern city is a center for the machine and tool industries; other products include armaments, toys, and electrical equipment.
*See also:* England.

**Birmingham** (pop. 907,810), largest city in Alabama, situated in the Jones Valley and protected by mountains to the southeast and northwest. Located in a region rich in coal and iron, it manufactures numerous iron and steel products, including pipes, stoves, cotton gins, diesel engines, and electrical equipment. Birmingham was founded and incorporated in 1871, on a site where railroads from 4 directions met in a cotton field. It is now an important rail and air terminus and has a port of entry accessible from the Gulf of Mexico through a channel. The city is also an important educational center, being the site of Miles College, Howard College, Birmingham-Southern College, and the University of Alabama Birmingham (UAB).
*See also:* Alabama.

**Birney, James Gillespie** (1792-1857), U.S. abolitionist. Birney, who came from an old slave-owning family, freed his slaves in 1834. He launched the abolitionist newspaper the *Philanthropist* in 1836, became executive secretary of the American Anti-Slavery Society in 1837, and founded the Liberty Party, standing as its presidential candidate in 1840 and 1844.
*See also:* Abolitionism.

**Birth,** the climax of gestation (the development of a child or other baby mammal within its mother's body) and the beginning of an independent life. In humans, a normal birth proceeds in 3 stages. Mild labor pains caused by contractions of the muscles of the uterus are usually the first sign that a woman is about to give birth. The contractions push the baby downwards, usually head first, which breaks the membranes surrounding the baby, causing the amniotic fluid to escape. In the second stage of labor, stronger contractions push the baby through the cervix and vagina, or birth canal. This is the most painful part and usually lasts less than 2 hours. Anesthetics and analgesics are commonly administered at this time, and delivery is aided by hand or with obstetric forceps. In some cases, the baby must be delivered by a surgical procedure called cesarean section. As soon as the baby is born, its nose and mouth are cleared of fluid and breathing starts, whereupon the umbilical cord is cut and tied. In the third stage of labor, the placenta is expelled from the uterus and bleeding is stopped by further contractions. The exact mechanism by which labor is initiated remains unknown; however, recent research indicates that hormones both from the placenta and from the mother's pituitary gland play important roles in the onset of labor.
*See also:* Reproduction.

**Birth control,** prevention of conception in order to avert unwanted births. There are various contraceptive, or birth-control, devices, including condoms, spermicidal jellies, diaphragms, intrauterine devices, and pills taken by women. Surgical sterilization (for men: vasectomy; for women: tubal ligation) is also possible. Diverse methods of birth control have become increasingly widespread in the 20th century, especially in industrialized countries.

**Birth defect,** congenital anomaly; structural or severe functional defect present at birth. Birth defects cause about 10% of neonatal deaths. A major anomaly is apparent at birth in 3-4% of newborns; by the age of 5, up to 7.5% of all children manifest a congenital defect. The incidence of specific congenital anomalies varies with a number of factors: (1) Individual defect (common malformations such as cleft lip and cleft palate occur in 1 in every 1,000 births). (2) Geographical area (because of factors such as differences in the genetic pool or the environment). For example, the occurrence of spina bifida is 3-4 in every 1,000 births in areas of Ireland, but under 2 in 1,000 in the United States. (3) Cultural practices: where marriages between relatives are frequent, the incidence of certain defects increases. (4) Certain prenatal problems. Scientists estimate that about 2.5-3% of infants born annually in the United States begin life with major birth defects; counting minor types of defects, the percentage increases to 7-10%.

**Birthmark,** skin blemish, usually congenital. There are 2 main types: pigmented nevuses or moles, which are usually brown or black and may be

raised or flat; and vascular nevuses or hemangiomas, local growths of small blood vessels, such as the "strawberry mark" and the "portwine stain." Although harmless, they are sometimes removed for cosmetic reasons or if they show malignant tendencies.
*See also:* Mole.

**Birthstone**, gemstone associated with a month. The ancients allotted a birthstone to each month and believed that it would influence anyone born in that month. The stones and the qualities they were thought to impart are: *January*, garnet (loyalty); *February*, amethyst (sincerity); *March*, blood-stone (courage); *April*, diamond (innocence); *May*, emerald (love); *June*, moonstone (health); *July*, ruby (contentment); *August* sardonyx (married happiness); *September*, sapphire (clear thinking): *October*, opal (hope); *November*, topaz (faithfulness); *December*, turquoise (prosperity).

**Bishop, Billy** (William Avery Bishop; 1894-1956), Canadian military flier, credited with shooting down 72 German airplanes in World War I. In 1917 he was awarded the Victoria Cross, Britain's highest military decoration, and the Distinguished Service medal.
*See also:* World War I.

**Bishop, Elizabeth** (1911-79), U.S. poet and translator of Brazilian poetry, widely acclaimed for her succinct style and lyricism. Her books include the Pulitzer Prize-winning *North and South—A Cold Spring* (1955), *Questions of Travel* (1965), and *Geography III* (1976).

**Bismarck**, one of the most powerful German battleships of World War II. It had a speed of 30 knots, carried eight 15-in (38.1-cm) guns, and displaced more than 45,000 long tons (45,700 m tons) of water. It was sunk in May 1941 after eight different British ships bombarded it about 600 mi (970 km) off the French coast. A 1989 inspection of the sunken ship by U.S. researchers indicated that the Germans might have caused it to go down themselves to prevent its capture.
*See also:* World War II.

**Bismarck** (pop. 83,831), capital of North Dakota and seat of Burleigh County, on the Missouri River. In the mid-19th century, the original settlement was a busy river port and fortified center for the region. It had a brief boom as a supply depot for the Black Hills gold rush of the 1870s, and was the western terminus of the Pacific Railroad until 1879. The city became territorial capital in 1883, and in 1933, its skyscraper capitol was completed. There are rich lignite and petroleum deposits in the vicinity. Bismarck is also a market for grain and livestock.
*See also:* North Dakota.

**Bismarck, Prince Otto von** (1815-1898), German political leader who was instrumental in creating a unified German state. Born of Prussian gentry, he entered politics in 1847 and became premier of Prussia in 1862. In 1866 he defeated Austria in the Austro-Prussian War, creating the North German Federation, which excluded Austria. The Franco-Prussian War (1870-71) resulted in the defeat of France and the creation of a German empire under Prussian hegemony. Bismarck was made imperial chancellor and prince

(1871). Although Wilhelm I was nominally the kaiser (emperor), Bismarck held real power and ruled as a virtual dictator. Under his regime, the German economy flourished, and German power expanded internationally. He was forced to resign in 1890 after the accession of Kaiser William II.
*See also:* Germany.

**Bismarck Archipelago**, group of mountainous islands in the Pacific Ocean, northeast of New Guinea, comprising New Britain, New Ireland, the Admiralty Islands, and many smaller islands. During World War II the Japanese captured the islands and made the area their center of defense in the southwest Pacific. After the war the islands were handed back to Australia and are currently administered from New Guinea. Most of them are covered with jungle vegetation and some have active volcanoes.

**Bismuth**, chemical element, symbol Bi; for physical constants see Periodic Table. Bismuth was known to the ancients and in early times was confused with tin and lead. It was shown to be distinct from lead in 1753 by Claud J. Geoffroy. Bismuth is sometimes found native, as the minerals *bismite* and *bismuthinite*. It is obtained as a byproduct of the refining of lead, copper, and tin. Bismuth is a grayish-white, hard, brittle, low-melting metal. It is the most diamagnetic of all metals and has the highest Hall effect of any metal. It has a low thermal conductivity and a high electrical resistance. Bismuth forms low-melting alloys that are widely used in fire detection and fire extinguishing systems. Bismuth and its compounds are used in powerful magnets and, in medicine, as antisyphilitics and anti-infectives.

**Bison**, any of several species (genus *Bison*) of ox-like animals of the family Bovidae. Bison may weigh half a ton and stand 6 ft (1.8 m) tall. The American bison, often miscalled the buffalo, once grazed the plains and valleys of Mexico to Canada in herds of millions and was economically vital to Native Americans. Hunted ruthlessly by European Americans, it was almost extinct by 1900. There are still a few herds in U.S. and Canadian national parks and population calculations determine that there are about 15,000 bison in the United States and an equal number in Canada.

**Bissau** (pop. 109,000), capital, largest city, and major port of Guinea-Bissau. It is located at the mouth of the Geba River on the West African coast. Its main exports include coconuts, rice, peanuts, hardwood, palm oil, and shellfish.
*See also:* Guinea-Bissau.

**Bithynia**, ancient country of Asia Minor, in what is now Turkey. The Persians conquered Bithynia in the 600s B C, but the country became independent after Alexander the Great's destruction of the Persian empire. Bithynia was independent from the 3rd century B C until 74 B.C when Rome annexed it. It declined in the 2nd century A D

**Bitterling**, minnowlike fish of the family Cyprinidae, found in the fresh waters of Europe and Asia Minor. It is remarkable for its association with freshwater mussels. In the breeding season the female develops a 2-in (5-cm) tube with which she deposits her eggs inside a mussel. The milt (sperm), deposited by the male near the mussel, is drawn in through the mussel's respiratory siphon to fertilize the eggs. Meanwhile the mussel releases its larvae, which cling to the skin of the female bitterling and are carried around before dropping to the bottom.

**Bittern,** any of several species of migratory birds of the heron family. The U.S. bittern ranges from 2 to 3 ft (61 to 91 cm) tall. Its brownish color blends into marshland reeds, allowing it to feed upon its diet of fish, frogs, mice, and insects.

**Bitternut,** medium to large-sized tree (*Carya cordiformis*) of the walnut family, which grows mostly in low wet woods. Its name is derived from the tree's bitter-tasting nuts. Thin-shelled and cylindrical in shape, they contain a fat white kernel. Bitternut wood is used for making wooden crates and furniture.

**Bitter root,** any of several small perennial plants of the family Portulaceae, with long edible roots. It is also called tobacco root because of the tobacco odor generated when cooked. Bitter root has a fat stalk and produces a single rose-colored or white flower. It is the state flower of Montana.

**Bittersweet,** either of 2 unrelated woody vines: U.S. bittersweet (*Celastrus scandens*) and European bittersweet (*Solanum dulcamara*). The U.S. bittersweet grows up to 20 ft (6 m) in height, and has tiny greenish flowers and a woody stem. In late autumn yellow pods split open, displaying red and yellow waxen berries. European bittersweet is rarely more than 8 ft (2.4 m) high. Its flowers vary from violet to light blue and sometimes white. The vine produces poisonous berries and leaves. It is native to Europe and Asia.

**Bitumen,** general term for naturally occurring hydrocarbons (compounds of hydrogen and carbon). It commonly refers to solid or semisolid compounds like pitch, tar, and asphalt. Bitumen products are widely employed to coat timber to protect it from water, and to seal roofs, arches, walls and floors. *See also:* Coal; Hydrocarbon.

**Bituminous sands,** sands containing natural bitumen deposits. The heavy oil extracted from these sands is converted to synthetic crude oil by refining. *See also:* Coal.

**Bizet, Georges** (1838-75), French composer, best known for his opera *Carmen* (1875), one of the most popular in history. He also wrote symphonies and incidental music for other operas.

**Björling, Jussi** (1911-1960), Swedish operatic tenor who specialized in Italian opera, especially works by Verdi and Puccini. *See also:* Opera.

**Bjørnson, Bjørnstjerne Martinius** (1832-1910), Norwegian poet, critic, novelist, dramatist, and politician, winner of the Nobel Prize in literature (1903). Initially concentrating on themes of Norwegian history, he later wrote about modern social problems. Among his writings was the novel *Flags Are Flying in Town and Port* (1884).

**Black, Davidson** (1884-1934), Canadian anthropologist who discovered the early human species later known popularly as Peking man. He was professor at Peking Union medical college in China until his death.
*See also:* Anthropology.

**Black, Hugo Lafayette** (1886-1971), U.S. politician and jurist, associate justice of the Supreme Court (1937-71). A supporter of the New Deal, Black was appointed to the Supreme Court by President Franklin D. Roosevelt. Although he was a former Ku Klux Klan member, he became a leader of the Court's efforts to extend civil rights.
*See also:* Supreme Court of the United States.

**Black, Joseph** (1728-99), Scottish physician and chemist. He investigated the properties of carbon dioxide, discovered the phenomena of latent and specific heats, distinguished heat from temperature, and pioneered the techniques used in the quantitative study of chemistry.
*See also:* Chemistry; Heat.

**Black Americans** *See:* African Americans.

**Blackbeard** (d. 1718), English pirate whose real name was probably Edward Teach or Thatch. A privateer in the War of the Spanish Succession, he later turned to piracy in the West Indies and along the Atlantic coast, until he was killed by the British.

**Blackberry**, prickly bramble (genus *Rubus*) of the rose family, native to north temperate regions of the world, that produces an edible fruit. Some varieties, including the loganberry and boysenberry, are cultivated to be sold fresh, frozen, or canned, and are used in beverages, liqueurs, and preserves.

**Blackbird**, any of several dark-colored perching birds of the family Icteridae, including the red-winged blackbird and the yellow-headed blackbird. Blackbirds may survive temperatures as low as 20°F (–6°C). They travel in huge flocks (as many as 5 million birds) and eat fruit, insects, and worms, and often do serious damage to crops.

**Blackbuck** (*Antilope cervicapra*), antelope of India and Pakistan. Once numbering millions, there are now only a few thousand left in the plains and woodlands where they live in herds. The females and young are yellow-fawn with a white eye-ring; the adult males are dark brown, stand about 32 in (81 cm) tall at the shoulder, and bear spiral horns up to 2 ft (60 cm) long. Blackbuck are very swift and used to be hunted with cheetahs.

**Black Codes**, laws enacted after the Civil War in the states that had formed the Confederacy. These codes were aimed at preserving white supremacy after the demise of slavery. Some codes persisted into the 20th century, despite constitutional amendments guaranteeing equal rights for former slaves.
*See also:* Civil War, U.S.

**Black Death**, common name for an epidemic of bubonic plague that swept through Asia and Europe in the mid-14th century, perhaps halving the

population of Europe. Caused by a bacterium, the disease was carried by flea-infected rats. Its economic effects were far-reaching, among other things fanning flames of superstition and religious prejudice.
*See also:* Bubonic plague.

**Black-eyed pea** *See:* Cowpea.

**Black-eyed Susan,** hardy annual or biennial coneflower (*Rudbeckia hirta*), the state flower of Maryland. Sometimes called yellow daisy, it bears 20 to 40 orange-yellow ray flowers around a group of darker brown florets.

**Blackfish,** common name given to any of various dark-colored fishes, including the black sea bass found along the Atlantic coast of the United States, the Alaska blackfish found in streams and ponds in Alaska and Siberia, and the tautog, found in the Atlantic Ocean from New Brunswick, Canada, to South Carolina.

**Blackfoot tribes,** North American plains tribes of the Algonquin linguistic family. The Blackfoot, named for their black-dyed moccasins, were originally hunters and trappers in what is now Montana and the Canadian provinces of Alberta and Saskatchewan. The disappearance of the bison (killed off by white settlers), a smallpox epidemic, and wars with whites reduced the Blackfoot population. Blackfoot today are farmers and ranchers in Montana and Alberta.
*See also:* Algonquins.

**Black Forest,** wooded mountain range in the province of Baden-Württemberg, southwestern Germany. An area of great scenic beauty, it is an important tourist attraction, with lumber, clock, and toy industries.

**Black Friday,** term referring to 2 particular financial disasters that occurred on Fridays. The most famous was Sept. 24, 1869, when speculators Jay Gould and James Fisk tried to corner the gold market with the connivance of government officials. The market collapsed, and many were ruined. The second Black Friday was Sept. 19, 1873, when a collapse of the New York Stock Exchange led to a panic.
*See also:* Cornering the market; Stock exchange.

**Black haw,** small tree or shrub (*Viburnum prunifolium*) of the eastern and southern United States. It grows up to 15 ft (4.6 m) high. After a frost, its bluish-black berries can be eaten.

**Black Hawk** (1767-1838), Native American leader of the Sauk tribe, who opposed the movement of European settlers westward to Illinois. A treaty had been signed by the Sauk and Fox tribes in 1804 ceding lands east of the Mississippi River to the United States, but Black Hawk declared that the Sauk had been tricked and that the contract was invalid. In 1832, he and his warriors fought to regain their land. Black Hawk and his 2 sons were captured in 1833 and moved to a reservation near Fort Des Moines.
*See also:* Indian wars.

**Blackhead** *See:* Acne; Pore.

**Black Hills,** mountain range in South Dakota and Wyoming, famous for the Mount Rushmore National Memorial. Here, the heads of 4 past U.S. presidents are carved out of the mountainside. The Black Hills are rich in minerals, including gold. Their highest point is Harney Peak (7,242 ft/2,207 m). *See also:* Rushmore, Mount.

**Black hole,** according to current astrophysical theory, the final stage of evolution for very massive stars following complete gravitational collapse. In theory, a star with a mass more than 3 times that of the sun could collapse to an indefinitely small size. The gravitational field of such an object would be so powerful that not even electromagnetic radiation (including visible light) could escape. Black holes, if they exist, would have to be detected by their gravitational effects on other bodies and by the emission of X- and gamma rays by objects falling into them. A black hole would therefore bear some resemblance to the initial state of the universe in the big bang theory. *See also:* Astronomy; Star; Big bang.

**Black Hole of Calcutta,** prison cell in which 146 British captives were incarcerated on the night of June 20, 1756, after a battle between British and Indian troops during which the Indian forces captured a British fort. Some of the prisoners suffocated in the 14 ft (4.3 m) by 18 ft (5.5 m) room. John Holwell, a British survivor, alleged that 123 of the 146 had died, but subsequent research suggests that there were probably about 15 deaths.

**Black Kettle** (1803?-68), Cheyenne chief known for his efforts to live peacefully with European settlers. Despite this, his people were subjected to unprovoked attacks by U.S. troops. In Nov. 1864 nearly 300 men, women, and children in southeastern Colorado were massacred by troops led by Col. John Chivington. Black Kettle escaped and moved to a settlement in what is now Oklahoma. In Nov. 1868 General George A. Custer led an attack that killed Black Kettle, along with as many as 100 of his people.

**Blacklist,** list of persons, companies, or organizations who are disapproved of and are to be boycotted.

**Black lung,** disease caused by inhaled dust which collects in the lungs and may eventually destroy them. Black lung has two forms, simple and complicated, and is found among coal miners and sandblasters. Symptoms are wheezing, coughing, and a higher incidence of lung infection.

**Black market,** illicit dealing in scarce commodities or currencies, in defiance of rules for rationing and price restrictions. In the United States, black market operations did not appear on a large scale until strict price controls and rationing were introduced during World War II. After the war, black market operations ceased for the most part as government controls were lifted. A black market also operates in countries where there is a shortage of reliable foreign currencies such as dollars or marks and people are prepared to pay above the official exchange rate to obtain them.

**Black Mountains**, range of the Blue Ridge Mountains in western North Carolina and highest of the Appalachians. Their highest point is Mount Mitchell (6,684 ft/2,037 m).
*See also:* Blue Ridge Mountains.

**Blackmun, Harry Andrew** (1908- ), U.S. lawyer named to the U.S. Court of Appeals in 1959 and appointed Supreme Court justice by President Nixon in 1970. Blackmun has upheld liberal positions on civil and reproductive rights while remaining conservative in other respects.

**Black Muslims**, popular name of a U.S. black nationalist movement (originally called the Nation of Islam) founded in Detroit in 1930 by Wali Farad, who rejected racial integration and advocated thrift, hard work, and cleanliness. Under Elijah Muhammad (1934-75), the Black Muslims became a major force in the African-American community, demanding the formation of an independent Black nation in the United States. In the 1960s a split between Elijah Muhammad and Malcolm X, a Black Muslim minister and the group's most prominent leader, undermined the strength of the Nation of Islam. Malcolm X was assassinated in 1965, and when Wallace Muhammad succeeded his father as leader of the group in 1975, he turned the organization into a non-political association whose beliefs are closer to those of orthodox Islam, changing its name to the American Muslim Mission. A splinter group bearing the original name, the Nation of Islam, continues to uphold Elijah Muhammad's teachings.
*See also:* Malcolm X; Muhammad, Elijah.

**Black Panther Party**, U.S. black political movement founded in Oakland, Calif. in 1966, advocating self-defense of the African-American community and revolutionary change in the United States. Under the leadership of Eldridge Cleaver, Huey P. Newton, Bobby Seale, and others, the Panthers opened community centers and bookshops as well as doing legal battles with the authorities. Their often violent rhetoric was used to justify armed attacks that resulted in the death of many Panther leaders, such as Fred Hampton in Chicago. The influence of the party was weakened by internal factional disputes in the early 1970s, and by the 1980s its influence in the black liberation movement had ended.

**Black Power**, slogan coined in the mid-1960s by militant black activists, particularly Stokely Carmichael of the Student Non-violent Coordinating Committee (SNCC), to give voice to and inspire a growing black pride and aspiration for political power. A significant turning point in the history of Black Power occurred at the 1968 Summer Olympics when U.S. athletes receiving medals for their victory raised their fists in sympathy for this movement. It has evolved a multiplicity of meanings ranging from awareness of African-American economic potential to cultural and political organization.
*See also:* African Americans; Carmichael, Stokely.

**Black Prince** *See:* Edward the Black Prince.

**Black Sea**, tideless island sea between Europe and Asia, bordered by Turkey, Bulgaria, Romania, Ukraine, Russian Federation and Georgia and linked to the Sea of Azov and (via the Bosporus) to the Mediterranean. It covers 181,000 sq mi (468,790 sq km) and is up to 7,250 ft (2,210 m) deep. The Danube, Dniester, Bug, Don, and Dnieper rivers all flow into the sea. The chief ports are Odessa, Sevastopol, Batumi, Constanta, and Varna. The Black Sea coast is an important resort area.

**Black September,** name applied to various armed groups within the Palestine Liberation Organization. Named for the civil war in Jordan in Sept. 1970 that led to the expulsion of all Palestinian guerrilla groups from the country by King Hussein, groups called Black September claimed responsibility for or were implicated in many violent acts in the 1970s, including the killing of 11 Israeli athletes at the 1972 Olympic Games in Munich.
*See also:* Arafat, Yasir; Palestine Liberation Organization.

**Black Shirts,** nickname given to Fascist Party activists in Italy. They were organized by Benito Mussolini in 1919 and seized control of the Italian government in 1922, forcing King Victor Emmanuel III to appoint Mussolini as leader.
*See also:* Mussolini, Benito.

**Blacksnake** (*Coluber constrictor*), nonvenomous snake common in almost every part of the United States. One of the largest North American snakes, it is 4-7 ft (120-210 cm) long. The adult is a deep slate-black color, while the young are pale gray with grayish-brown patches. Sometimes known as the "racer," this snake can move along the ground as fast as a running human can run and can climb trees with ease. Its food consists mainly of lizards, frogs, mice, and birds. The eggs, usually a dozen or more, are encased in a leathery shell. Also referred to as blacksnakes are the pilot black snake (*Elaphe obsoleta*) of North America and various black snakes of Australia (genus *Pseudeschis*).

**Black Sox Scandal,** ironic name for 1919-20 baseball scandal that led to radical reorganization in the administration of the sport. It broke out when Edward Cicotte of the Chicago White Sox confessed to accepting a bribe to influence the outcome of the 1919 World Series. He named 7 other team members allegedly involved. All 8 were suspended for a season but were cleared of fraud.

**Blackstone, Sir William** (1723-80), English jurist, author of *Commentaries on the Laws of England* (1765-69). Educated at Oxford, Blackstone was admitted to the bar in 1746 and in 1758 became the first holder of the new chair in English law at Oxford. The *Commentaries*, whose influence was considerable in the United States as well as England, forms a compendium of English law up to the 18th century.

**Black studies,** in U.S. education, program of study of the culture, history, and literature of African Americans, initiated to correct the omission of such information from traditional scholastic disciplines. These courses were added to high-school and university curricula as a result of black protests of the 1960s.

**Blackwell, Antoinette Brown** (1825-1921), U.S. social reformer and Congregationalist minister. A graduate of the theological seminary of Oberlin College, she became an itinerant preacher. In 1853 the Congregational church in South Butler, N.Y., made her its pastor. She thus became the first woman in the country to be formally appointed pastor of a church. Blackwell was a writer as well. Her best-known book was *The Sexes Throughout Nature* (1875).

**Blackwell, Elizabeth** (1821-1910), English-born U.S. physician, first woman to be granted a medical degree in the United States. Refused admission to various medical schools, she graduated from the Geneva (N.Y.) Medical College in 1847. In 1857 she and her sister opened the New York Infirmary for Women and Children, which was entirely staffed by women, and in 1868 she helped found its Women's Medical College. Returning to England, she taught at the London School of Medicine for Women.

**Black widow,** poisonous spider (genus *Latrodectus*) of the Americas. Adults are black and have red or orange hourglass-shaped marks on their abdomens. The adult female is 0.5 in (1.3 cm) long and often devours the smaller male during mating. The bite of the black widow can cause considerable pain, swelling, and nausea, but is rarely fatal to healthy adults.

**Bladder,** muscular sac in the lower abdomen of all mammals that stores urine produced by the kidneys. Urine is carried to the bladder through 2 tubes called ureters and is emptied through the urethra by the contraction of a sphincter muscle. The term is also used to designate any similar organ in plants or animals; for example, the swim bladder in fish and the vesicles in some seaweeds.
*See also:* Kidney; Urine.

**Bladder, gall** *See:* Gall bladder.

**Bladderwort,** aquatic plant (genus *Utricularia*) found in tropical and temperate zones that traps insects, larvae, small worms, and protozoa in air-filled sacs attached to its stems and roots. In medical history, the plant has been used for the treatment of eczema and other allergic skin conditions.